Introduction to Speech
Communication

Introduction to Speech Communication

John F. Cragan
David W. Wright

John K. Boaz
Vincent Hazleton, Jr.
Herb Jackson
Ted R. Jackson
Catherine Wenc Konsky

Johnny I. Murdock
William D. Semlak
Ralph L. Smith
George E. Tuttle
Wenmouth Williams, Jr.

Illinois State University

Waveland Press, Inc.
Prospect Heights, Illinois

For information about this book, write or call:

Waveland Press, Inc.
P.O. Box 400
Prospect Heights, Illinois 60070
(312) 634-0081

Photographs in this book are courtesy of Illinois State University Photo Services and *The Vidette*.

Library of Congress Catalog Card Number 80-52302
ISBN 0-917974-45-X

Printed in the United States of America.

Contents

Preface

Our approach to the basic course in speech communication is grounded in two beliefs. First, the introductory course should adequately describe communication theories, and second, the course should increase and improve the oral communication skills of the student. This textbook represents only one component of the educational process in speech communication. Instructor lectures and student speech exercises are necessary elements in meeting the major objectives of a speech communication course. This book contributes to the overall objective of the course in three ways: 1) it defines the basic elements of speech communication; 2) it traces the origin and development of six different clusters of communication theories; and 3) it indicates important communication skills to be practiced, with special emphasis on how to prepare and deliver speeches.

The faculty in the Department of Communication at Illinois State University shared equally in the writing of this textbook. The content of this book represents, in our judgment, the "basic" subject matter for a beginning course in speech communication. We have included in the textbook subject matter for the basic course that tends not to undergo rapid change over time. We have not included student exercises and simulations in this book because of their transitory nature; in fact, the exercises we use in our own course change from term to term.

We would like to thank the thousands of Illinois State students who have provided helpful criticism at the end of each semester that over the years has contributed to the evolution of our basic course and the development of this textbook.

John F. Cragan
David W. Wright
Normal, Illinois
July 1980

Introduction

1

Overview of Communication
A Personal Introduction

John F. Cragan

Hi! How are you? My name is John Cragan. My wife, Betty, and a few old friends call me Johnny. My mother would never let anyone call me Jack and when she was mad at me she would yell, "Come here this minute, John Francis."

Betty and I have two children (Katie and Keary). We live in an old house with a big dog (Sean) and one very mean cat (Tiger). When there is a thunderstorm the girls, the dog, and the cat all pile into our bed. I kind of like it but I act like I do not.

I wish I could meet you personally but it is not possible to step out of the written pages and talk face-to-face with you. Also, it might be quite embarrassing for both of us. You might be sitting in your dorm room spilling coke and pizza all over this page as you cram for the final examination in your basic speech communication course. You might even be mad at me for wasting your time with all of this "chit chat." If you could step through the pages of this book into my study, I would be quite embarrassed. You would see me scratching this page on a yellow legal pad that has tea and wheat toast crumbs all over it. Furthermore, I'm sitting in my "writing" coat, hat and shoes. You see, I can't write unless I wear these old things.

I have been trying to engage in an interpersonal conversation with you but I feel my stomach tightening up. I am afraid of communication

3

failure. A lot of fears are rushing through my head. If I could see your face or hear just one comment from you, I would know if I should continue risk-taking by disclosing more personal information. But written communication is not very well suited for interactive interpersonal discussions and it makes it difficult for me to adapt my behavior. And besides, you are not reading for enjoyment or to make new friends, you are reading for results. You want a clear, concise explanation of speech communication in terms of useful theories and specific skills so that you may become a better communicator, so what is this textbook author trying to say?

Well, I am really trying to say "hi" and welcome to college but I am also saying that face-to-face speech communication uniquely allows for immediate adaptive behavior on the part of the communicators and that speech communication has many distinctive, sometimes competing functions, that often occur simultaneously in one message so it is difficult to say what we mean and even more difficult to ensure that you understand what we mean to say. But we work hard throughout this book to use the print medium to explain speech communication principles and skills. I hope that you find this book enjoyable and useful.

Hopefully we have designed a textbook that will satisfy your many needs as a communicator. If you are like most Americans and me, you have some deep-seated fear about speech communication. In fact, national surveys repeatedly find that the number one fear we have is the fear of giving a public speech. This is true despite the fact that about 70% of our waking hours are involved in some form of communication. National surveys also report that college students want to improve their interpersonal communication skills. College seniors want to improve their interviewing skills as they seek their career job when corporations come to campus looking for college graduates who can communicate effectively and efficiently within work groups. In short, there are a lot of reasons why you should be intrinsically interested in improving your communication competency.

This book provides you with an explanation of the different types of human communication and details advice on how you might improve your communication skills. I truly believe you can become a better communicator if you practice the speech skills that are presented in this book and those which are part of the basic course you are probably taking right now.

Definition of Speech Communication

Speech communication is the study of the process people use to transmit messages to each other. Historically, the discipline is focused on how people use verbal and nonverbal symbols to induce cooperation. However, in the last thirty years the scope of speech communication has expanded to include, in addition to persuasive communication, the sub-areas of interpersonal communication, small group communication, information processing communication, conflict resolving communication, and mass communication. Thus, the task of providing a meaningful introduction to the theories and practices of speech communication is complex. In order to provide a more complete definition of speech communication, there needs to be an explanation of the different types of human communication.

Interpersonal Communication is person-to-person dialogue for the purposes of improving the quality of our relationships. Interpersonal skills deal with such things as how to initiate, develop, and terminate relationships. Interpersonal communication is different from role-to-role communication. This chapter starts with an interpersonal monologue. The section seems "odd" in that our culture tends to dictate that only role-to-role communication (professor to student) communication should occur in textbooks. Also, the Personal Introduction Section was barely interpersonal communication because the medium (written communication) does not allow for immediate interaction between people.

Small Group Communication is a form of role-to-role communication in which a few people (three to thirteen) engage in communication interaction over time generally in face-to-face settings. These people have common goals and norms and have developed a communication pattern for meeting their goals in an interdependent fashion (Cragan and Wright, 1980). Small group communication skills focus on how to achieve the three basic outputs of group productivity, membership satisfaction, and group consensus. For example, there are sixteen leadership communication behaviors that need to occur in group discussions in order to maximize productivity.

Information Processing Communication is concerned with the efficient and accurate transfer of information from source to receiver. The communication skills inherent to this form of communication between people centers on the understanding of the six human elements (thought, perception, memory, attention, language and listening). In addition, information processing theories explain machine-to-machine communication and person-to-machine communication, but we do not examine these other uses of information theory in this book.

Persuasive Communication is intentional communication designed through the use of symbols to affect change in others. Television commercials are a daily reminder of this form of speech communication. Persuasive communication skills are the various strategies used to construct messages and present them to receivers so that their attitudes, beliefs and values are changed in the way the sender intended. The use of rational arguments and emotional appeals are two sets of communication behaviors that we call persuasive communication.

Conflict Resolving Communication is a specific form of role communication that takes place when people involved in a dispute have both motives to cooperate and motives to compete. The three most common examples of this type of communication are called bargaining, mediation, and arbitration. Some of the communication skills associated with conflict resolution are good faith bargaining, non-polarizing communication, signposting, and flexible communication.

Mass Communication is the use of print and electronic medias to transmit interpersonal, informational and persuasive messages to large groups of people. In this book we do not explain how to construct mass mediated messages but instead describe how mass communication developed in our culture and how it influences us as members of the mass audience.

Speech communication is a symbolic process that functions in several different and often synonymous ways. We use communication to create a symbolic identity for ourselves and others through person-to-person conversations. We attempt to influence others through the use of language systems. We work cooperatively through small group communication. We bargain and negotiate where possible. We transmit information from sender to receiver. In our technocracy all these forms of communication are processed through mass media channels.

Basic Principles of Human Communication

There is not a general theory of speech communication but as the previous section indicated there are identifiable sub-areas of speech communication that have theoretical explanations that spell out basic communication skills to be learned. But there exists some tension between these different theories. For example, persuasive communication theories seek to explain how people can manipulate and control each other through the use of symbols, while interpersonal communication theories advise against the use of manipulative communication behaviors. However, there are some principles that are common to all forms of speech communication. This section presents the most important ones.

Speech communication is a systematic, symbolic code. We communicate through the use of our verbal and nonverbal codes. The verbal codes carry most of our cognitive meaning while the nonverbal codes carry most of our affective meaning. Yet we are not sure how thoughts and words relate to each other. Most of our language appears to be learned but humans are not only symbol users but symbol creators.

How we create language and thought is still unresolved. However, at the practical level, it is clear that our means for conveying thought is a language code that is shared by a group of people. Chapter 3 provides an in-depth analysis of our communication codes.

Speech communication is a continuous, adaptive process. In face-to-face communication, it is very arbitrary and difficult to indicate where a conversation starts and ends. What is clear is people continually react and adjust to the messages they receive from each other. In public speeches we call this speaker adaptation. In information processing we call it reaction to feedback. In interpersonal communication the adaptation is often so fast and continuous that it is impossible to sort out the discreet messages and the reaction to them. This is particularly true when affective meaning is examined in the nonverbal code. The dynamic nature of speech communication is very important. A textbook can only be changed about every four years, while face-to-face communication can be instantaneously responsive to feedback.

Speech communication is interactive. Computer technology is allowing mass communication systems to become more adaptive by making them more interactive. Computer-controlled two-way cable systems are now allowing people to literally talk back to their TVs, however, interaction does not necessarily mean that adaptation will occur. In Chapter 8 we will discuss some of the problems of reducing conflict when people are interactive but not adaptive. Certainly one of the universal characteristics of all speech communication is its interactive nature.

Speech communication is intentional. Although it is true that all behavior communicates and thus we cannot *not* communicate, the study of speech communication focuses primarily on intentional communication. While much of our communication is spontaneous, it is still, for the most part, intentional. We intend to build certain relationships or transmit specific information or persuade or work cooperatively with others and we use language codes to accomplish these ends. Thus, most of speech communication that is worth studying is intentional communication.

Speech communication is risk-taking behavior. The fear that we feel in some communication situations is real. This speech anxiety or apprehension can be minimized as we learn the skills associated with each type of communication. Making a persuasive public speech is risk-taking. That is why Chapter 10 is devoted to the nuts and bolts of how to prepare and deliver a public speech. Seeking to meet new people is risk-taking. A complete withdrawal from this risk is to become a recluse, or in an extreme case, catatonic. So speech communication is risk-taking behavior but this book is designed to reduce that risk.

An Overview

Certainly one of your greatest expectations of an introductory course in speech communication is to improve your ability to give a public speech. Although the entire book works toward helping you become a better communicator, Chapter 10 maps out a step-by-step process of speech preparation that should ensure your success in making a public speech. Chapter 10 details a twelve-step formula for preparing and delivering speeches that is a sequential series of recommendations that we are sure is a workable schemata to use. Most of the advice that we present on speech preparation has been accumulated by scores of speech communication professors for literally hundreds of years. While you may not formally use each step for brief, informal presentations, the twelve-step system is the best approach to adopt for a major presentation.

The advice in Chapter 10 will only become meaningful if you actually use the system in preparing one of your classroom speeches. The classroom environment is a safe laboratory to publicly practice your speech skills so we hope that you will use our twelve-step procedure in preparing at least one of those speeches. Once you have used our system, you will undoubtedly make adaptations until you have your own procedure that works best for you. Of course this is your goal — a preparation procedure that ensures that the speeches you make in your career will be good ones.

The two most common types of speeches that you will find yourself giving are informative and persuasive speeches. Chapters 6 and 7 are devoted to explaining the information and persuasive theories that are usable to a student of communication. These two chapters also make numerous recommendations on how you can better design your intentional messages whether they are of an informational or persuasive nature.

Chapter 6 examines the six critical elements of information processing that impact on your ability to transmit clear, accurate, and effective messages. In this chapter we make suggestions on how you as a sender or a receiver of messages can transfer information better. Chapter 7 analyzes the three basic approaches to human persuasion (rational, psychological, dramatistic) that you can use as a basis for constructing persuasive messages.

Most of your day-to-day communication can be classified as interpersonal. Chapter 4 has two goals: (1) to explain the characteristics that go into making you a more competent interpersonal communicator; and (2) to show how communication functions in building better interpersonal relationships. We think you will find this chapter to be the most enjoyable one in the book, enjoyable partly because you will easily relate to the ten knowledge and skill behaviors that a confident interpersonal communicator should possess and partly because the chapter explains the five major factors that are involved in developing interpersonal relationships. In total, we trust that the chapter makes some clear recommendations to you on how you can become a more skilled interpersonal communicator.

As we indicate in Chapter 2, we Americans have a cultural history of making group decisions. We are all expected to be competent small group communicators. Thus, Chapter 5 is concerned with describing the roles that are played in small discussion groups and with specific emphasis on guidelines you can adopt in your effort to become a better group discussant. We make specific recommendations on how you can be a better group leader and also how you can perform the other necessary roles in small group communication. The chapter also details prescriptive meeting procedures you may want to use that are designed to produce communication patterns that work best towards solving various group tasks. You should note that much of the group communication behaviors that are recommended in Chapter 5 are quite different from the communication behaviors advocated in the interpersonal, information processing, persuasion, and conflict resolution chapters. This does not mean that these other forms of communication do not occur during the life history of a small work group. Indeed, some interpersonal communication will occur as well as periods of argumentation and information transferring. Chapter 5 merely focuses on the communication that is unique to the small group process. In fact, each of the six different types of communication that we describe in the *Dimensions* section of the book are explained in separate chapters not because any random large "chunk" of communication is purely one type of communication, but because it is easier to see the complexity of human communication and understand the many skills involved if each of the six dimensions are presented in a separate chapter.

In a free society such as ours, it is natural that more open, verbal conflict will take place. Also, our society has formalized much of this communication combat. Chapter 8 deals with the role communicators play in the resolution of conflict. We have focused Chapter 8 on the special communication skills that you may well want to develop for conflict resolution. For example, the chapter describes the five basic communication styles that most of us use when we are engaged in conflict resolution. You may want to determine which style you use when you are trying to resolve conflict, or more importantly, you may want to change to another communication pattern that through classroom exercises appears to be a better way for you to communicate in these situations.

In Chapter 9 we do not prescribe a set of communication skills that you could adopt in order to communicate more effectively in the mass media channels. Instead, we outline the historical development that produced our mass media in an effort to explain how it has become such a dominant part of our lives. Since most of us are acted upon by the message creators of the mass media, we believe that it is useful to present you with theories that explain what effects the mass media is having on us, the members of the mass audience. Finally, we end the chapter with specific suggestions on how you can protect yourself against some of the harmful effects of the mass media. While Chapter 9 in part explains how the mass media functions in our acculturation process, Chapter 2 is devoted exclusively to a discussion of how culture influences, and, in fact, determines many of our communication patterns. Also, Chapter 2 highlights the many difficulties we encounter in cross-culture communication. We begin our book with our chapter on culture and communication in order to emphasize that even when we are confident communicators in our own culture, we are not assured that we can speak effectively across cultures. In other words, most of our interpersonal and persuasive communication skills are culture-bound. In fact, some of these skills when used in cross-cultural communication may be counter-productive. Finally, in this chapter, we try to point out to you how most of the communication practices that we teach in American colleges are "dictated" by our culture.

In addition to culture, communication codes make up the second set of basic elements in human communication. Just as we often overlook the influences of culture on communication patterns, we tend to take for granted the common symbolic code people need to share in order to communicate. In Chapter 3 we provide a close examination of our verbal and nonverbal codes. We look at how they interact in order to allow us to talk to one another. In general, Section 2 is constructed to provide a necessary background for your understanding and development of American communication skills that should prove helpful in your effort to improve yourself as a communicator.

Summary

Speech communication is the process people use to transmit messages to each other. There are six distinct dimensions to speech communication: (1) interpersonal communication, which is person-to-person dialogue for the purpose of improving the quality of our relationships; (2) small group communication, which is a form of role-to-role communication that a small group of people use in order to meet their common interdependent goals; (3) information processing communication, which is concerned with the efficient and accurate transfer of information from source to receiver; (4) persuasive communication, which is intentional messages designed to affect change in others; (5) conflict resolving communication, which takes place when people involved in disputes have both motives to cooperate and to compete; and (6) mass communication, which is the use of print and electronic medias to transmit messages to large groups of people. Although there is no general theory of speech communication, there are five basic principles of human communication: (1) speech communication is a systematic, symbolic code; (2) speech communication is a continuous adaptive process; (3) speech communication is interactive; (4) speech communication is intentional; and (5) speech communication is risk-taking behavior.

References

Bormann, E., & Bormann, N. Speech communication: an interpersonal approach. New York: Harper & Row, 1972.

Brooks, W. Speech communication. Dubuque: Wm. C. Brown Co., 1978.

Cragan, J., & Wright, D. Communication in small group discussions: a case study approach. St. Paul: West Publishing Co., 1980.

DeVito, J. Communicology: an introduction to the study of communication. New York: Harper & Row, 1978.

Larson, C. Communication: everyday encounters. Belmont: Wadsworth Publishing Co., 1976.

McCroskey, J., & Wheeless, L. Introduction to human communication. Boston: Allyn and Bacon, Inc., 1976.

Scheidel, T. Speech communication and human interaction. 2nd ed. Glenview: Scott, Foresman and Company, 1976.

Zimmerman, G., Owen, J., & Seibert, D. Speech communication: a contemporary introduction. St. Paul: West Publishing Co., 1977.

II

Basic Elements of Communication

2

People, Culture and Communication

Ted R. Jackson

People, culture and communication are entwined. Human beings are unique among the species because we use culture and communication to literally make us what we are. Men and women use communication to create their culture. Language, both verbal and nonverbal, is the medium we use in communicating our culture and ourselves. More will be said in Chapter Three about how we acquire and develop such language.

Language and people have been subjects for communication research for centuries. But it has only been in the last two decades that a focus has been drawn to culture and its impact on communication. Culture is the collective whole of language, symbols, rituals, myths, institutions and values that we use to organize ourselves into a particular society. Culture is such a pervasive influence upon our lives, and the way that we communicate, that we are not consciously aware of it until we come into contact with people from another culture. In more homogeneous societies, such as Japan, culture's impact is so unconsciously pervasive that there is no word or term in the language to express it.

Learning the language of another culture is often the simplest step in the intercultural communication process. Learning the culture of others is far more complex, but it is probably far more important as a factor in effective communication.

The jet aircraft, bringing relatively cheap transportation, and the growth and rapidity of mass communication, have had the greatest influence in creating an intercultural awareness. Millions of American tourists, multi-national corporation workers, Peace Corps people, students, educators and government workers have made the global trek with their cultural baggage in tow. "Cultural shock" has probably been the most common experience for all. While most cultures hold some values in common, such as the safety and welfare of the individual, it is the values not shared which pose the greatest barriers to effective communication. Many Peace Corps members have returned home in frustration and despair when they discovered that the people with whom they worked in the host country did not share their value about technology.

Knowing about, and understanding another culture is no guarantee of successful communication. Since all people are so immersed in their own culture it is easy to develop what sociologists call "cultural ethno-centrism," that is, a sense of cultural superiority. When a person or society seeks to impose their culture upon others it can be termed *cultural chauvanism* or *cultural imperialism*. Much of the tension and conflict generated between the United States and Russia during the last generation may be attributed to this trait. Though we know a great deal about each other's culture, the manner in which we order our economic and political lives is vastly different, with both sides claiming superiority. For example, a woman from the United States who is strongly allied with the women's rights movement in her country would come into strong conflict with men from Japan, or the Middle East who hold different views about the role of women in society. Such disagreements do not occur because of cultural ignorance, but because of cultural awareness. Both the men from those societies and "liberated" United States women would claim cultural superiority in any conflict in communication over that issue.

Acquiring Culture

How do human beings acquire culture? We don't acquire it by taking Culture 3 in high school. Nor do we acquire it by taking Culture 101 in college. We start acquiring it from the day we are born.

It has been said in Chapter 1 that communication is a process. It is continuous, on-going, dynamic, and systemic. Just as it is impossible not to continously communicate, either verbally or nonverbally, it is just as difficult not to behave, think or communicate outside of one's cultural framework without a concerted effort to do so.

The methods which are used to acculturate the individual from permitted to overstep it. For example, in the 1960's and early 1970's, the outer limits of United States culture were bombarded by those who opposed the war in Viet Nam, and by participants in the civil rights movement. This country was founded on the basis of protest of grievances. When a proper hearing and settlement of those grievances has not been forthcoming, public demonstrations are a part of our cultural history. The right to assemble and protest grievances became a key article in the Bill of Rights in our Constitution. The right to assemble and form a broad range of religious views and political philosophies through freedom of speech and religion is protected by the First Amendment to the Constitution. Political freedom is given great latitude in peace times, but less in times of war and crisis. Religious freedom is granted great latitude in both peace and war.

Individuals may be acutely aware of their personal values, but only vaguely conscious of the cultural value that permitted or even shaped the personal value. We take for granted the practice of religion in a multitude of faiths and sects. Our culture has tolerated a broad spectrum of activities in the practice of religion. The Jehovah's Witness sect has taken to court and won a number of law suits permitting them to propogate their religion. Two such practices involve going door-to-door to spread their beliefs and refusing to pledge allegiance to the flag in public school rituals. More recently, the actions of some sects may challenge the outer limits of religious freedom in our culture in much the same way political freedom and free speech has in the past. The People's Temple suicides and murders in Jonestown, the recruiting practices of the Moonies and Hare Krishna, the founding of a nation wide Christian Broadcasting Network by Rev. Robertson at the taxpayers' expense, have been actions which are causing concern among many in our society. If such actions result in a religious backlash we will be forced to examine the cultural value which permitted the rise of such practices.

An Outline of Value Orientations

SELF

Individualism-interdependence

| 1. individualism | 2. individuality | 3. interdependence |

Age

| 1. youth | 2. the middle years | 3. old age |

Sex

| 1. equality of sexes | 2. female superiority | 3. male superiority |

Activity

| 1. doing | 2. being-in-becoming | 3. being |

THE FAMILY

Relational orientations

1. individualistic   2. collateral   3. lineal

Authority

1. democratic   2. authority-centered   3. authoritarian

Positional role behavior

1. open   2. general   3. specific

Mobility

1. high mobility   2. phasic mobility   3. low mobility, stasis

SOCIETY

Social reciprocity

1. independence   2. symmetrical-obligatory   3. complementary-obligatory

Group membership

1. many groups, brief identification, sub-ordination of group to individual   2. balance of nos. 1 and 3   3. few groups, prolonged identification, subordination of the member to the group

Intermediaries

1. no intermediaries (directness)   2. specialist intermediaries only   3. essential intermediaries

Formality

1. informality   2. selective formality   3. pervasive formality

Property

1. private   2. utilitarian   3. community

HUMAN NATURE

Rationality

1. rational   2. intuitive   3. irrational

Good and evil

1. good   2. mixture of good and evil   3. evil

Happiness, pleasure

1. happiness as goal   2. inextricable bond of happiness and sadness   3. life is mostly sadness

Mutability

1. change, growth, learning
2. some change
3. unchanging

NATURE

Relationship of man and nature

1. man dominating nature
2. man in harmony with nature
3. nature dominating man

Ways of knowing nature

1. abstract
2. circle of induction-deduction
3. specific

Structure of nature

1. mechanistic
2. spiritual
3. organic

Concept of time

1. future
2. present
3. past

THE SUPERNATURAL

Relationship of man and the supernatural

1. man as god
2. pantheism
3. man controlled by the supernatural

Meaning of life

1. physical, material goals
2. intellectual goals
3. spiritual goals

Providence

1. good in life is unlimited
2. balance of good and misfortune
3. good in life is limited

Knowledge of the cosmic order

1. order is compre-hensible
2. faith and reason
3. mysterious and unknowable

Anthropologists Kluckhohn and Strodtbeck (1961) and intercultural communication scholars Condon and Yousef (1975) have approached the study of cultural norms from the viewpoint of value orientations. Kluckhohn saw five sets of value orientations as important and the latter expanded them to twenty-five. The assumption behind their approach is that as inhabitants of this planet there are certain conditions and situations which we all face in common, and that as cultures and sub-cultures we develop a value orientation in the process of dealing with those conditions.

The value orientation approach to the study of culture seems to have merit over other methods. Some psychologists have studied man as a creature who seeks to satisfy basic needs. But this system fails to explain why people in different cultures meet those needs in vastly different ways, or why some needs become secondary to some and primary to others. Dorothy Lee (1959) states the problem of the basic needs approach as follows:

> ...the need for food of a member of American society is far greater than that of the members of most other societies. Curiously enough, we also find that though a laborer on a New Guinea plantation needs a minimum diet of seven pounds of yams, plus a stated amount of meat, an Arapesch in his own hamlet, working his fields, climbing up and down steep mountain sides, working hard at ceremonials, can live a meaningful life and procreate healthy children on three pounds of yams a day, and almost no meat...when the Arapesch gardens inefficiently in company with his brother-in-law, and when he plants his fruit tree on someone else's distant land, he multiplies his exertions and minimizes his subsistence so as to achieve a maximum of social warmth... When he takes his pig to another hamlet, and asks someone else's wife to feed and bring it up, what need exactly is he satisfying? And is this need greater than the general human need for food? And does its satisfaction supply a substitute for caloric intake?

She concludes that such questions may appear nonsensical, but they demonstrate the necessity for an almost endless list of needs when studying a culture from this approach.

Condon and Yousef (1975) admit that the value orientation method may have limitations, such as being deductive, whereas other methods tend to be inductive, and may not provide a sufficient number of sets for each value orientation, but they argue that it has advantages. "We have a structure and vocabulary that can be used as a standard for comparing different cultures and for describing variations within a single society." Their structure provides for the building of cultural values around the following concepts which are common to all: *self, family, society, human nature, nature* and *the supernatural.* Each category within the structure has subsets on which a continuum of values are placed. For example, in developing self concept in a particular culture one's *age* is a factor. When placed on a continuum of youth, middle years, to old age, a particular culture may build its values around youth. In this society, great attention and expense would be lavished upon youth. As members of that culture grow older they engage in activities and behaviors to "stay young." They engage in physical exercise, wear wigs, get hair transplants, get facelifts, wear make-up. When they retire they live independently from their children, both for their own privacy and the desire not to be a "burden" on their children and grandchildren. Thus in being a member of such a culture one's self concept is heavily influenced by the value placed upon youth. Jack Benny never got older than "39." Zsa Zsa Gabor is still "25," and in the 1960's a few said "don't trust anyone over 30." At the opposite extreme, in another culture, an individual's self concept may be developed around the value of old age. Youth, while loved and cared for, is not the most valued age. Value is attributed to maturity, experience and age. The young are to "be seen but not heard." One develops status and respect in the culture as he grows older. In some African societies, where there is no written language, the oldest members of the group or tribe are the ones responsible for preserving and passing on the history of the tribe to younger members. It would be unthinkable for them to be independent and live apart from their children and grandchildren in their old age. One's concept of his or her importance would be built around the value of growing older.

While one may be tempted to characterize the dominant culture in the United States as being youth oriented, it is probably more accurate to say that there are subcultures with value orientations at all points on the continuum from youth-middle age-old age, and the middle years may be those we value most highly for some functions. For example, in business and government, we entrust vast powers for decision making in the hands of those between ages of 35 and 55. We may want our presidents to be "youthful" but not "young." Presidents Theodore Roosevelt and John Kennedy were on the borderline of being "too

young" when they were elected with their ages in the early forties.

A full description of Kluckhohn's and Condon's value orientation systems cannot be given here. A brief summary of related and derived concepts will be offered with the belief that it will provide some insight to the reader into the manner in which we have developed values which we hold, but seldom think about.

Self

Age has already been discussed as being a factor in the development of an individual's self concept in his or her culture. One's sex is equally important. Placed upon a continuum, values would be built around equality of the sexes, female superiority or male superiority. In this country government policy mandates equality of the sexes, especially in economic spheres of our society and in some social areas such as education, but there are subcultures which build their value of self upon female or male superiority.

Sex is a factor which has become a revolutionary force around the world to cultural attempts at stability. Its effects will be felt more in the future than it has at the present time. In this country laws requiring sexual equality have been in effect only in the last decade. The Equal Rights Amendment to the Constitution, which it is hoped by its supporters, will bring a better enforcement and speedier implementation of those laws, has yet to pass. Whether the Equal Rights Amendment passes, or not, the trend toward sexual equality is well established. Women are increasing in numbers in the work force and in the different kinds of jobs that they perform. They are now being admitted to the military services and military academies, serving as firefighters and on police forces.

While the role of women is changing world-wide, with the possible exception of Israel, the pace is not as great as it is in this culture. Prosser (1978) noted the following exchanges in a discussion at a recent intercultural communication conference involving Americans and Japanese which took place in Japan. They were discussing roles of husbands and wives in their respective countries. An American wife remarked about her husband:

> He wouldn't prepare the meal, but he does the dishes, which he feels competent to do. Would this happen in your society? [Response:] No. certainly not. I consider myself lucky to have a husband who allows me to pursue my own interests. I don't want to put extra burdens on him. What Florence's husband did could never happen in my own home.

When asked how she felt about it she replied:

> It is my life—and I can't change that...I don't feel any injustice

Property is the last of societal generated value orientations to be discussed. Cultures value property from *private, utilitarian* and *community* orientations. American culture places great emphasis on private property. It becomes the standard by which many Americans measure success. This value gets inculcated into us at a very early age. Most American parents don't buy toys for "the" children. They give specific toys to specific children. They become private property and if other children, or brothers or sisters want to play with them, permission of the owner must be obtained.

Some observers of our culture claim that we place a higher value on private property rights than we do on human rights. This may be true if our laws are a reflection of our values. In most states a bank robber would receive a long prison sentence of 20 years or more, while a murder sentence might be quite short depending upon the circumstances.

While our culture highly values private property, others value it only in a utilitarian way. Nomadic tribes, both in the United States and the Middle East, look upon land to be used and the idea of privately owning it would be as strange as privately owning the air around us. Property is looked upon as something to be used to sustain life or to make it easier, but it is never viewed as a personal possession.

A third value orientation toward property is to communally own it. We tend to think of this as a value orientation shared only by the Communist countries, however, in our culture we place a considerable value on public parks, public buildings, museums, lakes and streams. It could not be argued that this value orientation is as prevalent in this country as it is in the socialist societies. An attempt has been made here to isolate some areas where cultural values are generated. They have been identified and described as separate entities, however, it should be understood that there is considerable overlapping in the way in which values are created from self-concept, to family to society.

Human Nature

Cultures also generate value orientations around their concepts of *human nature* according to Condon and Yousef. Two of those dimensions will be discussed here — *good and evil*, and *mutability*.

Good and Evil: This is not necessarily a discussion of good and evil from the religious viewpoint, though religion has an influence. It is rather a consideration of those behaviors that members of a culture engage in which reflect an interpretation of human nature as being *good*, a *mixture of good and evil*, and basically *evil*. For example, it would appear that cultures that develop a compulsive need to develop elaborate security systems, not only for the nation but for personal property, do not view human nature as basically good. The security systems may not reflect a value orientation that man is basically evil — the value orientation reflects a view that man is part good and part evil. A bookstore owner who creates a detection system to control shoplifting may not reflect a view that man is evil. It probably reflects a view, however, that there are a few among us whose makeup tips the scales toward evil to the extent that he should be on guard in protecting against shoplifting.

I suppose the ultimate example of a view of human nature as essentially evil would be the early Christian Crusaders who would place their wives in chastity belts while they went out to make war against the evil heathens.

Though we can observe certain behaviors in cultures that reflect a clear value orientation there are other situations where it is ambiguous. Deception is often viewed as an evil attribute in human nature. Yet, when deception is employed to undo or defeat evil it is not viewed as evil. If an embezzler uses deception to take your money it is evil. If the police use deception to lay a trap to capture the embezzler, that is good law enforcement. The taking of the life of another human being is evil, but killing in self defense goes unpunished in most circumstances and is apparently not evil. A person who would go out in the streets and gun down 25 armed policemen would be evil. A person in wartime who would go into battle and gun down 25 armed enemy soldiers would be valorous.

When good and evil are viewed from a religious perspective interpretations of human nature differ considerably. For example, early American fundamentalist religions viewed man as basically evil and self-recognition of that state of being was necessary for redemption. At the other extreme Unitarians would take the view that there is more good in man than there is evil, and if that side of his nature is nurtured, cultivated and appealed to his behavior will reveal the prevalence of good over evil.

Mutability as a dimension of human nature has to do with its *change, growth* and *learning*, to *some change*, to its *unchanging* nature. American culture overwhelmingly reflects a value orientation toward a changing human nature. Our technological development has added impetus to this value—that man can alter his destiny, that the human living and working condition does not and must not be a state of abject misery. We are also learning through education and experience that certain segments of our culture should not and cannot be consigned to certain predetermined roles. We are learning that minorities can perform functions in society other than doing menial tasks. We are learning that women have other dimensions to their human nature beyond the scope of bearing and rearing children, cooking and housecleaning.

The strength of this value orientation in our culture is one of the reasons for some of our most frustrating communication failures when dealing with cultures who view human nature as unchanging. One of the most chronicled failures is the young Peace Corpsman who successfully communicated the viability of new technology to relieve the burden of human drudgery only to have it rejected because the local populace believed that human suffering was the plight of human nature. If a culture believes that human nature is immutable, that we are placed on earth to undergo certain tests of human endurance, then changes in human nature are doomed to failure as we know them.

Nature

Condon and Yousef discuss four orientations through which we derive values from nature. Two of them will be considered here.

Relationship of man and nature has dimensions of *man dominating nature, man in harmony with nature,* and *nature dominating man.* The chief value orientation in American culture quite obviously is man dominating nature. Some of the feats are rather mind boggling when one pauses to reflect upon them. The Tennessee Valley Authority controls, and has made placid, one of the most destructive rivers in the world. The Tennessee River and its tributaries annually wrought millions of dollars in damages to those cities located near their banks. Now they add millions of dollars to the economy of the area from vacationers who enjoy the many lakes that were built to control the river system.

What we have done to dominate the air and space is the stuff of science fiction. Ever since the Wright brothers, and later Lindbergh's solo flight across the Atlantic, America's fascination for, and creativity with conquering the space above us has seemed compulsive. Perhaps no other culture on earth would have supported a leader, as we did John F. Kennedy in 1961, when he initiated a program that he claimed "would put an American on the moon" within ten years. We not only walked on the moon, today we probe the stars. Some seriously speculate about the possibility of building colonies in space. Space scientists claim that it can be done and that it is only a matter of time until the technology is feasible. Who are the likely candidates for such space colonies? They could very well be those who live in, or will live in, those structures which are being built that permits man to live out his life and have all his needs met under one roof. One such edifice has plans for a small lake and a park around which the structure will be built.

Though the major value orientation in American culture is man dominating nature, there is a growing sentiment in our society that perhaps we have gone far enough if not too far — that our domination of nature is in fact destroying it, and that we should learn to live with it in harmony. Such sentiment has resulted in the establishment of a federal agency, the Environmental Protection Agency, to serve as a watchdog over some of our more questionable conquests of nature. One of its powers is to require an environmental impact study of actions which might endanger nature. One such study resulted in halting a nearly completed dam by the Tennessee Valley Authority when it was discovered that a small fish, called the Snail Darter, would be destroyed because its only known habitat was the river on which the dam was constructed.

Private organizations such as the Sierra Club and Green Peace are much more alert than the federal government in monitoring man's destructive impact on nature. Such organizations were very influential in creating the Environmental Protection Agency and the Alaskan Wilderness Act, which sets aside several million acres of Alaskan wilderness to be free from commercial exploitation.

There are also small pockets of the third value orientation with respect to man's relationship to nature, that of nature dominating man. One finds in insurance policies exclusions from coverage of "Acts of God." The implication is that there are some forces in nature that man cannot control, that they control man, such as hurricanes. Perhaps this is not a value orientation as such but is a recognition that at this time man can't control all aspects of nature, but perhaps may be able to do so in the future. We have people researching possible ways to control hurricanes.

Probably other than the United States, Canada and Western Europe, the other cultures of the world have a stronger value orientation toward man living in harmony with, and man being dominated by nature. Japanese art and theatre reflect a strong sentiment toward man living in harmony with nature. Such terminology as "third world," "developing nations," and "underdeveloped nations" is the invention of the United States and Western Europe. It reflects our value orientations. To dominate nature, man must develop technology, but the development of technology doesn't come free. Man pays the price in the destruction of his environment. We enjoy the comfort of speeding in jet planes to distant cities and lands. In doing so we slowly destroy the ozone and subject ourselves to increased rates of cancer and respiratory diseases. We enjoy our automobiles, but the air smells of burned gasoline which destroys our health. The farmer values pesticides which help increase his yield, but the price is paid in the increased pollution of our lakes and streams, and in the death of fish and to the birds which eat the poisoned insects, resulting in a more "silent spring." We value the development of superhighways, shopping centers, airports, new housing and industrial projects. In so doing we destroy the land which has provided sustenance to man and animal throughout the ages, but will be denied to future generations, when the need for it will be greater. We treasure appliances and gadgetry from furnaces, refrigerators, dishwashers, air conditioners, to hair dryers which create creature comforts. These require an ever increasing supply of energy to operate, and we pay the price in scarring the earth with strip mining, by polluting our beaches with oil spills from tanker accidents and offshore drilling mishaps, and by polluting our environment with radioactive wastes that will last for centuries. Increasingly we rely upon chemicals to advance our lifestyle, but we pay the price by polluting the waters upon which we depend for life and pleasure. Four million of the fourteen million acres of commercial shellfish waters in the United States have been abandoned due to chemical pollution in the last few years. Underground water supplies serving one half of the population of this nation are threatened by poison, from indiscriminate dumping practices of chemical companies.

Is it possible that we have never stopped to pause and reflect upon the cost of "development" as we know it? Given the different value orientations of many cultures with respect to human nature and nature, is there any question as to why some cultures are "developed" and others are "undeveloped"? If the farmer in central Africa perceives the planting and raising of his crop as primarily a function of nature he will react differently to nature than the farmer from another culture who perceives the process as essentially mechanical.

As long as the "undeveloped" societies maintain value orientations that nature dominates man they are likely to remain undeveloped from our viewpoint, but the environment benefits from that result.

Different value orientations toward nature have given rise to extensive communication problems for many Americans for centuries. Some of the greatest breakdowns in relations with the American Indian tribes, from the outset until today, has been over differing viewpoints on nature. The Indians could never understand why the settlers wanted to personally "own" the land, or why they killed more game than was necessary for food, or why they cut down more trees than was necessary for building homes and cooking food. Nature, to the Indians is basic to their religion, and to see it exploited in ways that appear to them to be destructive is demeaning.

Concept of time is also an orientation around which cultures develop values with respect to nature. The dimensions are *future, present* and *past.* Probably all of us have heard the expression "time is money." This is an indication that time is a very valued commodity in the United States. Though there may be certain characteristics of our culture which reflect a value for all three orientations, when one studies the behavior of Americans, the conclusion must be that we value the future more than the past or present. This is a likely extension of our emphasis on youth, doing activity, our views on a changing human nature, and man's domination of nature. We may treasure today, but we spend vast amounts of time and energy planning for the future. Probably most college undergraduates don't like to read books such as this one, take exams, or write term papers. They do it because they believe that it will have a future payoff. Almost every organization, business, or government, and many families, have short or long range plans for the accomplishment of certain goals. We save for the future, we buy insurance to cover any future problem or emergency. A few people go so far as to plan their own funeral. Anticipation of the future is so pervasive that retirement is often a problem. So much effort is placed on the future that when it arrives, with respect to retirement, people have difficulty coping with it. They have spent so little time on valuing the present that it becomes a problem in learning to value it when they have it in abundance.

As mentioned earlier there are orientations which value the present and past in our culture. The "now" generation of the 1960's and early 1970's and the "beat" generation of the 1950's were minority segments of the culture who rejected the "rat race" to "get ahead" in our society and focused upon an appreciation of the present. Most such movements — if indeed they can be called movements — are short lived. Many of those who were "turned off" in the 1960's are leading conventional lifestyles today. One of the slogans of the "now" generation was "don't trust anyone over 30," but Tom Hayden, who was one of the leaders of the movement, ran as a serious candidate for the United States Senate in California in 1978. One would not expect to see the slogan nor his involvement in the counter-culture a centerpiece in his campaign.

Likewise there are pockets of orientations valuing the past, but when compared to other cultures they can't be interpreted as very significant. With respect to family history only a small minority can trace family roots beyond a few generations. In less mobile cultures many can trace family history over periods of hundreds of years. Alex Haley, the author of *Roots,* helped verify his family's history by talking to an African tribal historian who was able to cite the date that Haley's ancestor, Kunta Kinte, was stolen into slavery hundreds of years ago.

When alert Americans visit Europe, they are immediately aware of the value placed on tradition with respect to buildings and monuments. This writer had the experience of staying overnight in England in a hotel over 500 years old. It would probably be impossible to locate a single structure in this country that is of that age. Greeks and Italians spend great energy and effort to preserve remains from ancient Greek and Roman culture. In Athens one can see the olive tree that Athenians claim grew in Plato's yard and the cave where Socrates was imprisoned and later drank the hemlock. One's head buzzes with confusion trying to separate history from mythology when a Greek stands at the remains at Delphi and points to the crack through which the oracle spoke. Greeks are so engrossed in their history and tradition that they don't bother to separate the two. A Greek's self concept is shaped by his history. To be Greek means to be free. A Greek would never be loyal to his government, because such loyalty would be bestowed upon an impersonal institution. Instead he would be loyal to Greece as the motherland which represents people, and thus freedom. Governments make laws which restrict freedom, likewise it becomes an obligation to a Greek to try to outwit the law, to escape its thrust, by doing so one is free.

We have seen how concepts of time, and how it is valued, has a tremendous impact upon our behavior, and thus how we communicate.

The Supernatural

There is strong similarity between the value orientation growing out of man's relationship with God and his relationship with nature. Therefore only one of the dimensions will be discussed here to illustrate how man develops values from this orientation.

The *providence* variable has dimensions of *good in life is unlimited, a balance of good and misfortune,* and *good in life is limited.* Quite obviously the prevailing orientation in the United States is that good in life is unlimited. Good in life is limited only by man's ingenuity and knowledge. This idea is reflected in much of our behavior and thinking. Perhaps every generation in our history has believed that the life and well-being of the next generation would be better than their own. Parents struggle and make sacrifices in order to provide their children with opportunities so that they would have a better life than the parents had. In contrast to the view that God controls the destiny of man our motto tends to be, "God helps him who helps himself." For example, when faced with a draught the American Indian farmer would pray to the Rain God for rain, whereas the modern farmer will seed the clouds and make it rain.

In many cultures the supernatural and nature tend to be one and the same. When Peace Corpsmen suggested to a group of farmers in India that they switch from wooden to iron plows they were appalled that anyone would advise them to tear the flesh of their mother with knives. The Maya Indians in Yucatan build altars in the field at planting time and pray for a successful crop. In other words, there are cultures that believe that man is completely at the mercy of his devine creator and there is need for continuous ritual in life to let the Gods know that you realize that fact.

Between the two extremes is the middle orientation that believes that there is a balance sheet kept by the supernatural of good and evil. This view is that for all the good in life there is an equal amount of misfortune, and if the books aren't balanced in this life they will be balanced in the next one. Some religions warn that rich men cannot enter "the kingdom of heaven," because they haven't "paid their dues" in an equal amount of misfortune.

Value orientations have been discussed here as though they were discrete entities. It would be a mistake, however, to try to tie a particular value orientation to a specific communication behavior. They have been broken down here only for the sake of discussion. In actuality, all of the orientations come together as one, in determining how an individual will function in a particular culture.

Value orientations about self, family, society, human nature, nature and the supernatural have an all pervading influence upon how we communicate and behave within our own culture. Likewise, our knowledge of how other cultures have developed different values from the same orientations will influence our ability to communicate interculturally.

Communication is Culture Bound

If we are to gain such insight to enable us to engage in intercultural communication, it would be wise for us to remember that the concept of communication itself is culture bound. For example, in our society we communicate in many different settings. When we are taught communication, and when we study it, we do it from a framework of settings which are unique to our culture. For example, in our culture we teach interpersonal communication because the individual must develop and use such skills in order to function successfully within our society. These skills are necessary in relating to family members, in relationship building, in seeking a mate, and in seeking and maintaining employment. Strong interpersonal communication skills would not be as important to an individual who comes from a culture which is more formal in family and other relationships, or where intermediaries often make the decisions in selection of marriage partners and in finding employment.

In our society we study small group communication because communication within the small group meets a cultural need. Outsiders who have observed us often conclude that we are probably the most small-group, or committee oriented, nation on earth. We value individualism highly, but where decision-making is involved, the individual will dare not make the decision without the input of a group. People in our society who have great personal power of decision-making, such as the President of the United States, or heads of corporate giants would not think of using that power without first using the group communication process to provide input into the decision. The outsider trying to function in our culture would probably be ineffective unless he understood the strong value we place upon communication within the small group. Likewise, we would not communicate well in those cultures where decisions are often made on the basis of custom, tradition, or religion, if we demanded that such decisions employ the small group process.

We study conflict resolving communication in our society because so many areas of our culture are adversarial in nature. Though our economic system is not always competitive in the market place, it is often competitive with respect to the way it functions with regard to labor and management. Teachers and school boards often relate to each other in adversarial situations. In such conditions it is important to the individual in our culture to be able to employ communication skills in bargaining and negotiating that will satisfy his self interest without destroying the opposition. These situations are often called win-win, or lose-lose. In other words, each side compromises and gains something, but not everything, or loses something, but doesn't lose everything. Each side realizes the necessity for the opposition's existence for its own welfare.

There are, however, some situations in our culture that are win-lose in the adversarial relationship. This is true in all of our political election system and in much of our legal system. In our political election system the candidate either wins or loses. In the legal system cases are often won or lost in court. In many cases where the evidence isn't strong in support of the original charge, the two sides will plea bargain. There is still a winner and loser, but on a reduced charge. Since we value competitiveness in many key areas of our culture, we place a high priority upon studying communication strategies to resolve the conflicts. When we rub elbows with such cultures as Japan, which is not nearly as competitive in communication relationships, we are often viewed as being overly aggressive. In Japan, labor and management have established a cooperative, as compared to our adversarial relationship. Their legal system is also a more cooperative one than ours. Thus, in our society the need to study conflict resolution communication has a high priority due to our cultural values, whereas in Japan the need for such communication emphasis would be low.

Historically, our nation has bestowed recognition and prestige upon outstanding public speakers. Before the development of mass communication, the public speaker, whether politician, theologian, or social pioneer, commanded the attention and respect of the American people. The public speech, or debate, were the chief sources of knowledge and entertainment to those living on our frontiers in the 19th century. In 1858 the Lincoln-Douglass debates in Illinois drew thousands to each of the seven occasions on which they debated. It should therefore come as no surprise that our culture values effective public speaking. While it may be true that contemporary America can offer no equals of Patrick Henry, Daniel Webster, Abraham Lincoln, Frederick Douglass, Franklin D. Roosevelt, John F. Kennedy, Martin Luther King,· or Hubert Humphrey, it does offer contemporary Americans an opportunity to hear a person such as former Congresswoman Barbara Jordan who can enunciate the American dream.

Since we value the public speech in our culture from an historical perspective, we study the methods which produce its effectiveness.

Again, a culture which placed less value upon public decision making, or the influence of the individual's persuasive ability upon the decision making, would not place as high a priority as we do upon public speaking skills.

The last form of communication that we stress in our culture that will be considered here, is mass communication.

Of all the forms of communication, mass communication has perhaps the most pervasive influence upon our lives. In our culture it is imperative that we study it and try to assess its effects. At this writing that task is impossible. We do believe that radio, television, motion pictures, newspapers, magazines, stereo records, tapes, and books offer the greatest opportunity for bridging the gaps of misunderstanding in intercultural communication. If, however, we are to capitalize upon this opportunity the mass media will require considerable innovation. For example, one of the major problems of the electronic mass media is the ease with which it stereotypes cultural characteristics. Examples of racial and sexual stereotyping are abundant in the electronic mass media. But, this also has its advantages for research and innovation. It is very easy to replay this form of communication for such research with the aim of making the media reflect a more accurate image of cultural characteristics. As Margaret Mead has suggested, the mass media may be the instrument through which future generations bridge the void in intercultural communication.

All of our communication is literally a communication of our cultural values. Our cultural values determine what we communicate and how we communicate it.

Summary

Our culture and our communication are closely entwined. We spend considerable time studying communication, but we seldom think of culture until we come into contact with one other than our own, and when that occurs the focus is usually upon differences. Often the evaluation is negative.

Culture is a combination of our language, symbols, rituals, myths, institutions and values. We start acquiring our culture at an early age. We acquire it intitially from the family and later through institutions.

Most nations around the globe have much more cultural homogeneity than we have in the United States. It is therefore important for us to become more aware of cultural differences within our society if we are to communicate effectively. Those cultural differences grow out of orientations from which we derive our values. Those orientations are self, family, society, human nature, nature, and the supernatural.

References

Bloomington Daily Pantagraph, Jan. 19, 1979, p. A-9.

Condon, J.C. and Yousef, F. *An Introduction to Intercultural Communication.* Indianapolis: Bobbs-Merrill, 1975.

Kluckhohn, F.K. and Strodtbeck, F. *Variations in Value Orientations.* Evanston: Row, Peterson, 1961.

Lee, D. *Freedom and Culture.* Englewood Cliffs: Prentice-Hall, 1959.

Mead, M. *In Culture and Commitment: A Study of the Generation Gap,* 1970.

Prosser, M.H. *The Cultural Dialogue.* Boston: Houghton-Mifflin, 1978.

3

Communication Codes

Vincent Hazleton, Jr.

It is a truism among students of communication that "meanings are in people not in words." While there is a lot of truth to this statement, it must be qualified. Without words and nonverbal behavior, "meaning" would be a "meaningless" concept. What the statement should be understood to "mean" is that meanings are not transferred directly from person to person. Meanings are sent in messages and meanings are attributed to messages. Sometimes the meaning sent is not the meaning attributed. This is because meanings are coded in messages.

In order to understand a message that is intended, a receiver must know the code that the sender of a message is using. In this chapter we will examine the two types of codes used in human communication: verbal and nonverbal. We will examine elements and characteristics of each, the communicative functions each performs, and examine problems that arise in the use of each.

Verbal Codes

Many philosophers and scientists have observed that verbal codes may be the distinguishing characteristic of the human species. While many animals may communicate in a rudimentary fashion using vocal signals (i.e. birds sing, dolphins whistle), no other animal possesses so elaborate and rich a signal system as a human language. Verbal codes, unlike other aspects of behavior, exist for no other purpose than communication.

Try to imagine what it would be like to try and communicate what you are experiencing now without using some oral, visual, or tactile form of verbal code. It would be impossible. While a great amount of information about affective and emotional states is conveyed nonverbally, the transmission of cognitive information is dependent almost entirely upon the use of verbal codes. Poetry, drama, the existence of complex organizations and intimate relationships would all be impossible without the use of verbal codes.

Because verbal codes are the primary vehicle for human communication they are important to study. The purpose of this section is to provide you with an understanding of verbal codes and how they function in the communication process. First, the concept of verbal code is defined. What is a verbal code? Second, the characteristics of the elements that make up verbal codes are examined. Third, the concept of meaning is considered. Fourth, the functions which you use verbal codes to perform are identified. And finally, problems that arise in communication from the use of verbal codes are discussed, with the intention that hopefully, in the future you can avoid or at least understand some of these problems of communication.

Verbal Codes Defined

Verbal codes consist of (1) shared sets of symbols and (2) shared sets of rules for combining symbols into understandable utterances. The emphasis in this apparently simple definition is first of all upon the notion of sharing. Without a shared system of symbols and rules communication is impossible. Even within a particular verbal code such as American English there are specialized symbol systems used by certain groups that are not shared by all speakers of the language. While it is often frustrating to communicate with someone who does not speak American English, it can be equally frustrating to attempt to communicate with an attorney or medical doctor because of the specialized symbol systems that they use and with which most people are not familiar. For example, to a physician, a broken blood vessel might be a hematoma, and to an attorney, a divorce might be a marriage dissolution suit.

The basic component of verbal codes is the symbol. A symbol is an arbitrarily selected and learned stimulus which serves as a representation of something else. Words are the most common symbols. That the symbols that represent particular objects are arbitrarily selected accounts for the wide diversity in human verbal codes.

The arbitrary nature of symbols becomes particularly apparent when examining the symbols which different cultures select to represent naturally occurring sounds. For example, American children represent the sound of a barking dog with the symbols "bow wow", while Japanese children represent the same sound with the symbols "wan wan", and Finnish children represent the same sounds with the symbols "hau hau". While there may be some similarity between the sounds the children make and the sounds the dog makes, the representations chosen for the three verbal codes are clearly different, and it is unlikely that the speaker of one verbal code would recognize the intended meaning represented by the use of the appropriate representation in either of the other verbal codes.

The fact that a single symbol may have many meanings and that the meanings of symbols change over time are also evidence for the arbitrary nature of symbols. Much humor is dependent upon use of words with more than one meaning. Puns are examples of humorous word play. A symbol that has acquired an additional meaning in recent times is "waste". During the Vietnam war, the term waste came to be synonomous with "killing". The significance of the use of the term "waste" to symbolize death is considered later in this chapter.

That verbal symbols are learned stimuli implies two things. First, it implies that verbal codes are acquired, not innate. While there appears to be some innate propensity for humans to acquire verbal codes, the particular verbal code acquired is a function of the culture in which a person is raised and that person's physiological capabilities. For example, we are not surprised that children born in Spain are likely to speak Spanish, or that children in Illinois say "you guys" while children in Louisiana say "y'all". Second, it implies that verbal codes as "stimuli" must take some physical form, either graphic, oral, or tactile to be communicated.

The rules that are used to combine symbols into understandable utterances are of two types: grammatical and contextual. Grammatical rules specify permissable relationships between symbols. That is, they specify what symbols may go together and in what order. The importance of word order in determining meaning is clearly demonstrated by considering the difference between a *blind Venetian* and a *venetian blind*. In both cases, the first word serves as an adjective modifying the following noun. In the first case, the referent is understood to be a citizen of Venice, a city in Italy or perhaps California, who cannot see. In the second case, the referent is understood to be a type of window covering. Yet the symbols are the same.

The creativity that is a product of the use of verbal codes may in large part be attributed to the flexibility provided by grammatical rules. The creative potential of grammar is seen easily. With just 5 nouns and 5 verbs, it is possible to construct 25 two word utterances. If you assume that nouns are also capable of functioning as the object of verbs, it is possible to construct 75 three word utterances. Now consider that most verbal codes possess many thousands of symbols which perform other grammatical functions, such as adjectives, adverbs, prepositions, conjunctions, etc. In fact, it has been estimated that if you were to take the English language, it would take ten trillion years just to utter all the possible 20 word sentences (Farb, 1973).

The contextual rules which govern the use of verbal codes specify which symbols and utterance types are appropriate and permissable for a given communication situation. There are rules for fighting, joking, loving, and learning. These rules are implicit rather than explicit. You learned them as children and tend to become aware of them only when a rule is violated. As children you were probably taught that it is "polite" to use the terms "sir" and "ma'am" when addressing adults. In addition to learning what is appropriate, you also learn what is inappropriate. You are aware of what is rude, crude, and impolite in a large variety of communication situations. Imagine how your teacher would react if you addressed him or her as "Hey, you."

To summarize what has been said so far, in order for communication to be effective and efficient, it is necessary for people to share a set of symbols and a set of rules for combining those symbols into grammatically and situationally appropriate, and therefore understandable, utterances. Hope I understand you that all. (The preceding sentence should be read as "I hope you understand all that." If it was more meaningful to you in its original form, please do not continue, but return to the beginning of this section and read it again.)

Elements of Verbal Codes

Verbal codes, like people and cultures, are born, evolve or change, and die. Fifty years ago, no one spoke fortran. Today, computer experts around the world can communicate with each other using fortran and other computer languages. The original meaning of the word dumb was "unable to speak". Today, dumb is usually considered to mean "stupid". Today, there are no native speakers of Latin or many native American languages. In order to understand these processes and to understand the problems involved in using verbal codes, it is necessary to have an understanding of the basic elements which make up verbal codes and how these elements interact in the communication process.

All oral verbal codes can be broken down into units of sound called phonemes. These are the most basic elements of verbal codes. More simply, phonemes are the consonants and vowels that make up a language. Phonetic regularities are an important part of every language. People frequently make judgements about speakers' cultural background or social status because of how they say things.

Verbal codes have been observed to consist of as few as 11 and as many as 67 different phonemes (Russell & Russell, 1971). For example, all the words in the English language can be said using between 35 and 45 different sounds. The exact number necessary depends upon the dialect of the speaker. On the other hand, the Hawaiian language consists of only 13 different phonemes. This accounts for the number of long words and the melodic sound of the Hawaiian language.

With minor exceptions, phonemes are only meaningful in combination. The smallest meaningful unit of sound is called the morpheme. When you think of meaning you usually think of words. However, not all morphemes are words. "Man" is an example of a morpheme that is also a word. By adding "ly", another morpheme, to to the noun man, the adverb "manly" is created. If you add "un", another morpheme, to the adverb "manly", you would create an adverb whose meaning is the opposite of manly. Most suffixes and prefixes are morphemes but not words.

From phonemes and morphemes, words are constructed. Verbal codes consist of two types of words: *function* words and *content* words. *Function* words inform you of the grammatical structure of utterances. That is, they tell you how content words are to be understood. For example, upon hearing an article such as a, an, or the, a listener expects to hear a noun or an adjective/noun combination. *Content* words, on the other hand, have cognitive referents. That is, they have meaning which is independent of their grammatical class. In the sentence, "the dog and cat chased a mouse," the words "the", "and", and "a" are function words. "Dog", "cat", and "mouse" are content words.

The smallest unit of verbal codes used for purposes of communication is the utterance. Utterances may consist of a single word or many words. Utterances are the smallest unit of speech which can stand alone as meaningful in a conversation. Utterances depend heavily upon context for meaning. That is why it is difficult to understand overheard bits of conversation.

✳ Communication involves two or more people and is therefore a cooperative process. The construction of meaningful utterances is dependent upon adherence to and understanding of what Grice (1967) calls the cooperative principle. Simply, speakers try to be informative, truthful, relevant, and clear, and listeners interpret what speakers say on the assumption that they are adhering to these principles. According to Grice, in living up to the cooperative principle, speakers normally try to satisfy four maxims. These maxims specify how speakers should contribute to a conversation. They are:

✳ (1) **Maxim of Quantity**. Make your contribution as informative as is required, but no more informative than is required.

(2) **Maxim of Quality**. Try to make your contribution one that is true. That is, do not say anything you believe to be false or lack evidence for.

(3) **Maxim of Relation**. Make your contribution relevant to the air of the ongoing conversation.

(4) **Maxim of Manner.** Be clear. Try to avoid obscurity, ambiguity, wordiness, and disorderliness in your use of language.

By obeying these maxims, a speaker can construct meaningful utterances. More importantly, by using these maxims as an interpretive framework, listeners can interpret utterances as meaningful. How this is done is discussed in some detail in the following section.

Meaning

"What do you mean? I didn't understand you." How often have you heard or used these two utterances. In this section, the concept of meaning is discussed. How messages mean is not completely understood. There are many sources of meaning in most messages. Here meaning is examined on two levels. First, meaning as it applies to words is considered. Second, meaning as a product of utterances is discussed.

It was noted earlier that the meaning of function words is grammatical. They tell how content words are to be interpreted, whether the word is singular or plural, or whether it is a noun, adverb, or adjective, etc. Content words, on the other hand, mean on two different levels. The *denotative* meaning of content words refers to the objects or activities which are the literal referents of the word. It is effective to think of the denotative meaning of a word as its literal "dictionary" meaning. The *connotative* meanings of words refers to the emotional or evaluative response that words evoke from listeners. The difference between connotative and denotative meanings is easily seen by comparing synonyms, words which supposedly have the same meaning. Consider the words "prostitute" and "whore." While both words have the same denotative meaning, their connotative meanings are different. Most people would consider "whore" to have a more negative connotation than "prostitute." What would you rather be called, a student, an undergraduate, a pupil, or a scholar? By selecting from sets of synonyms with different connotative meanings, a communicator may express many different meanings while ostensibly, on a denotative level, saying the same thing.

Imagery is another aspect of word meaning. Imagery refers to the capacity of words to evoke mental images of things or events. Some words arouse a sensory experience, such as a mental picture or sound, very quickly and easily, whereas other words may do so only with difficulty or not at all. Figures of speech, such as similes and metaphors can be used to increase the imagery of messages. Consider the following examples: (1) My roommate is terribly messy, or (2) My roommate is as messy as a pig. Which evokes the clearer and stronger image? Probably the second. Messages which are high in imagery are more concrete and are more likely to be correctly interpreted. Messages which are low in imagery are abstract and subject to multiple interpretations. Research seems to indicate that messages which are high in imagery are more likely to be remembered (Kausler, 1974) and that persuasive messages which enhance imagery through the use of devices such as similes and metaphors tend to be more persuasive (Bowers & Osborn, 1966; Reinsch, 1971).

Intensity refers to the attitudinal information conveyed by the verbal code. That is, the degree to which someone likes or dislikes someone or some thing, or the extent to which someone agrees or disagrees with a point of view. By examining messages for their intensity, it is possible to determine whether someone feels negatively or positively about something and the degree to which they are emotionally involved. Intensity is determined by the use of adjectives, adverbs, and connotative meanings of words. Compare the intensity of the following two sentences, both of which convey positive affect. I had a somewhat nice time during spring break. I had a very wonderful time during spring vacation. Sometimes small changes in the choice of words can result in large changes in meaning.

The more emotionally involved a person is in a subject, the more likely he or she is to use intense language in talking about it. Research shows that using intense language may not be a good idea in most persuasive situations. Speakers who use highly intense language are judged to lack objectivity. On the other hand, speakers who try to appear totally objective and try to avoid using evaluative words may appear unconcerned and also may fail in their persuasive attempts. Messages of moderate intensity appear to be most persuasive.

If your goal is to activate or motivate an audience that already agrees with your point of view, the use of intense words may be an effective strategy. The use of intense language in such situations may increase an audience's perception of issue importance. One social group that has effectively used this strategy is the anti-abortion movement. Their messages appear to be directed at people who are either neutral or slightly against abortion initially. They use highly intense messages, referring to abortion as murder, and have been extremely effective at motivating people to action. Pro-abortionist groups on the other hand, tend to use neutral terms in referring to abortion and tend to use intense words in describing the effects of unwanted children.

Words may also be ambiguous or vague. A word is ambiguous if it has two or more meanings. The sentence, he wears a light suit in summer, is an example of ambiguity. The sentence may be interpreted to mean that he wears a lightweight suit or that he wears a suit made of light, such as a halo. The correct interpretation of ambiguous messages is dependent upon knowledge of the communication context. In fact, most communication problems that are attributed to ambiguity actually occur because they are heard out of context or because the sender and the receiver have defined the context differently.

Vagueness is similar to ambiguity. A word is vague if the parameters of its meaning are unclear. While ambiguous messages result in radically different interpretations, vague messages result in different but related interpretations. The statement, I like older women, is vague. While the major thrust of the statement is clear, I like women, the parameters of the meaning of "older" are undefined. After all, how old is older? Vague messages, like ambiguous messages, are interpreted on the basis of context or prior experiences and attitudes.

The deliberate use of vagueness is called equivocation. Politicians frequently use equivocation as a communicative strategy. Because vague messages are generally interpreted from the framework of the audience members' values and prior perceptions, a politician can use the equivocation strategy to create a single message which audiences with differing view points find appealing or at least unoffensive.

The processes by which words are created and given meaning and by which current words acquire new or different meanings are complex. By combining existing words or using them in new and different fashions an infinite number of different meanings can be expressed. Take for example, the word "waste." The common meanings of the word waste are: (1) to use or expend thoughtlessly, and (2) garbage. During the American involvement in Vietnam, waste was used as a synonym for "kill." Grunts (U.S. infantry) wasted (killed) gooks (Vietnamese). Why was waste used as a synonym for kill? No one can say for sure. Perhaps, waste conveyed more accurately feelings that American soldiers had about the war and their role in it than the word "kill."

Arriving at the meaning of an utterance is not a simple function of adding together the meanings of the words from which the utterance is constructed. It is possible to say something and mean exactly its opposite. Listeners utilize the maxims of the cooperative principle, discussed earlier, in addition to their knowledge of word meanings, to determine the meanings of utterances. Consider the following exchange between student and teacher.

Dr. Hazleton: Papers are due Tuesday.

Janey: Dr. Hazleton, my typewriter is broken.

Dr. Hazleton: I have a typewriter that works.

On the surface, three things have been said, Janey has asserted that her typewriter does not work, and Dr. Hazleton has asserted that papers are due Tuesday and that his typewriter works. Both have actually implied much more than that. Both expect the other to adhere to the maxim of relation. So each statement must be interpreted as relevant to the ongoing conversation. If Dr. Hazleton assumes that Janey's assertion is relevant, he will realize that she means she cannot meet the Tuesday deadline because her typewriter is broken. If Janey recognizes Dr. Hazleton's second utterance as relevant, she will realize that it is possible for her to use Dr. Hazleton's typewriter and that he still expects her paper on Tuesday. Can you predict the next utterance? How likely is it that Janey would ask to borrow Dr. Hazleton's typewriter? By applying the maxim of relation and using the first utterance to define the context, both Janey and Dr. Hazleton were able to understand the meanings implied by the other. In addition, the maxims place constraints on the permissable contributions that each can make to the conversation. The response alternatives that Janey has as options are limited, if she is to make a meaningful contribution to the ongoing conversation.

Failure to adhere to the maxims can result in misunderstandings. Take a violation of the maxim of quantity.

> John: The school board requested the teachers to stop drinking at school.
>
> Bill: I didn't know there were teachers drinking at school. Isn't that against the law?
>
> John: There aren't any teachers drinking. There are students drinking at school.

When John told Bill the teachers were to stop drinking, he was not as informative as he could have been, and Bill understood him to say teachers were drinking at school. By violating the maxim of quantity, John misled Bill. The misunderstanding could have been avoided if John had inserted the word students before the word drinking in his first utterance.

Unintentional violations of any of the maxims can result in communication problems. The sentence, they sent the supplies over a week ago, violates the maxim of manner. Depending on how the words are grouped, it can be understood in at least two different ways. Sentences such as, the supplies arrived over a week ago and the supplies are over a week late, would both meet the maxim of manner and result in unambiguous messages. Violations of other maxims are equally serious. It would be difficult or impossible to exchange information if you could not tell what was true or false, if speakers did not obey the maxim of quality. Have you ever participated in a conversation where one of the participants frequently made comments about topics which other participants had finished discussing earlier? Such violations of the maxim of relation are both confusing and irritating.

Not all violations of the maxims result in misunderstandings. By blatantly and obviously violating maxims while still adhering to the cooperative principle it is possible to mean the opposite of what is said. Many things are said, indirectly. Sarcasm, understatement, and irony are examples of situations where the implied meaning of an utterance is the opposite or different from the simple interpretation of the utterance. Have you heard anything like the following example?

Janey: How was your blind date last night?

Susan: He didn't spill anything on me.

Susan has violated the maxim of quantity, she is not giving as much information as the question required. By focusing upon what appears to be an irrelevant attribute, she has communicated to Janey that she did not think too highly of her date. Thus, apparently senseless utterances can be interpreted as perfectly sensible, when listeners recognize the cooperative intent of speakers and take into account their knowledge of the speaker and their knowledge of communication rules. These two elements, shared experience and shared knowledge of the verbal code, are perhaps the most important factors in understanding meaning.

Functions of Verbal Codes

Messages are used to do things. Verbal codes are tools through which social activities are accomplished. They are also used to achieve personal goals. Halliday (1973) identifies seven functions which can be performed using verbal codes. He identifies an instrumental function, a regulative function, a representational function, an interactional function, a heuristic function, an imaginative function, and a personal function.

The instrumental function represents attempts to manipulate the environment through the use of verbal codes, to initiate events. Each of us has basic needs and desires which we attempt to fulfill through communication. This is perhaps the most basic of functions. In order to survive, a child must be able to convey information concerning needs for food and/or warmth. As we develop, our needs and desires become more complex and we need a larger repertoire at our command in order to meet these needs. Statements which begin with "I want" or "I need" appear to fulfill the instrumental function.

The regulative function refers to attempts to control events when they happen, rather than to cause events to happen (instrumental function). Through the use of verbal codes we regulate social roles and status. Also, complex patterns of rules are developed to control behavior. The existence of these patterns is made apparent by

observing communication behavior. Status, for example, may be inferred from the use of titles or simply observing patterns of inter-action. Individuals of higher status, control interaction and are also deferred to by individuals of lower status. "Talking down" to some one is a way of indicating lower status and thereby controlling their behavior. You may know what it is like to be treated like a child, or to be treated like a little brother or sister.

The regulative function may also be performed with respect to the self. How many times have you talked to yourself while performing a task? Many students find reading aloud or copying to be an effective learning strategy. After all, if you learn from observing others, why can you not learn from observing yourself? When you talk to yourself, you are also listening, and when you write, you are also reading. This constitutes a self-feedback loop, which can be used to regulate behavior, a use of verbal codes to perform the regulative function.

Verbal codes are used interactionally to ensure maintenance of social structure. That is, verbal codes are used to identify and maintain social groups. Slang, jargon, and rituals are all examples of verbal codes used instrumentally. Vocabulary and dialect are two important clues concerning group membership. The more frequently individuals communicate and the more isolated they are from other individuals and groups, the more likely they are to develop and use verbal codes uniquely. For example, close friends frequently appear to use a verbal short hand, seldom using complete sentences to communi-cate. In much the same way, members of professions, trades, and social organizations, develop jargon and use specialized symbols which allow them to communicate more effectively and to identify each other as members of "the group".

Failure to use instrumental language properly can be considered bad manners or identify you as an outsider. A great deal of the ritualistic communication in which we engage, such as greetings and good-byes, performs this function. For example, not greeting a friend in public is generally considered bad manners. The greeting is not "informative" but it does serve to identify two people as friends or acquaintances. The greeting informs the participants to the conversation and observers that friendly behavior is appropriate and to be expected.

The representational function refers to the use of verbal codes to exchange or deliver information. Individuals use verbal codes to make knowledge claims about themselves, about the world in which they live, and about others. Simple statements, such as, "I went to a movie" or "There is the chalk" are examples of utterances which perform the representational function.

Communication may also be used to acquire information. The heuristic function refers to verbal codes used as a tool to acquire understanding or knowledge. Verbal codes allow you to ask questions and construct answers. By linking old concepts with new ones, you increase understanding, create simpler ways to communicate complex ideas, and in general increase the effectiveness of attempts in relating to others. This function is the basis for education. Through this function it is possible to learn without doing. This results in potentially important savings in time and effort.

The way a person speaks is a part of his or her self. In a sense everyone uses verbal codes uniquely to express the self. Everyone develops a style of speaking. This is the personal function, the way in which verbal codes reflect the individual personality. Expressions of mood, feelings, and emotions are examples of this function. However, in most situations where there is the opportunity for individuals to improvise the content of their messages, the messages will perform the personal function, they will reflect the individual's style of speaking.

Finally, verbal codes are used to discuss and create the imaginary. Philosophical systems, fictional literature, and word games are examples of the imaginative use of verbal codes. Through imagination, both play and creative work can be performed. Many of the ways in which people organize perceptions are based upon symbols developed through performance of the imaginative function. Existentialism, pragmatism, communism, and democracy, all of which may seem real and tangible are in reality abstract products of imagination, made real through the use of verbal codes.

It may be difficult in a particular instance to classify an utterance as performing a single function. This is because most utterances are multi-functional. While giving or seeking information, an utterance may also define the social relationship between speakers, identify the next speaker, or reflect the emotional state of the speaker. In fact, some utterances do all of these things.

Problems

At the beginning of this chapter, it was observed that the message sent is not necessarily the message received. The very characteristics that make verbal codes useful for communication also make communication breakdowns possible. Breakdowns occur not simply because of the codes, but because of the ways in which individuals use verbal codes. In this section, five common problems which can interfere with effective communication are examined. These problems are inference-observation confusion, bypassing, allness, frozen evaluation, and indiscrimination.

Codes only imperfectly represent what is actually observed and only a small portion of what is actually observed can be communicated. These principles are easily demonstrated by observing how two different people describe an event they have both observed. Invariably, both will describe the event differently. In addition, it is likely that they will both report elements or aspects of the event which did not occur or were not present. It is this tendency to create information on the basis of observation which is the source of inference-observation confusion.

Consider the following possible events. Upon seeing a fire truck, with its siren on, arrive at a neighbor's house, you might tell someone that there is a fire next door. If you saw someone run from a store with a sack of money, followed by other people, you might yell, "Stop, thief" and join the chase to catch the thief. If you are told that your fiancee was seen on a date with your best friend, you probably would be upset and accuse your fiancee and your friend of "cheating on you." If your teacher frowns while you are giving a speech, you might tell a classmate that the teacher did not like your speech. In each of these situations, an inference is made based upon an observation, there is a fire, the man running is a thief, your fiancee is cheating on you, and your teacher does not like your speech. There are, however, other equally reasonable explanations for each event. Perhaps the fire engine is on a test run. Perhaps the man with the sack of money is the store owner, and he is being chased by thieves. Perhaps a surprise party is being planned. Perhaps your teacher has indigestion—after all, there are many reasons for frowning.

Much of communication is about inferences based upon observation. Statements of inference are easily confused with statements of observation. There is nothing in verbal codes which allows a listener to automatically identify either. This does not mean that you should not make inferences, but that you should (1) be aware when you are making an inference, (2) calculate the probability that the inference is correct, and (3) distinguish between inferential and observational statements in your own communication. Utterances which begin with, "I think", "there may be," "there is probably", and other similar statements indicate the presence of an inference to listeners.

Because we cannot report all that we perceive or all that there is to perceive, we engage in a process of abstraction. That is, we focus upon only selected aspects of objects and experience. The problem of allness occurs when people fail to realize that their responses to reality are abstractions and that the messages they encode are also abstract. More specifically, allness occurs when a person thinks that it is possible to know and say *everything* about something; that a particular message conveys all that needs to be said about a topic. People who are prone to engage in this type of behavior frequently seem arrogant, intolerant, or close minded.

It is not easy to cope with the problem of allness. However, there are several things that you can do to minimize the problem with respect to your own behavior. First, be aware of how the abstracting process is reflected in your own behavior. Be humble, rather than defensive in your behavior. If it is not possible for others to know everything, it is not possible for you either. Second, recognize that abstraction is inevitable and attempt to develop empathy so that you can understand how others abstract and communicate about reality. Seek feedback to determine if your messages are understood and to determine if you are understanding the messages you receive. Finally, remember that no one ever has the last word, it is always possible to say more, etc.

Bypassing occurs when individuals use the same word while meaning different things and when individuals use different words to mean the same thing. Imagine two friends discussing another friend, Tom. Everything proceeds smoothly until one friend mentions that he saw Tom's girlfriend, Sue. The second friend replies that Tom's girlfriend is Sally. It turns out that both are correct. They have been talking about Tom Jones and Tom Smith, without realizing it. Has something like this ever happened to you? Or imagine a Southerner on vacation in the North. He wants a hot dog for lunch. He would not think of ordering a coney; he doesn't know what one is.

One reason that bypassing occurs is that people assume that words have a single correct usage. Many words have multiple usages, particularly slang words. Also usages change over time. A second cause of bypassing is the belief that words have meaning. As it was noted before, meanings are attributed to messages, meanings are not directly transferred between people. You can only understand the meaning of messages with respect to your own experience and knowledge.

There are several strategies for coping with and avoiding problems of bypassing. First, and perhaps most important, remember that words have multiple meanings and that meanings are assigned by people. It is wise to sometimes check and see if you share a common vocabulary or experiences with others before you attempt to communicate with them. Second, the use of paraphrasing, restatement, and questioning can be effective ways of identifying instances of bypassing while communicating. Finally, try and become sensitive to the ways in which situational and verbal contexts serve to limit and define the ways that messages are to be interpreted.

Frozen evaluation occurs when people do not recognize how people and objects change over time. After all, as we all know, "you can't teach an old dog new tricks" and "a leopard can't change his spots". Both of these statements are symptomatic of a frozen evaluation viewpoint. This viewpoint assumes that labels are always accurate.

Frozen evaluation is more of a people problem than an object problem. The categories that people are placed in and the labels that accompany them can seriously affect their lives. Teachers, for example, expect students to live up or down to their reputations. If they expect a student to have a writing problem, they are more likely to find fault with that student's writing. In the same way, students who have heard that Professor Stephens is boring may not listen as effectively as students who have heard nothing about Professor Stephens. Professor Stephens may be boring, but on the other hand, how can a student make an accurate judgement if he or she has not been listening. Outliving or living up to the expectations which are attributed on the basis of verbal labels can be difficult. No one is always entertaining and witty. Ex-criminals will always be criminals in the minds of some people.

The only way to cope with frozen evaluation is to realize that people do change. They mature. They learn. They remember. They forget. It is wise to occasionally assess the validity of the labels that you use to identify and categorize others. They may need changing.

Indiscrimination is similar to frozen evaluation. It occurs when you generalize the attributes of groups to individuals. Indiscrimination is the basis for stereotyping. It involves the neglecting of differences and emphasizing of similarities.

Thinking is made more efficient through processes of categorization and generalization. These processes of categorization and generalization are the basis for indiscrimination. If a small child is bitten by a dog, she or he may assume that all dogs bite and develop a fear of all dogs. In the same way, you may attribute particular characteristics to members of the opposite sex, members of particular social groups, or members of other races. While there may be some validity to the association of the attribute with the group (some dogs do bite), no attribute applies universally to all members of a group.

The solution to the problem of indiscrimination is to look for unique-ness. Also, you should attempt to assess the validity of the stereotypes that you have learned. Many stereotypes are learned second hand as folk lore or myth, and have little basis in reality. Having no other information about an individual, you may communicate with them on the basis of cultural or social stereotypes. However, you should be sensitive to the feedback which tells you whether or not the stereo-type applies and you have communicated the message you intended.

Nonverbal Codes

Paradoxically, nonverbal codes are both simpler and more complex than verbal codes. The objective of this section is to explain the para-dox. Specifically, this section has four objectives. First, nonverbal codes will be defined: What are nonverbal codes and how do they differ from verbal codes? Second, the different dimensions of non-verbal codes will be examined: What aspects of human behavior are used to communicate nonverbally? Third, the functions of nonverbal communication will be examined, focusing upon the question: What is communicated nonverbally? Finally, communication problems generated by nonverbal messages will be considered.

Nonverbal Codes Defined

✻ Nonverbal communication is defined as *the product of a continuous, multi-dimensional, affective message system.* The meaning of this definition is probably not immediately apparent to you. Nonverbal codes are more difficult to define than verbal codes and are perhaps best understood in terms of how they are different from verbal codes. Perhaps the most apparent way in which verbal and nonverbal codes differ is in terms of content.

While most of the cognitive content of our communication is conveyed by verbal signals, much of the affective content of communication is conveyed by nonverbal signals. Affective content includes information about the emotional state of the communicator, the communicator's evaluation of objects, and the communicator's relationship with other communicators. Based upon non-verbal messages you may decide that a speaker is confident, nervous, or angry, that a speaker likes or dislikes a topic, or that a relationship is public and formal or private and intimate.

While it is possible to convey cognitive messages nonverbally, such messages tend to be both simple and short. Examples are moving the head to signal yes and no. While such simple cognitive messages may be communicated nonverbally it would be difficult and awkward to convey complex messages. This should be apparent to anyone who has played Charades. Imagine trying to explain nonverbally that you cannot go on a date because you have relatives in town.

In a similar way, while verbal messages may contain affective information, they tend to be the primary source of cognitive information, and only a secondary source of affective information. Take for example, the message, I like you. Depending on the nonverbal messages accompanying the verbal message, the message will be believed or disbelieved, and not only that, a receiver will also make judgments about the degree of liking based upon the nonverbal message.

The importance of nonverbal messages in communicating affect has been demonstrated by Mehrabian and his colleagues (Mehrabian and Wiener, 1967; Mehrabian and Ferris, 1967). Mehrabian studied the effects of variations in verbal messages, vocal cues, and facial expressions upon perceptions of attitude. He found that the vocal cues and facial expressions were more important than the verbal messages in affecting judgments about attitudes.

Nonverbal communication is continuous, while verbal communication is discrete. It is easy to identify the basic units, such as words and sentences from which verbal messages are constructed. It is difficult to identify basic units of nonverbal messages. There are two reasons why such a task is difficult. First, words have referents which are distant in time and space. Understanding verbal messages is only

partially dependent upon the immediate context for appropriate interpretation, while understanding nonverbal messages is always
dependent upon context. Second, verbal messages have beginnings and
endings, while nonverbal messages do not. The sender of a verbal
message has some ability to determine and control the receiver's
access to his or her communication. Access to nonverbal messages is
not dependent upon the sender, but on the receiver of communication.
The saying, that "you cannot not communicate" is obviously most true
with respect to the nonverbal code.

Verbal messages are usually oral or graphic. Only infrequently are
both methods used simultaneously. In contrast, nonverbal messages
are almost always multidimensional. Body movement, physical
appearance, vocalics, space, artifacts, time, and touch may all be used
to convey nonverbal messages. The characteristics of each of these
dimensions is discussed in the next section of this chapter.

Each of these dimensions is independent of the others. Thus, they
may be used to send the same or different nonverbal messages simultaneously. This makes possible two things. The ability to send the same
message using more than one dimension increases the probability that
the message will be received and correctly interpreted. The ability to
send different messages using different dimensions at the same time
increases the variety and types of meanings that can be communicated
nonverbally. For example, using facial expressions, voice, and body
together, it is possible to communicate both surprise and anger or
surprise and joy at the same time. Many of the nonverbal messages
sent represent blends based upon the simultaneous use of more than
one dimension of nonverbal codes.

Dimensions of Nonverbal Codes

The significant dimensions of nonverbal codes include kinesics,
touch behavior, proxemics, vocalics, physical appearance, time, and
artifacts. Each of these can either be manipulated prior to interaction
or during interaction and sometimes both. Manipulations prior to interaction help define the communication setting and provide a frame of
reference for communicators to use in the process of attributing
meaning. Manipulations during interactions are directly interpreted as
messages about the on-going interaction. Each of these dimensions is
discussed in this section.

Kinesics

Kinesics includes all forms of body movement with the exception of
touch that are used to communicate nonverbally. This includes

movement of the head, face, neck, trunk, shoulders, arms, hands, hips, legs, and feet. Because of the large number of body parts that communicate through movement, an almost infinite number of kinesic messages can be constructed. This would seem to make the study of kinesics impossible, however, it is possible to identify or categorize kinesic behaviors in terms of the functions they perform. Ekman and Friesen (1969) identify five categories of kinesic behavior: emblems, illustrators, affect displays, regulators, and adaptors.

Emblems are nonverbal signals which have clearly defined verbal translations. Because their meanings are commonly understood, we frequently substitute emblems for verbal signals. Have you ever been asked a yes/no question while talking to someone else on the telephone? Rather than interrupting your telephone conversation, you probably responded with an emblem. You may have moved your head up and down to signal "yes", from left to right to signal "no", or you may have moved your hand from left to right at approximately chest level to signal "not now, I am busy".

Emblems may be either conventional or arbitrary. Conventional emblems mimic behavior and their meanings may be recognizable across cultures. For example, raising a hand to an open mouth is quickly recognized by anyone as a message about food or eating. However, like symbols, the relationship between some emblems and their meanings is arbitrary. The V for victory or peace and the circle formed by touching thumb and forefinger for A-OK are examples of emblems whose meanings are arbitrary. It is unlikely that someone unfamiliar with our culture would understand their meanings.

Illustrators are movements which accompany and modify our understanding of verbal messages. For example, to illustrate the fact that you have three main points you might hold up three fingers. These are intentional behaviors which may accent, repeat, complement, or contradict parts of verbal messages. Illustrators do not occur in the absence of speech and usually do not have a literal verbal equivalent.

Affect displays convey information about the emotional states of communicators. The face is the primary source of affective information. Research (Ekman, Friesen, and Tomkins, 1971) has identified six emotions which are the basis for affect displays: surprise, fear, anger, disgust, happiness, and sadness. Communicators may blend these basic displays to produce a wide range of expressions. For example, think of the different ways you would react to a happy surprise or to a sad surprise. Affect displays may be either intentional or unintentional. We tend to have a great deal of faith in the information leaked by unintentional affect displays.

Regulators are those kinesic behaviors which are used to regulate social interaction. Because they are learned from childhood, we are seldom aware of our use of regulators. These behaviors are discussed in more detail in the section on functions of nonverbal behavior.

Adaptors are kinesic behaviors which satisfy physical or psychological needs. Scratching and nose picking are examples of adaptors whose function is to fulfill a physical need. We tend to be aware of these types of adaptors and their use is frequently culturally regulated. They are most likely to occur in private or in intimate situations. In contrast, we are frequently unaware of the psychological adaptors that we use. In public, the use of psychological adaptors is likely to be a reaction to stress. Nervous speakers for example, are frequently unaware that they are playing with coins in their pockets or performing some other adaptive nonverbal behavior to help manage their nervousness. Impressionists depend heavily upon the ability of audiences to recognize the adaptive behaviors which characterize famous people.

Touch Behavior

Despite its limited potential for communication of complex messages, touch appears to be an extremely important form of nonverbal communications. Some researchers claim that frequent touching is necessary for normal human development. Institutionalized children, for example, who are likely to be touched less than children raised in a normal family environment, tend to learn to talk, and walk later than is average. In addition, touching plays an extremely important role in the development of intimate and sexual relationships. Touch is used as a means of expressing, sympathy, solidarity, friendship, and sexual arousal.

Typically, people engage in a wide variety of different types of touching behavior, each used to communicate a limited message. Argyle (1975) identifies sixteen different behaviors common in Western culture. The behaviors listed by Argyle include: patting, slapping, punching, pinching, stroking, shaking, kissing, licking, holding, guiding, embracing, linking, laying-on, kicking, grooming, and tickling. Each of these behaviors usually is directed at a limited area of the body. For example, you are more likely to pat someone upon the head or back than upon the chest or leg.

Other factors such as sex and situation may affect touching behavior. For example, in our culture, it is permissable for males to pat females upon the buttocks. Such behavior is usually considered appropriate only under private or semi-private circumstances. Females are less likely to pat males, particularly in front of others, and patting of the buttocks by members of the same sex is generally considered taboo. A notable exception to this taboo is male athletes engaged in team sports. However, such behavior is considered appropriate only during a game.

Perhaps because of its intimacy potential, the use of touch is highly normative. Research indicates that while the bodies of Americans are highly accessible to friends who are members of the opposite sex, access is limited for members of the same sex and family members.

Proxemics

Proxemics is the study of man's use of space. Basically, there are two types of space: territory and personal space. Territory is geographic space which individuals consider as their own. Territory remains stationary and does not travel with individuals, although individuals are likely to have territories that they claim and defend in most places they frequent. Man's need for territory is quite apparent. Anyone who shares a room knows where her territory is and where the roommate's territory is. Students are likely to sit consistently in the same desk during the course of a semester. Even husbands and wives tend to sleep consistently on one side of the bed or the other and refer to that side as "my" side.

Personal space refers to the space immediately surrounding individuals. Hall (1959) identifies four subcategories of personal space: public, social-consultative, casual-personal, and intimate. According to Hall, public space includes that distance between approximately twelve feet and the limits of visibility. Only infrequently do we communicate with individuals in public space. Social-consultative space includes the distance between four and twelve feet. Formal communication, such as business transactions are likely to occur within this area. The casual personal space extends from one and one-half to four feet from the body. Most social conversation occurs within this area. Intimate space includes the space approximately within eighteen inches of the body and the body itself. Only those with whom we are socially intimate are allowed within this region.

The actual sizes of the subcategories of space identified by Hall are not fixed, but vary in relation to a number of factors. Burgoon and Saine (1978) identify three classes of variables which affect the use of personal space: people characteristics, interaction characteristics, and environmental characteristics.

Sex, age, status, culture, liking, and personality are examples of people characteristics which affect the use of personal space. Men maintain greater personal distances than do women or mixed couples. Individuals stand closer to people of approximately their own age than they do with those younger and older when communicating. As status increases, the distance between communicators is also likely to increase. People of Latin America and the middle east tend to maintain a much smaller conversational distance than Americans. Naturally, we stand much closer to individuals we like than individuals we don't like. Finally, introverts maintain a greater social distance than extroverts.

Formality and purpose are examples of interactional characteristics which affect the use of personal space. The more formal a situation is, typically, the greater the social distance. Individuals who are cooperating are likely to be closer together than people who are competing.

Environmental characteristics such as the amount of space, number of people, and arrangement of furniture also affect the use of personal space. For example, people in a crowded elevator behave much differently than two people in an elevator.

We are most aware of norms concerning territoriality and personal space when they are violated. When territory or personal space is intruded upon, individuals will either try to chase the intruder away, increase the psychological distance, or retreat. If a student in a crowded class changes seats in the middle of a semester, she is likely to receive some hostile glances or hear, "that's my seat." Psychological distance is increased by treating individuals as if they were objects and did not exist. In elevators, individuals look at the ceiling or stand back to front so that they can avoid eye contact. When personal space is invaded in an uncrowded environment, the response is likely to be retreat.

Vocalics

The voice is also a tool of nonverbal communication. Vocalics includes all nonlinguistic aspects of the vocal signal. Elements of vocalics are voice quality, vocal characterizations, and vocal qualifiers. Vocalics may convey information about such things as the personality of a speaker, the speaker's confidence or emotional state, or the speaker's feelings about the topic of communication.

Voice quality is a function of such factors as: pitch range and control, lip control, rhythm control, and resonance. Voice quality is often linked to judgments about personality. Voices may be described as sexy, masculine, forceful, weak, nasal, tense, breathy, etc.

Vocal qualifiers are such things as intensity, duration, and pitch. Vocal qualifiers are used to complement and accent verbal messages. By varying the loudness (intensity) of speech speakers can draw attention to and emphasize desired aspects of messages. The same things can be done by varying the duration of sound. For example, if you wish to convey the idea that something was done slowly, you might prolong the word slow-ly.

Vocal characterizations are such things as laughing, crying, belching, moaning, groaning, and yawning. Typically, such behaviors are taken as clues concerning the emotional or physical state of the communicator. For example, listeners who yawn are judged to be bored and giggling may be seen as a sign of embarrassment.

Physical Appearance

Evidence of its importance is the fact that each year Americans spend millions of dollars to alter their physical appearance through the use of plastic surgery, diet, exercise, grooming aids, clothing and cosmetics. Unlike some other aspects of nonverbal behavior such as the use of space, touch, and kinesics, physical appearance is seldom manipulated during interaction. The manipulation of physical appearance typically occurs prior to interaction. The unemployed "dress-up" for interviews, people, put on their "party" or "church" clothes, males and females diet or exercise to become more attractive.

If we do not manipulate physical appearance during communication, you might ask then why is it an important element of nonverbal communication? The answer is simple. In face-to-face situations, we are aware of a person's physical appearance before we interact with them. Thus, personal appearance plays a role in initial impression formation, and has an initial effect on the nature of social interaction. For example, an interviewer for an accounting firm stated that the first thing that he always does in an interview is check to see if the interviewee's shoes are polished. He would never consider hiring a person that did not polish his or her shoes for an interview.

There is a large body of research which demonstrates the advantages of being physically attractive and the disadvantages of being physically unattractive. For example, attractive females have been found to be more effective at persuasion than unattractive females. In the area of courtship, physical attractiveness has been observed to be an important variable in predicting a desire to continuing dating someone following a blind date. In addition, attractiveness has been found to influence mock jury decisions, teacher's assignment of grades, and mate selection (Knapp, 1978).

In our culture there are strong stereotypes associated with body shape. Research (Wells & Siegel, 1961) has examined how individuals respond to each of three extreme body types: endomorphs, mesomorphs, and extomorphs. Endomorphs are soft, round, overweight people. When shown a silhouette of an endomorph, subjects judged that such a person was likely to be judged older, shorter, more old-fashioned, less strong, less good looking, talkative, warm-hearted, sympathetic, good-natured, dependent on others and trusting of others. Mesomorphs are bony, muscular, athletic people. They were judged to be masculine, adventurous, mature, tall, good-looking, and self-reliant. Ectomorphs are tall, thin, fragile people. Ectomorphs were judged as suspicious of others, ambitious, nervous, tense, quiet, pessimistic, and less masculine than others.

Body color, body odor, hair, and clothing are also aspects of physical appearance which can take communicative significance. These and other elements of physical appearance can be taken to communicate such diverse things as occupation, political orientation, degree of formality in a given social situation, or sexual interest. Again, this underscores the potential importance of physical appearance as a dimension of nonverbal behavior.

A note of caution is in order at this point. While the research indicates that physical appearance can significantly affect subsequent communication, relatively little is known about the effects of communicating with someone over time on perceptions of physical appearance. Getting to know someone frequently results in changing your opinion concerning their attractiveness. After all, beauty is in the eye of the beholder.

Time

Time is manipulated to convey information about status and importance. If you can make someone wait for you, it is likely that you are of higher status. If you ask that a meeting be held immediately, it is likely that the topic of the meeting is important. Time is an intangible. We cannot see it, taste it, or touch it. Yet, we are all aware of it. Time can be used to communicate indirectly by speeding things up or by slowing them down and by violating or conforming to the expectations of others about how time should be used.

The importance of time varies from culture to culture. Different cultures develop different norms concerning the use of time. Thus, concepts such as late, early, on time, later, in a little while, and soon may take on different meanings in different cultures. For example, to be "on time" in the United States a person should not arrive more than a few minutes, perhaps five, before or after the agreed upon time. In some Latin cultures, a person may be considered on time when he or she is as much as an hour late.

In addition, events carry with them certain expectations about time. Being late for a date is not necessarily the same as being late for a business appointment. Such expectations are generally widely known within cultures. This is easy to demonstrate. Poll your classmates. Ask them how late a person must be before they are "late" to class or "early" for a date. In both cases there should be considerable agreement.

Artifacts

Sometimes people manipulate objects in the environment for purposes of communication. Generally artifacts communicate in two ways. First, they are used to regulate communication by constituting the communication context or situation. Second, they are used to signal status or characteristics of communicators. Both are important elements of communication.

Situations or contexts can exert a powerful influence on behavior. For example, it has been observed that people drink more in dimly lit bars where country music is played. In contrast, people drink less in bright bars that play disco and rock music. Similar effects can be observed for communication. Most public buildings, such as airports, are designed to discourage communication. Chairs usually face in a single direction, or are uncomfortable distances apart, and generally they are in an open area so that conversations may be easily overheard. In the same way, people view the living room as an appropriate place for formal entertaining, and family rooms as a place to be used for informal entertaining.

Artifacts also communicate status and other personal information. In the business world, the size, location, and furnishings of a person's office may tell you a lot about his or her status. In the federal bureaucracy, for example, the size of desks and the type of desk and chair is dictated by GS ranking. GS 15's have larger and nicer desks than lower ranking civil servants. In fact, in Washington, D.C. there are people whose only job is to make sure that no one has office equipment better than they are supposed to have.

Size, color, shape, texture, lighting, temperature and arrangement are ways in which artifacts and environment can vary. Consider the different communication environments in which you live and work. How does each affect your communication? What makes an environment intimate or formal? How do important people convey status? What types of persons ride a ten-speed bike or drive a Porsche? Your ability to answer each of these questions reflects the knowledge that all of us have and use to communicate nonverbally through artifacts.

Functions of Nonverbal Signals

When we engage in a conversation we use both verbal and nonverbal signals to communicate. While most of the cognitive or referential content of our communication is conveyed by verbal signals, much of the affective or evaluative content of communication is conveyed by nonverbal signals. That is, we depend upon nonverbal signals to make sense out of what has been said. Knapp (1978) identifies six functions that nonverbal signals perform in relation to verbal behavior. According to Knapp, we use nonverbal behavior to repeat, complement, accent, substitute for, contradict, and regulate verbal behavior.

Repeating the information increases the likelihood that it will be received and understood. Thus repeating information nonverbally increases our probability of communicating successfully. Frequently, we repeat our verbal messages without being aware of it. How often do you move your head from left to right when saying no, or up and down when saying yes?

Nonverbal signals are also used to modify or elaborate upon the meaning of verbal messages. When someone says that they are happy, they may be just happy, or very happy. The speaker's posture, facial expression, and manner of speaking combine to tell how happy he really is, or how unhappy he is. Nonverbal behavior that is complimentary allows us to make judgements about the speaker's attitude and/or intentions. Is a speaker serious, does he intend to do what he says? To a large extent judgements about such issues are based on an assessment of nonverbal behavior.

Nonverbal behavior is frequently used to accent or highlight aspects of verbal messages. In speaking, you cannot underline or use italics to draw attention, but you can use a "dramatic" pause or raise, or even lower the volume of your voice. If you are mad at someone, you may shake your fist and scowl at them as you speak. Thus, nonverbally, we indicate what we consider most important.

Sometimes nonverbal communication is used instead of verbal communication. When someone is busy and is asked a question they may respond with a shake of the head or a gesture. When you see someone across a crowded room, you may substitute a wave of the arm or some other gesture for a verbal greeting in order to avoid being rude. Sometimes we substitute because the nonverbal message can be a much more efficient and eloquent means of conveying particular meanings. The conspirator's wink and the touch of consolation are both effective and efficient substitutes for verbal messages.

As long as verbal messages agree with nonverbal messages, we depend primarily upon the verbal message to interpret the primary meaning of what is being communicated. When the nonverbal message contradicts the verbal message, we depend heavily upon the nonverbal message for purposes of interpretation. Sarcasm is an example of behavior where nonverbal behavior is used deliberately to signal that the true meaning of the verbal message is the exact opposite of its literal interpretation. It is difficult to believe that the speaker whose hands tremble and voice breaks is not nervous even though he says he is confident and calm.

The dependence upon nonverbal cues when verbal and nonverbal messages conflict is easily explained. Verbal behavior is perceived as consciously planned, under the control of the speaker. Nonverbal behavior on the other hand is less easily controlled because of its multimodal nature. Because it is perceived as difficult to "fake" and more spontaneous, we have considerable confidence in our judgements on the veracity of nonverbal messages. This does not mean that our judgements are always accurate. Some individuals are effective at masking deception and other individuals are poor interpreters of nonverbal cues.

Nonverbal behavior plays an important role in the regulation of social interaction. How do you know that it is your turn to speak in a group discussion? How do others know that it is your turn? Researchers have identified numerous nonverbal signals that are used to signal that it is, or is not someone else's turn to speak, and cues that signal a desire to speak.

Five cues have been identified which signal that a speaker desires to continue speaking in a conversation (Duncan, 1972). These are: (1) the continuation of a gesture; (2) facing away from the receiver to avoid eye contact; (3) inhaling audibly; (4) maintaining a similar pitch level for several successive words; and (5) filling pauses with non-meaningful vocalizations, such as "uh" or "and". This last behavior, the use of vocalized pauses, which is considered undesirable in public speaking is often simply a carryover from conversational behavior. It is so automatic that many beginning public speakers are unaware that they fill pauses when speaking.

Three types of cues signal that it is our turn to speak. Body orientation and gaze are the cues with which we are most familiar. In a classroom when a teacher asks a question you know that you are to answer if the teacher finishes the question looking directly at you. In addition to body orientation and gaze, certain vocal cues signal the end of a turn at talking. A drawn out or stressed final syllable, a rising intonation pattern when a question is being asked, or a falling intonation pattern for other utterances all indicate a willingness to allow others to speak.

Listeners also play an important role in the regulation of interaction. Among cues that listeners use to signal a desire to speak are: gazing at the speaker, nodding of the head, and forward leans (Wieman, 1973). In addition to signaling their desire to speak, listeners also provide feedback to the speaker about how the speaking turn is going. Nonverbal behavior used to regulate the behavior of the speaker is called "backchanneling" (Duncan, 1972). Through backchannel behaviors, listeners can indicate, among other things, recognition of a speaker or topic, degree of interest in a speaker or topic, that the pace of speaking is adequate or should be modified.

Research by Wieman (1975) indicates that sensitivity to and the ability to use regulatory nonverbal behaviors is closely related to perceived "communication competence". Speakers who interrupt others, pause for longer than three seconds, or change topics without the appropriate nonverbal signals are perceived as less competent communicators. It might be fair to say that the communicator who is not sensitive to the use of regulatory nonverbal behavior does not know the rules of syntax of interaction.

Problems

There are two important potential sources of error in nonverbal communication. The first is a problem of control or leakage. The second is a problem of focus or segmentation.

As was noted earlier, there are many different dimensions of nonverbal codes which can operate independently and simultaneously. This can pose a problem for communicators. Communicators are frequently unaware of the nonverbal messages that they are sending. Communicators frequently leak unintended nonverbal messages. This is particularly true for important or stressful situation in which kinesic adaptors are likely to be used. Receivers may not recognize a particular behavior as adaptive. They may think that it is intended and therefore interpret it incorrectly. For example, when thinking, I frequently frown. On occasion, students or members of my family have assumed that I was frowning at them. The solution to this problem is rather simple from one direction and complex from the other. As receivers of nonverbal messages, we should make a habit of first checking other dimensions of nonverbal behavior to see if they are conveying a similar message. Second, it is sometimes useful to point out the inconsistencies between messages. While it takes time to do this, it may be worthwhile if by doing this you avoid an incorrect interpretation of a message. My wife, for example, has learned to ask "Why are you frowning?" By seeking additional information to determine if her original interpretation was correct, misunderstandings occur less frequently.

This problem is more complex from the standpoint of the sender of nonverbal messages. The problem arises when you are unaware of the nonverbal messages you are sending. The only solution is to try and become more aware of your own nonverbal behavior. This is not easy, but there are two things that may help. First, try and learn about your use of nonverbal behavior from your friends. Friends are frequently willing to describe how you behave nonverbally. For example, as a form of adaptive behavior, I frequently "play" with a piece of chalk while lecturing. I was not aware of this behavior until my students told me about it. In the same way my wife made me aware that I frown when thinking and now I warn people about it to avoid miscommunicating. A second strategy is to practice being aware of your nonverbal behavior when communicating. If you are to be successful at this, you should begin with simple situations, situations that are not stressful. The more you practice the better you will become and you will find that being aware of your nonverbal behavior is less difficult than you might think.

The second major problem with nonverbal codes is focus or segmentation. Unlike verbal codes, the nonverbal code does not consist of discrete, easily recognized parts. Concepts such as words, sentences, and paragraphs are not meaningful when talking about nonverbal messages. As communicators, we are faced with the problem of determining what is the meaning or referent of nonverbal messages. Because nonverbal messages do not have easily recognized beginnings and endings, this can be difficult. While the meanings of nonverbal messages are always relevant to ongoing interaction, sometimes the actual referent of a nonverbal message is something said immediately preceding a current message or its referent may be the next message a communicator intends to send. Also, nonverbal messages are complex in that they may represent information from many different dimensions. For example, our understanding of a nonverbal message may take into account proxemics, kinesics, or vocalics or all three. Thus, what a person focuses upon and how that experience is segmented, plays an important role in determining the meanings that they attribute to nonverbal messages. This problem is best dealt with by developing awareness and seeking explicit feedback. Try and become sensitive to individuals focusing habits and seek information when you are unsure about nonverbal messages.

Summary

We communicate using verbal and nonverbal codes. Most of the time, both codes are used simultaneously to communicate. Verbal codes consist of shared sets of symbols and shared sets of rules for combining symbols into understandable utterances. Nonverbal codes are the product of a continuous, multidimensional, affective message system. Verbal codes convey most of the cognitive content of communication. Nonverbal codes carry most of the affective content of communication.

Verbal systems consist of phonemes, morphemes, words, and utterances. There are rules which we all learn as children which allow us to transform phonemes into morphemes and words, and words into utterances. The four maxims of Grice's Cooperative Principle are an example of the social rules which are a part of all verbal codes.

The meaning of verbal messages can be discussed at two levels: words, and utterances. Connotation, denotation, imagery, intensity, ambiguity, and vagueness are ways that the meanings of words can differ. The meaning of utterances is tied to knowledge of the social rules of communication. Knowledge of the maxims of quantity, quality, relation, and manner allow us to interpret utterances with direct and indirect meanings.

Verbal codes are tools through which social activities are accomplished. Specifically, there are seven functions of verbal codes. The functions are: instrumental, regulative, representational, interactional, heuristic, imaginative, and personal.

The very characteristics of verbal codes that make them useful for communication make problems possible. Inference-observation confusion, allness, bypassing, frozen evaluation, and indiscrimination are communication problems which arise from the misuse of verbal codes.

Nonverbal messages are multidimensional. We can communicate nonverbally through kinesics, touch behavior, proxemics, vocalics, physical appearance, time, and artifacts. Each of these dimensions is used differently and varies with respect to the potential for manipulation. Manipulations during interaction are interpreted as messages about the ongoing interaction.

We depend upon nonverbal messages to make sense out of what has been said. Knapp identifies six functions that nonverbal signals perform in relation to verbal signals. Nonverbal behavior is used to repeat, complement, accent, substitute for, contradict, and regulate verbal behavior.

There are two problems involved in using nonverbal codes for communication. The first is a problem of controlling behavior, leaking messages. The second is a problem of focusing upon nonverbal behaviors or segmenting behaviors. Both problems are best coped with by seeking feedback about your interpretation of the meanings of nonverbal messages and developing self-awareness of your own nonverbal behavior.

References

Argyle, M. *Bodily communication.* New York: International Universities Press, 1975.

Bowers, J.W. & Osborn, M.M. Attitudinal effects of selected types of concluding metaphors on persuasive speeches. *Speech monographs,* 1966, *33,* 147-155.

Burgoon, J. & Saine, T. *The unspoken dialogue: An introduction to nonverbal communication.* Boston: Houghton Mifflin, 1978.

Duncan, S. Some signals and rules for taking turns in conversations. *Journal of personality and social psychology,* 1972, *23,* 283-292.

Ekman, P. & Friesen, W.V. The repertoire of nonverbal behavior: Categories, origins, usage and coding. *Semiotica,* 1969, *1,* 49-98.

Ekman, P., Friesen, W.V. & S. Tomkins, Facial affect scoring technique: A first validity study. *Semiotica,* 1971, *3,* 37-58.

Farb, P. *Word play: What happens when people talk.* New York: Alfred A. Knopf, 1973.

Grice, H.P. William James Lectures, Harvard University, 1967. Published in part as "Logic and conversation." In P. Cole & J.L. Morgan (Eds.), *Syntax and semantics, Vol. 3: Speech Acts.* New York: Seminar Press, 1975, 41-58.

Halliday, M.A.K. *Explorations in the functions of language.* London: Edward Arnold, 1973.

Hall, E.T. *The silent language.* Garden City, N.Y.: Doubleday, 1959.

Kausler, D.H. *Psychology of verbal learning and memory.* New York: Academic Press, 1974.

Knapp, M.L. *Nonverbal communication in human interaction.* New York: Holt, Rinehart, and Winston, 1978.

Mehrabian, A. & Ferris, S.L. Inference of attitudes from nonverbal communication in two channels. *Journal of consulting psychology,* 1967, *31,* 248-252.

Mehrabian, A. and Weiner, M. Decoding of inconsistent communications. *Journal of personality and social psychology,* 1967, *6,* 108-114.

Reinsch, N.L., Jr. An investigation of the effect of metaphor and simile in persuasive discourse. *Speech monographs,* 1971, *38,* 142-145.

Russell, C. & Russell, W.M.S. Language and animal signals. In N. Minnis (ed.) *Linguistics at large.* New York: Viking Press, 1971.

Wells, W. & Siegel, B. Stereotyped somotypes. *Psychological reports,* 1968, *23,* 1175-1178.

Wiemann, J.M. *An exploratory study of turn-taking in conversations: verbal and nonverbal behavior.* Unpublished MS thesis, Purdue University, 1973.

Wiemann, J.M. *An exploration of communicative competence in intial interactions.* Unpublished PhD. dissertation, Purdue University, 1975.

Dimensions of Communication

4

Interpersonal Communication

Catherine Wenc Konsky
Johnny I. Murdock

How much time do you spend each day talking to other people? No doubt you spend a lot of time talking with and listening to friends, teachers, acquaintenances, co-workers, and family members. On a given day, we communicate one-to-one with many people. This is interpersonal communication. Yet we receive little formal instruction in the nature and functions of interpersonal communication—how to initiate, develop, and, in some cases, terminate relationships. We learn by trial and error. Unfortunately, this type of learning can be costly in terms of personal feelings, friendships, desired relationships, and often ends in failure. We have all experienced the gut level feeling, "I blew it." This chapter has two goals: (1) to explain the characteristics of the competent interpersonal communicator, and (2) to look at the role of communication in building interpersonal relationships.

A Basic Overview

Approaches

Historically, communication scholars focused on public communication, especially informative and persuasive speaking. Basic books contained pragmatic advice on how to speak to groups of people. Beginning around 1960, our society became concerned with issues related to the quality of life and self-development. Many communication theorists shifted to a focus on interpersonal communication. Instead of concentrating on speaker-to-audience variables, the focus became person-to-person variables. The issues in interpersonal communication center on how to use communication to improve the quality of our associations with others.

Three approaches to or traditions in interpersonal communication show the development of today's pragmatic approach to the subject. Initially, researchers borrowed some assumptions from *behavioral psychology* to guide explorations in interpersonal communication. The approach was to isolate what variables (i.e., causes) would produce selected interpersonal outcomes (i.e., effects). Some researchers studied the effects of language intensity. They wanted to know how people would differentially react, for example, to the statement, "I'm upset about...," versus the statement, "I am mad as horse feathers about...." In terms of language, personality, perception, and situational context variables, they did find effects. However, this approach did little to improve interpersonal relations at a quality of life level. It was too manipulative in that it stressed controlling the reactions of others by changing one's own behavior.

Individuals such as John Powell (1969), John Stewart (1977), and Carl Rogers (1961) reacted negatively to the behavioral approach. They led in the development of the *humanistic tradition* which stressed selected quality of life values such as being open to others, honest with others, supportive of others, and empathic with others. Students were assured that if they would openly and honestly discuss their feelings, motives and self with others, the others would reciprocate and their lives would be improved. Unfortunately, the others didn't always reciprocate honestly; in fact, the honest communicator frequently found himself or herself being manipulated. While there were the good interpersonal experiences, there were also the bad. The desired quality of one's interpersonal life was seldom achieved.

Both traditions proved inadequate because each ignored a crucial issue. Causes and effects are important, values of openness and honesty are important; but both traditions were blinded by the speaker-receiver model of public communication. Each assumed that as one person changed his or her behavior in relation to another, the other would respond in the desired fashion, and the interpersonal relationship would improve. Both traditions more or less said, "You can do it, baby," and ignored the wisdom of what became a popular song, "It takes two." We needed an approach which, while incorporating individual considerations, focused on relational parameters and expectations.

General Systems Theory represents a third approach that, while incorporating concepts from the behavioral and humanistic traditions, finally defined the nature and scope of interpersonal communication. Developed by Ludwig Von Bertalanffy to explain the complex inter-relationships of elements and components in biological organisms, General Systems Theory has been usefully applied in engineering, computers, and management (Ruben and Kim, 1975). General Systems Theory has been ingeniously applied to interpersonal communication by theorists like Paul Watzlawick (1967) and Virginia Satir (1967, 1972).

They define interepersonal communication as a highly complex system where variables such as perception, individual similarities and differences, goals, time, communication climate, and social rules meet. Interpersonal communication is viewed as a *transaction* — the system of variables and their interrelationships which can explain and predict dyadic behavior. The *behavioral* tradition emphasized linear causes to effects; how one variable (e.g., anxiety) influences behavior (e.g., hand-shakes) in initial meetings. The *humanistic* tradition emphasized openness and honesty (i.e., how candor contributed to feelings of self-worth). Both traditions are incorporated into *General Systems Theory*. However, since the theory focuses on transactions between two people, other variables are considered and *mutuality* becomes an issue.

Because interpersonal communication is defined as a transaction, one cannot just consider person A and person B. Rather, the relation-ship must be studied. Both persons simultaneously send and receive messages; mutual and divergent goals are examined; social rules as they influence behavior must be considered; and so on. From the systems perspective, it is essential to focus on *interpersonal trans-actions.*

While this may seem overly complex and confusing to you, the transactional view of interpersonal communication, the focus on rela-tionships, has produced (1) the theoretical structure of this chapter, (2) many of the concepts discussed, and (3) several of the applications suggested. Finally, the transactional view reminds us that human communication and relationships are, in fact, complex.

Interpersonal Relationships

The transactional perspective defines interpersonal communication as the *mutual relationship between two persons.* A *mutual relationship* denotes that verbal and nonverbal messages are simultaneously exchanged between the members in a transaction, and it *connotes* the complexity of the process. Interpersonal communication occurs within a wide range of interpersonal relationships; relationships that vary from temporary to permanent, from acquaintances to lovers. The *Interpersonal Relationship Continuum* in Figure 1 represents the relational range in which we function as interpersonal communicators.

Figure 1. Interpersonal Relationship Continuum

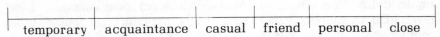

| temporary | acquaintance | casual | friend | personal | close |

We intuitively recognize that our relationship with a salesperson at the bookstore is somehow qualitatively different from that with our roommate or spouse. List the names of ten people you know; then place them on the continuum. If the names are at different locations, we are willing to bet that after a moment's reflection, you will realize that the communication in your transactions with each is also different. The topics we talk about and the degree to which we are willing to discuss various issues change as a function of where a relationship is on the continuum.

We need to realize further that relationships change in many ways over time. Persons who are acquaintances sometimes become friends. Persons who were once friends sometimes move back to acquaintances (e.g., a friend joins a fraternity and you don't). Other factors such as interest, personal priorities, external events and competency skills affect how relationships develop and where they are on the relationship continuum.

Before we turn to the major issues of this chapter, we want to comment on the concept of *uniqueness*. Each of us is unique, (i.e., unlike any other person) and we want others to realize this fact. You do not like professors to respond to you as just a student. Professors like students to treat them as a person and not just a role. Due to such factors as time and effort, we can't treat every person as unique. Therefore, while we are going to discuss competencies, skills and strategies related to interpersonal communication, one must remember that the concepts can only be effectively applied when we are willing to acknowledge each other's uniqueness.

Interpersonal Communication Competence

Our goal should be to become *competent interpersonal communicators.* Competence has two dimensions — *knowledge and skills. Knowledge* includes our awareness and understanding of the numerous variables which affect human relationships. *Skills* involve the ability to pragmatically apply, consciously or even unconsciously, our knowledge. In this section, we will review the major variables which research has shown are related to interpersonal competence. It is important to realize that knowledge and skills exist in a reciprocal relationship — as our knowledge is improved, we refine interpersonal skills; conversely, as our skills are developed, our knowledge is developed via experience.

To the extent possible in this chapter, we plan to describe the ideal interpersonal communicator. Why should we make the effort to acquire new knowledge and improve skills? At one level, improving competence will give us greater understanding and control over our lives. At a second level, improving competence will improve our relationship with people we love or like. At a third level, improving competence will permit us to cope with the numerous demands frequently made upon our lives by peers, friends, relatives, co-workers, superiors, etc.

Researchers have identified numerous variables to which the competent interpersonal communicator is sensitive. The competent interpersonal communicator possesses the knowledge and skills listed in Table 1. We have devoted the remainder of this section to discussing this view of competence.

1. *What is the self?* Basically, *the self as used here means our perception and awareness of ourselves as unique persons.* Suppose we were required to describe our *self*. We could immediately provide a demographic description including race, sex, religion, academic major or degrees, political affiliation, and hobbies. Although it would be somewhat more difficult, we could describe our personality (e.g., shy or aggressive), beliefs (e.g., there is a God), values (e.g., honesty is good in relationships), morals and ethics (e.g., murder is sinful), and goals (e.g., earning $20,000 two years after graduation). With some effort, we might even relate two or more concepts together, such as explaining that while a major goal is earning a good income, we want to help others (i.e., offered as one explanation for becoming a lawyer).

None of us would find the task easy, and we probably wouldn't feel that the description captured the real self. We rarely think of who we are or where we are going. Life's activities fill each day. We do this, we do that, we talk to others, and seldom ask, "Who am I?" However, if we have little knowledge of self, then how can we function effectively in relationships with others? The answer is simple, "We can't."

At the skill level, we must learn to practice introspection. Occasionally, events almost force us to question, analyze, and evaluate the self. In some instances, we realize that we are not satisfied and we ask, "Why?" Suppose the person is a business major and realizes that his or her major courses are boring. This realization may result in introspection as the person evaluates his or her goals and values. In other instances, relational conflicts and crises may lead to self evaluation. Suppose a person is happy in his or her relationship with another, but learns that the other person is unhappy. A common reaction is to blame the other person, but the competent communicator will question his or her perception of and goals for the relationship. Other events may force introspection, but the competent communicator does not let events dictate self evaluation. He or she periodically evaluates the self. This introspection may occur once a month, twice a year, or once a week. The frequency is not the key issue. The issue is that for the competent interpersonal communicator introspection is a consciously selected and practiced activity.

Table 1

Dimensions of Competence

Knowledge of	Skills Involving
1. Self	Introspection (questioning, analyzing, evaluating your behavior, thoughts, and feelings)
2. Roles	Sensitivity to, control over own, ability to switch
3. Individuality	Recognition of fairly invariant and temporary characteristics of self and others
4. Satisfactions and Goals	Directional awareness of purposes (specific tasks, sharing, relational develpment)
5. Context	Adaption to physical and social settings
6. Relational history	Awareness of how the past influences the present
7. Time	Sensitivity and response to developmental stages, sequences, and changes in relationships
8. Communication climate	Management of communication codes and behaviors to create, maintain, or modify desired relational environments
9. Rules	Identification of social parameters and modification in relational environments
10. Relational Complexity	Synthesis; flexibility in coping with the transactional nature of interpersonal relationships

2. *What is a role?* Theoretically, *a role is a set of formal and informal expectations* we have about concepts like friend, mother, professor, roommate, boyfriend, spouse, etc. Very basic formal expectations are found in dictionary definitions. Formal expectations

can always be written because they are generally true of everyone who occupies a given role. Such formal expectations can be very complex. Examples include university handbooks which spend a lot of time defining the rights and responsibilities of professors, and company manuals which define the roles of supervisors, managers, and vice-presidents. In addition to such formal role expectations, informal expectations also develop on the basis of our experience. Each of us has experiences with our mother, our father, our professors and our friends. That is, formal expectations are expanded, modified, and changed due to personal experience.

While the distinction between formal and informal expectations is theoretically useful, we do not normally think of our roles (e.g., professor or student) in terms of theory. Each of us has a conceptualization of friendship, for example, and would find it difficult, if not impossible, to separate our formal and informal expectations. However, the competent interpersonal communicator knows that we occupy roles in our interpersonal relationships, and that differences in our perceptions of roles are probably the result of experiences which have produced different informal expectations.

At the skill level, the competent communicator is sensitive to the characteristics of a wide variety of roles, and to relational disagreements concerning roles. He or she is sensitive to disagreements which frequently result from different informal expectations. Take the case of two roommates who disagree over whether they can use each other's cosmetics, shaving cream, and/or toothpaste. The conflict is probably the result of differing informal expectations about the definition or role of a roommate. The competent communicator also consciously controls the roles he or she is willing to occupy in a relationship with another. Bill assumes that his friendship with Sam includes the role of confessor; Sam does not make that assumption. Control means that Sam does not allow Bill to place him in that role and can explain to Bill the difference between friend and confessor. Finally, the competent interpersonal communicator knows and controls the switching of roles with different persons. Mary knows why and in what ways she behaves differently with her mother, Dave who works in the same office, Harold whom she dates, and Mary her roommate.

3. *What do we mean by individuality?* People are not merely a series of roles. *Roles must be qualified by individuality. Individuality covers the relatively invariant aspects of the self and temporary states which can change a person.* Suppose Vince has two roommates who are also friends. While the roles are the same, Vince does not communicate with both in the same way nor on an identical set of topics. He makes an effort to adapt to the individual beyond the level of role.

At the skill level, one can illustrate this competency by looking at the relationship of a professor with students. If the professor is to adequately fulfill his or her role, all students should be treated the same in terms of the quality of work and expected behavior in the classroom. However, when two students turn in late papers, one due to laziness and the other because of real sickness, we can agree that the professor ought to treat each differently. In short, *the competent communicator is willing to modify his or her roles to fit the uniqueness of another.* He or she expects the same from others.

4. *What are satisfactions and goals? Satisfactions and goals are desired outcomes.* When they are obtained, the interpersonal communicator is satisfied or happy. We can achieve and obtain a wide variety of satisfactions and goals through interpersonal relationships. Goals can be very simple. We might ask to borrow a classmate's notes. The goal is to obtain information. In fact, obtaining information is at least a temporary goal at various times during all relationships. We ask a salesperson for information about a product, we ask for and give a lot of information during the initial stages of a relationship, and we get and give information with friends, spouses, professors, etc. Other goals are somewhat more complex or difficult to achieve. A goal may involve completing some task (e.g., completing a paper), getting to know another better (e.g., talking with a new acquaintance at lunch), planning time (e.g., agreeing on plans for the evening with a date), developing a relationship (e.g., mutual self-disclosure), resolving relational conflicts (e.g., seeking a mutually acceptable solution), and so on. Relationships must develop or identify mutual and/or compatible goals. *The competent interpersonal communicator is sensitive to his or her goals, the goals of the other, and the relational goals which are shared.*

While goals are anything we want and attempt to achieve or obtain, satisfaction refers to our assessment of the success or failure of such attempts. In a student/professor relationship, the goal of the student might be only to obtain a high grade. If successful, he or she is gratified; if not successful, he or she is dissatisfied. The student probably also wanted to gain knowledge about the subject matter of the course. If he or she got a "c," but learned a lot, the satisfaction assessment is probably mixed. If another student taking another professor for the same course obtained an "A," but learned very little, the gratification assessment will also be mixed. In one case, the assessment is that while the professor is hard, the course is interesting. In the other, the professor is easy, but the course is a waste of time. Which professor would you take? In contrast, if the student got a "c," and learned very little, the satisfaction assessment will be negative. In the future, he or she will avoid that professor.

A given interpersonal relationship can involve numerous goals. In such a relationship, some goals are obtained and some are not achieved. A satisfaction analysis is the decision-making process where we decide to maintain, modify, or terminate the relationship because overall the relationship is rewarding or punishing in terms of goal achievements, and/or because new relational options appear more rewarding. When Mary says to Bill, "On balance, I think we get along," she is giving her decision based on a satisfaction analysis.

At the skill level, the competent communicator is aware of the goals in a given transaction and his or her relationships. His or her communication behavior is goal directed. If asked, the competent communicator could list all or most of the main goals in a relationship. He or she could further explain why, from his or her satisfaction analysis, the relationship is or is not achieving the various goals. Suppose Sally is going to a party where she expects to meet some friends she has not seen for three months. Her goals will probably be to: (1) have fun, and (2) renew the friendships. Much of Sally's communication with the friends will center around their activities during the last few months. Humor, discussion of mutual friends, talk about T.V. shows, and mutual updating will dominate the transactions. In order to reach both goals, Sally will probably avoid serious topics of conversation (e.g., politics or religion) and meeting new people. She will focus her behavior on actions which are compatible with both goals.

In relationships, the competent communicator considers relational goals, whether or not they are being reached, his or her feelings of satisfaction, and comparisons of the rewards and punishments of a given relationship with other existing or potential relationships. Mary has been dating Arnold for five months. She likes Arnold. While she enjoys being with Arnold, she realizes that she doesn't feel able to relax or to be completely honest with him. She realizes that she is often more relaxed around several different friends. After some thought, Mary realizes that although being with Arnold is fun because they enjoy many of the same things, Arnold is highly opinionated and she has been tense out of a subtle fear of causing an argument. What will Mary do? She may try to modify the relationship and her behavior to reduce this tension. She may decide that other existing or potential relationships appear more rewarding and terminate the one with Arnold. Her final choice is not the issue. It is important that she consciously make a decision in terms of her goals when assessing her feelings for Arnold.

5. *What is context? Context has both a physical and a social dimension.* The *physical dimension* includes location (e.g., an office vs. a living room), the use of space, furnishings, and other environmental factors such as color, temperature, and music. These nonverbal elements often affect our interpersonal relationships in subtle but meaningful ways. For example, assume that you walk into a doctor's office for consultation. The office is spacious and furnished with an examining table, a small desk in the corner, and three arm chairs surrounding a small table. After the examination, the doctor motions you to sit in one of the arm chairs to discuss the health issue. Contrast this physical setting with one in which the spacious office is dominated

by a massive desk. There are no comfortable chairs, rather two office chairs are positioned directly across from the doctor's desk. The doctor talks to you from behind the desk. These differences in the use of space and furnishings are likely to affect the communication and perhaps the expectations of both the doctor and the patient.

The *social dimension* is defined in terms of the *primary* and *secondary functions that situations* serve in a particular society. For example, the primary function of the work situation is to accomplish tasks while the primary function of the lunch hour is to eat a meal. However, both the work situation and the lunch break have secondary functions. These secondary functions are manifest in discussions of political issues and personal attitudes in the office and work issues at lunch. If a worker asks his supervisor for a raise over lunch instead of during regular working hours, he is making a choice related to the social context.

An initial step in developing skills in this area is to become more observant of context. The competent communicator can isolate those elements of physical and social context that have the highest probability of accounting for differences in the outcome of a transaction. Take the example of a marriage proposal. It might be made in a living room during half-time of a televised football game or during a candlelight dinner at an expensive restaurant. Which would you prefer? Generally, a marriage proposal during a football game would be labeled as inappropriate behavior because it does not fit the context. A marriage proposal during a candlelight dinner would be labeled as appropriate because it does fit the context. If you went to lunch with a new acquaintance, and the person read the school newspaper instead of talking with you, how would you feel about the person?

Differences in physical and social context can affect the mutual perception of a transaction. It is important to realize that difficulties can occur when two communicators fail to agree on which physical context and social context is appropriate for a particular transaction. If John plans a classic romantic evening for his marriage proposal, but Mary prefers more nontraditional contexts for special events, context might be a problem for these two communicators. It is not context itself, but our expectations related to context that prove most troublesome. The competent communicator recognizes the impact of context in interpersonal relationships and chooses contexts for mutual satisfaction.

6. *What is relational history? A relational history is the sequence of transactions that begins when two people meet and continues throughout their relationship.* Relational history emphasizes that previous transactions influence future transactions. Suppose Phil tells Laura about his financial woes related to college. Her response is sarcastic. We predict that Laura's behavior will influence what Phil is

willing to discuss with her in the future.

The key concept in understanding how a relational history develops and affects an interpersonal relationship is perception — an active and often unconscious process of structuring events and attributing meaning to them. Too often we are tempted to contend that we know what *really* happened or what someone *really* meant only to find out that the other person's perception or view of the situation is completely different from ours. For example, your roommate comes in and finds you studying. After a simple "Hi," he or she goes into another room and starts reading a magazine. You perceive this behavior as avoidance and begin to wonder why he or she is so aloof, when in fact your roommate intends the silence to be a gesture of thoughtfulness because he or she does not want to disturb your studying. Each of you *constructed* a reality that did not match the other's. No one is right or wrong. What each person in the relationship *perceives* about the events that make up the relational history has a critical role in shaping future events.

The perceptual process occurs primarily on the unconscious level and involves three processes: (1) leveling, (2) sharpening, and (3) distortion. It would be impossible for a communicator to remember every event that contributed to the total we call relational history. In fact, it isn't necessary. If you are dating someone, you need not be able to catalogue and analyze each time you went out or talked in class. To manage all these events we use a technique called *leveling*. That is, we tune out those events that have little or no significant impact on the relational history as we perceive it. That's why one person in a relationship sometimes remembers an event like a particular date while the other vaguely recollects it, if at all. Leveling enables us to reduce large numbers of events by selecting, even if unconsciously, certain ones to remember.

A second process we use in developing a relational history is *sharpening*. This involves remembering certain events in essential detail and attributing relational significance to them. Think back to a time when you made a flip response only to learn that later the other person took it seriously. Such sharpening can be problematic if both individuals do not attribute the same level of significance to a statement.

The third process we use in developing a relational history is *distortion*. This occurs when a person wrongly attributes meaning to a particular behavior. A classic example of distortion occurs when a husband sends flowers to his spouse as a gesture of love and she begins to question what he's done to make him guilty enough to send flowers.

On a skill level, the competent communicator can identify the processes of leveling, sharpening and distortion that occur in his or her relationships. This does not mean that a communicator analyzes everything that happens in a given relationship. Such a pattern of monitoring one's behavior would be counterproductive, not only because it would take too much time, but also because a preoccupation with analysis takes the focus off actual experiences. We should strive to isolate and analyze those aspects of the relational history that are most important to its continued development. In addition, the competent communicator realizes that each relational history is unique. For example, Todd has just joined Business B as a middle manager. He left Business A because one of his subordinates was promoted to a position he wanted. He has begun to observe that Matthew, one of his subordinates, works long hours without additional compensation. Todd reasons that Matthew is working for promotion to Todd's job when, in fact, Matthew is motivated by his dedication to produce a quality product. This distortion on Todd's part will figure significantly in the Todd/Matthew relational history from Todd's perspective. Being sensitive to the impact of the past on the present is an essential skill that we develop over time by communicating to test the accuracy of our perceptions.

7. *What is time?* Time as used here does not refer to an identifiable number of hours or days. *Time refers to the stages and behaviors which sequently occur in most interpersonal relationships.* When two people meet, initial discussions center on demographic variables (e.g., my major is political science), general personal histories, mutual friends, and interests. This stage, frequently referred to as an *initial encounter*, may last five minutes or through several transactions over an extended period. Both persons are subjectively conducting a *similarity or compatability* analysis. If the analysis suggests that the other person is enough like me in terms of attitude and interests, a decision is often made to develop a relationship. The competent communicator does not attempt to develop relationships until satisfied with the information gained at this initial stage. Moving to the developmental stage does not end the gathering of information for similarity analysis; however, other topics and activities enter the relationship. When John and Martha discover that they both like musicals, among other information, in the initial stage and John wants to further develop the relationship, he asks Mary to attend a musical. Such a sequence is a predictable pattern. A competent communicator would not ask a person to attend a musical before learning whether he or she likes musicals.

At the skill level, the competent communicator is sensitive to the stages of relationship development, self disclosure patterns, relational conflict sequences and social inclusion parameters. He or she probably would not be able to articulate all these sequences, yet he or she follows the sequences and is immediately aware of their violation. Have you ever been in this position? You have recently met a person and know little about him or her. You encounter the person at a party, and he or she begins to tell you about very personal and intimate events in his or her life. You probably felt uncomfortable. Why? The person had violated the sequential pattern by which self-disclosure develops in a relationship. While we will more fully consider self-disclosure later in this chapter, the competent interpersonal communicator follows the time sequenced stages and knows when they are violated.

8. *What is communication climate?* By communication climate we mean *the relational environment that constrains and controls the kinds of messages that communicators exchange.* For example, in his last job Brian discussed very few of his work related ideas with his boss. Yet in his current position Brian has had many informal discussions with his boss about a wide range of work related issues. His willingness to discuss in one job setting and not the other is primarily a function of communication climate. Brian's job experiences illustrate the *two extreme types of communication climate — high risk and low risk.* All of our interpersonal communication occurs in a climate somewhere within these two extremes.

In a high risk climate, the communicator must be careful of what he or she says because the norm is one of judgment and evaluation. As a result, the communication is guarded. Brian simply didn't feel safe in discussing his ideas for change with the first boss. *In a low risk climate*, the communicator realizes that equality and not evaluation is the norm. Even though Brian was the subordinate, the second boss valued his opinions and ideas. Because Brian could identify differences in communication climate in these two work settings, he was able to adapt his verbal and nonverbal communication appropriately.

As two individuals develop a relationship, the communication climate develops somewhere between the extreme of low risk and the extreme of high risk. While most of us have probably not thought of our communication in a particular relationship in terms of climate, we have an intuitive sense that the same communicative behavior is neither appropriate nor effective in all contexts. This is no accident. Our appreciation of the role of communication climate in interpersonal relationships is based on understanding two interrelated variables — *openness and trust.* Communicators learn how open or candid they can be in discussing their feelings and attitudes with others. For example, over time Mike learns that he can discuss politics freely with George, but not religion because George tends to judge negatively those people who don't share his views on it. In other words, *as the anticipation of evaluation increases, openness decreases.* In addition to openness, trust plays a major role in defining the communication climate. Trust is built through communication and the development of a relational history where one feels that there is low risk when revealing information. As a result, trust influences what is discussed, how topics are discussed, and one's willingness to discuss candidly. If Diane trusts Beth, she believes that she can really say what she feels about abortion to Beth without any fear that Beth will think less of her if they disagree. *As risk decreases, trust is likely to increase.*

On a skill level, the competent communicator can identify the verbal and nonverbal behaviors that characterize low risk and high risk climates. That is, he or she recognizes indicators of respect, empathy, and support in contrast to indicators of manipulation, evaluation and defensiveness. Eric and Jon have been friends for two years. Their interpersonal communication has produced a relatively *low risk climate. Their verbal behavior demonstrates mutuality through conditional and inclusive phrases* like "Do you think?," "We could," "I think." Eric and Todd, on the other hand, have been friends for five years, but their interpersonal communication has produced a relatively *high risk climate.* If we tuned in on one of their discussions we would likely hear *absolute and exclusive phrases indicating a one-sided and evaluative climate* like "You can't" and "I won't." In each of these relationships, the nonverbal communication, especially paralanguage, will also have an effect on the type of communication climate that is produced. Which climate would you prefer?

The competent communicator realizes that even though we might prefer it, not every one of our interpersonal relationships can be low risk. Therefore, the same level of openness and trust is not appropriate in all relationships. We do not expect an individual to be as open and trusting to a casual acquaintance as to his or her spouse. In addition, because the communication climate is developmental, the competent communicator must adapt his or her messages while recognizing that time and other factors (e.g., violation of trust) can change the existing climate.

9. *What are rules? Rules are relational guidelines that dictate the parameters of acceptable and unacceptable behavior in a given situation. These rules exist on two major levels — societal (e.g., those rules developed by society) and relational (i.e., those rules unique to a particular relationship). Such rules can be stated in terms of do and do not or can and cannot. On the societal level,* we did not tell jokes at a funeral; we refer to superiors or teachers by their title and last name (e.g., Dr. Henson or Ms. Thorpe) unless they indicate that we can use their first name; and we congratulate the bride and groom at a wedding rather than telling them that they've made a stupid mistake. *On the relational level,* you might be painfully aware of the fact that your spouse abhors any conversation before breakfast. In another relationship, the rule might be spirited conversation from the moment of awakening. Most of us would find it difficult to articulate the rules that govern our relationships because often we are not consciously aware of how central these rules are to our behavior. From childhood on we learn, primarily through trial and error, how to behave according to societal and relational rules. If you still have any doubt about the importance of rules in our interpersonal relationships, focus for a moment on your reaction to the following instances: another person staring at you in a restaurant, someone you don't know sitting down right next to you in an otherwise empty lecture hall, two people

discussing a personal problem in a crowded elevator. Each of these examples should strike you as inappropriate because they represent rule violations at the societal level. It is when we sense a violation that we are usually able to specify the rule.

The competent communicator need not be able to list all the societal and relational rules that govern his or her relationships. *Rather, the focus should be on the development of two key skills*: (1) a sensitivity to rule violations, and (2) the ability to articulate the unique rules for a specific relationship. These skills will enable communicators to discuss the impact of rules on their relationship as the need arises, and to make modifications in their communication patterns. For example, Joe senses that his communication with his wife Jean has changed, but he's not exactly sure why he feels this way. As Joe analyzes their communication over the last few months, he realizes that a unique rule has been violated. Both Jean and he have been rushing in after work and beginning to take care of household responsibilities without stopping to discuss their day. While it might not seem important, these few minutes provided a relaxed, sharing atmosphere that each enjoyed and needed. At this point, Joe approached Jean about the change in their communication pattern, and both agreed they had unconsciously violated a rule that contributed positively to their relationship. As competent interpersonal communicators, they resolved the issue by being sensitive to the rule violation and taking steps to alter their communication.

10. *What is relational complexity? Relational complexity is the term*

we use to describe the essence of any interpersonal communication situation. While we have presented and discussed the knowledge and skills in Table 1 in a linear fashion, they really represent factors that are highly interactive. To attempt to rank order the concepts in terms of their impact on an interpersonal communication situation is not useful because their impact does not occur in a hierarchical top-to-bottom order. In fact, any change in one of the variables can change the situation, sometimes dramatically. *Relational complexity denotes that interpersonal communication is a process which is constantly changing as a function of the nine other key variables.*

Let's construct a hypothetical example to illustrate the complexity. Mr. Rohr and Ms. Rohr, a college freshman, are discussing use of the family car on Saturday night. Mr. Rohr is Ms. Rohr's father (roles). Their discussion is taking place in the kitchen (physical context) after a pleasant dinner (social context). Each wants the family car (goals) and is aware of the other's immediate purpose. Their communication in the past has been based on reasonably accurate perceptions with minimal distortion (relational history). In addition, a unique equality rule has developed insofar as each individual perceives he or she can say whatever he or she feels, except for constraints provided by the societal rules in the situation. The climate is supportive because Mr. Rohr and Ms. Rohr have managed their verbal and nonverbal communication to create an emphasis on problem-solving and not on competition. Even with this brief example, we recognize that to change any element can change the situation significantly. What if Ms. Rohr were Mr. Rohr's spouse, the discussion occurred as soon as Mr. Rohr walked in the door after a hectic day, or the relational history were marked by frequent misperceptions?

The competent communicator develops three basic skills in order to manage relational complexity: (1) analysis, (2) synthesis, and (3) flexibility. For a given relationship, the competent communicator should be able to analyze a given relationship in terms of the nine variables listed in Table 1 (i.e., What are the role relationships, primary rules, relational history, etc.). Relational complexity also demands synthesis or an ability to see the relationships between these variables. Finally, based on analysis and synthesis, the competent communicator develops flexibility. By flexibility we mean the ability to adapt communication behavior to the demands of the situation. We must guard against the tendency to look for *the* set of principles to apply in all interpersonal communication situations. However, more fruitful is the development of a repertoire of skills which are used according to the evaluation of a particular situation or relationship.

At this point, it might appear that becoming a competent interpersonal communicator is a hopelessly complex and unmanageable venture. However, developing interpersonal communication competence takes time and effort as well as a persistent refinement of our skills. We might draw an analogy to learning to drive a car. Think about the first time you got into a car and had to consciously think about putting the key into the ignition, stepping on the accelerator, shifting gears, applying pressure to the brake pedal, etc. Initially, perhaps you felt first a bit overwhelmed, but were determined to master the skills. Then there was driving straight ahead, and turning right and left. Backing up demanded a bit more practice, but it was parallel parking that probably demanded the most effort to master. As you practiced, many of these behaviors were incorporated into a series of steps that you eventually performed unconsciously. Even though these behaviors are now relatively automatic, there are times when you must focus consciously on the skills and adjust your driving patterns (e.g., when moving from dry pavement to icy pavement).

Similarly, as interpersonal communicators we struggle with the basic skills like what to say when you first meet someone, how to make small talk at a party, or how to maintain appropriate eye contact during a conversation. In fact, you have probably managed all three of these skills simultaneously. Then there was talking with your friend who is upset because she just broke up with her boyfriend, who is worried because she just blew an exam, or who is anxious because she has a demanding job. The skills required in each of these instances are not always applied at a conscious level. Once we become reasonably competent communicators in a given relationship, we (like the driver) do not depend on conscious analysis and synthesis. However, there are times when we become consciously aware of our skills and their application (like on an icy road). This shift to the conscious level is likely to occur when we develop a new relationship or perceive significant changes in an existing relationship (e.g., your best friend doesn't want to talk much any more, your favorite opposite sex friend hasn't asked you out in weeks). The competent interpersonal communicator is sensitive to the need for flexibility.

Pragmatic Applications

We have spent considerable space discussing the competencies of the ideal interpersonal communicator. So far, we have ignored one central issue, "How are these competencies used in interpersonal relationships? At an abstract level, the competencies are used in processes relating to the initiation, development and, when necessary, the termination of interpersonal relationships. Within these processes the competent interpersonal communicator is aware of and sensitive to a host of factors: (1) conversation topics for initial encounters, (2) factors involved in interpersonal attraction, (3) information sharing, (4) self-disclosure, (5) mutual relational expectations, (6) individual priorities, (7) language variables, (8) nonverbal variables, (9) relational conflict inevitability, (10) resolution and maintenance strategies, (11) relational evaluation, and (12) fifteen to a thousand other factors. Rather than attempting a review of the numerous issues associated with these eleven factors, we have focused on (1) interpersonal attraction, (2) matching expectations, (3) self-disclosure, (4) verbal and nonverbal codes, and (5) interpersonal conflict. These five factors are among the most important ones involved in developing interpersonal relationships. Our purpose is to provide a pragmatic analysis of how the competent interpersonal communicator functions in these key relational areas.

Interpersonal Attraction

What attracts us to another person, or what are the key factors in interpersonal attraction? While these questions have been extensively researched, no comprehensive answers are available. The chemistry of attraction can be only partially explained. We will look at three factors: (1) attractiveness, (2) attitudes and values, and (3) personality.

Although some want to deny it, physical attraction is a crucial factor, especially during initial transactions. Research has shown that consciously and unconsciously the initial visual impression influences interest in the other. The length of time and topics we are willing (want) to discuss in a transaction are partially determined before one word is spoken. Obviously, physical looks and beauty are variables related to attraction. However, the old saying, "Beauty is in the eyes of the beholder," qualifies any blatant generalization about good looks. When two people meet and like what they see, physical attraction has had an effect. It includes hair styles (i.e., short or long hair), clothes (i.e., casual or formal; jeans versus slacks), posture (i.e., straight or slouching), etc. We cannot deny the power of the initial visual impression.

Attitudes and values cover a broad range of topics. Included are hobbies, social preferences, interests, academic views, social views, political beliefs, religious memberships, and even preferred foods. While the crucial topics vary from person to person, a moderate-to-high degree of similarity must occur on such topics. Most of us do not attempt to learn the political preferences of the other before dating him or her, but many individuals attempt to learn the religious preference (i.e., catholic, jew, aethiest, protestant) before or on the first date. We like to have interpersonal relationships with those who are similar to us—they like to do what we like and they value what we value. When two people meet, the initial transaction often focuses on revelations about hometowns, majors, social preferences and music (i.e., low intimacy information). In essence, we can label this transaction as the initial similarity analysis. The analysis continues in later transactions, but it is part of the attraction system.

Personality influences attraction, but not in just one way. Martha and Edward are both aggressive but not domineering individuals (e.g., assertive and cooperative). They may enjoy an interpersonal relationship. Howard and Sally are both aggressive and domineering (i.e., assertive and uncooperative). Both will attempt to control a relationship. Fortunately, interpersonal attraction, if it occurs at physical and attitudinal levels, won't last long. Karen is aggressive and domineering, but Larry is nonagressive and compliant (i.e., unassertive and cooperative). They may well be attracted to each other. Larry will have a person make the decisions he likes to avoid, and Karen achieves her desire to be the boss. *Two persons with similar personalities may be attracted to each other, two similar personalities may result in mutual unattraction, two dissimilar personalities may lead to attraction, and two dissimilar personalities may result in an attraction failure.*

Dissimilarity resulting in an attraction failure needs some clarification. Arnold is aggressive but not domineering (i.e., assertive and cooperative). Kristen is neither aggressive nor domineering (i.e., nonassertive and cooperative). While there may be initial attraction, the prognosis is not favorable. Kristen will be happy, but Arnold will begin to be frustrated. He will want to share the decision-making and control in the relationship; Karen will want him to control the relational choices. Sooner or later Arnold will probably terminate the relationship. Kristen will be hurt and not understand why Arnold has rejected her.

The competent interpersonal communicator knows his or her physical preferences, but doesn't let such biases prevent the formation of friendships. While the perfect person would have no physical biases, a less than perfect communicator can only work to control the negative effects. For intimate personal relationships, physical attraction remains an important variable. The competent interpersonal communicator knows his or her attitudes, values and personality well enough so that he or she can seek and identify others who match at an attraction level. *The competent interpersonal communicator can be more tolerant, but we like what we like in others.* What we like is not easy to control or change. We can to some degree control such factors, but even if we could control all factors, few of us would want to completely eliminate them.

Matching Expectations

In an interpersonal relationship, we attribute meaning to verbal and nonverbal cues in order to determine whether the other person's perception in a particular transaction matches ours. Basically, we are

asking, "Does he or she see this the way I do?" Competent interpersonal communicators do not require that perceptions always
match. *However, the competent communicator recognizes that
perception forms the basis for his or her expectations of what ought to
happen, what the other ought to do, what the other person ought to say,
and so on. When expectations don't match, problems are likely.* Take
Joshua who loves Ann and values marriage. Based on his expectations,
he thinks they ought to get married. Ann loves Joshua and also values
marriage. But she considers marriage to be a lifetime commitment she
is not ready to make. She thinks they ought to wait to get married, and
expects Joshua to feel the same way. In contrast Joshua reasons,
"Since she doesn't want to get married now, she doesn't really love
me." His conclusion is based on mismatched expectations. These two
people need to share information about their expectations so that each
understands the other's perspective. We have here a case of different
perceptions of love and marriage creating mismatched expectations.
Let's look at another case. Harry and Sam were friends in high school
and have planned to share a dorm room. When they arrive on campus,
Harry says, among other things, "Let's try to keep the room half-way
clean." Sam responds, "Sounds reasonable." Three weeks later after
Harry has cleaned the room twice, the blow-up comes. During the
argument, Sam states, "Cleaning the place every two or three weeks is
enough; every week is overdoing it." At the center of the problem are
mismatched expectations, each has a different expectation about the
meaning of "half-way clean."

We need to examine how perceptions are shaped. (*Two key factors affect each individual's perception of a particular transaction: (1) the perceived nature of the issue, and (2) the perceived consequence of the issue.*) The nature of the issue varies along a continuum from issues that are considered unimportant (e.g., what we eat for dinner) to issues that are considered crucial (e.g., whether we invest our money in a speculative venture). The consequence of an issue varies along a continuum from low (e.g., what movie we see Saturday night) to high (what city we move to after graduation). Figure 2 is a Perception Grid that we can use to plot two people's perceptions relative to each other. For example, Al and Bob are roommates. Al grew up in a large family with an average income. He values a budget highly and feels that money should be spent for necessities. The rest should be saved. In contrast, Bob grew up in a relatively wealthy family and sees little reason to budget. He likes to spend freely. Al and Bob contribute money to pay expenses jointly for rent, utilities, food and extras like snacks, entertaining friends, etc. Let's plot their perceptions. For Bob, money is relatively unimportant and of low consequence (Position B). For Al, it is quite the opposite (Position A). While the distance plotted here is not any absolute measure of how far apart their perspectives are, it illustrates that there is a significant difference. Unless Al and Bob share information about their perceptions of money, each is likely to form some misleading expectations about how the other thinks the pooled money should be spent. In actual relationships, it can take quite some time to realize that misunderstandings are caused by mismatched expectations.

IMPORTANT ⟶ ✳ Figure 2. Expectation Grid

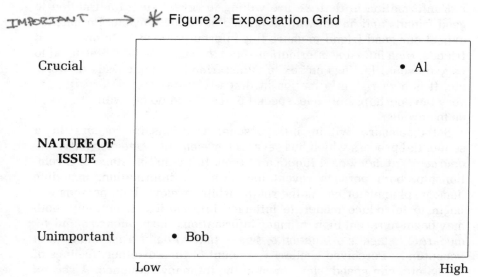

We do not mean to imply that matching expectations for every trans-action is realistic or necessary. However, even when the issue is unimportant but of some consequence, a person prefers that his or her expectations are matched. For example, Marty always leaves the cap off the shampoo in the shower. No one in the apartment perceives this to be a critical issue in their relationship as roommates. Yet the other roommates expect, probably unconsciously, that the shampoo will be capped. When Jeff gets into the shower and finds watered down shampoo, he probably becomes quite aware of the violated expectation because it is of relatively high consequence at the moment. The competent communicator appreciates the distinction between consequence and importance as well as their interface.

Self-Disclosure

Self-disclosure is a key factor in interpersonal relationships. When we self-disclose, we share with others our beliefs, thoughts and feelings about a given topic. In essence, we provide information about the self. We can categorize this self information on an intimacy continuum. Low intimacy information about the self probably includes feelings about sports, music, food, current fashion, etc. It is low risk in the sense that we are willing to reveal it in most relationships and do not care if the information is passed on to almost anyone. Moderate intimacy information about the self probably includes beliefs and feelings about politics, religion, family relationships, etc. It is medium risk information in that we are willing to reveal such information to good friends and do not want it passed on to just anyone. Rather, we expect our good friend to share this information only with other good friends. High intimacy information about the self is usually restricted to very personal feelings on sex, another friend, a major issue at work, etc. It is high risk information in that we reveal such information to very few, perhaps only one, special persons and do not want it passed on to anyone.

Self-disclosure within interpersonal relationships occurs in a sequential process which has several key elements. One element is the degree of intimacy as a function of time. In the initial stage of a rela-tionship, both persons reveal low intimacy information, including demographic histories. As the relationship develops, both persons will begin to introduce moderate intimacy information. Eventually, both may begin to reveal high intimacy information. The sequence of low-to-moderate-to-high is a function of time — time to build trust and mutual acceptance. Perceived similarity, amount of time together, feelings of liking, etc. can speed, slow, or stop the intimacy sequence. A second key element is reciprocity. That is, as the level of intimacy develops, it is a mutual development. When one person begins to reveal moderate intimacy information, the second person must reveal the same type of information if the relationship is to continue to develop. If the second person responds to the moderate intimacy information with low intimacy information (e.g., shifts the topic to a new movie) and/or negatively evaluates the information, the relationship will not continue to develop, although it may continue to exist (e.g., two persons can continue to work at adjacent desks). The sequential elements of reciprocity and intimacy level as a function of time are two key elements in developing relational self-disclosure.

The competent interpersonal communicator is aware of the elements and processes in self-disclosure. He or she is aware that self-disclosure involves risks when revealing moderate and high intimacy information. Further, given a continuing relationship, the level of intimate information and degree of explicitness (i.e., general statement to personal examples) defines the relationship on an impersonal-to-personal-to-very-personal continuum. How does the competent interpersonal communicator use all this knowledge?

He or she is aware that the development of an interpersonal relationship in terms of self-disclosure follows a trial-balloon — reciprocity — surveillance — trust spiral once the dyad moves beyond low intimacy information. Bill and Mary met through some friends over lunch in the cafeteria. Over the next week, they chat occasionally, learn of mutual friends, and build what might be labeled as a casual-social relationship. Mary decides that she wants to get rid of the casual aspect and move the relationship toward a friendship-male/female. During the next transaction, she discusses her feelings about family relationships and illustrates her point by referring to some neighbors in her hometown (i.e., moderate intimacy information at a medium degree of explicitness). If Bill responds with a general comment, "Yeah, you are very perceptive about the William's," and shifts the discussion to the lecture he just heard in basic speech, Mary as a competent communicator would realize that Bill wants the relationship to remain casual-social. If Bill reciprocates Mary's self-disclosure, Mary would tentatively view the relationship as moving in the desired direction; she might even offer one or two more trial balloons as long as Bill reciprocates.

However, Mary would surveil the environment for feedback as it relates to trust. Suppose she hears from Sue (a mutual friend), "Bill mentioned to Fred that he really enjoys talking with you." She gets positive feedback which helps develop trust. Suppose Sue said, "Bill told Fred you certainly have definite views on family relationships," or suppose she hears nothing about the conversation for a week. She has received somewhat neutral feedback, and will probably offer more trial balloons until she is more sure of Bill's feelings. Suppose Sue states, "Bill told Fred you have some weird ideas on the family." She has received negative feedback, and will probably reevaluate Bill and her relationship with him.

Assuming the relationship develops to a close-personal level where even high intimacy information is discussed with a lot of explicitness, surveillance becomes more difficult since neutral and negative feedback are the only possibilities (i.e., high intimacy information is not to be discussed outside of the relationship). This is why the mutual trust necessary for high self-disclosure is developed over time, and why once trust is violated, it may be almost impossible to rebuild.

Mary, as a competent interpersonal communicator, knows how to proceed up this trial-balloon—reciprocity—surveillance—trust—self-disclosure spiral. Of course, dates with Bill, mutual needs and goals, and relational rule development will also affect the process. For various reasons, we develop few relationships with a high self-disclosure norm. The competent interpersonal communicator controls his or her self-disclosure behavior to match the goals and expectations of a given relationship.

Verbal and Nonverbal Codes

Verbal and nonverbal codes powerfully influence the development of interpersonal relationships. We know others and they know us through communication, both verbal and nonverbal. From a relational perspective, the verbal code serves two main functions: (1) to define the relationship, and (2) to control relational outcomes. In terms of relational definition, the use of pronouns is one key indicator. Jim and Sarah have been dating each other for six months. Lately, it seems that most dates have ended in what we politely label discussions. Both like each other, but both are frustrated by the tension developing in the relationship. On Sunday afternoon, after a frustrating date on Saturday night, Sarah meets Jim for lunch. They begin to discuss their relationship and feelings. Sarah's statements cover, "I feel...," "Our options are...," "How do you feel about...?" Jim's statements are, "I think...," "You feel...," "I don't...."

Notice the difference in relational definitions. Jim states his position and his perception of Sarah's position. Sarah states her position, asks for Jim's position, and mentions their options. From an analysis of pronouns, we find that Jim's pattern is I-You and Sarah's is I-We-You. Jim's pronoun usage suggests that there is no mutual relationship. Sarah's use of we indicates that she either wants or believes there is a mutual relationship. While it would be dangerous to conclude from one transaction that Jim and Sarah perceive their relationship differently, their use of pronouns hints at relational definition.

In order to control relational outcomes, the competent communicator can employ two skills, restatement and requests for clarification. When someone says, "I hear you saying that" or "You seem to mean," that individual is restating his or her understanding of the other's statement or position. This skill is particularly useful after perceived mutual agreements about relationships, rules, etc. (e.g., "We agree to discuss this problem tomorrow"). At a basic level, restatement requires the other person to agree or disagree with our perception of what was said. Restatement enables us to control relational outcomes insofar as we test the accuracy of our perceptions. A second skill is requests for clarification. The competent communicator doesn't assume he or she knows the position or perception of the other person. Rather, he or she asks (e.g., "What do you think about...."). This skill is very useful in learning if the expectations of the other person match our own. Like restatement, asking for clarification is likely to produce fewer surprises in a relationship. Competent interpersonal communication demands the use of these verbal skills. However, we do not mean to imply that analysis of pronouns, restatement, and asking for clarification are to be employed in every transaction. In fact, such overuse of the skills would be counterproductive.

From a relational perspective, the nonverbal code functions (1) to define the realtionship, and (2) to promote relational understanding. In order to define the relationship through the nonverbal code, the competent communicator must first employ the basic skill of observation. Because nonverbal cues not only come from many dimensions — space, gesture, and touch, to name a few — but also often occur simultaneously, the competent communicator must become consciously aware of what's happening, where, and when. Jane and Joann work together at a pizza parlor. They are in a few classes together and have been to a few of the same parties on campus. If we had unlimited time to observe their use of the nonverbal code, we would probably find that (1) their touching behavior is limited; (2) when they touch, it is usually on the arms, hands, or shoulders. In other words, Jane and Joann follow, although probably unconsciously, society's norms for touching. The norms are: (1) generally, don't touch others; and, (2) if you do touch, do so only on nonintimate body regions. By employing the skill of observation, we might conclude that Jane's and Joann's relationship is casual. We can determine, although not with absolute certainty, the nature of a particular relationship by observing nonverbal behavior in context. For purposes of illustration, we have discussed only one aspect of the nonverbal code as used by Jane and Joann. However, the competent communicator would not limit himself or herself to only one dimension of the code in defining the parameters of a relationship.

To promote relational understanding, the competent communicator employs the skill of interpretation. This skill requires determining what a particular nonverbal behavior means to a given communicator in the relationship. John and Marcia are sitting by the fire in the apartment living room. It's been quiet for a few minutes. Marcia thinks, "He's ignoring me. We don't seem to have anything to talk about." John is thinking, "What a great way to spend a cold evening. We can relax without needing to talk." If both John and Marcia fail to interpret the silence the same way, their relational understanding is affected negatively. John thinks things are great, and Marcia thinks they could be much better.

The competent communicator knows that different interpretations (why is this happening?) of a particular nonverbal dimension are possible. Among other interpretations, John and Marcia could conclude that the silence means: "I don't know," "I don't care," "I didn't hear you," "I'm thinking," or "I'm ignoring you." The final interpretation should be based on observation of the nonverbal behavior in context and in conjunction with the verbal code. Accurate interpretation determines relational understanding. This is important because greater relational understanding leads to greater relational satisfaction—a highly desirable product of competent interpersonal communication.

Interpersonal Conflict

An old myth about interpersonal relationships is, "Two individuals who like (love) and trust each other can get along in a sort of natural harmony. Interpersonal conflicts represent the failure of one or both persons to like or trust." We will not review here all the reasons why this is false. Problems of perception, misunderstanding, individual changes, and competing demands and goals, among others, cause conflicts in interpersonal relationships. A synthesis of the theory and research on conflict now yields the following axioms:

1. Interpersonal conflicts are inevitable.

2. How interpersonal conflicts are managed causes relational confirmation, deterioration, or destruction.

3. Although communication can be a cause of conflict, communication is the only means by which interpersonal conflicts can be satisfactorily and mutually resolved.

Although the first axiom may seem odd, differences develop between two people in a relationship. Two ideal interpersonal communicators would probably never have a conflict; however, no one has ever found one perfect interpersonal communicator. In fact, it is our closest relationships which can produce the most rewarding conflicts. As Thomas Oden observed, "It is precisely the intimacy most deeply nourished by affection that is most capable of constructive conflict or 'fair-fighting.'

Stated concisely, the intimate relationship is emotionally warm, yet conflict-capable." (Oden, 1974).

Since interpersonal conflict is inevitable, we will focus on the strategic management of such conflicts. As an initial observation, we must remember that conflict produces psychological stress and emotional arousal. Raised voices, loaded language, and sarcasm often are the products of this arousal.

Strategic Principle 1: Speak in a normal voice. Use language which reflects your feelings and position, but which avoids emotional ventilation. There is a great difference between saying, "You lazy nerd! You are as responsible as an alley cat. Look at your clothes strewn around this room." and saying, "Al, look! I'm not the greatest in keeping the room clean, but I get embarrassed when friends drop by and find clothes lying all over the place." Communicate your feelings, communicate your position, don't communicate negative reactions and evaluations which derogate the other person. The competent interpersonal communicator rationally selects language and avoids emotional reaction.

Strategic Principle 2: Be specific! Identify the behavior or problem you perceive as the conflict. Do not trot out a laundry list of 20 gripes. All too often the following sequence happens. Mary has a comlaint about her relationship with Sue. Perhaps she is not very tactful in stating her position. Perhaps she is tactful. In any case, instead of responding to Mary's grievance, Sue counters with one of her own. Mary raises a third conflict; Sue raises a fourth. Half an hour later, both have listed all their tensions, misperceptions, and grievances. While nothing has been resolved, both feel hurt, frustrated, and blame the other. No matter who raises the conflict, the competent interpersonal communicator keeps the discussion focused on the issue of the conflict, and blocks the introduction of additional grievances.

Strategic Principle 3: Relational conflict is a dyadic affair. Never raise a conflict in front of others if you value the relationship. Bill and Mary are at a dinner with Laura and David. Bill learns that Mary wants to go to a play Saturday night. He has a different activity planned. Instead of saying, "We might have a potential problem concerning Saturday. Let's talk about it later," Bill tells Mary why he thinks the play is a stupid idea and insists on his activity. Mary disagrees. With the audience of Laura and David, chances are the conflict will escalate and neither will compromise. Like high intimacy information, the competent interpersonal communicator knows that conflicts should be resolved within the dyad. After the dyad has repeatedly failed to resolve the conflict, a third party may be consulted; however, this should be agreed to jointly as a general rule.

Strategic Principle 4: Select an appropriate time for the discussion. If you are super angry, wait until you cool down. If you perceive the other person is tired or angry, wait for a better moment. In short, select a time when you and the other person can more or less (emphasis on the *more*) rationally deal with the conflict. For example, when Carla walks into the room after a hard exam and Sue, without asking how she did on the test, proceeds to chew her out for using all the shampoo, she has violated this principle.

Strategic Principle 5: When you learn you are wrong, admit it. When a compromise is possible, either offer it or accept it when offered by the other. A natural way to view interpersonal conflicts is as a win/lose proposition. If Bill wins, Mary loses, or visa versa. A more productive question is, "What's more important, this conflict or this relationship." We are not advising that you give in merely to preserve the relationship—conflicts need to be rationally and equitably resolved. However, relational goals must remain at least equal to individual goals and needs if the relationship is to survive.

Strategic Principle 6: When the conflict is resolved or tabled for discussion, summarize any mutual agreements, and then reaffirm the relationship. Suppose we have Diane and Frank. They have been married for two years, both work and Diane usually gets home at 6:00 and Frank around 7:00. Frank arrives home. Diane isn't there. Time passes! Around 9:15, just before Frank calls the police, Diane walks in. Frank learns that she has been shopping with a friend from work and blows up. He keeps saying, "Why didn't you call me?" Diane, realizing she is in the wrong, apologizes. In one case, Frank says, "OK," then turns on the TV. In another case, Frank says, "Hey, clown, I love you," and hugs Diane. Which relationship do you think will last?

Interpersonal conflicts can be productive or destructive for the individuals and relationships. If you really practice these six principles, we promise you more productive outcomes.

Summary

We began with a transactional approach to the study of interpersonal communication. From this perspective, interpersonal communication focuses on mutual relationships between two persons. Within a wide variety of one-to-one relationships (i.e., from temporary to permanent, from acquaintances to lovers), each of us functions as an interpersonal communicator.

Our question throughout this chapter has been, "What does it take to become a competent interpersonal communicator?" At the most basic level, the answer was that a competent interpersonal communicator must acquire a knowledge of key variables which affect interpersonal communication, and then develop the skills necessary to pragmatically apply such knowledge. In terms of knowledge, we discussed the variables of (1) self, (2) roles, (3) individuality, (4) satisfactions and goals, (5) context, (6) relational history, (7) time, (8) communication climate, (9) rules, and (10) relational complexity. In terms of skills, we offered some suggestions on how a knowledge of each variable may influence one's approach to and behaviors in interpersonal relationships.

Certain processes, stages, and variables occur within many, if not all, interpersonal relationships. We explored the factors that a competent interpersonal communicator would review and consider during the development of an interpersonal relationship. We included a discussion of (1) interpersonal attraction, (2) matching expectations, (3) self-disclosure, (4) verbal and nonverbal codes, and (5) interpersonal conflict.

A crucial assumption throughout this chapter is that the development of interpersonal communication competency will change how each of us communicates with others. As we develop our competencies, we will find ourselves more sensitive to and aware of others. This change will allow us to communicate more effectively (i.e., express our intentions, positions, feelings) with others.

This chapter provides you with the basics for developing your own interpersonal communication competency. Some of the specific communication skills (e.g., the restatement skill, self-disclosure skills, conflict resolution strategies) you can begin to practice immediately. Other skills (e.g., sensitivity to roles and rules) will take some time and effort to develop. The effort is worth it. As you improve your interpersonal communication through developing competency, you will find your interpersonal relationships more productive and rewarding.

References

Alberti, R.E., & Emmons, M.L. *Stand up, speak out, talk back: the key to self-assertive behavior.* New York: Pocket Books, 1975.

Bach, G.R., & Wyden P. *The intimate enemy.* New York: Avon Books, 1968.

Bateson, G. *Steps to an ecology of mind.* New York: Ballatine Books, 1972.

Berscheid, E. & Walster, E.H. *Interpersonal attraction.* Reading: Addison-Wesley, 1969.

DeVito, J.A. *The interpersonal communication book.* 2nd ed. New York: Harper and Row, 1980.

Doolittle, R.J. *Orientations to communication and conflict.* Chicago: Science Research Associates, 1976.

Filley, A.C. *Interpersonal conflict resolution.* Glenview:Scott, Foresman, and Company, 1975.

Gibb, J.R. Defensive Communication. *Journal of communication.* 1961, 11, 141-148.

Johnson, D.W. *Reaching out: interpersonal effectiveness and self-actualization.* Englewood Cliffs: Prentice-Hall, 1972.

Jourard, S. *The transparent self.* rev. ed. New York: D. Van Nostrand, 1971.

Knapp, M.L. *Social intercourse: from greetings to goodby*. Boston: Allyn and Bacon, 1978.

Levy, R.B. *Self-revelation through relationships*. Englewood Cliffs: Prentice-Hall, 1972.

Miller, G.R. (ed.) *Explorations in Interpersonal Communication*. Palo Alto: Sage, 1976.

Miller, G.R., & Steinberg, M. *Between People*. Chicago: Science Research Associates, 1975.

Oden, T.C. *Game free: a guide to the meaning of intimacy*. New York: Harper and Row, 1974.

Powell, J.S.L. *Why am i afraid to tell you who i am?* Niles: Argus Communications, 1969.

Rogers, C.R. *On becoming a person*. Boston: Houghton Mifflin, 1961.

Ruben, B.D. & Kim, J.Y. (eds.) *General systems theory & human communication*. Rochelle Park, New Jersey: Hayden, 1975.

Ruesch, J., & Bateson G. *Communication: the social matrix of psychiatry*. reprint, ed. New York: W.W. Norton, 1968.

Satir, V. *Conjoint family therapy: a guide to theory and technique*. rev. ed. Palo Alto: Science and Behavior Books, 1967.

Satir, V. *Peoplemaking*. Palo Alto: Science and Behavior Books, 1972.

Smith, D.R., & Williamson, L.K. *Interpersonal communication: roles, rules, strategies, and games*. Dubuque: Wm. C. Brown, 1977.

Stewart, J. *Bridges not walls*. 2nd ed. Readings: Addison-Wesley, 1977.

Watzlawick, P., Beavin, J., & Jackson D. *Pragmatics of human communication*. New York: W.W. Norton, 1967.

Wiemann, J.M. Explication and test of a model of communication competence. *Human communication research*. 1977, 3, 195-213.

5

Small Group Communication

David W. Wright

One of the most common dimensions of communication involves human interaction in the small group. If you were to sit down and write a list of all the small groups to which you belong, you certainly would have written several pages. School groups, church groups, families, sororities, study groups, athletic teams, and many more are just a beginning of a representative list of everyday life groups to which we belong. The mere fact that we converse with each other in small groups to such a great extent makes the study of small group communication important for everyone. This chapter details and explains many aspects of communicating in small groups which you encounter on a daily basis.

First, a brief historical background of small group communication highlights speech and small group traditions that influence group processes. Next, selected theories of small group communication are examined from both interdisciplinary and within-the-field perspectives. These theoretical considerations in turn provide an understanding of small group concepts and variables that are applicable to the process of interacting in small groups. The third section of the chapter focuses on specific uses of small group communication. These uses have immediate and direct application to the groups in which you participate daily. A summary of the most important theoretical concepts and useable small group practices closes the chapter, while emphasizing the role of small groups in everyday life.

Historical Background of Small Group Communication

This introductory section deals primarily with the speech and small group traditions that form the historical foundations for our study of small group communication. In addition, the process of communication itself is viewed as an influence on the historical underpinnings of small groups. From our brief examination of these traditional influences, basic small group definitions and kinds of small groups are presented.

The speech tradition as historical background for small group communication has essentially two strains. They are the continued use of oral presentations in small group settings and our study of discussion methods. The first strain, oral presentations in small groups, has at its foundation the notion of practice. Traditionally, oral presentations have been given in such formal discussion settings as conferences, conventions, committee meetings, and the like. Making certain that speakers in these formal group situations are fluent, well-prepared, and well-organized has been a perennial concern for speech communication scholars. Even since the time of the Greeks when a major concern of rhetoricians was deliberative speaking, the attention to the practice aspects of speechmaking has been emphasized in group discussion environments.

The second major strain of the speech tradition, the study of discussion methods, also can be traced back to our Greco-Roman heritage. Not only were the ancients concerned with rhetoric, the effective use of speechmaking in a presentational and often persuasive

way, but with the theory and application of the dialectic. The dialectic is the effective use of the dialogue—the continual use of the question and answer method with its primary object being the search for truth. The many dialogues included in the works of Plato are splendid examples of the dialectic. This pattern of questioning and answering found in the dialectic is at the heart of our study of discussion methods. How a group discussion progresses from beginning to end has been viewed not infrequently as a way of thinking. In group situations the reflective thinking method as applied to discussion has been the most predominant influence on the speech tradition. The most famous proponent of reflective thinking in this century has been John Dewey (1910). His suggested steps of reflective thinking are in reality a structuring of the dialogue, a set patterning of questions and answers in a discussion.

Thus, we see the two strains of the speech tradition of small group communication as having the same base: the Greeks' treatment of rhetoric and dialectic nearly 2500 years ago. The continual practice of oral presentations in speech situations can be traced directly to our rhetorical foundations, while the study of discussion methods is firmly rooted in the dialectical method. Possibly in no other communication dimension do the two ancient pillars of speech, rhetoric and dialectic, blend together as much as they do in the study of small group discussion.

The small group tradition which forms another historical foundation for examining small group communication is much younger than the above-discussed rhetorical and dialectical strains of the speech tradition. To begin with, the small group tradition may be viewed from a broad interdisciplinary perspective. A variety of academic fields contribute to the small group tradition, including psychology, sociology, organizational management, information theory, and the like. The structural explanation of what a group looks like and how it is formed is a result of this interdisciplinary influence on our study of groups.

Psychologists would have us emphasize the behaviors of individual members that compose groups. For example, what personality characteristics it takes to distinguish leaders from nonleaders has been a continual research question. Other kinds of questions that have intrigued psychologists include: how dominant or submissive should group members be? does intelligence affect the performance and participation of individuals in the group? to what extent does anxiety detract from a participant's effectiveness? As one can see by this sampling of research questions, psychologists are concerned with what behaviors of individuals affect member performance and the like. The influence of the field of psychology on the study of small groups thus is primarily *individual-based*.

On the contrary, sociologists have been primarily concerned with viewing the small group from a *group-orientation*. Such areas as the formation of group norms, the development of group membership, the effect of certain group membership on other groups, have all been treated by sociologists. The notions of what are secondary and primary groups in general have been applied to small groups in particular. In addition, the whole notion of the structure of a group has been a major research area; specifically, the use of sociograms to describe how individuals relate and interact with each other inside a given group. Not only are we trying to look at a collection of individuals, as the psychologists essentially do, sociologists have added the dimension of a group in which the individuals relate and organize.

Thus, another aspect of the interdisciplinary influence on the small group tradition comes from the field of organizational management. During the twentieth century, and particularly since World War II, organizational management has been concerned with groups. When one observes both large and small companies, it is easy to identify various groups that compose the organization. For example, a manufacturing company typically has at least the following departments (groups): sales, production control, quality control, shipping, billing, accounting, etc. In all probability these basic groups are made up of other groups (generally called subgroups). Also, these groups seek some kind of organized relationship with each other. Finding these kinds of relationships among various groups and departments that make up companies is one of the primary areas of study in the field of organizational management.

Information theory has been another kind of interdisciplinary influence on the small group tradition. Information theorists have typically looked at groups in a systematic way; i.e., they have analyzed the structure and composition of groups by looking at what went into the group and what came out of it. It would not be unusual for an information theorist to quantify the "bits of information" given to individual members of the group as input and then analyze these bits of information as they were processed and as to what group outcomes were produced.

The attention to processing information in groups has probably been influenced more by the interdisciplinary nature of communication than any of the above-mentioned fields taken separately. Communicating in the small group goes beyond the individuals who make it up, the group structure as a whole, the relation of groups in organizations, and input-output perspectives. The communication orientation of small groups provides explanations of how groups process information through the dynamics of interaction. The individual group member must accept at least some responsibility for the communicative behaviors of small groups. The speech, small group, and communication traditions provide ample historical background to serve as a foundation for the study of small group communication. More specifically, they serve as a solid base for the fundamental definitions of small group processes used in this chapter. Further, the definitions given below are deemed appropriate for the general kinds of groups that most individuals interact within during their everyday life group experiences.

The basic definitions given here will help you to distinguish between the concepts of small group, small group communication, and small group discussion. A *small group is defined as having three required* attributes: (1) *size* (2) *structure of the group and (3) individual responsibility to the group*. The issue of size has been a legitimate concern to small group researchers as well as lay practitioners. Typically, a small group has been defined according to the size criterion as ranging from 3 to 15 persons. Small group researchers have been fond, especially in laboratory settings, of describing the group in terms of 5 persons. Other have found that a tendency toward subgrouping (dividing into more than one group) occurs as early as 7 members and certainly by 9 members. General agreement, however, seems to be found for describing the group as being comprised of a minimum of four persons and a maximum of nine; the preferred optimum size, at least to this author, is 5-7 members in a group. A second necessary characteristic for a group is that it have some discernable structure. Typically, this structure includes some common goals and interests that are the concern of a group in a face-to-face situation. A third necessary criterion for a small group is that its individual members feel some responsibility to it; i.e., participants recognize the group's existence and share in its successes and failures. A *small group, then, may be defined as 5-7 group members who recognize a face-to-face structure and accept some responsibility for the group's actions.* The definitions of small group communication and small group discussion assume at least the majority of the characteristics of the definition of small group given here.

Small group communication is defined as *the group system in which members interact and are interdependent upon each other within a small group structure*. Key parts of this definition are those relating to interaction and interdependency. When communicating in a small group it is assumed that all members will interact, to at least a minimal degree, and that these interactions will relate, at least in part, to other group members. This latter notion of relating the interactions of members to the group is called interdependency. Not only do members in the group system process information through interaction, they do so in a mutually dependent pattern.

The definition of small group discussion is more specific than either of the other two key definitions cited above. *Small group discussion* is defined as *the process whereby 3 or more people overtly think and work together in order to share information or solve a problem within a small group interaction context.* In addition to being a small group and being a communication system that emphasizes interaction and

interdependency, the small group discussion definition emphasizes the ability of group members to *overtly* think and work together; that is they may not necessarily like the individual members of the group or share other common interests, but they do work together hard enough to achieve some goal achievement through the discussion process. The above definitions of small group, small group communication, and small group discussion are appropriate for the kinds of small group of which we find ourselves members everyday.

There are three basic kinds of small groups: *task, encounter, and consciousness-raising*. The task group is probably the most common for most of us. Typical task groups are work groups at the office, study groups, athletic teams, and the like. The major objective of task groups is goal achievement of some kind and usually requires at least a simplistic form of small group discussion. Encounter groups are usually socio-emotionally oriented. Bull sessions, therapy groups, human potential groups are all examples of encounter groups. These kinds of groups require at least some level of small group communication. Consciousness-raising groups include such organizational groups as the National Organization for Women (NOW) and the Gay People's Alliance. Hopefully, the group structure provides some maintenance features of what we expect from a small group.

Regardless of the kind of group, one studying groups must be aware of the group's history. If the group has never met before, we identify the group as being a zero-history group. Most natural groups have developed a history of sorts and are categorized as on-going in nature. We generally find that most work groups have a group history and understand that they should try and achieve group goals. However, what is and what should be in task-oriented small groups varies a great deal of the time for many reasons. Some of these reasons for varying behaviors which utilize small group processes will be better understood after reading the next section of the chapter which examines selected theories of small group communication.

Selected Theories of Small Group Communication

This section presents three general classes of small group communication theories. They have been chosen for their representativeness and fundamental knowledge base in order to aid you in your general understanding of small group communication. The essential concepts that have been derived from the three general classes of small group theories, as well as key variables that have been measured, are highlighted at the end of this section. The first small group theory, Lewin's Field Theory, gives us an understanding of groups from a psychological perspective. The second general theory classification looks at the small group from systems and interaction approaches; George Homans and Robert Bales respectively are the two representative theorists to view the group in this way. The third general category of small group theories examines the contributions of major communication theorists and how they view human interaction in the small group context.

Lewin's Field Theory

Kurt Lewin's Field Theory examines the small group from two psychological bases; phenomenology and Gestalt psychology. Phenomenology observes the behavior of individual group members from the standpoint of the behavior itself; namely the source of group behavior is found in individual persons and not the environment (Shepherd, 1964, p. 24). Gestalt psychology is based quite simply on the proposition that the whole is greater than the sum of its parts; for Lewin this meant that the group product was unique and not just a summation of the individuals' collectivity. In other words, Lewin's Field theory has two psychological bases: phenomenology which is individually-oriented and Gestalt psychology which is group-oriented. This solid theoretical foundation allows the student of small groups to view the group from the standpoint of the individual's behavior in the group and from the position of the group as a whole.

Below are listed some of the basic concepts of Lewin's Field Theory. Lewin's understanding and perception of these concepts are undoubtedly part of the reason that he has been acknowledged as the "father of group dynamics." Your grasp of these concepts will help you to better realize the importance of this individualized social psychological approach to small group communication.

1. *life-space*. This unique concept can best be explained in terms of our knowledge of communication theory. Just as each individual carries around a "personal space bubble" that increases and decreases in size as one moves from environment to environment, so does a group member possess an area immediately around him in the group situation which we call "life-space."

2. *position and goals*. Just as each group member possesses "life-space," they do so in relation to other group members and their respective "life-spaces." This relationship between each member's life-space is called *position*. Each member has an individual and group *position* toward everyone else's life-space. The position that each person's life-space occupies will influence where he or she stands in relation to his or her personal *goals* and the group's *goals*. The following diagram illustrates the relationship of *life-space, position,* and *goals*.

In the diagram the circle around each letter represents a group member and his or her respective life-space. The *position* of the group members toward the *group goal* is about the same for Members A, B, C,

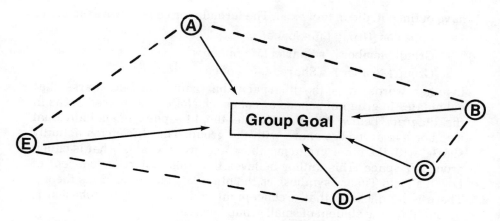

and D; obviously Member E's position is much further away. Also notice the dotted lines between each member's position in the group. Again Member E is much further away from any other member's life-space; on the other hand, Members B&C positions are very close to each other. One interpretation could be that Members B&C are in fairly close agreement regarding both personal and group goals. On the other hand, Member E is probably individually far apart from the other group members just as he is toward the group goal; perhaps he is an alienated member of an on-going group or a newcomer to an already established group.

3. *locomotes.* In order for the group members to move toward personal and group goals from their life-space positions, it is necessary to have some motion mechanism. In Lewin's Field Theory the motion mechanism takes the form of *locomotes*; i.e., influences that move the group toward its goals. In speech communication we categorize locomotes as leadership functions. The next section of this chapter contains detailed descriptions of leadership functions that must be performed in the group.

4. *barriers.* It certainly is not uncommon to find *barriers* in the group's way when individual members and the group as a whole try to accomplish personal and group goals. These areas of conflict must be minimized, if not eliminated, in trying to move individuals' life-spaces into more favorable positions when seeking goal attainment. It is usually necessary to perform certain leadership functions (*locomotes*) in order to remove interpersonal and task barriers in the group.

5. *cohesion.* This is a key concept, in this author's opinion, of Lewin's Field Theory. In fact by understanding the above concepts of Field Theory, we can now classify the major small group variable, cohesion, as "group life-space." If group members share their individual life-spaces, that area becomes known as group life-space. In addition, this belongingness and togetherness achieved by sharing members' life-spaces could not be achieved unless a small group, as we

have defined it, did in fact exist. The formula for cohesion is as follows:

Cohesion (Group Life-Space) =

Group Member A's Shared Life-Space +

Group Member B's Shared Life-Space + etc.

In other words, it is the life-space that each member shares that culminates in group life-space or cohesion. Notice the shared areas in the diagram below; these illustrate the life-space each individual member has agreed to share with the group. That life-space actually shared with the other group members and group goal is what is called group life-space. This author believes that this major key concept of Lewin's Field Theory synthesizes the other key concepts of his theory. There is no question that a conceptual understanding of cohesion is essential for the student of small group behavior.

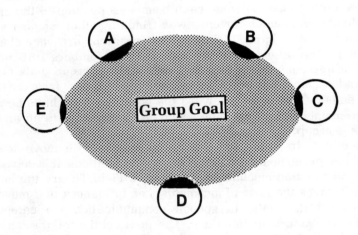

Systems and Interaction Theories

The second general class of small group theories ties together the systems and interaction approaches. The leading proponent of the systems approach has been George C. Homans, particularly his writing included in *The Human Group* (1950). The most significant outside influence on small group communication scholars' research has been Robert F. Bales. The impact of his *Interaction Process Analysis*, or I.P.A., on the development of interaction theory has been tremendous (1950).

The major assumption supporting systems theory is the statement that the small group *is a system*. Homans identifies two systems for us: *internal and external*. The internal system focuses on statements made by members in a face-to-face group context. These include statements of *interaction* ("Who would like to suggest some ideas first?"), statements of *activities* (I'll think of something after I go and get another cup of coffee!"), and statements of *feelings* ("I think that's lousy that you won't share your ideas with the group until you satisfy your 'caffeine fit'"). Obviously, statements made in groups that you belong to are more intelligent (sometimes anyway?!) than those mentioned above; however, the notion that statements tie the group together into an internal, working system is a basic tenet of Homan's theory.

In explaining the external system, it is best to acknowledge that statements made within the group (internal system) are in part a result of outside groups to which we belong. All of us belong to permanent kinds of on-going groups: ethnic, religious, racial, age, economic, political, and sexual. These permanent types of groups that we carry around with us from one internal system to another comprise the external system of an individual. The impact of the external system of each individual on the internal system of a group is a major factor in a group developing norms.

Homans suggests that a group goes through three phases: *elaboration, differentiation, and standardization.* These three modes of group development are seen in the statements that group members make in small groups to which they engage in face-to-face interaction. For example, the topic in one discussion group (internal system) may be smoking. One member of the group might belong to a religious group (external system) that believes tobacco is an unhealthy and irreverant habit. This member may make a statement regarding smoking activities of another group member. This group member may in turn suggest through *elaboration* that his forefathers regarded the sale of tobacco as an economic necessity. A third group member may *differentiate* these individual values based on the norms of the other two members' respective external systems. However, all other group members may suggest through statements or sentiments that they prefer that smoking not take place in meetings of their discussion group. This represents *standardization* of a group norm in the internal system.

Bales, on the other hand, as the major exponent of the interactionist theory does not separate the group into an internal and/or external system. Rather he views the small group as an entity in which task and social dimensions of the group are the major considerations. In order to get a handle on these two basic dimensions of small groups, Bales developed an observational system (IPA) by which he could categorize task and social kinds of acts. Shepherd defines the unit "act" in the way that Bales and most others using IPA do as "verbal and nonverbal behavior of a person which is communicated to at least one other person in the group and which has an observable beginning and end." (Shepherd, 1950, p. 29). Twelve categories of "acts" were classi-fied into four major headings: Positive Actions, Negative Actions,

Questions, and Answers. The first two headings account for "acts" in the social realm, while the latter two headings emphasize "acts" in the task dimension. What is so important to Bales, and the many people who have studied his interaction schema, is the delicate balance between task and social aspects of a small group. Many work groups might emphasize task behaviors, while others might exhibit interaction patterns that are socially-oriented. What is the right "task-social balance" for one group might be entirely wrong for another.

These two approaches (Homans and Bales) that make up the second class of small group theories are much more sociological in their derivation and composition than Lewin's Field Theory could ever be. First of all, Homans and Bales start by analyzing the group or system as a whole and then identify interaction components. Both theorists already accept the collection of individuals as being group-like whether they are or not. In addition, while Homans has his "statements," Bales has his "acts;" each theorist then is focusing on how the system and its interrelated parts interact in the context of the human group.

Communication Theorists

Although the speech communication discipline has been influenced to no small extent by group theorists from other fields, certain group communication scholars have made significant contributions to our study of small group processes. Those selected theorists included here are Barnlund and Haiman, Bormann, Fisher, and Gouran.

1. *Barnlund and Haiman.* As Lewin has been acclaimed as the "father of group dynamics," Barnlund and Haiman have generally been regarded as the predominant speech theorists to introduce group dynamics into our study of small group discussion. Their trend-setting discussion text, *The Dynamics of Discussion* (1960), became a major influence on those in the field of speech who wished to include the study of group dynamics within the realm of small group discussion study. A major stream of influence they made upon the field was their concentration on what leadership behaviors are performed by group members in general and leaders in particular. Their attention to leadership functions has influenced this author to no small extent when they are discussed later in the chapter.

2. *Bormann.* Ernest G. Bormann was among the first to suggest that discussion and group processes could be taught side-by-side. His book, *Discussion and Group Methods*, served as an impetus for speech scholars to recognize the importance of group methods in task groups (Bormann, 1969). Bormann also contributed a role emergence explanation of how groups form and operate. This theoretical position has been helpful to this author in discussing group roles in the next major

section of the chapter.

3. *Fisher.* One of Bormann's doctoral students, B. Aubrey Fisher, furthered his mentor's attention on task groups by focusing on their decision-making processes. Of particular note were the four phases of group development that Fisher suggested occur in ad hoc and natural groups (Fisher, 1970). These four phases include Orientation, Conflict, Emergence, and Reinforcement. The four stages of group development helps the student understand that different kinds of communication behaviors occur at different points of the discussion agenda and group's history.

4. *Gouran.* The most prolific contributor to the speech communication literature on small group communication is Dennis S. Gouran. This speech scholar has concentrated on studying major group outcomes such as consensus, quality of decision, and member satisfaction. A key means by which Gouran has tried to influence small group scholars is his attention to certain communication behaviors (notably orientation behavior) that affect major small group outcomes (1969). In general Gouran's research, along with that of the other speech communication scholars cited above, has contributed to our knowledge of major concepts and variables derived from communication theories. These key small group concepts are discussed below.

Major Small Group Concepts and Variables

In a number of instances, the small group concepts discussed below have also been measured extensively as small group variables. However, some concepts (such as cohesion and member satisfaction)

Figure 1

Key Small Group Concepts Model

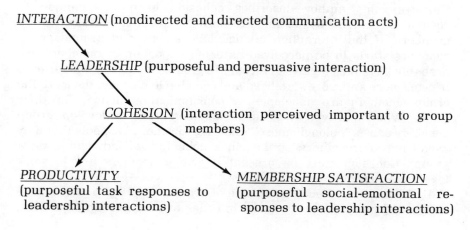

INTERACTION (nondirected and directed communication acts)

LEADERSHIP (purposeful and persuasive interaction)

COHESION (interaction perceived important to group members)

PRODUCTIVITY (purposeful task responses to leadership interactions)

MEMBERSHIP SATISFACTION (purposeful social-emotional responses to leadership interactions) have proven to be extremely difficult to operationalize as testable small group variables. Therefore, the student of small group communication should be aware that the concepts presented here have not been uniformly measured as variables in laboratory and field experiments. Nevertheless, the writings of respected scholars, accompanied with an equal dose of common sense, have lead communication researchers to consider the following concepts important to the study of small group processes. The concepts considered primary to the study of small group communication include: interaction, leadership, cohesion, productivity, and membership satisfaction. Figure 1 shows these five key concepts and their unique relationships to each other.

1. *Interaction*. Communication interaction is the most pervasive and dynamic variable that is studied in small group communication. More specifically, communication interaction includes all non-directed and directional acts, both verbal and non-verbal, that are communicated in the group. Interaction includes everything that is said by any group member and individuals' overt verbal and nonverbal behavioral reactions. In essence, interaction is the form and content that the process of communication takes in small groups.

2. *Leadership*. Interaction units that are purposeful and persuasive are categorized as leadership influences in small groups. In order for an act of interaction to be called a leadership act, it must *influence* significantly one or more member's behaviors in the group. If leadership has been found to be synonymous with any other social psychological concept, it indeed has been the concept of influence. Leadership, in terms of small group communication, can be defined as *any significant influence upon the group by any group member*. Small group leadership, then, is purposeful and pervasive interaction rather than being random in its direction.

3. *Cohesion*. The variable that makes a group a group is cohesiveness. If a group does not have cohesion (i.e., possess group lifespace), we have only a collection of individuals and not a group entity. One way this author describes cohesion in a way unique to communication is by examining how interaction affects group members. If the interaction taking place among and around group members starts to be perceived as being important to members, we probably have the makings of a real-life group. As interaction patterns become more and more stabilized and sensible to a group, the more the group members are developing a communication history for their group. When this type of group history continues to develop, group members sense "belongingness" and "togetherness" aspects that they would not share otherwise (i.e., in a collection of individuals vs. a group). Cohesion must be present if group members are to work together as a group.

4. *Productivity*. A major outcome of group work is to achieve some stated and unstated group goals. In order to attain group objectives,

purposeful task responses must occur. Typically, the group members move toward the accomplishment of group goals through the performance of task leadership functions (e.g., seeking ideas, seeking idea evaluation, etc.). Normally, individual members of small groups try to find the areas in which they agree and disagree. When conflict occurs regarding task achievement, members try to resolve it for the benefit of the group. When areas of agreement are found in the task domain of the group, this consensus should be overtly recognized by all members of the group. In other words, there is a great deal of give-and-take between group members as they work toward the accomplishment of their group goals.

5. _Membership satisfaction_. The purposeful social-emotional responses to leadership interactions are identified as membership satisfaction. Not only do we wish the group to come up with a group product, but we want to have enjoyed as individuals the group experience in reaching the group's task objectives. Social-emotional satisfaction of individual members is a necessary outcome of small group communication. If we do not expect to gain anything individually from the group experience, is it enough just to achieve a group product? Most people would say no, especially after several group experiences that did not offer membership satisfaction to its participants. Thus, we define _member satisfaction as the degree to which group members are satisfied with the group experience._

Although other small group concepts are believed to be important, and have in fact been researched extensively (e.g., consensus, quality of group product, conflict, etc.), it is believed that the five small group concepts presented in Figure 1 are indeed prerequisite to satisfactory group functioning. Of course, when we apply certain concepts to particular kinds of groups, we find that the emphasis may change a great deal. For example, in a task group we always expect a group product; whereas in an encounter group, membership satisfaction may be more important than the actual goals achieved by a group. It should be noted further that key small group concepts will vary in their importance when applying knowledge about them to groups with a history and one-time meeting groups. In the latter instance, that is groups with little or no history, the concepts of task leadership and group productivity may take precedence over cohesion and member satisfaction. On the other hand, cohesion is a central concept to on-going groups. The key point here is that small group concepts must be situationally applied to kinds of groups, as well as groups with varying histories.

Specific Uses of Small Group Communication

The first two sections of the chapter provided an explanation of the historical background of small group communication and major theories that have influenced our study of small group processes. In the latter section key concepts and variables that have been derived from selected theories were explored as they related directly to communication in the small group. The current section on specific uses of small group communication emphasizes the *application* aspects of small group theory and research. The reader should know that the discussion principles recommended for general and specific usage here are solidly grounded in small group communication theory and/or recurring experience in everyday group situations. The first major part on general usage infers that the discussion principles presented will have application, for the most part, to a number of groups. The second part of this major section of the chapter is oriented toward both informal and formal group techniques that are unique to special group situations.

Application of Discussion Principles for General Group Usage

The discussion principles presented below are usually applicable to a number of small group settings and various kinds of small groups. The information furnished to the reader should be immediately applicable by the reader to one or more groups to which he or she belongs.

A. *Purposes of small group communication.* The three general purposes of small group communication are *ventilation, information-sharing,* and *problem-solving*. Whenever a group gets together, it is usually to accomplish one of these purposes. To some extent, these three purposes could overlap in any one group and within the context of one group meeting. In fact, this overlap of the three general purposes of small group discussion is probably healthy in most on-going groups. The reason that one purpose is dominant in most groups is the fact that groups generally agree on what major goals they are trying to achieve.

We have all experienced ventilation in small group communication. Recall the last examination that you took in this or any other class. Remember how you ventilated your feelings about the test to other class members after leaving the examination room. It was almost like a contest on seeing who could talk first (e.g., asking what questions you got right, what was the answer to Question 5, etc.). Ventilation is a healthy purpose of small group communication that is applied almost daily. As an individual you need people to talk to and with a great deal of the time. We are able to vent out feelings in group situations. Many times, this behavioral act of "group cleansing" or catharsis could very easily become a first step in trying to solve an individual's personal problem in a group. Such group settings as bull sessions in dormitories and Alcoholics Anonymous meetings provide group ventilation vehicles for individuals who need them.

Information-sharing is a second major purpose of small group communication. One good reason for groups to meet is to share information. Although the actual dissemination of information among the group members does not necessarily make them brighter, the information provided is generally much broader in scope and certainly more prolific than that information which would be gathered by one individual. This broader exposure to information quite often stimulates understanding and increased ideation in the group. This in turn leads to better group ideas. Good examples of groups who engage in information-sharing include conference and work groups in business and industry, educational workshop groups, graduate seminars, and government "think-tank" groups. This sharing of information in a group setting also provides the payoff of learning through participation. No doubt, when you share information in your group discussions in this class, you will be benefiting from a knowledge perspective as well as division-of-labor bases.

Problem-solving is the purpose of small group communication that groups, if they have the necessary time, get together for the most often in work-related situations. This is especially true for on-going task groups in organizations. Common examples of groups who frequently engage in problem-solving are school boards, sales meetings, and governmental task forces. The emphasis is on trying to achieve group solutions which most members find acceptable to themselves personally and agreeable to the group as a whole. In essence, a group solution to a problem represents one to which group members have arrived through consensus and the decision is felt to be one that all members of the group can "live with." Problem-solving in groups is a time-consuming activity. Often the purposes of ventilation and information-sharing overlap with problem-solving. And yet, this most complex purpose of small group communication can bring immeasurable satisfaction to the group members because they shared in formulating the decision.

B. *Leading Group Discussions.* In order to accomplish the purposes of small group communication, there must be adequate leadership in the group. The leadership dimension is probably the one that small group scholars like to investigate and discussion practitioners wish to apply most frequently. The advice given here on leadership is mostly reflective of who does the leading (i.e., the leader) and what the people leading do in discussion groups (i.e., perform leadership functions).

There are several basic assumptions one must make when writing about group discussion leadership. The first fundamental assumption that one makes is that leadership is synonymous with influence, i.e., as we have hinted at before, leadership *moves the group.* Thus, small group leadership is defined as *any significant influence upon the group by any group member.* Hopefully, this influence is positive and moves the group toward the group goals and not away from them. Our definition of group leadership also assumes that the concept of *leadership* and the notion of *a leader* are not the same thing. Significant influences upon the group may be performed upon the group by *any* group member, not just a single individual called the leader. Another very important assumption is that in order to have leadership, one must have followership. The best way to find out whether you are leading the group discussion is to notice whether anyone is following; if you have no followers, you cannot be labeled the leader either in theory or in practice. The last general assumption is that the best leadership combines the qualities of *who* is leading the group with *what* leadership functions are being performed. These fundamental notions about small group leadership in general are important as we cover the primary dimensions of discussion leadership below.

There are essentially three kinds of small group leadership: the designated leader, the emergent leader, and the leaderless group. The designated leader is a leadership style in which one person has been named the leader of the group from its very first beginnings. In many formal groups the highest ranking officer (i.e., club president, discussion moderator of a radio forum, department head, etc.) is perceived as being the leader of the group. In these kinds of groups, this positional leader is definitely viewed as being the leader in name, if not in fact. The designated leader has usually been formally recognized outside the immediate group as being the leader. This kind of recognition quite often gives more attention to the leader in name than the followers (i.e., leaders many times in fact) that helped to sustain the designated leader's perceived power base to influence members both in and outside of the group. There have been some cases where the designated leader is a strong leader throughout the group's history and other instances where the positional leader has fallen on his or her face during the first few critical moments of the discussion.

A second kind of small group leadership is the idea of the emergent leader. This style of leadership is prevalent in groups that have formally designated leaders and those that do not. The key to understanding the emergent leader is to recognize that whatever his or her source of influence, it has been gained from *within* the group. In order for a leader to emerge in a group, he or she must have adequate followership. If someone tries to emerge as the leader and receives no support, the person has not in fact become the leader. On the other hand, if a leader emerges and has strong support from his followers, then the emergent leader is a leader in fact and may even be strong enough to depose a designated leader if there was one in the first place. In group situations where there was no designated leader, it is typical for one or more members to try and emerge as the task leader of the group. Having successfully separated leader contenders from nonleaders, a good way for the emergent task leader to gather and maintain support is through the aid of a "lieutenant." (Bormann and Bormann, 1976). This lieutenant, usually well in tune with the social-emotional needs of the group, serves as a major follower to the emergent leader and gathers additional followership support from other group members.

The leaderless group is a third variety of small group leadership. In this kind of leadership condition, there never was a designated leader. The general assumption is that what leadership moves have to be done will be diffused equally throughout the group; we identify this type of leadership as *shared leadership*. In this author's opinion, shared leadership that grows out of the leaderless group condition is very idealistic and not very common. In fact, the leaderless group condition with no history of an appointed leader probably facilitates the emergent leader kind of small group leadership. Further, the *leaderless* group should not be confused with the *leadershipless* group. The distinction between the two is a critical one for the following reasons: (1) there is no assigned leader in the leaderless group, but there is leadership, and (2) the leadershipless group not only has no assigned leader, but is void of leadership as well.

A word or two is in order about the climates that promote each of the above-mentioned kinds of leadership. Only a democratic climate, that is where some control is exercised over the process decisions of the group and not the content decisions, can foster all three major forms of small group leadership. An autocratic climate, on the other hand, finds only the designated leader style of leadership operative as this individual controls both the process and content decisions of the group. Hopefully, you will be able to experience all kinds of leadership in many of the group discussion in which you participate.

In addition to the kinds of leadership cited above, another dimension of small group leadership that is vital to consider is the area of leadership qualities. It has long been held that certain people have a much better chance of being a leader in the group because of the particular repertoire of qualities or traits that they possess. Certain personality variables such as self-assertiveness and extroversion have been deemed important qualities for the effective small group leader (McGrath and Altman, 1966, p. 62). In fact, many of the task and social-emotional capabilities of leaders have been highlighted in Stogdill's *Handbook of Leadership* (1974). Although we recognize the importance of the individual qualities that leaders bring with them, we cannot underestimate the status the potential leader has in a particular group and his or her ability to perform leadership functions effectively.

The key to leading group discussions, whether one is designated as the leader or not, is to emphasize *what* needs to be done in the group to move it towards the goals of the group. These leadership moves are called leadership functions. These communication leadership

behaviors that need to be performed in the small group have been categorized as follows: task functions, procedural functions, and interpersonal functions. The latter type of functions are performed to service the social-emotional needs of individual members of the group. Procedural functions are necessary to maintain the group's identity and keep the general group operations moving. Task functions are goal-achievement in their orientation and work towards the attainment of a group product.

There are six specific leadership functions in the task area. They include:

1. *contributing ideas* — a new or fresh idea is presented for the first time in the group;

2. *seeking ideas* — asking members of the group to suggest new and fresh ideas;

3. *evaluating ideas* — opinions expressed about ideas which further their consideration by the group or eliminate them;

4. *seeking idea evaluation* — asking members of the group to evaluate ideas already presented;

5. *making the general more specific* — when an idea becomes too "heady" or complex, examples are given to make the contribution more specific;

6. *making the specific more general* — when an idea becomes buried in "nitty-gritty" details and needs to be made more general for the sake of understanding.

The six task leadership functions cited above occur quite naturally during the course of a group's history. Caution should be exercised, however, to make certain that enough ideas are presented in the discussion and that they get a full and critical airing in the group's deliberations.

The five following leadership functions are considered crucial in the procedural area:

1. *goal-setting* — the establishment by the group of its goal and the acceptance of members to work toward goal attainment;

2. *agenda-making* — the "map-making" function in small groups which assists the group in accomplishing its goals in an orderly fashion;

3. *clarifying* — eliminating verbal communication barriers through restatement and other basic communication strategies;

4. *summarizing* — the verbal "adding up" at each stage of the agenda to insure that the group's main points are in order and not forgotten;

5. *verbalizing consensus* — stating out loud those points to which the members of the group agree.

Unlike task leadership functions, procedural functions need constant attention in the group. Remember that not all members of the group always agree with what has been said and where the group is going; therefore, it is always wise to actively pursue group operations through the verbal performance of procedural functions.

There are also five functions that comprise leadership behavior in the interpersonal area. They are:

1. *regulating participation* — regulating your own or someone else's participation by calling on group members to speak, etc.;

2. *climate-making* — providing and maintaining a positive group atmosphere in which each member has a sense of "psychological safety;"

3. *instigating group self-analysis* — having a "discussion about the discussion" in order to analyze significant points in the group's history;

4. *resolving conflict* — minimizing discussion obstacles at either the ideational or interpersonal level;

5. *instigating conflict* — intentionally magnifying disagreements in the group in order to facilitate full consideration of group and individual goals.

One must always remember that group members are human beings working on human group needs. It is essential, then, to satisfy the social-emotional needs of individual members through the performance of interpersonal leadership functions throughout the discussion.

In order to capsule some of the information presented above regarding the leadership of group discussions, the following general leader techniques are offerred. It should be remembered that in most cases the suggestions given below are appropriate whether one is the designated leader or not.

1. *Work toward the group goals.* By staying on track and following the agenda, groups can reach their goals in an efficient manner. Groups are formed to achieve group products; therefore, members have an obligation to work towards accomplishing task objectives agreed to by the group.

2. *Ask questions.* If you don't understand an idea or it seems unreasonable, question it. If not enough ideas have been presented, in your opinion, seek new ideas and have the group fully explore them by adequately evaluating them through questions.

3. *Stay on the agenda.* Avoid tangents unless they are meaningful to the group's goals. By staying on the agenda, groups can accomplish their goals within given time constraints.

4. *Perform procedural functions.* In most groups, adequate summarizing and agenda-making do not get done unless the designated leader or another member actively and frequently performs these procedural functions.

5. *Think before you talk.* Especially in problem-solving discussions, it is extremely important for group members to monitor their own participation by evaluating their comments before they make them. This is particularly appropriate for "class" task leadership.

6. *Don't try to be the leader in every group to which you belong.* Many group situations are very situation-bound. They require a unique balance between who the leader is and what needs to be done. Varying small group leadership helps to maintain this delicate balance in different group situations.

C. *Participating in Group Discussions.* One of the keys to a good discussion is active participation by the group members. Although leadership is often singled out as the most recognizable feature in determining whether a group is successful or not, we all know that adequate followership and participation are necessary for the group to move toward achieving its goals. In fact, it is the very principle that a certain amount of roles are necessary to be played by the participants that has lead many small group researchers to recognize the importance of followers and participants in group discussions.

One way of looking at participative roles in group discussions has been to identify those which are predetermined and those which are emergent in nature. *Predetermined group roles* are typically more formal, more structured, and more format-determined than *emergent participative roles*. The latter role-types endorse and encourage spontaneity, multidimensionality, and heterogeneity in the group. An example of a predetermined group role would be the moderator of a panel discussion. For example, the formal responsibilities of the moderator commonly include: a) regulating participation, b) introducing the topic and the participants, c) being in charge of pre-planning the physical relationships, d) summarizing and verbalizing consensus, and e) directing the question and answer period. A participant's role in a panel discussion might well include the following formal behaviors: a) responding to the moderator's directions and regulations, b) handling the subject matter, c) avoiding time-consuming tangents, and d) being an active respondent to fellow members' comments and questions. In other words, much of the formal structural nature of the panel discussion *predetermines* the role behavior of the designated leader (moderator) and the participants. Predetermined group roles are often quite obvious in one-time meeting groups that adhere to strict, formalized procedures.

Emergent participative roles, on the other hand, are considerably less formal, less structured, and less format-determined than predetermined group roles. A number of emergent roles are classified by their task and interpersonal orientations toward the group. Examples of such roles are tension-releasers, dramatizers, idea evaluators, information contributors, clarifiers, and climate-makers. A major difference between predetermined and emergent roles is that the latter type usually occurs in an on-going group that has a history. Obviously, in many group discussions we will see some blending of predetermined and emergent roles.

Regardless of the major classification schema for group roles, we recognize that the existence of such roles are vital to the group's success. Shepherd has suggested that there are five features to a successful group: objectives, role differentiation, norms, membership, and communication (1964, pp. 122-124). This author would contend that such characteristics, and ones like them, depend to no small

Chart 1

Features and Roles in a Good Group

Features of a Good Group	*Roles Necessary for a Good Group*
Group Goals and Purposes	Idea generator, information provider, clarifier, contributor, evaluator
Group Role Differentiation	Task leader, social-emotional leader, lieutenants, tension-releaser
Group Norms and Standards	Conflict resolver, blocker, central negative, mediator, negotiator, opinion leader
Group Membership	Cohesion builder, conflict resolver, playboy, central negative
Group Communication	Stimulator, regulator, summarizer, interactor

extent on the development of roles in the small group. Chart 1 clearly identifies features and roles that constitute a good discussion group. As one can see, there are many roles that must be assumed by group members in order to have a good group and reach goal attainment. Obviously, some roles are more important than others (e.g., task leader) and numerous roles can be played by any member (e.g., a task leader can be a regulator, summarizer, and clarifier, etc.).

In addition to the above explanation of why group roles are so important to the creation.and life of a small group, certain general guidelines can be followed to help you become a better participant in small group discussions. These include:

1. *Select the group roles that are best for you and the group.* If you are by your very nature a good information provider, try to assume this as one of your roles in the group discussions of which you are a member.

2. *Work for the group's good.* Your participation should have at its touchstone your honest intent at doing your best to accomplish the group's goals.

3. *Ask questions.* If you aren't sure which direction the group is going, ask other group members; chances are that sometimes they wanted to ask the same questions.

4. *Stick to the group's business.* Don't go off on tangents; always try to stick to the group's announced and perceived goals. Group discussion is a time-consuming effort to begin with; don't waste time by going off on unnecessary tangents.

5. *Be an active participant.* This should be a key participation principle. No doubt you are in the group for a specific reason. Help the group but with your participation. Active participants make discussions come alive! Be an active participant and enjoy your group experiences!

By following the above-mentioned guidelines and having a clear understanding of the importance of both predetermined and emergent group roles, you should now be able to become a much more effective participant in small group discussions.

D. *Thinking and Working in Groups.* When individuals get together to do group work, they obviously need some mechanisms by which they can think and work in small groups. How individuals *think* in groups is through the use of group thought patterns. The way in which group thought patterns are implemented into the group mechanism to give it some sense of process order by which to *work* is called an agenda system. Although there are numerous group thought patterns and a long list of agenda systems available to groups, only several of each will be introduced here.

The three fundamental types of thought patterns that are commonly used in small groups include: a) intentional thinking, b) reflective thinking, and c) creative thinking. *Intentional thinking* emphasizes the persuasive powers that members use on one another to try to persuade each other on what position or solution to accept. *Reflective thinking* is nonintentional in nature and tries to reflect an organized sequence that one goes through from problem identification to solution implementation. Much of the attention paid to reflective thinking in groups is a result of the impact of John Dewey's famous five steps of reflective thinking on explaining individual thought. (Dewey, 1910). Many speech scholars feel that "how we think" reflectively as individuals can be incorporated into agenda systems that small groups use to think and work together. *Creative thinking* is a mode of exploration which reorganizes past thoughts and produces new or fresh ideas more or less spontaneously in groups. Certain specific discussion techniques such as brainstorming aid the group in generating creative ideas.

These three kinds of small group thought patterns are incorporated to some degree in the agenda systems used by members to do group work. Some agenda systems are more specific in orientation and others deal with the complex issue of problem-solving in groups. One agenda system that can be used equally well by one-time meeting and on-going groups alike is the "Wright 494" Agenda System. The ten steps of the "Wright 494" Agenda System are presented in Chart 2.

Chart 2

The Ten Step "Wright 494" Agenda System

1. *Ventilation* — period of primary tension for the group.

2. *Clarification of Problem and Establishment of Group Goals* — definitions and limitations occur here.

3. *Analysis of Problem* — according to facts, probabilities and values.

4. *Establishment of General Criteria* — basic minimum standards necessary for considering general solutions (e.g., feasibility, utility, etc.)

5. *Suggesting General Solutions* — typical solutions for this problem area; include "brainstorming" for solution ideas at this stage.

6. *Evaluation of Solutions According to Steps 3 & 4* — if proposed solutions do not meet general criteria, disregard for remainder of this problem-solving discussion.

7. *Development of Situational Criteria* — group standards and norms appropriate to this specific problem area.

8. *Evaluation of Solutions According to Step 7 Criteria* — situational criteria play important part in narrowing solutions in order to select best solution for this particular problem area.

9. *Select Solution(s)*—the *best* solution(s) for this specific problem area.

10. *Implement Solution(s)*—*how* will the solution(s) best be adapted and actually put into practice.

As one can see from the detailed agenda system presented in Chart 2, there are many considerations that must be made in going from the top to the bottom in a problem-solving discussion. Although the "Wright 494" Agenda System is heavily detailed in its solution-orientation, there are others that are focused more on the problem and idea generation. Still others are extremely simple and provide an ample agenda system. For example, Maier's Formula is a simple two-step agenda system: Decision-Making = Idea Getting and Idea Evaluation (Maier, 1970, p. 182).

No matter what agenda system is adopted by the group, the group itself will always adapt, modify, and create agenda systems for their own particular needs. This natural tendency, for on-going groups especially, to develop agenda systems unique to the situation and individuals in the group is indeed a good one. In fact, most real-life groups are better at developing ways that they can think and work together than in selecting the "correct" agenda system. This author would continue to recommend that groups follow their own best path and adopt a certain agenda only when dictated by the situation.

Special Uses of Small Groups

This division of the chapter deals with both informal and formalized group techniques that are unique to special group situations. Whereas those principles suggested for general discussion usage above are hopefully applicable to a number of cases, the formats and techniques presented here are highly situational and rule-governed. The two major categories of prescriptive patterns covered in this section are discussion formats and discussion techniques.

A. *Discussion formats.* A discussion format is a prescribed pattern which by its very nature dictates the flow of information within a discussion, participation interaction, and the breadth and depth of individual participation. Five discussion formats will be examined: round table, panel discussion, symposium, lecture-forum, and parliamentary procedure. Although this list of formats is far from all-inclusive, it is a highly representative one for the beginning small group student.

1. *Round table.* The round table format is a typical discussion pattern for small groups. The discussion usually takes place around a table and does not usually have a time limit as do other format types. Typically, there is no audience observing the behavior of round table

participants. The round table is therefore *a private discussion format which takes place in a closed seating arrangement.* The exchange of ideas is quite open, interaction is extensive, and participants feel free to probe in depth for the best individual and group ideas.

2. *Panel discussion.* The panel discussion is a group communication event that is *coacting* in nature. A panel discussion is *a coacting session in which group members interact among themselves and with an audience on a controversial discussion question.* A stage play and a panel discussion are very similar in that they are both communication events that emphasize coaction. Just as the actors interact on stage with one another during the course of the play, the production is being done for the benefit of an audience. Thus, the flow of information within a panel discussion is not as free as it can be in a round table. A moderator generally calls on participants who are expected to know certain aspects of the problem better than others. Likewise, when participation is regulated, as it usually is, both the content and form of a panel discussion can come off sounding "too rehearsed" and lacking spontaneity. When this happens we usually say that the panel was a "pseudo discussion." Good panel discussants, and moderators of them, hopefully try to avoid this basic pitfall of the panel discussion format.

3. *Symposium.* A symposium is a *series of short speeches on different aspects or pro and con positions of a controversial topic.* Just as a panel discussion is put on for an audience, so is a symposium. However, the symposium is even more tightly controlled than the panel.

The moderator introduces each symposium speaker and regulates the length of each presentation as best as he or she can. The symposium is a good format for disseminating information, but a poor one for group interaction. It is a preferred discussion pattern for so-called experts on a topic because they do not have to respond immediately, or perhaps ever in this setting, to other speakers' views.

4. *Lecture-forum*. A lecture by itself is not a discussion format. If the audience has the ability to ask and answer questions either during and/or after a lecture presentation, we have what is known as a *forum*. The forum can and should occur within every public discussion format. In order to get the proper evaluation of ideas, it is necessary to have the opportunity to do it. A forum period following a lecture or any other public discussion format provides the audience with the capacity to ask questions.

5. *Parliamentary procedure*. This public discussion format emphasizes the method by which the content and form of exchanging ideas is controlled. As many of you know, only one piece of business can be dealt with at a single time when following parliamentary procedure. The way business is carried out in public meetings is through the use of main motions or resolutions. All other motions must relate to the motion on the floor or the way in which the business of the meeting is carried out. A chairperson typically presides over meetings, with the able assistance of a parliamentarian armed with a copy of *Robert's Rules of Order*. The chairperson regulates participation by who is recognized to speak and what is considered *germaine* to the discussion at hand. The system of parliamentary procedure favors the principle of the majority. Typically, a majority vote (or a ⅔ majority) will carry the day. The importance for the student of small group discussion in knowing the "ins and outs" of the parliamentary procedure format is to prepare oneself for group meetings in which this pattern is used. Many times the group communication participant will have to know parliamentary procedure to protect his or her rights and to enable him or her to find a way in which to participate effectively.

B. *Discussion techniques*. There are numerous discussion techniques that can be applied to enhance idea production and increased group participation. Three discussion techniques that accomplish these dual objectives and are treated here are brainstorming, nominal group discussion, and buzz group technique. Although numerous other special techniques could be examined, these three have immediate application to your work and school environments.

1. *Brainstorming*. The ideational technique of brainstorming emphasizes the *quantity* of ideas produced in the initial phases of a discussion; whereas, the *quality* of ideas are evaluated at a later time (Wright, 1972, p. 42). Typically, a group is divided into smaller groups of 5-7 people for brainstorming sessions. Group members throw out *any*

ideas on the brainstorming topic without fear of evaluative appraisal and/or reprisal! This free-wheeling exchange of ideas can produce a large amount of ideas in a very short period of time. Advertising agencies use the brainstorming technique to generate new advertising slogans and campaigns. Obviously, these ideas are scrutinized carefully, often to the tune of *many* dollars, after the quantity of ideas has been produced. But after all, isn't it nice to have such a large list to select possible "best idea" and "best solutions" from? This large amount of initial ideas would not have been so plentiful if group members had not benefited from "hitchhiking" off of other members' ideas. When used properly, the brainstorming technique can be one of the best ideational friends a group could have.

2. *Nominal group discussion.* The nominal group discussion is also a group ideation technique; however, it is quite a bit different in its scope. The nominal group is a collection of individuals who are a "group in name only." In order to get a fairly even number of ideas from each group member, the nominal group discussion (NGD) can be used. First, a designated leader asks the group members to write down three or more concerns related to a topic. Second, the leader calls on each member in sequence to have the member present one of his or her ideas each time he or she is called upon. Third, each member can ask questions of other members after all ideas have been presented and placed on a master list. Fourth, each participant prioritizes the ideas by ranking them. The result is that a group list of ideas has been produced and placed in order of importance. A further result is that each participant has had the opportunity to share through fairly equal participation in the production and ranking of group ideas.

3. *Buzz group technique.* This is another technique in which large groups are broken into smaller groups of 5-7 persons. This is done for two main reasons: 1) to increase participation by group members, and 2) to facilitate a division-of-labor for the larger group in order to achieve the overall group goals. The above two reasons are in fact the rationale for the existence of buzz groups. If a key-note speaker is asked to present a 20 minute speech to stimulate an audience of 200 persons in discussing a problem area, it would be rather difficult to have a meaningful discussion after the speech among all of the members of the audience. In order to have meaningful small group communication, we divide the audience into buzz groups of 5-7 people. Each member of the group can now *actively* participate in a group discussion on the problem area. Perhaps various groups could be assigned to analyze various aspects of the problem, therefore facilitating the division-of-labor principle.

In each of the above discussion techniques, one can easily see how the chances of producing a large number of ideas through active member participation can be facilitated in small groups. These task-oriented discussion techniques are certainly not the cure-all for all of our problems; however, they do give us a good way to generate ideas and solutions for consideration. When well used, selected discussion formats and techniques can offer meaningful communication choices to members of small groups.

Chapter Summary

This chapter has introduced the beginning student to one of the most complex areas of study in human communication; that is, interacting and participating effectively in small groups. Speech and small group traditions provided the foundations for exploring small group communication historically. Basic differences were seen to exist between our definitions of small group, small group communication, and small group discussion. When the major kinds of groups (task, encounter, and consciousness-raising) are considered in light of small group definition as well as history of the group, we understand how important it is to have a solid handle on the major concepts that comprise our study of small group communication.

Representative theorists (including Lewin, Bales, Homans, Barnlund and Haiman, Bormann, Fisher, and Gouran) were examined in lieu of their theoretical and research contributions to the small group literature. Key concepts that are crucial to our study of small group communication were discussed in some length. The five most important concepts for the beginning student of small group communication to know were identified as follows: interaction, leadership, cohesion, productivity, and membership satisfaction.

The last half of the chapter dealt with specific uses of small group communication. This section examined in detail those discussion principles which could be applied across groups. First, the basic purposes of small group communication were presented. Small group leadership dimensions were discussed in detail, with special attention to leadership functions. After examining important roles necessary for effective participation in group discussions, various group thought patterns and agenda systems were presented as ways members of small groups can think and work together. A subsection on special uses of small groups concluded the body of the chapter with a treatment of five discussion formats and three discussion techniques.

Although there have been many books written about small group communication and literally thousands of studies conducted in the area of small groups, one can feel fairly confident that the material presented in the chapter above grasps the essence of small group communication for the beginning student. The reason that this author makes the above claim is two-fold. First, the acknowledgment that the various theoretical underpinnings of small group communication is highly interdisciplinary recognizes that certain concepts and variables studied will be more important in certain situations for particular students than in others. Second, the theoretical principles examined in this chapter pertaining to small group communication can be applied in everyday life situations.

The difficulty for the student, then, is to make the right theoretical choices and apply them correctly to the given situation. The probability for doing this is greatly enhanced by experiencing a great deal of small group situations and participating in groups for a considerable length of time. This position seems particularly important when considering work groups in organizations. By experiencing the application of various leadership conditions, meeting procedures, and other communication aspects of work groups *over time*, it seems to this author that we will increase our probabilities of applying the right small group theories to our organizational environments.

Hopefully, your small group communication experiences will support this fundamental proposition.

References

Bales, R.F. *Interaction Process Analysis.* Reading, Mass.: Addison-Wesley Publishing Co., 1951.

Barnlund, D.C. and Haiman, F.S. *The Dynamics of Discussion.* Boston: Houghton Mifflin Co., 1960.

Bormann, E.G. *Discussion and Group Methods.* New York: Harper and Row, Publishers, 1969.

Bormann, E.G., and Bormann, N.C. *Effective Small Group Communication.* 2nd edition. Minneapolis: Burgess Publishing Company, 1976.

Cragan, J.F. and Wright, D.W. *Communication in Small Group Discussions: A Case Study Approach.* St. Paul, Minn.: West Publishing Company, 1980.

Cragan, J.F., and Wright, D.W. Small group communication research of the 1970's: a synthesis and critique. Paper presented at the annual convention of the Speech Communication Association, Minneapolis, Minnesota, November 3, 1978.

Dewey, J. *How We Think.* Boston: D.C. Heath, 1910

Fisher, B.A. Decision emergence: phases in group decision-making. *Speech Monographs,* 1970, 37, 53-66.

Gouran, D.G. Variables related to consensus in group discussions of questions of policy. *Speech Monographs,* 1969, 36, 387-391.

Homans, G.C. *The Human Group.* New York: Harcourt, Brace, 1950.

Lewin, K. *Field Theory in Social Science.* Edited by Dorwin Cartwright, New York: Harper Brothers, 1951.

Maier, N.R.F. *Problem Solving and Creativity in Individuals and Groups.* Belmont, California: Brooks/Cole, 1970.

McGrath, J.E., and Altman, J. *Small Group Research: A Synthesis and Critique of the Field.* New York: Holt, Rinehart and Winston, Inc., 1966.

Shepherd, C.R. *Small Groups: Some Sociological Perspectives.* Scranton, Penna.: Chandler Publishing Company, 1964.

Stogdill, R.M. *Handbook of Leadership.* New York: The Free Press, 1974.
Wright, D.W. The utilization of brainstorming for the derivation of discussion
    topics. *MSA Journal*, 1972, 7, 42-43.

6

Information Processing

George E. Tuttle

The purpose of this chapter is to provide clear understanding of how we perceive that humans are able to handle information obtained through the senses, particularly the visual and auditory senses. Our understanding of how that process functions has evolved during the last fifty years. The evolutionary modifications have not occurred in isolation of general social forces.

People's perspectives have led to change as the society in which they live has changed. Many of the forces operating to change society are catalytic forces in changing the way communication occurs and the way communication is viewed. Current critical forces would include: a technological explosion descending from an earlier industrial revolution; a reordering of economic motivations from a need-service base to a want-get base; a shift in world wide political forces from nationalism versus internationalism to a coexistence of both national and international forces. Consequently, the availability of data delivery and the personal to national need to process data has changed how we function and how we conceptualize and react to the forced changes in function.

The examination here will follow three stages: first, a review of the historical development of information processing view of human communication which will lead to a description of the functions of that process in contemporary society; second, identification and analysis of critical elements of information processing in human communication as it occurs via the oral mode; and third, speculation on the means to maximize information processing in order to achieve efficiency in transaction and transfer of information.

Throughout this and subsequent chapters, the terms "model" and "process" will appear often. A model is a way of conceptualizing the essential components and their relationships in communication. A process is some on going, dynamic, and interactive set of related events.

Historical Development

If a magical time capsule would allow travel back in time for a short fifty years, the then prevailing how explanation of the domain of human communication would be a classical model surviving with little fundamental change over 2,000 years since the Greek philosopher and teacher, Aristotle. Several Aristotelian concepts are still useful today in explaining manipulative communication behavior and will be treated at greater length in chapter seven.

The Aristotelian model of how is essentially a linear model with three component parts: speaker, speech, and audience. The model includes a speaker or someone who is capable of conceiving and originating an orderly and selected set of data, constructs, and reasons. Further, the model includes the speech or an orderly and selected set itself which is moved from the speaker or originator to the audience or destination. Finally, there is an audience or an other who is the destination capable of understanding and who is motivated to respond to the orderly and selected set. The Aristotelian how model, although not sufficient today, has contributed to the evolutionary progression of information processing. The three components in the how model are still three fundamental components in any contemporary perspective on information processing. Now they are commonly called by scholars "source," "message," and "receiver." The linearity of communication has undergone two distinct changes such that it hardly exists in contemporary how explanations of process.

If the magical time capsule could transport us from the 1920's to the 1940's, we would find the world drastically changed by technological, economic, and political forces. Demands for data were accelerated and the time frames for satisfying the demand were considerably shortened. The telephone, telegraph, and radio became permanent fixtures. The computer was still on the horizon. Data had to move from board room to board room, administrative office to administrative office, person to person, terminal to terminal in a matter of minutes.

Therefore, the way we view how information should be structured, constructed, and exchanged had to undergo modification.

Shannon and Weaver developed a mathematical model for perceiving communication which met the needs of engineers whose concern was transmission of signals. The Shannon and Weaver model (1949) includes the component of "noise." Essentially, "noise" is a term referring to any signal which becomes a stimuli competing with or interfering with the intended signal transmission through the channel between sender and receiver (see figure 1).

Figure 1

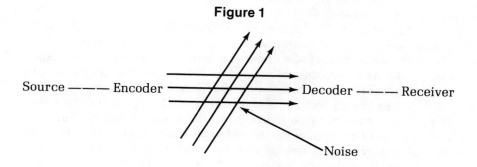

Adapted from Claude E. Shannon and Warren Weaver. *The Mathematical Theory of Communication*, Urbana, University of Illinois Press, 1949, p. 5

In making the analog between Shannon and Weaver's mathematical model with its concept of noise to human communication it is easy to recognize that noise may be both internal and external signals which interfere with transmission of the message. Internally, the signals are likely to be thoughts running through the mind of the person. The person might be mentally focusing on what happened the day before, what is planned in chemistry class the next day, how one plans to list income on a financial aids form or an income tax return. Externally, the signals are likely to be competing physical stimuli—that is— words, sounds, movements. A freight train passing by an open window would make it difficult for one to explain a lesson to a class or to hear the code symbols from an IBM service representative explaining the upkeep of a computer.

Implicit in the concern for noise is the reason for concern. In the case of Shannon and Weaver's mathematical model, the concern was to achieve fidelity; that is, accurate reproduction of electrical signals received from an output source. Returning to the analog with human communication, it is obvious that noise is a factor which interferes with the fidelity of transmission; that is, accurate reproduction through the neurological system to the mind of stimuli at an output location (a receiver).

Within a few years, the Shannon and Weaver transmission model was modified by Wilbur Schramm (1955) into a model of communication which contained components useful in accounting for human features and forces in the communication process. Particularly important in the Schramm model is the notion of field of experience. That is, there are events in the past of both sender and receiver which mold and shape the particular way in which the person views or perceives every stimuli. The most important contribution of this model is the suggestion that meaning must take place in the realm where fields of experience belonging to source and receiver overlap or are similar enough to be "shared."

The concept of field of experience suggests that for one person in the act of communication, either source or receiver, the meaning of the signal received through the channel is molded by experiences. Experiences are those events which have or make a lasting impression on either the conscious or subconscious mind. The extent to which experiences are similar, represents the extent to which understanding of symbols can occur (see figure 2). In the situation where there is a source (S) with a surrounding field of experiences (FOE) and a receiver (R) with a surrounding field of experiences (FOE), meaning can occur with those symbols which tap into the area of overlapping fields of experience.

Figure 2

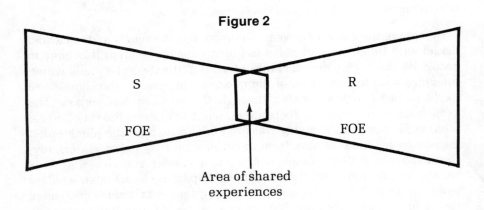

Area of shared
experiences

The model has utility when communication between individuals or groups is analyzed. A person who grew up in a rural, provincially oriented great plains community has had a somewhat different set of personal and group experiences than a person who grew up in the North side of Chicago or the Watts region of Los Angeles. Even a person growing up in a small community on the east side of the Montana Rockies has had a different set of life experiences than a person growing up and or living on the west side of the Montana Rockies. When two individuals of such different backgrounds communicate by constructing messages and transmitting through the channel of spoken word, the two individuals will have very little commonality in their past experiences from which they can construct meaning.

Experiential factors other than geography do account for the varying shape of perspectives on the world and the verbal and nonverbal code systems representing the perspectives. The CBer in today's popular culture has a set of code symbols whose meaning comes only from being a part of the culture which participates in CB communication. Consider the following dialog:

A. "Mercy sakes, good buddy, did you eyeball the seat covers on that beaver?"

B. "Seat covers on a beaver?"

A. "Yea, in that rubber ducky."

B. "Seat covers on a beaver in a rubber ducky?"

A. "Yea. Mercy sakes, that beaver must have been in a hurry for a cup of coffee."

B. "A beaver, in a rubber ducky, going for a cup of coffee?"

A. "Hey, you ain't no good buddy."

The Schramm concept of field of experience, then, provides a theoretical perspective on the processing of information by humans which accounts for diversity and confusion. A considerable portion of interpersonal and intergroup conflict of the decade between 1965 and 1975 can be considered in large part a consequence of failure to locate "shared" fields of experience by parties communicating.

Concurrently with the Shannon and Weaver and the Schramm perspectives to explain how information gets processed, a meaning centered perspective was developing. The general semanticist's perspective developed by Alfred Korzybski, Wendall Johnson, and S.I. Hayakawa (1972) focused on non-Aristotelian systems as a how explanation of communication. The general semanticists argued for a view of communication based on the behavioral consequences of code symbols (words). They argued the utility of knowing and predicting how a receiver is likely to react (behave) in response to a given code symbol. Several of the general semantics group concepts are useful in extending the Schramm shared experience concept.

The general semantics set of explanations begins with the notion of symbolism. Hayakawa observed that: "the process by means of which human beings can arbitrarily make certain things may be called the symbolic process." (1972).

In addition, this perspective drew upon an earlier Korzybski analog between the physical world and the verbal symbolic world stating that the verbal world ought to stand in relation to the extensional world as a map does to the territory it is supposed to represent. The general semanticists then stated that: "the symbol is not the thing symbolized;" "the map is not the territory;" and "the word is not the thing." Therefore, the physical stimuli can have a variety of symbolic meanings and yet never be an exact likeness to what is symbolized. The word "chair" is not the same as the object "chair." In addition, the word "chair" can have more meanings than the object "chair."

Today, the general semanticist's perspectives as how explanations of human communication have led to the admonition that meanings are in people. The implication for a contemporary view of information processing is that data which might be transmitted, is limited in its meaning to the forces which shape and mold source and receiver processing.

If the magical time machine could advance forward from the 1940's to the mid 1950's, we would find that a new phenomenon and a corresponding new how explanation of communication has made an impact on society. The computer quickly became a fixture rather than a novelty. People had to begin talking to computers and other machines as well as about those machines. The idea of people talking to machines has some interesting analogs for explaining the how of information processing. One of the most fundamental components of that analog is the notion of feedback. Basically, feedback is a return response to an initial stimulus. It may be viewed from both a corrective and a qualitative perspective.

Initially, the machine notion of feedback as corrective was adapted to human communication. In order to talk to a machine, people must develop and use a precise languages as well as perfectly logical sequences. After communication is initiated and before termination, exchanges between man and machine are essentially corrective in nature. The machine is programmed to accept communication and then make choices among clearly programmed options. If the machine is not given precise information it will request more information. The person omitting as simple a symbol as a slash when talking to the computer will soon discover the computer responding possibly even with an analysis of where the directions were insufficient for execution. Thus, feedback between man and machine is essentially corrective communication (see figure 3).

As the notion of feedback was applied to explain human communication, it took on a wider dimension than just the corrective dimension of man talking with machines. To be successful, the precision and logic have to have stylistic characteristics of high fidelity and control. Applied to humans communicating with other humans, that means that people will have to function alternately as source and receiver to refine the context and the symbols in the context. Further, people will have to attend to and select from stimuli representing the

Figure 3

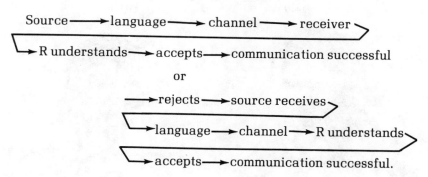

message. In some cases, receivers will have to construct their own frame of reference. Thereby, it is possible to limit, expand, or amplify data transmitted or exchanged between humans.

In human communication, feedback has come to have several operational nuances. First, feedback is viewed as response of the listener to the speaker's signal. Second, feedback is viewed as reinforcement when in the form of response to a response. Third, feedback can be viewed as internal mechanism control.

In the final analysis, the concept of feedback as borrowed from, and modified from, human-machine communication is a how theory from both an observer and a participant perspective. The human

application of the feedback concepts make it possible, for example, to observe groups and recognize why and how leadership, cohesion, and teamwork evolve among group members. It also enables people to engage in group activity with greater success.

Two models for explaining communication of humans developed within the speech communication discipline have provided useful contributions to understanding verbal communication acts as information procession. The first of these, the Berlo model (1960), caused scholars to think and reflect on the notion of process when referring to human communication. The Berlo model synthesized many of the earlier contributions from several academic fields. The impact of Berlo is twofold: one, he stresses the intent of the communication is to influence (thus, his is an extension of the older Aristotelian model); and second, he focuses on several important components in the process rather than just one component. The latter carries the implication that somehow the component parts must interact with each other rather than stand in isolation. Berlo identified four components worthy of consideration: source, message, channel, and receiver. Each component part contains various subordinate component parts. Understanding the source and the receiver means considering such factors as communication skills (speaking and listening), attitudes, knowledge, the social system, and the cultural system. Three factors comprise the message: content, treatment and code. Five channels are available through which messages can travel: sight, hearing, touch, smell, taste.

Perhaps the most complete contemporary model of the communication process is the Becker model (1971).* This model represents an interactive and systemic perspective on the evolutionary art of trying to understand how humans engage in information processing (see figure 4). Parts are interactive when one influences the choices and behaviors of the second. Parts are systemic when they are observed to be in a predicted relationship with other parts.

Figure 4

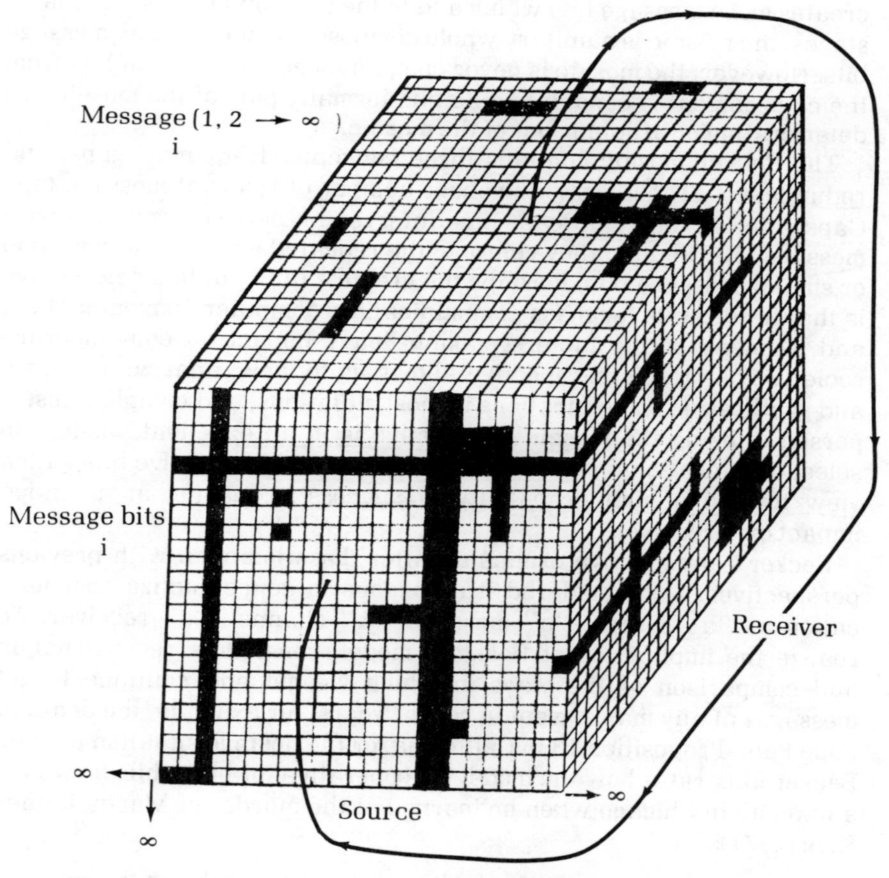

Becker developed what he called a "mosaic" model of human communication. The mosaic concept accounts for the substantial mass

*Sam Becker, "Rhetorical Studies for the Contemporary World," in Lloyd Bitzer/Edwin Black, *The Prospects of Rhetoric.* © 1971, pp. 71. Reprinted by permission of Prentice-Hall, Inc., Englewood Cliffs, New Jersey.

of information from many sources which must be accounted for in the contemporary electronic, high speed society. The message becomes message bits in the sense of small, fragmented, and incomplete "bits and pieces" of a large whole. The mosaic is a way of using a single picture composed of many small pieces of substances which "fit together" to form a pattern of wholeness. In isolation, each piece would be rather meaningless; but, when the pieces are fit together into the mosaic an organized whole exists that has meaning. Communication, then, is exposing many small pieces of information received from many different sources and in many different situations over a period of time where the communicant, in response to others, creates more message bits which add to the developing mosaic. In later stages, the mosaic is a unitary whole composed of many, many message bits. However, the mosaic is never complete, because input of bits from the environment is constant while bits formally part of the mosaic are deteriorating or dropping out of the mosaic.

The Becker mosaic contains three concepts: frequency, gaps, and redundancy. Frequency is the sheer number of relevant message bits. Gaps refer to the significant time intervening between contacts with message bits. Redundancy refers to the repeated exposure to the same or similar message bits. Perhaps the greatest utility of this perspective is that it accounts for mass communication, computer communication, and as many of the factors making heavy impact on contemporary society. The mosaic perspective allows us to view, analyze, criticize, and synthesize communications in most situations, and complexities. A person utilizing the mosaic perspective is in an excellent position to select organizational patterns, support bits, and illustrative bits with a view toward a high probability of success in making an intended impact on a receiver.

Becker's perspective originated after dissatisfaction with previous perspectives. He considered it erroneous to conceptualize communication as "a" source, "a" message, "a" channel, "a" receiver. To realize the implication of Becker's model, consider a reconstruction and comparison of the ways in which we got and continue to get messages of any major event in recent years; for example, the death of Pope Paul, Proposition 13 in California, or the hostage situation in Iran. Becker illustrates how the model was operative for him while he was in a taxi cab in Chicago when he learned of the murder of Martin Luther King (1971):

> The message, set-the front slice of the cube-might be the set of messages about the Martin Luther King murder. The ordinate represents all of the possible bits in that message set; the abscissa represents all possible sources. The darkened cells indicate that, at that point in time, those particular message bits are not available from the sources....

Thus the front layer of the cube represents the message bits about King which can be found at one point in time from each possible source.

The other slices of the cube represent other message bits — the Arab-Israeli conflict, the student power movement, the field of speech, and so on.

The way in which educated people view communication has evolved considerably in the past fifty years. We have gone from a source centered, linear perspective to a complex matrix mosaic which includes the notion of feedback and gives relatively equal emphasis to source, message, and receiver variables. The evolved perspective is in part a response to and inclusive of the contemporary technological, economic and social forces.

At this point it is possible to begin the formulation of an information processing perspective. This perspective is different from the persuasive perspective in several respects. First, the information processing perspective does not assume social influence as a necessary direct goal or purpose but does recognize that social impact may very well occur. Second, the information processing perspective assumes the utilization of corrective feedback to increase fidelity of the exchange rather than for correction of strategic choices by source and receiver.

The remainder of this section will provide further explanation of information, processing, information processing, and the functions of human information processing.

Information

Generally, we take the term information to mean data and facts. That perception of the term is not incorrect. However, information has a broader meaning in the context of information as a communication form. The broader meaning is more useful. Information refers to an amount of choice which enables a reduction of entropy. Entropy is a measure of uncertainty, that is, a measure of how little is known about any given entity or idea. As bits and pieces of data are recognized then the quantity of unknown is reduced. Or, referring to Becker's model, more squares in the mosaic become clear and visible. For example, the scientists's knowledge of the planet Saturn is not too considerable. There have been estimates of size, distance from other heavenly bodies. However, it could be said that considerable entropy exists. Recent rocket probes by the United States and the USSR have produced massive amounts of bits about atmosphere, gases, temperature, etc. Too many bits exist for the average person to process all at one time. However, if one selects some of the bits relating to temperature and examines those bits, the amount of entropy will be reduced. The bits themselves do not constitute the information. The recognition of some kind of pattern in the bits enables one to select between judgement categories of hot, warm, cold. The act of choice as dictated by the configuration of bits constitutes information. Given the above explanation, it should be obvious that to say "63°F, 68°F, 70°F, 61°F" is not information but represents bits; whereas, to say "the temperature is moderate in human comfort terms" is information. The individual temperature readings are data (bits). The bits can lead to reduction of uncertainty about something (less entropy) and thereby become information.

A second perspective for understanding the full meaning of information is to consider source categories. That is, where do the bits come from which allow choices to be made? There are essentially two sources: first hand experiences (including observations and thoughts) and second hand bits. In everyday lay terms we often use the phrases "first hand information" and "second hand information" to refer to the sources of information. In reality, they are the source of bits which allow the formation of information.

Processing

Processing means that several parts are ongoing and interacting. Usually a process has the four elements of action, change in time, progress or advancement over time, and a goal. Processing can be an interaction of variables within a receiver of communication. Processing can be an interaction between two or more persons engaged in an act of communicating. In either case, the process will contain the four elements.

Information Processing

The term information processing refers to the ongoing, interacting way in which a human internally handles bits of information, or it refers to the ongoing, interacting way in which two or more humans handle bits of information among themselves. One can process information from a source perspective or from a receiver perspective. In terms of a purely humanistic notion, it is necessary for success to have some understanding of how receivers process information. From a goal oriented communication notion, it is necessary for success to have some understanding of those factors which affect a receiver's processing of information. Considering the second reason for interest, we know that such factors as time, relationship between stimuli and attitudes, relationship between stimuli and previously known information, relative strengths of competing stimuli, the contextual relationship of the stimuli are factors critical to the way a receiver of a message processes information. As suggested earlier, information processing is the reeducation of the unknown (entropy) through choices. The choices are made by acts of selection in some deductive or inductive sequence toward reduced entropy.

How can such a process be explained in simple terms? Consider a helpful illustration. A teen-ager brings to a parent a piece of written communication (containing numerous bits) providing information about a ski trip over a holiday break from school. As one might expect, the parent selects two bits of written stimuli in the early stage of processing as points of focus: cost and chaperone plan. By contrast, it is probable that the teen-ager had first selected bits of written stimuli focusing on a description of the events of the trip (that is, learning to ski, meeting new friends, staying at a lodge). Being a clever communication strategist, the teen-ager precludes the adult's area of entropy with important bits — willingness to pay for the cost of the trip and having the resources to pay the cost. The bits are provided with appropriately selected verbal and nonverbal stimuli. In other words, the teen-ager states it clearly and appears sincere. The bits have provided information and entropy is reduced. At this point the parent progresses to another stage in the process by recalling other relevant stimuli. The parent recalls that the teen-ager has a history of financial solvency and accuracy as well as a very frugal selection of ways to spend money. The act of comparing the written bits in another stage in the information processing causes further reduction in entropy. The illustration could go on to the question of whether the teen-ager had considered all of the factors regarding having a good time (such as, if friends were going on the trip).

At this point the reader should be able to expand a knowledge of information processing by completing the extensions of the illustration above. In fact, the reader should be able to construct an example from their own recent experiences.

Functions of Human Information Processing

It will be helpful to understand why humans need to process information. There are essentially two reasons which constitute the foundations of human information processing. First, humans want to transfer information from one person to another person. In the transfer functioning process, individuals or groups seek to create awareness of something in a receiving individual or groups which approximate the awareness in the source individual or group.

The transfer function has behavioral implications for both the source and the receiver in the communication act. The source will want to select communcation symbols (bits) and orderings of the sets of symbols which will achieve the highest fidelity and reduce entropy.

The receiver will want to arrange internal attitudes and perceptions such that high fidelity and a reduction of entropy can occur. The transfer function can be observed in such situations as the following: a supervisor explaining the steps for operating a machine; a basketball coach explaining how to overcome a full court press; a nurse explaining how to replace a bandage on an injury; a librarian explaining the procedure for operating a computer search terminal for bibliographic listings. It should be an easy task for the reader to add five or ten similar examples to the list of situations which represent the transfer function.

The second function, or reason for processing information, is a transaction function. This is one in which the individual or groups seek to build relationships through mutually satisfactory exchanges of information. In order to achieve the desired goal, it is necessary to exchange bits about the self and to exchange perceptions (also bits) of the other (s).

This transfer function also has behavioral implications for both the source and the receiver in the communication act. The implications include willingness to be both source and receiver of message bits plus a willingness to internalize a rational thinking process. The transactional function can be observed in such situations as the following: a husband and wife considering a budget item; a fire officer and a fire fighter reviewing departmental goals; members of a college class at a reunion recalling their college years. It should be an easy task for the reader to add five or ten additional examples to this list of situations which represent the transactional function.

In summary, information has been considered as an amount of choice which enables a reduction of entropy. Data and facts (bits) are the constituents of information. Processing has been described as on going and interacting. Information processing has been defined as the on going, interacting way in which a human internally handles bits of information or the way in which two or more humans handle bits of information between themselves. Two functions of transfer and transaction have been identified and described.

Critical Elements of Information Processing

The second section of this chapter will focus on six important elements which are critical to the information processing in humans which occurs via the oral channels. Each element will be examined for its impact on the process.

Impact of Thought Processes

The way in which a source and a receiver think will cause considerable influence on the cognitive interpretation of data. It is clear that both source and receiver must place data into some meaningful configuration and the configuration must be somewhat shared between the source and receiver for meaning to occur in the transfer or transaction. The impact of thought is best understood as the notion that consistency of thought configurations produces maximum fidelity and reduction of entropy.

There are essentially two categories for describing thought processes: nonrational thought and rational thought. Nonrational thought is the use of intuition, so called psychic powers, and other non-reasoning means to treat data and arrive at conclusions. Essentially, very little is known about how these types of thoughts operate. Their existence is beginning to be hinted at in scientific literature; but the predictability and fidelity is so unknown, the types in the nonrational category must still be viewed as outside the realm of scholarly knowledge about human methods of information processing. In other words, two humans may indeed be able to share a meaning via psychic exchange of stimuli at some level which can not be observed or measured by present means; but, until considerably more systematic observation is available we are unable to discuss the impact of this category of thought processing on human communication.

Much more is available concerning the second category, rational thought. Centuries of speculation and systematic observation are available which enable scholars to make observations about impact with greater confidence in their conclusions.

Rational thought refers to the use of reason to treat data and arrive at a conclusion. One rational procedure is called deductive in nature because the known conclusion is the obvious result of treating data (bits) in sets or chains which descend from a general level to a specific level. Deductive reasoning involves the utilization of formal logic. In formal logic, there are three constituent parts: a major, general premise; a minor, specific premise; and a conclusion. Chaining occurs when the conclusion of one deductive set becomes the major premise of another deductive set. A common illustration of the deductive procedure is the following:

> Tight money supply in the national economy tends to pro-
> duce high interest rates for the consumer.
> The Federal Reserve System has recently raised the prime
> lending rate ¼ percent.
> Those of us who are consumers can expect to pay higher
> interest rates on most loans.

Although the process of deductive reasoning is often followed by sources and receivers in a communication transfer or transaction, it is much more common for the deductive process to be abbreviated omitting one or more of the three parts. To the extent that individuals and or individuals in groups are utilizing the deductive procedure in parallel form between them, then it is possible to have a degree of successful attempts at human communication. Although the general impact of deductive procedures is made here, more specific treatment and description is available in chapter seven.

A second rational procedure is called inductive in nature. Inductive processing of information involves treatment of bits by moving from specific to general. That is, many specific examples or instances are identified. Taken collectively, the individual bits allow one to generalize. For example, scientists may make laboratory tests with a new drug on hundreds of rats and then on a specified number of human subjects. If the drug works in a significant number of instances, the scientist may be willing to argue that the drug is satisfactory for use on the market. In everyday processing, a student of the stock market may observe in the *Wall Street Journal* that stock in company X has followed a decline for five straight days, that stock in a blue chip company Y has followed a declining trend in four of the last five days, that stock Z, a utility, has declined sharply for the last four days in a row. Therefore, the student of the market may conclude that the market generally is on the down side. That processing of information may cause the individual to make a statement to another person intended to influence the behavior of the second person. As a third example, consider the processing of data you receive about the quality of food in the dormitory cafeteria. After hearing a similar message from four or five sources, you will likely conclude something about the quality of the food. That inference is a product of inductively processing information. To the extent that a source and a receiver utilize the inductive procedure in parallel manner, then we have a degree of success in human communication. Although the general impact of inductive procedures has been identified here, more specific discussion of the impact is considered in chapter seven.

Impact of Perception on Information Transfer and Transaction

When humans communicate with or via machines there is a purely logical processing of information. No other factors have an impact once the logic system is selected. Such is not the case with human communication. Several factors exert strong impact upon the processing of bits in a message by the source and or the receiver. One such factor is perception.

Perception is the view one has of the reality around them. It is the set of experiential references from which one constructs meaningful views from the data and stimuli presented. Essentially, perception refers to the way in which one looks at the hard data available. There are several important factors which influence how the frame for viewing data is constructed. Some factors are a part of the environment in which the stimulus originate, thus, outside the receiver. For example, physical conditions like distance and competing stimuli are influencing factors.

An early view of perception suggests that there is an additive effect to the accumulation of data which allows the beginning of a construction of a frame of reference in the mind of the receiver. Asch (1946) suggests two general models of impression formation. One model predicts that a final impression is the sum of the impressions of individual stimuli. A different model suggests that as a receiver begins to process data there is an immediate organization of all the incoming stimuli into a perceptual whole. Asch's latter model provides a why explanation for stereotyping and indexing.

Later research suggests that something about personality type might be a factor in how individuals perceive data. Research by Luchins (1957) and by Mayo and Crockett (1964) provide evidence to argue that cognitively complex people have a differentiation of traits, a subtlety of relationships among traits, and a tolerance for contradictory information not tolerated in the processing method by cognitively simple subjects. Yet, additional research points to personal ego involvement as a factor which affects the perceptual frame of reference. McCrosky, Burgoon, (1974) and others have been able to postulate that highly ego involved persons or persons highly ego involved on a particular topic will have a very limited range of options within the topic scope which they can accept. In other words, the latitude of acceptance is inversely related to the degree of ego involvement.

A more contemporary view extends impression formation to the notion of cognitive complexity as a factor in perception. This view postulates a relationship between social (exterior) and cognitive (internal) factors shaping perception. The work of Delia (1974) and others suggests that a socially cognitively complex individual has the capacity to perceive in a more complex frame whereas a socially cognitively simplistic individual has only a limited capacity to perceive.

There is little doubt that human processing of information, unlike machine communication, is highly affected by the variable of perception. What's more, the variable is present in all situations in which human communication occurs. The exact ways in which this variable operates is still only partly understood and represents a viable area of inquiry.

Operational implications are important. First, the source of a message must consider what is known about the social, cognitive, ego characteristics of a potential receiver. If such consideration does occur, then the source person is able to select verbal and nonverbal code symbols which have high probability of being processed by the receiver in a way which will facilitate the transfer of meaning. Second, the receiver of a message must be willing to provide feedback to the source. In giving feedback, the original receiver must recognize what is known about the other party so that verbal and nonverbal code symbols will be selected which will have high probability of being processed as intended.

Impact of Memory on Information Transfer and Transaction

Classical theorists identified five canons of rhetoric meaning five factors very important to the process as it was known and perceived in that period. During the centuries, one of the canons, memory, was virtually dropped from the canons of rhetoric. Today communication scholars seldom refer to the canons of rhetoric. However, among the modern concept of variables, attention has been refocusing on memory; but, the reason for focusing is different today. The classicist considered memory from a source perspective. It was something the speaker had to do — carefully memorize the message to be delivered. Today's communicologist is more concerned with the implications of memory from the receiver perspective. How does a receiver retain data bits? How can data bits be recalled for integration with other data bits? What is the capacity for storage of data bits? Clearly, the computer era has produced a reshaping of the how explanation of human communication from a processing perspective. Contemporary interest by the general public in the variable of memory is attested by a rash of popular games utilizing memory as a function of the game. The most contemporary is a toy released in fall 1978, Simon Says.

From the process view, memory is important for the storage capacity factor. Data must be stored temporarily, and it must also be stored for longer periods of time. Such capacity must be viewed as a limitation on the human as a communicator.

Memory really is not a single variable, but rather a general term for several kinds of memory. William James suggested two kinds of memory, primary memory and secondary memory. Immediate knowledge of the past is an example of primary memory. For example, the data which a person can recall by exerting effort about an important homecoming game one week after the game illustrates primary memory. Momentary awareness of a present experience is an example of secondary memory. Recall of the third digit in a string of four digits ten seconds after receiving the stimulus is an illustration.

Sperling (1963) suggests a static perspective of memory. He points to three stages. The first stage is simply total sensory image awareness of events just ended. A second stage is short term recall which contains limited information which can be extracted from rapidly decaying sensory images. The third stage is permanent or long term storage and recall of a large capacity. Indeed, the three stages very likely involve different functioning of the human neurological system. It is clear that the capacity for memory is not equally distributed in individuals nor is the capacity equally distributed across stages in the same individual. As we later examine methods for maximizing the communication process, it should be kept in mind that the potential for benefit from one or more methods probably also varies among individuals.

The length of time that a set of data can be retained such that recall on demand is possible is referred to as the span of memory. There is evidence that immediate memory appears to be limited in most people by the number of items, regardless of the information content complexity of the item. Therefore, it has been suggested that the apparent memory span could be increased by a recoding process called "chunking." By using a coding system and grouping data, it is possible to extend the retention with a string of code words. What is true of discreet bits of information is probably also true of rather limited sets of data. The mind seems to be limited in its capacity to recall a long chain of the items (sets of data). The "chunking" concept seems to be a means by which the mind can expand the quantity of sets of data which can be stored and recalled.

The implication of the way the mind operates by chunking is that a source in a communication act can increase the probability of effective communication transfer or transaction by placing data and ideas into groups or chunks. In fact, recent attention to memory by psychologists has verified a very old rhetorical concept of organization. If the source is careful in grouping data and sets of data in a pattern which is likely to conform to the memory patterning of the receiver, communication will be enhanced.

The goal in communication is to be effective and efficient. In pursuit of that goal, there are three factors which can be expected to increase the effectiveness of receivers' potential to gain from a communication event: structuring, ordering, and mnemonic devices.

Structuring. Structuring is defined as the provision of a form and configuration to a set of data. Structuring involves utilizing what is known about the process by which the mind chunks data. From the receiver's perspective structuring means taking bits provided by a source and regrouping into a manageable fashion.

Ordering. Ordering is defined as the particular pattern sequence chosen for chunking available data. There are some orders which seem more compatible with the mind's processing of information.

One method of ordering is the primacy order. This method recognizes that some chunk of data placed at the beginning of a string of chunks will have greater probability for recall by the subject than chunks appearing somewhat later in the string. An explanation for such a factor functioning is that the mind attends more to an item of early encounter and attends less to subsequent encounters. Therefore, the primacy event is more likely to be transferred to longer term memory systems. Another explanation is that retention does not decrease with contact between one event and similar events when the target event is presented first.

A second method of ordering is the recency order. This method recognizes that some chunks of data placed at the end of a string of chunks will have greater probability for recall by the subject than chunks appearing somewhere earlier in the string. The explanation for this phenomena is that the most recent stimuli has made the most telling impact because of its recency and is most likely to be recalled when the subject wishes to recall data relative to a given subject.

There doesn't seem to be much basis for considering either primacy or recency as the predominant model to explain how memory functions as a factor in human information processing. But it does appear fairly certain from contemporary research in the field of speech communication and in the field of psychology that either method is superior to placement of chunks of data in the middle of a string of chunks for facilitating recall from memory.

The implication for a source of data in a communication event is in the value of knowing how processing is likely to occur in the intended receiver. Such knowledge will allow the source person to construct an order and structure with ideas and data so there is a maximum chance of achieving the intended transfer or transaction. Specific application of this implication is available in chapter seven.

The implication for the receiver of data in a communication event is that knowing how memory functions as part of human information processing will allow the individual receiver to increase their own efficiency as a processor. Whether or not data has been ordered and structured by a source, the receiver can use one of several devices or techniques to aid memory — or improve listening.

Mnemonic Devices. All mnemonic devices seek to provide a relationship between the data to be learned and some previously learned schematic method. One category of devices seeks to enhance simple, direct recall. Some of the oldest mnemonic devices provided by the Roman Quintilian in the *Ad Herennium*, include rehearsing and searching for unique or isolated features. Rehearsal involves simply repeating mentally bits that have been heard. Searching for uniqueness means what it says, finding some small feature which makes one bit or set of bits different from another bit or set of bits. As an example of the method, consider the task of learning a vacation milk delivery route door to door that a delivery person must master quickly. That can be done quite effectively in one day by identifying some unique feature of each home on the route or of the home's immediate surroundings. The feature must be some distinctive item such as shape of a roof or size of an evergreen. Similarly, if one is listening to a message containing a list of reasons for buying a product it would be helpful to locate a distinctive feature about each item on the list.

Another old mnemonic method is to mentally establish a place-thing relationship. One may imagine that various items in a chain are mentally located in different locations. Moreover, the order of places will preserve the order of the things. Recall, then, occurs by visualizing each location and thereby discovering the object.

A second category of mnemonic devices seeks to systematically transform. Just as organization and structure are important for the source of a message, so it is for the receiver. In fact, it is important to the source, because it is important to the receiver.

Organization and structure are very fundamental methods of reducing large quantities of information such that the mind can handle all the data. Donald Norman (1969) summarizes studies which suggest that organization is the primary principle of memory for both short term and long term storage and recall. Norman further states a rule governing system to explain organization. Norman's sytem is summarized as follows:

1. Small basic units: The material to be learned must be divisible into small, self-contained sections, with no more than four or five individual items in any section.

2. Internal organization: The sections must be organized so that the various parts fit together in a logical, self ordering structure.

3. External organization: Some relationships must be established between the material to be learned and material which has already been learned, so that one fits neatly within the other.

In summary, this section has considered the fact that memory does have impact on the totality of information processing. Specifically, there are implications from both a source perspective and a receiver perspective. Finally, there are several mnemonic devices from which each individual must make a selection which works best for their individual information processing system.

Impact of Attention on Information Transfer and Transaction

Attention may be defined as the act of sorting out and selecting one stimulus from among competing stimuli. The act may be viewed as conscious and intentional although not necessarily desirable. At a basic level of communication, attention usually means giving recognition to a stimulus at the expense of other stimuli.

Along with several other factors considered in this section, attention is very important in the totality of the information processing in humans. There is a relationship between attention and memory, just discussed, which may be stronger than any other relationship between two factors considered in this section. What one attends to most firmly is likely to have a firmer place in the memory storage system and is most likely to be available for recall from the memory storage system. Therefore, attention plays a vital role in the information processing.

An understanding of the impact of attention on communication is best obtained by identifying the principles which seem to govern the way in which attention operates. Bryant and Wallace (1960) have suggested several principles which they labeled "laws" of attention.

The first principle says that "among competing stimuli, the stronger, the more intense stimuli is preferred to the weaker." If a person is speaking on the telephone and a loud program is blaring on television, the stimuli received over the telephone may not make a firm enough impact to be selected by the receiver's mind. In another instance, a person might be so engrossed in the detail of a story being told by a friend, that they fail to process the verbal stimuli from an instructor beginning a class meeting. Without some conscious effort on the part of the receiver, the principle will probably determine which stimuli are attended to by the person and subsequently stored in the memory.

The second principle says that "among stimuli which vary in size, the larger is preferred to the smaller." What better explanation is there for the contemporary fad for larger and larger television screens? Quite simply, the larger stimuli makes a greater quantitative impact on the sensory receptors.

The third principle says that "among competing stimuli, the moving one is preferable to the one at rest." The sensory receptors focus in on movement. Consequently, for years public speakers have been taught they should gesture when speaking, move physically from one location to another. Motion is very powerful. Certainly, the motion picture made a more dramatic impact than the viewing of still pictures or still slides.

The fourth principle says that "among two or more collections of stimuli, the group which is organized has preference over the group which is disorganized." We learn very early in our socialization that order is desirable. In fact, some would argue that the preference for order is an inate human trait. At any rate, most humans clearly demonstrate a preference for order in their lives. Whether by socialization or by inate quality, we attend more closely to the ordered set of stimuli and to a certain extent expect to find order.

The fifth principle says that "among two stimuli, one familiar and the other strange, the familiar one is preferred." The sensory receptors quickly focus on something which is closely related to bits which have already been stored in the memory. The more successful learning situations recognize this principle and systematically attempt to move from something known to something unknown but easily recognizable as similar to the known. Successful methods of teaching dance steps to groups utilize this principle.

Most teaching methods courses for education majors will advocate this principle as basic to providing instruction. A demonstration of assembling farm equipment to equipment dealers will utilize the principle. The validity of this principle as an important factor in attention has been demonstrated over and over. The reader could probably construct a long list of additional personal examples.

Attention has been defined as an act of sorting out and selecting stimulus from among competing stimuli. The act is conscious and intentional. Attention and memory are very closely related factors in the human information processing system. Five principles, "laws," of attention have been identified.

Impact of Language on Information Transaction and Transfer

Language is a common term scholars designate as a code symbol. Two basic code symbol systems, verbal and nonverbal, are discussed at length in chapter three. The impact of language on information transaction and transfer is in the role that symbolic interaction has on shaping the meanings of code symbols themselves when used by sources and receivers. According to the concept of symbolic interaction, a single stimulus does not have absolute, universally fixed meaning. Rather, the meaning comes from confirmation of two basic sources: 1) the context of the stimulus, and 2) the qualifying factors present in both source and receiver. Another complicating feature of language making an impact on information processing is the concept of levels of abstraction.

Eventually, the fact that language is not static but interactive in nature means that information processing in humans can not be described solely by a mechanistic, machine model. The most meaningful implication is to be aware of an enormous problem. We live in a highly complex, technical society where there is increased quantity of data (bits) available to be sorted, reviewed, stored, and recalled. The problem is complicated by the varied meanings which are typically possible with the usage of any code symbol. The problem is compounded even further by the number of individuals in the interactive event and the level of abstraction at which the participants choose to communicate.

Impact of Emphatic Listening on informaion Transaction and Transfer

Typically, at a high school level most people have become aware that talking and speaking are not the same thing. One is random whereas the other is purposive and systematic. Likewise, most people have become aware at the same level that hearing and listening are not the same thing.

Here, too, hearing is random whereas listening is purposive and systematic. Listening involves physical activity at a muscular, neurological system level. In addition, listening involves rational thought, selection, evaluation, and motive. How many misunderstandings have resulted from a dialog like the following:

A: You aren't listening.

B: Yes I am. I heard you.

A: If you heard me, why are you still doing X?

B: Because I didn't understand what you said.

A: But you said you were listening.

B: I was, but you were too far away and I couldn't understand.

A: Why didn't you ask what I said?

B: Why didn't you come and ask if I understood?

Skill in listening involves capacity to handle data, willingness to hear data, previous habits, and availability of explicit data in a message.

Listening is more than a single dimensional variable in information processing. Actually, there are two basic purposes for listening: pleasure and critical judgement. Although both types meet the criteria above, only the latter will receive attention in this work. What we normally call emphatically listening, that is conscious sharing of experience as we hear, is really the interactive effect of several other variables which affect information processing: perception, language, attention, and memory.

Frequently, we refer to the term "good" listening. That term is probably very misleading. Listening is neither good nor bad. Listening may be effective in terms of finding consistency of meaning between source and receiver.

The impact of listening on information processing is truly significant. Several studies have been completed which provide a startling picture of the proportion of time devoted to listening as compared to other aspects of communication. Rankin (1928) found that 68 adults divided their communication time as follows:

Listening	45 percent
Talking	30 percent
Reading	16 percent
Writing	9 percent

Today's society is even more orally dominated than it was in 1928. The proportions in listening and talking may in fact be much greater today.

The impact of listening on information processing is realized to be even greater when we recognize that effective listening habits must be consciously developed and utilized or they atrophy. Rossiter's study (1972) of upper level undergraduates and graduate students between

the ages of 20 and 60 found that the capacity for listening declines at some point between the beginning and end of the range. Atrophy of listening capacity may in fact be a consequence of major permanent forces in modern society. Nichols and Stevens (1957) have argued quite convincingly that in our culture people are taught not to listen by at least two factors. One, television commercials constantly repeat a message. Constant repetition of events is a central characteristic of television soaps and advertising planning. The effect may very well be to reduce the necessity to listen closely. Second, educational institutions consciously repeat information for students. Announcements in secondary and elementary schools are repeated. Directions are given again and again. The effect may very well be to reduce the necessity to listen closely. Recently we have even seen a cultural phenomenon which essentially says "don't listen to a message if it isn't what you want to hear." During the past ten years we have often witnessed situations where angry protesters refuse to allow a speaker to deliver a message if there is a chance the message will differ from what they want receivers to hear.

The societal barriers to effective listening add greater impact to the barriers to effective listening which are inherent in the process itself. There are measures which the individual can take to be a more effective emphatic listener. At least eight measures are available. The first six, discussed at length by Morlan and Tuttle (1976) are stated briefly here. First, "prepare yourself to listen." This would include making conscious effort to minimize or eliminate competing stimuli, determining a goal for listening, and being physically ready to listen. Second, "control the emotions." Consciously examine your biases toward the source or the expected topic to reduce the intrapersonally competing stimuli. If you are in an unfavorable emotional state for whatever reason, recognize that fact and make a conscious effort to control the impact of the emotions. Third, "listen for ideas and patterns of reasoning." This means avoiding the common temptation to just listen for facts. Strive to recognize ideas and patterns while noticing to what extent facts illustrate or prove an idea. Fourth, "listen to difficult material." Too often we are tempted to say to ourselves, "that's too complex for me to understand." Usually, that is not the case. It takes a conscious effort to listen to the abstract, complex, and unfamiliar information. Fifth, "avoid being critical of delivery." Unless you have as your purpose to be a rhetorical critic (which is a very respectable purpose) listening for aspects of delivery may be causing you to attend to relatively less important stimuli. Sixth, "use spare time wisely." If you recognize that the difference between physical ability of a speaker to deliver a message and the ability of the receiver's mind to process the message is at least a 3:1 ratio, you will want to use the "spare time" which is available to your mind. You might want to use some of that spare time to evaluate the facts and ideation present in the message or you might want to test the cognitive consistency of the various parts of the message.

Two additional measures for increasing the effectiveness of emphatic listening behavior are described by Weaver (1972). The seventh measure is to "reflect the message to the source." Quite simply, this means paraphrasing succinctly the last statement made to you or even making a summary of the entire conversation up to that point and then inviting a response to your feedback. This measure allows for correction and it also encourages the original source to continue with further extension of the message or to shift to another message. The eighth measure is to "try and determine whether your referents for the words of the source are about the same as the source's." Remember that concept referents, evoked by words, are usually subcategories with all the critical and noncritical attributes. Can you recognize to what extent you share those attributes? This is another intrapersonal activity which would make good use of the "spare time" available to the mind when it is processing a message.

Listening is certainly a very important factor in the human processing of information. It has been noted that listening is conscious and active rather than random and passive. It has been suggested that at least eight measures are available if one wants to increase the effectiveness and efficiency of their listening behavior.

Maximizing Information Processing Transaction and Transfer Functions by Source and Receiver

Maximizing as a Source

As a source, there are several kinds of analysis which will increase the probability of selecting and ordering code symbols which will result in clear instances of communication transaction and transfer. The source should consider self analysis, audience analysis, and message analysis.

The first and foremost analysis begins with the self. Examine your own knowledge of the subject of the intended communication to determine scope, depth, sophistication to which it can be developed. In addition, examine your own interests and commiment to the subject of the intended communication. If the interest is low, then two options are available: one, select a subject more interesting to you; or two, find a way to generate self interest in the subject. The latter might be achieved by asking yourself: "How would this subject relate to me now or in the future?", "Do I know anyone who is involved with this topic?", "What are some unique features about this topic?".

The second type of analysis is of the audience. This involves drawing some conclusions about many aspects of the people who will be the target of the message you intend to construct. Audience analysis involves asking yourself many questions about the person or group so that you have some idea of what the receiver wants to know or needs to know. Essentially, why will they want to listen? A more difficult part of audience analysis involves an examination of the kind of experiences the receivers have likely had to which you might make identification with code symbols. Asking and answering a lot of questions about audience experiences and attitudes will clarify what options are available to you for language, ordering, supporting.

Completion of the first two types of analysis allows completion of the third type of analysis — analysis of message construct options. All of the code symbol options are considered, and the ones best suited to the level of experience of the receivers are selected. This stage should also involve considering both cognitive and emotional "fit" of the code symbols. Likewise, this analysis allows you, as a source, to select from the available organizational patterns; such as, spatial, topical, chronological, logical, problem solving, and motivated sequence.

If you are a source for a message, and you have carefully considered the three types of analysis, then you have a right to feel satisfied that you have done everything possible to help the receiver process information in a manner consistent with your goals and purposes for initiating the communication.

Maximizing as a Receiver

As a receiver, you can play a vital role in maximizing the probability of effective communication transaction and transfer through two important methods: one, control of pre-attitude sets; and two, intentional responding (feedback).

A conscious effort must be made to control the attitude set which exists toward a subject or a person before a communication event takes place. The conscious effort begins by recognizing the existence of the set. Once the pre-set is recognized, then you may proceed to search for other possible perspectives which might be possible. Only after recognizing that there are in fact several perspectives can you begin to consciously put aside your own pre-set and approach a communication event with an open mind.

Responding to a message source with intentional feedback is another way a receiver can maximize the probablility of effective communication transaction and transfer. Returning meaningful stimuli represents intentional feedback. It is important to provide the source with the knowledge that a message has been received, processed, and understood. It also lets the source know if any of the above have not occurred. That knowledge is extremely important to the progress of the information output; thereby, the extension of the communication event. For the receiver to perform this function, it is necessary to want to offer feedback, to consider the standard meanings of verbal and nonverbal code symbols, and to consider the realm of shared experiences which can provide contextual meanings for the verbal and nonverbal feedback code symbols. Essentially, intentional feedback requires that you say to yourself, "I want to participate in the communication event in some meaningful way."

In summary, the way of explaining how humans communicate, especially via the oral mode, has evolved. The Becker model provides one of the most comprehensive models for explaining how information is processed within individuals and between individuals. Six elements important in the process are: thought, perception, memory, attention, language, and listening.

It is possible for a source to affect the efficiency of the processing of information by considering factors within self and within receiver. It is possible for a receiver to affect the efficiency of the processing of information by considering factors within self and within source.

References

Asch, S.E. "Forming Impressions of Personality." *Journal of Abnormal Social Psychology.* 1946, 41, 258-90.

Becker, Carl. "Rhetorical Studies for the Contemporary World." In Lloyd Bitzer and Edwin Black (Eds.) *The Prospects of Rhetoric.* Englewood Cliffs, New Jersey: Prentice-Hall, Inc., 1971.

Berlo, David. *The Process of Communication.* New York: Holt, Rinehart and Winston, 1960.

Bryant, Donald, and Wallace, Karl. *Fundamentals of Public Speaking.* New York: Appleton-Century-Crofts, Inc., 1960.

Delia, Jesse, Clark, Ruth, and Switzer, David. "Cognitive Complexity and Impression Formation in Informal Social Interaction." *Speech Monographs,* 1974, 41, 299-308.

Hayakawa, S.I. *Language In Thought and Action.* New York: Harcourt, Brace Jovanovich, 1972.

Luchins, A.S. "Experimental Attempts to Minimize the Impact of First Impressions." In C. Hoveland (ed.). *The Order of Presentation In Persuasion.* New Haven, Conn.: Yale University Press, 1957.

Mayo, Clara, and Crockett, W.H. "Cognitive Complexity and Primacy-recency Effects in Impression Formation." *Journal of Abnormal and Social Psychology,* 1964, 68, 335-388.

McCrosky, James, and Burgoon, Michael. "Establishing Predictors of Latitude of Acceptance-Rejection and Attitude Intensity: A Comparison of Assumptions of Social Judgement and Authoritarian Personality Theories.' *Speech Monographs,* 1974, 41, 421-426.

Morlan, Donald, and Tuttle, George. *Introduction to Effective Oral Communication.* Indianapolis: Bobbs-Merrill, Inc., 1976.

Nichols, Ralph, and Stevens, Leonard. *Are You Listening?* New York: McGraw-Hill, 1957.

Norman, Donald. *Memory and Attention.* New York: John Wiley & Sons, Inc., 1969.

Rankin, Paul T. "The Importance of Listening Ability." *English Journal,* 1928, 17, 623-630.

Rossiter, Charles. "Sex of the Speaker, Sex of the Listener, and Listening Comprehension." *Journal of Communication.* 1972, 22, 64-69.

Schramm, Wilbur, "How Communication Works." *The Process and Effects of Mass Communication.* Urbana: University of Illinois Press, 1955.

Shannon, Claude, and Weaver, Warren. *The Mathematical Theory of Communication.* Urbana: University of Illinois Press, 1949.

Spering, G.A. "A Model for Visual Memory Tasks." *Human Factors,* 1963, 5, 19-31.

Weaver, Carl. *Human Listening.* Indianapolis: Bobbs-Merrill, Inc., 1972.

7

Persuasive Communication

John K. Boaz

Persuasive communication is a sufficiently central instrumentality in our community lives that we begin this chapter by discussing briefly the role of persuasion in society. Next we trace historical approaches to persuasion which lead us from the development of rhetorical theory in classical Greece to a wedding in this century of that theory with modern psychological theories. The central purpose of this chapter is to describe three basic contemporary approaches to persuasive communication—the rationalistic approach, the psychological approach, and the dramatistic approach.

Role of Persuasion in Society

Society exists *in* communication. With this idea educational philosopher John Dewey calls our attention to the centrality of communication to our lives, to our society, and to our very social existence:

> Society not only continues to exist *by* transmission, *by* communication, but it may fairly be said to exist *in* transmission, *in* communication. There is more than a verbal tie between the words common, community, and communication. Men live in a community in virtue of the things which they have in common; and communication is the

way in which they come to possess things in common. What they must have in common in order to form a community or society are aims, beliefs, aspirations, knowledge — a common understanding — like-mindedness as the sociologists say. Such things cannot be shared as persons would share a pie by dividing it into physical pieces. The communication which insures participation in a common understanding is one which secures similar emotional and intellectual dispositions — like ways of responding to expectations and requirements (1916, p..5).

Communication is the process whereby we derive the essential agreements that constitute the nature of the society in which we live. The communication process is continuing and, therefore, the society is evolving, but at any point in time we can mark the givens — the heritage, the present, and the aspirations.

In a sense all communication is persuasive. To be sure, communication is expressive, but it is also intended to evoke response. The end of all communication is response, and all response is change. Every experience which we have leaves us altered in some way, and a communication event is merely one of the several events which we continually experience. The intention to produce change lies at the heart of persuasion. We should then attempt to define persuasion.

Persuasion is an intentional effort by symbolic means to effect change in others. Each of us is deluged daily with persuasive appeals. We ask and are asked to act, to give, to believe, to buy, to vote, to foreswear, and to sign on the dotted line. Advertising alone as a species of persuasion seeks our attention from radio and television to magazines, newspapers, billboards, the mail, and sometimes an occasional blimp. We cannot escape from participating in the process of persuasion, nor do we wish normally to avoid the process.

Democracy relies heavily upon persuasion, and skills in persuasion are a necessary concomitant of maintaining democratic institutions. Elements of the democratic system prevail throughout our social structures and institutions from the primary group to the national level. Thus, we have good reason to want to enhance our skills in persuasion. Indeed the alternatives to persuasion, coercion and force, we generally conceive to be too destructive and too costly for achieving common agreements and understanding.

We are receivers of persuasive messages to a far greater extent than we are persuaders ourselves. We listen more than we speak, as a general rule, and we read more than we write. Of the total time we spend communicating with others, the overwhelming amount is spent in the role of critical evaluator. Thus, while aiming to become a better persuader is a noble goal and one which we would encourage for students of persuasion, our suggestion to the reader would be to approach the study of persuasion from the standpoint of a critical evaluator of the persuasive process. In any event the principles of persuasion developed in the following pages remain the same for the persuader or the critical evaluator of persuasion.

Historical Approaches to Persuasion

We have noted that interest in persuasion is a concomitant of interest in democratic institutions and the democratic process. It should not be surprising, therefore, that the golden age of classical Greek democracy contributed substantially to the development of rhetorical theory or the theory of persuasion. It is unlikely that the rather comprehensive theory of persuasion that appears in Aristotle's *The Rhetoric* (fourth century, B.C.) sprang freshly to his fertile mind. Rather we can assume that he received from the oral tradition of handing down elements of culture a good deal of the theory which he so admirably categorized and elaborated.

It has been said that we are inclined to be Platonistic in our thinking whether or not we have ever heard of Plato, so pervasive is Platonic thought in western culture. Plato's approach to rhetoric is that of a moral philosopher. The *Gorgias* and *Phaedrus* are something more than treatises in dialogue form of the so-called art of rhetoric. These dialogues reveal basic elements of Plato's philosophy which in turn determine his position on rhetoric. We must first consider these fundamental philosophical notions in order to understand the basis on which Plato condemned rhetoric as he observed it in practice and on which he built what he considered to be noble rhetoric.

Plato is a rationalist. As such he stands in opposition to the sophists, the teachers of rhetoric in the fifth century, B.C., whose philosophical hallmark is skepticism. To the sophists, man is bound in a world of perception. Thus, they hold that no absolute physical principles can be inferred from observation, because perception is contingent and individual. By the same token they hold that morals and ethical values are relative, that they are determined by the individual, and that the events of life are essentially amoral.

Plato's position is largely determined by his doctrine of the two realms. He conceives of a realm or world of perception and a corresponding realm of ideas or forms. The realm of perception is the physical world, objective by virtue of its spatial and temporal construct. The realm of ideas he holds to be intimately related to the realm of perception, equally real and objective, but nonphysical, nonspatial, and nontemporal. The realm of forms is the ideal world which is the highest good and in which the physical world exists as a mere copy. Objectivity of the moral world lies in the realm of ideas. The moral world is the epitome of virtue manifest in temperance, courage, and wisdom.

Plato's ideal world is known through thought; indeed the forms are the objects of thought. Thus, thought leads us to truth and virtue. Persons by virtue of their innate relation with the ideal world are both good by nature and inclined toward the good as the source of their happiness. Therefore, insofar as people know the ideal through thought they are good and will good. The thought process is a creative act and is epitomized in dialectics, a form of discussion which emphasizes defining and analyzing concepts.

Plato condemns rhetoric first as a confused universal. Because it is not a universal, it has no ideal form and does not, therefore, participate in truth or virtue. Accordingly it cannot bring people into a state of greater happiness which is the highest goal of human action. Rather, rhetoric is explained as experience in producing a sort of delight, and not art or a creative act. Rhetoric is mere flattery and a counterfeit of a part of politics.

Elsewhere in the *Gorgias* Plato condemns rhetoric because it creates belief rather than knowledge. Belief, according to Plato, is a lower form of knowledge. Belief may be false but knowledge cannot be. The opinion of the multitude is no substitute for truth. Virtue consists in seeking the higher form of knowledge.

But perhaps his most important condemnation of rhetoric is in the area of morals. Plato feels that rhetoricians of his day had utter disregard for what he considered moral good. A fool and a flatterer cannot attain good because they have no knowledge of the good. Moreover, the rhetorician is concerned with personal freedom, power, show, and prestige rather than the truth. Finally, rhetoric gives greater power to the ignorant person rather than the person who possesses knowledge.

Throughout the criticism of the sophistic rhetoric in the *Gorgias* a good use of rhetoric is implied, and in the *Phaedrus* we find explicitly stated what Plato conceives good rhetoric to be. As we have seen, truth and virtue, knowledge and moral values, correspond with the highest good in Plato's philosophy. As we might expect the noble rhetoric is directed toward these two ideals.

Noble rhetoric, therefore, is based on knowledge. Rhetoricians must have knowledge of themselves, for fools can never attain what is good. Rhetoricians must have knowledge of what they propose to speak about, for those who are in ignorance cannot serve justice. And the rhetorician must have a knowledge of all kinds of persons for only by understanding the nature of each and how each is affected can the rhetorician undertake to arrange an effective means of persuasion. Thus, we have the cornerstone of classical rhetorical theory: the persuader must have knowledge of self, subject matter, and audience.

But knowledge of the truth is not enough. In the *Phaedrus* Plato points out that knowledge alone will not give you persuasion. "The perfection which is required of the finished orator is, or rather must be, like perfection of anything else, partly given by nature, but may also be assisted by art. If you have the natural power and add to it knowledge and practice, you will be a distinguished speaker" (1937, p. 273).

In outlining principles of the noble rhetoric Plato is brief but definitive. The rhetorical process is akin to the dialectic process of the Platonic dialogues. The rhetorician should begin with definitions, recognize debatable and nondebatable classes, and be able to break down ideas into their smallest categories. Organization should be governed by the principle of organic unity, that is to say, the beginning, middle, and end should be adapted to one another and to the whole. The style in which the rhetorician speaks should be appropriate and simple. Understanding is the goal.

Plato himself provides the best summary of his concept of true rhetoric:

> Until a man knows the truth of the several particulars of which he is writing or speaking, and is able to define them as they are, and having defined them again to divide them until they can be no longer divided, and until in like manner he is able to discern the nature of the soul, and discover the different modes of discourse which are adapted to different natures, and to arrange and dispose them in such a way that the simple form of speech may be addressed to the simpler nature, and the complex and composite to the more complex nature — until he has accomplished all this, he will be unable to handle arguments according to rules of art, as far as their nature allows them to be subjected to art, either for the purpose of teaching or persuading (1937, p. 280).

Aristotle, a student of Plato, shares Plato's concern for a discovery of the truth through discourse. Aristotle argues that truth is naturally inclined to prevail over its opposite. However, Aristotle's concept of rhetoric differs considerably from that of his teacher. Aristotle views rhetoric as an amoral tool, a tool which could be used for selfish or noble ends by good and evil orators alike. Moreover, he feels that truth must be given effectiveness in order to prevail. Rhetorical principles constitute the means for lending effectiveness to the truth. Thus, if truth does not prevail it is the fault of the orator for failing to use appropriate rhetorical means. Aristotle conceives of rhetoric functioning in an adversarial system. We might take as a model the American judicial system. There prosecution and defense are given equal opportunity to present the best possible case for guilt or innocence before a deciding audience, judge or jury of peers. Given advocates of equal rhetorical skills and talent, we assume within this system that justice will prevail. We assume that a better case can be built for the culpability of the guilty and the blamelessness of the innocent than their opposites and that an audience will perceive the just cause and respond accordingly — at least in most instances.

What then is rhetoric? Aristotle defines it in the opening pages of

The Rhetoric. Rhetoric is the "faculty of observing in any given case the available means of persuasion" (1954, p. 24). Persuasion takes place in various circumstances. Speakers vary, their purposes vary, occasions vary, and audiences vary. Thus, the persuader's strategy in shaping the message should be tailored to fit the circumstances of the particular situation. And what are the means of persuasion available to the speaker? Aristotle delineates three modes of persuasion: logical, emotional, and ethical. Logical proofs consist of adducing evidence and argument which appeal to the rational facet of a person's nature. Emotional proofs consist of associating the speaker's purposes with the needs, desires, and values of the audience. Ethical proofs consist in the audience's recognition of the intelligence, character, and good will toward the listener of the speaker.

Aristotle, like Plato, is a rationalist. Aristotle defines humans as "the rational animal." He feels that persons believe or act in response to good reasons for believing or acting. Thus, a major portion of *The Rhetoric* is devoted to analysis of the reasoning process whereby audiences are persuaded. Essentially logical proofs consist of evidence and argument. Aristotle cites laws, witnesses, contracts, tortures, and oaths as illustrative of the sources of evidence from which persuaders can develop arguments. Arguments in turn are of two sorts, inductive and deductive. Inductive arguments are those in which conclusions are drawn directly from evidence. Argument from example and argument by analogy are inductive in nature. Deductive arguments are those in which conclusions are drawn from other conclusions which in turn are inductively derived. Sign and causal arguments are deductive in nature. These forms of argument are discussed in greater detail later in this chapter under the rationalistic approach to persuasion.

The task of the persuader in an adversarial situation is to select those arguments which are most appropriate to develop one's own case and to refute given or expected counter arguments. Aristotle developed the notions of topics and status to aid the persuader in making those choices. The notion of topics is that there are general lines of argument which apply to a variety of specific propositions which might be advanced. Expediency and inexpediency, for example, is a topic or line of argument which could be adpated to any number of proposals. "My proposal is expedient and opposing proposals are inexpedient." Such a line of argument was one used by former President Ford in pardoning Richard Nixon; a pardon will put Watergate behind us whereas a trial could last for many months and still not resolve important questions. The notion of status is that there are critical issues involved in any controversy. Logical demonstration of one's case entails speaking to these issues. In considering a proposition of policy, such as passage of an equal rights amendment to the Constitution of the United States, a school debater knows that there are stock issues or questions which can be asked. These questions aid in identifying the real and critical issues in any proposition of policy. Are there signs that a significant problem exists? What causes the problem? Will the proposition being advanced solve the problem? Do the advantages of the proposal or proposed plan outweigh the possible disadvantages?

Aristotle also recognizes the involvement of the audience in the reasoning process of the persuader. Audiences do not merely coldly calculate the weight of evidence. Nor do they add up formally valid arguments. Instead audiences read their own experiences into the logical proofs advanced. Aristotle distinguished between the formulary syllogism of logic (all men are mortal; Socrates is a man; therefore, Socrates is mortal) and the rhetorical mode of logical proof which he called the enthymeme. Enthymematic reasoning entails audience involvement. The persuader may, for example, assert a generalization (redheads are hot-tempered) and expect that audience members will accept or reject according to evidence from their previous personal experience. Thus, audience analysis is crucial to the persuader in developing logical appeals.

The second mode of persuasion Aristotle identifies is emotional proofs. Aristotle's treatment of this mode consists in cataloguing and describing opposing human emotions such as mildness and anger, love and hate, confidence and fear, shamelessness and shame, pity and indignation, emulation and contempt, and benevolence and envy and their opposites. The task of the orator is to associate appropriately one or more of these compelling forces with the thesis or proposal. Like Plato, Aristotle attaches great importance to knowing one's audience. To that end *The Rhetoric* further characterizes persons of youth, age, and middle years, emphasizing that the persuader must approach different age groups with different sorts of emotional appeals.

A final mode of persuasion has to do with the personal appeal of the speaker. Aristotle asserts what many modern experiments have confirmed that quite apart from message there is persuasive appeal in the intelligence, character, and good will of the orator. That is to say, if the audience perceives the speaker to be a person who has keen intelligence, admirable character, and the best interest of the audience at heart, then that speaker is more likely to be a successful persuader than an orator having opposite qualities. One may view this mode of persuasion as requiring, as did the ancients, that the ideal orator is a good man speaking well, or, as do some contemporaries, that the ideal orator is the good image maker. In either event audience response is determined by source credibility, a dimension of persuasion we will explore more fully in connection with key variables in sources and receivers.

Viewing broadly the contribution of classical rhetorical theory to our contemporary conception of a theory of persuasion, we note the major divisions of rhetorical principle or canons of rhetoric: invention, arrangement, style, delivery, and memory. Invention has primarily to do with the analysis of the rhetorical situation or the means of preparing for persuasion. Invention is the process of selecting appropriate forms of support and establishing appropriate and artistically-conceived logical, emotional, and ethical modes of proof for persuasion. Arrangement has to do with the ordering of a persuasive message. Essentially the ancients advise dividing a speech into an introduction, an initial summary and narration of facts, proofs and refutation, and a conclusion. Style has to do with the speaker's selection of words, the arrangement of words into sentences and paragraphs, and the rhythm of the linguistic elements. Aristotle's criteria for good speech style are clarity, impressiveness, and appropriateness to the situation. The fourth principle, delivery, deals with the use of voice and body in presenting the message. Finally, memory has to do with the ways and means of remembering the major concepts and ideas of the message. It is interesting to note in passing that the ancients taught the use of mnemonic or associational devices to aid the memory in much the same fashion as many contemporary systems. What beginning student of music has not used the associational devices "FACE" and "Every Good Boy Deserves Fudge" to memorize the spaces and lines of the treble clef?

Finally, the ancients distinguished among the ends to which persuasive speech is addressed — legislative, judicial, and ceremonial or occasional. Legislative speaking is concerned with the formulation of policy to guide future action. Thus the arguments appropriate to such a purpose deal with the expediency or the harm of a proposed course of action. Judicial oratory is concerned with past action, and the arguments appropriate to this purpose deal with the justice or injustice of some action. Occasional speaking is concerned with assigning praise or blame and deals with the present; the arguments appropriate to this purpose deal with honor or dishonor, praise or blame. This type of division implies two important principles for persuasive communication. First, it is essential that the persuader clearly define the purpose or end to be sought in addressing a given audience. Second, clear definition of purpose enables the persuader to select and focus discourse upon those kinds or types of arguments that are most suitable to the task at hand.

Our contemporary theory of persuasion flows from a wedding in this century of classical rhetorical theory with modern psychological theory. Of particular importance in this connection was the appearance in 1915 of James A. Winans' *Public Speaking* which followed the classical canons of rhetoric, excepting memory, but incorporated the psychological teachings of E.B. Titchener, W.B. Pillsbury, E.L. Thorndike, and especially Harvard University's William James. It was James who asserted that "what holds attention determines action," and it was Winans who embodied this notion in

his very definition of persuasion: "Persuasion is the process of inducing others to give fair, favorable, or undivided attention to propositions" (Winans, 1917, pp. 191, 194). The utilization of empirical-experimental methodology has made possible the testing of a wide range of hypotheses relating to psychology, communication, and persuasion. Of particular note along these lines are the pioneer studies directed by Carl Hovland at Yale University and reported in *Communication and Persuasion* by Hovland, Janis, and Kelley (1953). Many of the specific generalizations and recommendations which are included in this chapter are based on the composite findings of Hovland and the many others who have followed similar research procedures.

Rationalistic Approach to Persuasion

A first basic approach to persuasive communication we label the rationalistic approach. This approach entails the identification, evaluation, and presentation of reasonable proofs for the persuader's thesis or proposition. You will recall that logical appeals constituted one of the classical modes of persuasion. Modern theorists often refer to this mode as argumentation. Ziegelmueller and Dause define argumentation as "the study of the logical principles which underlie the examination and presentation of persuasive claims" (Ziegelmueller and Dause, 1975, p. 4). Thus, argumentation is a critical as well as a persuasive tool. We can use argumentative principles to weigh the adequacy of logical appeals that are presented to us as well as to weigh the adequacy of logical appeals that we wish to advance to others.

Let us note, however, that there are limitations on our efforts to be reasonable, to think and act rationally. For one thing, truth, justice, and wisdom are elusive absolutes. We alluded in discussing historical approaches to persuasion to the conflict between the rationalism of Plato and the skepticism or philosophical relativism of the sophists. "The disagreement between Plato and the sophists over rhetoric was not simply an historical contingency, but reflects a fundamental cleavage between two irreconcilable ways of viewing the world. There have always been those, especially among philosophers and religious thinkers, who have emphasized goals and absolute standards and have talked much about truth, while there have been as many others to whom these concepts seem shadowy or imaginary and who find the only certain reality in the process of life and the present moment" (Kennedy, 1963, p. 15). Even the religious person is inclined to confess, "Now I see through a glass darkly; only then, face to face." The scientist comes close perhaps to assurance that he or she has a command of truth. We say, "He is dealing with natural law." Yet, in the realm of human affairs what is true, just, and wise is highly complex and very often open to doubt and question. In spite of our care in deliberation we still sometimes convict the innocent, pass harmful legislation, and reach poor personal decisions. The persuader does not deal generally with certainty but rather with varying degrees of probability.

The notion of probability is widely attributed to Corax and Tisias of Syracuse (5th Century, B.C.). Aristotle cites in *The Rhetoric* the classic example of argument from probability taken from Corax: If a weak man is charged with violent assault, the defense is that it is not probable that a weakling would attack a stronger man. On the other hand, if a strong man stands accused of assault on a weaker man, his defense is that it is not probable that he would do so knowing that people would surely think he *was* likely to do it. Aristotle adds that the first argument is genuinely probable whereas the second is not genuine but spurious. The second argument illustrates what is meant by making the worse argument seem the better (Aristotle, 1954, p. 160).

Moreover, faculty psychology (attribution of human acts to separate and distinct human faculties, such as intellect, emotion, and imagination) is long out of style. A contemporary view of the human nervous system is that higher cerebral functions are inseparably intertwined with the lower thalamic functions. An act of pure reason is meaningless.

Yet humans clearly have rational capacity, and this capacity is central to a definition of human kind. Humans can manipulate symbols and hence language. Language enables us to learn from the past, deal with the present well beyond an instinctual level, and project into the future. Language enables us to extend our experience beyond that which we personally and physically contact.

Moreover, our society generally demands rational action of us. As Crane Brinton puts it, "We are in the West still children of the Enlightenment" (1958, p. 213). We conceive of a rationally-ordered universe and within it "a rational science of the mind, of society, of business, of government, of ethics, and of international relations" (Randall, 1940, p. 255). Finally, McBurney and Mills observe, "The study and practice of argumentation...involves four basic assumptions which merit careful consideration." These assumptions are (1) propositions can be proved, (2) truth, justice, and wisdom are more powerful than their opposites, (3) rational decisions are to be preferred, and (4) emotional reactions are more easily enlisted in intellectually defensible causes (1964, p. 14).

Components of Logical Discourse

What, then, are the components of logical discourse? Logical proof consists of evidence and reasoning or argument. We begin with a disussion of evidence. Evidence constitutes the basis for argument. Evidence consists of facts, opinions, and material things. Evidence provides logical discourse with its vital connection with reality. General semanticists remind us that "the map is not the territory," that words are not things. That is to say, words, like maps, are abstractions of the real world. We must be sure that our discourse adequately reflects reality by being soundly based on valid evidence. We may assert anything that we wish or wish anything we assert, but it is through evidence that we are assured and may assure others of the soundness of our assertions. We may assert that the moon is made of green cheese, but it is the material evidence that United States astronauts have provided in the form of moon rocks that assure us that the moon is not made of green cheese. We may assert that unemployment is increasing or decreasing, but it is the factual information provided by the Bureau of Labor Statistics (assuming it is accurate) that bears us out or not. We may assert that coal gassification, atomic power plants, or Alaskan oil best promises to meet America's future energy needs, but it is the expert opinion of authorities in the field that we properly turn to for guidance.

Argument or reasoning is the second component of logical proof. Argument or reasoning consists basically of our interpretation of evidence. Reasoning takes two general forms: inductive and deductive. Inductive arguments draw conclusions directly from evidence. For example, if we know from factual or opinion evidence that six out of every ten Americans sampled feel that the President is doing a good job, we might infer that probably sixty percent of all Americans feel the same way. Deductive arguments, on the other hand, draw conclusions from other conclusions (often called premises) which in turn have been arrived at inductively. For example, if we accept the conclusion (premise) that "the best students get the best jobs," and if we accept the conclusion (premise) that "our university's students are the best students," then we can infer or reason deductively that "our university's students will probably get the best jobs." Both premises in this example of deductive reasoning theoretically could be arrived at by the inductive reasoning process. In this sense all argumentative conclusions can ultimately be inductively derived. In this sense, as we observed above, evidence constitutes the basis for argument.

Propositions

Argumentative discourse centers upon propositions which may be of three sorts: (1) propositions of fact, (2) propositions of value, and (3) propositions of policy. An example of a proposition of fact (that continues to be debated after more than a decade and a half and two official investigations) is that "Lee Harvey Oswald killed President Kennedy." That "a woman's place is in the home" is a proposition of value. That "the state of X should legalize no-fault automobile insurance" is a proposition of policy. Although propositions of value may entail debate over subpropositions of fact and propositions of policy may entail debate over subpropositions of fact and value, the main proposition which a speaker advances constitutes the ultimate conclusion the speaker wishes hearers to accept.

Issues

How, then, are propositions to be supported? What are the important subordinate arguments to be addressed? Issues serve as the crucial points in the analysis of propositions. The problem, then, is to discover the issues that are crucial to a particular proposition. One way of discovering or identifying these issues is through definitions. Take a proposition of fact, for example. The prosecution in a felony case at court is generally seeking to establish a proposition of fact, namely, that the defendant committed an act which is felonious under the laws pertaining to the jurisdiction. Such laws define various felonious acts, and it is the task of the prosecutor to show that the defendant's act meets the law's definition in all contested points. The issues in a proposition of value such as the illustration we gave above are more difficult to pin down. Obviously, the word "place" is the critical term; but legal definitions may not apply, dictionary definitions are themselves open to dispute, and subordinate questions of fact make the debate more complex.

So-called stock issues afford a tool for identifying the crucial, real issues in a proposition of policy. Presuming that it is logical to carry out a particular course of action only if there is sufficient need or advantage to act and a viable plan of action can be demonstrated, then need, plan, and advantages become crucial areas for analysis. Lee Hultzen (Bryant, 1958, pp. 109-110) capsulizes stock issues in the words "ill," "blame," "cure," and "cost." With any proposition of policy we are advised to ask first, "Is there an ill, a harmful situation, in the present state of affairs?" Next, "Who or what is to blame for this harmful situation? What is the cause of the ill or harm?" Next, "Will the proposal remedy or cure this ill? Will the course of action recommended affect the cause of the problem in such a way as to eliminate its harmful effects?" And finally, "Will the cure cost too much? Will the remedy be worse than the disease? Will the advantages outweight the disadvantages?"

Kinds and Tests of Evidence

Of the types of evidence identified above, facts and authority opinions are those most frequently found in persuasive communication. We will identify in the form of questions, first, some tests of factual evidence. (1) Is the evidence *relevant*? This test seems so self-evident as to be unworthy of mention. However, several years ago on a television commercial a leading nasal decongestant was deemed effective because it could be smelled through a wad of cotton, while a competing brand could not be detected in such a way. The evidence in that instance might have supported a claim for stronger odor, but hardly for shrinking swollen membranes of the nose. (2) Is the evidence *recent*? Nothing is as out-of-date as yesterday's newspaper, and dated evidence can lead us to poor conclusions in a changing situation. (3) Is the evidence internally consistent? That is, are there internal inconsistencies in the evidence? (4) Is the evidence in question consistent with other known evidence? (5) Is the evidence *sufficent*? A single case in point may be an excellent form of support for a generalization that is being advanced in making the generalization more concrete and vivid, but a single case in point is insufficient to support a generalization logically. (6) Is the evidence *verifiable*? How many myths have been perpetuated because neither sender nor receiver troubled to substantiate the authenticity of an alleged fact? Finally, we should remember that we are discussing facts as evidence in relation to an audience. The perception of audience members as to what is fact and what is not is crucial to the persuader in establishing a basis for inference, interpretation, or argument. "From the standpoint of argumentation, we are confronted with a fact only if we can postulate uncontroverted, universal agreement with respect to it" (Perelman and Olbrects-Tyteca, 1969, p. 67). At the same time, participation of audience members is frequently useful to the persuader in marshalling facts to support argumentative claims.

> Although the arguer should provide enough examples and realize the mistake of inadequate support, the other side of that coin needs to be remembered. The tedious repetition of examples for audiences who already know them can be injurious to the effectiveness of an argument. Therefore, arguers should remind listeners of what they already know and use that information as much as possible (Rieke and Sillars, 1975, pp. 104-105).

Statistical evidence affords the persuader a concise, convenient means of communicating a quantity or aggregate of individual facts or data. A happy compromise exists between presenting a single, concrete, and vivid example to support a generalization and presenting enough cases in point to demonstrate the generalization logically. That compromise is to present a single, typical case in point and statistical evidence to support the typicality of the case in point. Thus, we should also identify some tests of statistical evidence. The tests of relevancy, recency, internal consistency, external consistency, sufficiency, and verifiability apply here as well as to other forms of factual evidence. In addition, we should ask these questions: (1) Is the survey *method appropriate* to assure representativeness or typicality? One of the debacles of survey research was the Presidential poll of the now defunct *Literary Digest* in 1936. The *Literary Digest* projected Alf Landon to win over Franklin Roosevelt, whereas Roosevelt in fact lost only two states and won by a popular margin of 27,750,000 to 16,680,000. Clearly the *Literary Digest* did not contact the right people. Methods, such as those developed by the Survey Research Center of the University of Michigan for the 1952 Presidential campaign, control for the randomness, representativeness, and sufficiency of survey sampling. Unless such controls are present in the survey, results may well be questioned. (2) Is the statistical reporting properly *qualified*? A statistical expression of the average income of Americans or the annual incidence of home accidents in Wyoming may seem straightforward enough despite important ambiguities. Average income may be expressed in terms of mean (total divided by number), median (middle number in the range), or mode (number of greatest incidence). Incidence of home accidents may reflect only those requiring hospital treatment or those accidents occuring in the kitchen. (3) Are statistical comparisons based on *comparable data*?

Finally, we will identify in the form of questions some tests of authority opinions: (1) Is the authority *really an expert* on the questions under discussion? Is the authority in a position to know the facts relating to the topic? (2) Is the authority *physically, mentally,* and *morally qualified?* (3) Is the authority's testimony *internally consistent?* (4) Do other *experts agree* with the authority's testimony? Is there substantial agreement among the experts? (5) Is the testimony of the authority *consistent with other known facts?* (6) Is the authority an expert in the mind of the audience? Does the audience regard the authority as a credible source?

Kinds and Tests of Argument

Perhaps the most basic form of argument or logical inference is *reasoning from example.* This inductive form we call generalizing and the resulting conclusion, a generalization. In generalizing we draw a general conclusion about a class or population of things on the basis of evidence known about a representative sample of the class or population. The television networks which on election eve project winners on the basis of three or four percent of the votes already counted are reasoning from example. So was the *Literary Digest* in its 1936 predictions of a Landon Presidential victory over Franklin Roosevelt. Given the potential for fallibility in the process of generalizing, we should test such inferences with the following questions: (1) Are the examples *typical* of the whole class or population? The networks carefully select sample precincts for their projections to meet this test. The *Literary Digest* picked its telephone sample from names in telephone directories and other published lists. During the depression of the thirties there were apparently a good many voters who went Democratic who did not own telephones or appear on organization lists. (2) Have a *sufficient* number of examples been examined to warrant generalization? A failure to consider a large enough sample of the general population of things is a fallacy generally known as a hasty generalization. (3) Can contrary or conflicting examples be explained as atypical or unrepresentative? The incidence of unexplained contrary instances proportionately reduces the probability of the soundness of the generalization.

A second form of inductive argument is *reasoning from analogy.* An analogy is an extended metaphor in the sense that both metaphor and analogy are based on a comparison. Reasoning from analogy is based on the assumption that if two things, persons, or situations are alike in some known respects, then they are probably alike in some particular respect known about the one and not known about the other. "It worked for you; it'll work for me" is a popular expression of this form of argument. For example, "your low carbohydrate diet helped you lose twenty pounds; I think I'll lose too with a low carbohydrate diet."

Again we should test such inferences. (1) Are the two things being compared *alike in all essential aspects*? Successful and potential dieters may have brown eyes and love of the Beatles in common, but comparable eating habits, metabolism, hormonal balance, and the like are more critical points of comparison in dieting. (2) Are *differences* accounted for as nonessential or insubstantial? (3) Do *multiple* analogies lead to the same conclusion? We should distinguish at this point between the literal analogy and the figurative analogy. We have been discussing the literal analogy. A figurative analogy compares two different classes of things instead of two things of the same class. Comparison of the "seasons" of human life to the seasons of the year would be an example of a figurative analogy. Such comparisons unquestionably vivify discourse. We do not discourage their use, but we do point out that the figurative analogy is not a sound form of logical argument.

A first form of deductive argument is *reasoning from sign*. A sign is an indicator. The existence or absence of a sign suggests the existence or absence of a fact, condition, or quality that is not immediately apparent. For example, a freezing temperature registered on the thermometer indicates that there is likely to be ice on the pond and freezing road conditions. Such a relationship is natural and, therefore, reciprocal. That is to say, we may reason from seeing the thermometer that there is likely to be ice on the pond, and we may similarly reason from seeing ice on the pond that the thermometer will likely read a freezing temperature. Likewise, an American Automobile Association recommendation indicates that the restaurant receiving that recommendation is likely to serve good food. However, this relationship is conventional rather than natural, and, therefore, not reciprocal. A restaurant not bearing the AAA emblem may still serve good food; good food in a restaurant does not necessarily indicate that the establishment is AAA recommended.

Sign arguments are frequently used in persuasion to show the existence or absence of problems in a policy dispute. Should steps be taken to curb inflation or deflation, overheating or recession of the economy? Economists, businessmen, politicians, and others look to signs such as interest rates, employment figures, and indices of industrial output. Or to refer back to the Hultzen stock issues, sign arguments are frequently useful in demonstrating or disproving "ills" in a situation.

What tests can be applied to sign reasoning? (1) Is the sign relationship between substance and attribute *clearly established*? (2) Is the sign relationship *natural* or *conventional, reciprocal* or *not reciprocal*? Does the correlation exist necessarily, generally, or occasionally? (3) If the correlation exists generally but not always or only occasionally, are there *multiple* signs which lead to the same conclusion? Are contradictory signs taken into consideration?

A final and deductive form of argument is *reasoning from cause to effect* or causal argument. A cause is that which produces an effect, result, or consequence. In persuasive communication causal arguments are those which seek to link a particular cause and effect by demonstrating a general causal correlation. If, for example, we reason that X, a heavy smoker (cause), is more likely to contract lung cancer (effect) than nonsmokers, we do so on the basis of a general causal correlation between heavy smoking and lung cancer. That is to say, in everyday rhetorical discourse we might find the argument stated merely: "X runs a high risk of lung cancer because X smokes heavily." The general causal correlation in this example is unstated but assumed. A general causal correlation underlies all causal arguments whether the generalization is stated or not. Cast in a syllogistic mold the argument would be stated:

(general causal correlation)	Heavy smokers are more likely than nonsmokers to contract lung cancer, and
(specific cause)	X is a heavy smoker; therefore,
(specific effect)	X is more likely than nonsmokers to contract lung cancer.

Causal arguments are frequently used in persuasion to show the cause of problems in an existing policy or to project the future effects of adopting a new policy or course of action. To refer once again to the Hultzen stock issues, causal arguments are frequently useful in demonstrating or disproving "blames" or "costs" in a situation.

What tests can be applied to causal reasoning? We should examine the general causal correlation and ask (1) Are cause and effect *directly* and *closely related*? Crime may be linked to the evil instincts of humankind, pollution and overpopulation to ignorance, but these are distant and very general causes. The strength of causal argument lies in the closeness of cause and effect relationships. (2) Are there *multiple causes* which produce a given effect? Water pollution in a river, for example, may be produced by a combination of many causes. To control that pollution it is important to isolate the main cause or the major causes, to distinguish these from minor or insignificant causes. (3) Are there *multiple effects* produced by a given cause? In a complex situation where multiple effects are produced by a single cause, some effects may be beneficial while others are harmful. The sun's rays produce energy, warmth, and light as well as sunburn and sometimes blindness. People use guns for sustenance, protection, and sport, while guns are also involved in accidents and criminal acts. Gun control legislation, therefore, has advantages and disadvantages correlative to the beneficial and harmful effects of private ownership of guns. Major and minor effects should be assessed and with them associated values.

This last test is particularly useful in weighing or addressing the "costs" issue in a proposition of policy, the advantages and disadvantages.

Psychological Approach to Persuasion

A second basic approach to consideration of persuasive communication we label the psychological approach. The psychological approach entails the identification, evaluation, and presentation of motives for human action such as attitudes, beliefs, needs, and values. You will recall that emotional appeals constituted one of the classical modes of persuasion. Among the key variables in any persuasive situation which we discuss in this section are those which represent some modern conceptions of motives for human behavior and hence psychological bases for persuasive appeal. The psychological approach to persuasion emphasizes the cause and effect relationship between message (stimulus or cause) and listener reaction (response or effect). Notice the dominance of these themes in the following definition of persuasion: "Persuasion is conceived as that body of effects in receivers, relevant and instrumental to source-desired goals, brought about by a process in which messages have been a major determinant of these effects" (Fotheringham, 1966, p. 7).

We do not suggest by distinguishing the psychological approach from the rationalistic approach that the two approaches are discrete and mutually exclusive. Indeed many scholars include logical or rational appeals among the several types of appeals which may move listeners. Such appeals may be viewed as meeting a basic human need for cognitive consistency. The dominant theme in the rationalistic approach to persuasion is to insure logical adequacy, to offer sound reasons for belief and action. The dominant theme in the psychological approach is to insure that results or effects intended by the persuader are brought about by selecting the motive appeals most appropriate to a given audience.

Thus, identification and analysis of key variables in any persuasive situation is central to message preparation in the psychological aproach. Out of this analysis come decisions by the persuader for the best persuasive strategy, the best sorts of appeals, the most appropriate forms of organization and support, and the most suitable verbal and nonverbal style. We outline next these key variables.

Key Variables in Sources and Receivers

Attitudes. Attitudes are learned predispositions to respond in a certain way to certain objects, persons, or situations. Attitudes exist in

the minds of sources and receivers alike, and they tend to motivate our behavior and response. Attitudes are of importance to persuasive communication in that they motivate sources in their intention to influence others. In turn, receiver attitudes function to shape perception, acceptance, or rejection of persuasive messages. Indeed some scholars define persuasion in terms of attitude and attitude change. Simons, for example, defines persuasion as "human communication designed to influence others by modifying their beliefs, values, and attitudes" (1976, p. 21).

Attitudes held by individuals can be inferred by their expressions of opinion or other behavior. The Gallup Poll is a familiar means of periodically sampling American public opinion or attitudes about various current issues. When the Gallup Poll asks, "Do you approve or disapprove of the way the President is handling his job as president?" the response is an indicator of current American attitudes toward the President.

Attitudes may be thought of as having direction, intensity, and salience. The direction of an attitude refers to the positive, neutral, or negative feelings we hold toward an attitude object. If the Equal Rights Amendment is the attitude object, then the attitude dimension of direction might be expressed as pro-ERA, anti-ERA, or undecided as to the ERA. The intensity of an attitude refers to the degree of feeling we hold toward an attitude object. The attitude dimension of intensity might be expressed as very strongly pro-ERA, mildly pro-ERA, or neutral as to the ERA. The salience of an attitude refers to the degree of importance to our lives we attach to an attitude object. The distinction between intensity and salience in this example lies in the possibility that two people might be equally supportive of the ERA while one feels more strongly than the other that the ERA will make a real difference in that person's opportunities.

Although the aim of persuasion is to produce attitudinal and thereby behavioral change, sources may find receivers resistant to change. Part of the explanation for such resistance may lie in the factors just discussed. If there is great discrepancy, for example, between source and receiver attitude toward an attitude object, we can expect the receiver to be less apt to accept the receiver's viewpoint. Also, the persuader should recognize that attitudes generally do not function in isolation in motivating behavior. A given behavior is the product of interrelated attitudes and a situational context. For example, an individual may assent that donating blood to the Red Cross is a good thing but not actually do so for fear of pain, because of illness, or in light of inconvenience. The same individual might on another occasion donate blood because a loved one is in need of it.

Beliefs and values are closely related to if not subsets or components of attitudes. Beliefs, on the one hand, can be measured on a probability dimension. Martin Fishbein (1967, p. 183) has constructed a set of scales designed to measure belief. This instrument uses a seven-point scale between dichotomous adjectives such as true and false, possible and impossible, and probable and improbable to measure intensities of belief or disbelief in propositions of fact. Examples of beliefs that might be measured in this way are: "The Vikings discovered North America before Christopher Columbus" (past fact), "The United States faces an energy crisis" (present fact), and "Greater emphasis on preventive medicine will reduce the cost of health care" (future fact).

Values, on the other hand, can be measured on an evaluative dimension. Values are held in varying degrees of goodness or badness, shouldness or oughtness, and the like. Examples of value propositions are: "Individual benefits take precedence over community benefits," "Democracy is the best form of government," and "Saving is a virtue."

Attention. Attention theory concerns itself with how and why we attend to particular stimuli at a given time. The importance of attention to persuasion is obvious in that communication itself cannot take place unless sender and receiver are mutually attending to one another. Recognizing this fact Alan Monroe in recommending a psychological basis for speech organization incorporates an attention step as a first step in his widely taught "Motivated Sequence" (Ehninger, Monroe, and Gronbeck, 1978). We previously noted that William James asserted "What holds attention determines action," and that James Winans embodied this notion in his definition of persuasion: "Persuasion is the process of inducing others to give fair, favorable, or undivided attention to propositions" (Winans, 1917, pp. 191, 194).

Minnick defines attention as "...the process of selecting a particular stimulus of the many available in one's perceptual field and clearing one's sensory channels of competing information so that the selected stimulus is passed with minimal interference into the central nervous system" (1968, p. 53). Note that this definition describes attention as a process, something that is dynamic and variable. Viewed from the standpoint of a persuasive situation this definition implies that the persuader and his or her message are but two stimuli to which receivers can potentially attend. Sender and message are thus in a very real sense competing for the focus of audience attention, and audience attention having been gained the persuader must take steps to assure audience attention is maintained.

In seeking to gain and maintain audience attention persuaders must first consider needs and values of audience members. "Because a person's needs and values tend to focus attention upon stimuli related to those needs, a speaker can command attention if he connects his material with the motives and goals of his audience. Generally, the more urgent a need is the more sharply it restricts and focuses the attention" (Minnick, 1968, p. 64).

The persuader should next consider that there are factors that when present in stimuli involuntarily attract attention. These factors are intensity, contrast, novelty, movement and change, and repetition. The persuasive speaker should assess how these factors can be incorporated into both the delivery and the content of a message. For example, the speaker who moves and gestures appropriately is more likely than the stationary speaker to maintain attention. A novel anecdote, a striking statement, or a vivid example is likely to be an attention getting introduction.

Meaning. Meaning is often thought of as a constant or fixed commodity. To think that words mean what the dictionary says they mean, however, is a misconception of the nature and use of language. This misconception leads us to believe that by uttering certain words we can directly and completely transmit ideas from our mind to the mind of another person. To the contrary, S.I. Hayakawa reminds us, "The meanings of words are NOT in the words; they are in US" (1978, p. 280). That is to say, it is people who associate meanings with word symbols, and those meanings vary with the individual. At best we can hope through language to stir up meanings in others that approximate our own meanings as closely as possible.

Language is one means by which we convey meaning. Language has two dimensions of meaning that are commonly referred to as denotative and connotative. Denotative meaning derives from our understandings of the relationship between symbols and things to which symbols refer. Denotation has to do with the naming function of language. In English the word symbol "horse" stands for or names a thing or a group of things in the real world. The word "cheval" denotes the same thing in French as the word "horse" does in English, but "cheval" has no denotative meaning for us unless we understand this conventional relationship used by the French.

Connotative meanings derive from emotional associations we attach to words. The denotative meaning of the word "rabbit" is neutral, but the overlying connotations of "rabbit" may be positive or negative for different individuals. An enraged garden owner plagued by rabbits which elude his fence and pillage his lettuce may relish the thought of picking off one of those pests with a 22. On the other hand, a child with a pet rabbit, "Thumper," enamored of the Easter bunny and Joel Chandler Harris's Br'er Rabbit might be revolted at the thought of rabbit as a source of protein. Advertisers, as we know, are masters of connotation in selecting words to associate with products.

Meaning is also conveyed nonverbally. Without elaborating this mode of communication which is the subject of another chapter, suffice it to underscore here that meanings attached to nonverbal cues vary from individual to individual and from culture to culture. The finger signal formed by making a "V" of the upraised index and middle fingers may mean "victory" for a veteran of World War II, "peace" for a flower child of the Vietnam war era, and "two" for most Americans. However, a Frenchman may take this sign to mean "three" in that

French finger counting begins with the thumb signing "one," the thumb and index finger signing "two," and each of these plus the middle finger signing "three."

Ethos. Ethos or source credibility has to do with the personal appeal of the persuader. Andersen defines ethos as "the image of the source held in the mind of the receiver(s). Fully operationalized, ethos is the total of the receiver's(s') responses to all possible questions about the source" (1971, p. 218). We have noted that ethos is one of the three classical modes of persuasion and that quite apart from message there is persuasive appeal that derives from our positive or negative image of a source. We are more apt to believe a highly credible source than one with low credibility.

Andersen calls our attention to three distinctions implied by this definition. First, "ethos is determined by receivers" (1971, p. 218). In contrast to the classical view that ethos resides in the character, intelligence, and good will of the speaker, the contemporary notion is that source credibility is a function of the audience's image of the source. This discrepancy in viewpoint does not imply that source characteristics and audience image of them are necessarily unrelated but rather recognizes that two individuals may differ in their perception of a given source and that a single individual may change his or her perception of a given source.

Second, "ethos may change over time" (1971, p. 218). We may have a negative image of a source prior to a communication event but change to a positive image as a result of hearing what the source has to say, and, of course, the reverse may also be the case.

Third, "ethos is measured at different points in time as related to a given communication act" (1971, p. 218). Thus, persuaders can estimate their credibility prior to a communication event and plan an appropriate strategy. For example, a low credible source should take steps to enhance ethos by such means as arranging a positive endorsement, using good evidence, and attending to matters such as organization, style, delivery, and personal appearance.

By what criteria do receivers judge the credibility of sources? Analysis of semantic differential scales used to measure ethos has led various contemporary researchers to identify two to four dimensions of source credibility. Hovland, Janis, and Kelley (1953) identified expertness and trustworthiness. Berlo, Lemert, and Mertz (1966) identified safety, qualification, dynamism, and sociability. Andersen (1971) concludes that an evaluative and a dynamism dimension are the major constituents. Note the similarities between these contemporary dimensions and the Aristotelian constituents of ethos: intelligence, character, and good will.

Andersen observes, "The image that exists in advance of a given communication is based upon judgments about the source derived from 'experiences' *associated* with the source....Four categories seem of particular relevance: experiences with the source, either direct or vicarious; facts known about the source, particularly those that provide indication of referential class memberships; endorsements of the source offered by others; and immediate stimuli leading to the actual communication" (1971, p. 224).

Of intrinsic ethos Andersen continues, "Intrinsic ethos is the image of the source created during the process of message transmission. The stimuli arise from the source, the message, the occasion, the audience, and the channel" (1971, p. 227).

Needs. Needs are another source of motivation in individuals. If the persuader can successfully show that receiver needs will be met by the proposition being advocated, then receivers are more likely than not to accept and act upon the advocate's proposition. A widely accepted ordering of these needs which motivate us is that set forth by Abraham Maslow (1968).

Maslow's hierarchy of needs posits that a first order of needs which motivate behavior are *basic psychological needs* such as the need for air, water, food, etc. These needs are primary or prepotent in relation to other needs; these needs must be satisfied before other levels of need can effectively function to motivate behavior. A second order of needs Maslow calls *safety needs.* These needs have in common our requirement of a secure environment whether it be personal security, security in our home or job, or national security. A third order of needs is for *belonging.* This order recognizes that human beings are social beings and rely on primary groups such as the family and secondary groups such as work groups, church groups, and social groups to provide the individual with love, affection, and a sense of mutual support. A fourth order of needs is for esteem. These needs are for personal recognition, reputation, self-respect, and the like. At the pinnacle of the Maslow hierarchy is the need for *self-actualization.* Self-actualization refers to the need to realize one's potential. The Maslow hierarchy conveniently groups five orders of related needs while highlighting the idea that lower orders of need must be satisfied or largely satisfied before higher orders of need become effective motivating factors in behavior.

Key Variables in Messages

Organization. A popular recommendation to public speakers is to tell the audience what you are going to tell them, then tell them, and then tell them what you told them. In other words, speeches should have introductions, bodies, and conclusions. It is not unlike the classical expression of the notion of organic unity applied to speaking, namely, that every speech ought to be put together like a living creature, with a body of its own, lacking neither head nor feet, having both a middle and extremities, and arranged proportionately to each other and to the whole. Nor is this popular recommendation unlike Aristotle's observations: "A speech has two parts, you must state your case, and you must prove it." These parts are the body of the speech. "The introduction is the beginning of a speech, corresponding to the prologue in poetery and the prelude in flute-music; they are all beginnings, paving the way, as it were, for what is to follow." And finally, "The Epilogue [conclusion] has four parts. You must (1) make the audience well-disposed towards your self and ill-disposed towards your opponents, (2) magnify or minimize the leading facts, (3) excite the required state of emotion of your hearers, and (4) refresh their memories" (1954, pp. 199-218). In this section we shall discuss functions served by introductions and conclusions, alternatives for patterning the body of persuasive messages, some principles of outlining, and some reminders about the oral communication of transitions.

Introductions to messages can serve a variety of functions. (1) First and foremost the introduction should focus audience *attention* on speaker and message. Without such a focus of attention communication cannot take place. To be sure, even before the speaker begins some audiences may be inclined to attend because of the speaker's prestige or strong audience interest in the topic. In any case, the amount of attention material in the introduction should be tailored to the particular audience. Appeals to audience interests, needs, wants, desires, and values can help focus audience attention. Similarly intensity, contrast, novelty, movement and change, and repetition are elements to be incorporated into the content and delivery of the speech to gain and maintain attention. Specific techniques that draw upon these principles include the use of a familiar quotation, a startling statement, a vivid illustration, a relevant piece of humor, an item of curiosity, or striking statistics or facts. Other techniques include the use of a rhetorical question or some overt act such as a show of hands to invite audience participation and involvement. References to familiar ideas, interests, incidents, or individuals are other suggestions.

(2) The introduction should also establish *rapport* between speaker and listener. An important component of this relationship is the degree of credibility listeners ascribe to the speaker. In situations where speaker credibility is low or moderate, steps need to be taken to enhance that credibility. In a public speaking situation a glowing introduction, especially by a person respected by the group, is helpful. In any situation good organization, good evidence, good audience adaptation, good delivery, and good personal appearance are helpful. But in the introduction it is possible for the speaker to establish common ground directly with the audience and to establish his or her credentials tactfully. Take Ralph Zimmerman as an example. Ralph was a college student at Wisconsin State University—Eau Claire.

Ralph gave a speech in the Interstate Oratorical Association contest called "Mingled Blood," a speech about hemophelia, encouraging his listeners to give blood. Ralph was a hemophiliac, and this fact, as you can imagine, made all the difference in his credibility.

(3) The introduction is generally the appropriate place to set out the speaker's *purpose*, to guide audience response to the speech to follow. The exception to this recommendation is a situation in which the audience is hostile to the speaker's position, in which case a less direct method is probably appropriate. (4) The introduction may incorporate an *initial summary* or the main points to be developed in the speech. (5) The introduction may establish *background* of the subject area, showing the importance or significance of the topic. (6) The introduction may incorporate suitable reference to the *occasion*, other speakers, or notable members of the audience. In sum, the introduction should establish the groundwork for the message to follow, putting speaker and audience at ease with one another as much as possible.

Conclusions to messages should be direct or indirect requests for audience acceptance, commitment, or action relating to the proposition. The speaker may select one or more of a variety of techniques to accomplish this task. The message might be concluded with a final summary of main points, reinforcing the basic support for the proposition. The speaker might offer a direct challenge to the audience or indicate his or her own intentions. The speaker might conclude with a quotation or illustration embodying the concept of the proposition. The conclusion might offer some inducement to accept the proposition, or the message might be concluded with some basic and related emotional appeal. By whatever means, the conclusion should remind the audience of the response or end sought by the speaker through his or her message.

The body of the message in our view requires careful structuring. Although we will footnote this section with some evidence to the contrary, most speech communication scholars would agree that good organization is helpful to the persuader. A well organized presentation may, for example, enhance the credibility of the persuader. More basically, structuring or categorizing aids the individual in reducing the complexity of his or her environment, thus aiding in learning and recall (Bruner, Goodnow, and Austin, 1956, pp. 11-15). Therefore, we examine next some basic patterns which the speaker may select in arranging main points of the message.

A first set of patterns relates to our ways of perceiving. *Perceptual patterns* include the following: (1) *Time* sequence or chronological sequence utilizes time as an organizing principle. An outline based on time sequence might move forward or backward chronologically. The persuader seeking to establish his or her thesis as the logical extension of an historical series of events might use such a pattern. (2) *Space* sequence utilizes spacial perception as an organizing principle. We tend to place things from our vantage point in terms of left or right, near or far, up or down, and the like. This tendency is primarily a function of our visual perception. Thus, spacial patterning may be used to help audiences visualize the concept and content of the communication. (3) *Topical* sequence utilizes our inclination to group things and concepts according to their similarities.

A second set of patterns relates to the logical thought processes we discussed earlier. *Logical patterns* include the following: (4) *Inductive* sequence refers to an organizational pattern which moves from specific to general, from fact to inference, from supporting material to main points and ultimately in the conclusion to the persuader's thesis. As we have said, this pattern may be most useful in addressing a hostile audience. Cronkhite, in summarizing experimental studies on introductions and conclusions, concludes that "most audiences respond most favorably to a message in which the persuader does not state his purpose in the introduction, but rather uses that introduction to emphasize areas of agreement between himself and his audience — and then uses the conclusion to make an appeal for specific action" (1969, p. 195). (5) *Deductive* sequence refers to an organizational pattern which moves from general to specific, from inference to supporting fact, from proposition to main points to supporting material. (6) *Cause to effect* or *effect to cause* sequences parallel the form of argument after which they take their names. The same is true of the (7) *analogical* sequence.

A third set of patterns relates to the psychological approach to persuasion we are now describing. *Psychological patterns* include the following: (8) *Reflective thinking* sequence refers to the thought process John Dewey ascribes to the individual in acquiring belief or undertaking problem solving. He calls the process "active, persistent, and careful consideration of any belief in the light of the grounds that support it, and the further conclusions to which it tends" (1910, p. 6). The steps in reflective thinking include (a) perceiving a "felt difficulty," (b) locating and defining the problem, (c) suggesting possible solutions, (d) developing by reasoning the bearings of the suggestion, and (e) further observation and experiment leading to acceptance or rejection (Dewey, 1910, p. 72). Adapted to persuasive speaking the steps might be labeled (a) identifying the problem, (b) describing the problem, (c) identifying alternative solutions, (d) weighing alternative solutions, and (e) urging acceptance of and action upon the best solution. (9) Problem-solution sequence is a simplified version of the same pattern Dewey discusses. The problem-solution sequence lies at the heart of the pattern we outlined earlier in some detail, the (10) Monroe Motivated Sequence: (a) attention, (b) need, (c) satisfaction, (d) visualization, and (e) action.

Closely related to questions of sequencing and patterning are issues about primacy versus recency, climax versus anti-climax, and one-sided versus two-sided structuring of messages. Should the most important materials of the message be placed first or last, in a position of primacy or in the position that will be most recent in the recollection of the auditor? Experimental findings are divided on the question. "A fair comment is that the conclusion of a speech appears to be the position of greatest potency for retention, but that either the conclusion or the introduction is superior to the middle" (Eisenson, et al., 1963, p. 300).

Should the message move from strongest units or arguments to weakest or should a climax ordering be devised? Again experimental findings are divided as to which order produces greater attitude change and retention. "As with the primacy-recency factor, it is presently possible only to conclude that either one has merits, but that a decision on which one to use might best be made on other grounds, such as familiarity or complexity of the materials presented" (Eisenson, et al., 1963, p. 300). We would recommend that where source credibility is low or where audience interest in the topic is low that the anti-climax order be followed. Further, we would recommend the climax order for messages that have strong emotional content. All things being equal we would choose the climax order.

Should a one-sided or a two-sided message be presented? By one-sided we mean a presentation that contains only arguments favoring the proposition. By a two-sided message presentation we mean a presentation that includes arguments favoring the proposition and refutation of opposing claims. Experimental findings suggest a two-sided presentation is preferable when (1) the audience is well-educated (and presumably aware of the existence of the counterarguments), (2) the audience is likely to be exposed later to counterpropaganda, and (3) the audience is initially opposed to the speaker's proposition. Conversely, a one-sided presentation is more likely to be persuasive when (1) the audience is less-educated, (2) the audience is not likely to be exposed to counterpropaganda, and (3) the audience initially agrees with the speaker's proposition (Hovland, et al., 1949, pp. 201-27 and 1953, pp. 108-110). More recent confirmation of the effectiveness of two-sided messages comes from experiments (eg. McGuire and Papageoris, 1962) studying the effects of innoculation or forewarning. McGuire's use of the term "innoculation theory" comes from the biological concept of innoculating persons to make them resistant to disease. By analogy a two-sided message by introducing counterarguments and their refutation innoculates listeners to make them resistant to counterpersuasion.

Outlining is an important organizational step in message preparation. We offer just this brief advice about outlining. If the message outline is symbolized like this:

Introduction

Body

     I. (Main point)
        A. (Subordinate point)
           1. (Supporting material)
           2.
        B.
           1.
           2.
    II. (Main point)
        A. (Subordinate point)
           1. (Supporting material)
           2.
        B.
           1.
           2.
   III. (Main point)
        A. (Subordinate point)
           1. (Supporting material)
           2.
        B.
           1.
           2.

Conclusion

then, you should strive to maintain proper coordination, subordination, discreteness, and sequence in the outline. Main points ought to coordinate with main points, subordinate points with subordinate points. Likewise, A and B points ought to be subordinate to the I, II, and III points which they support. Individual points in the outline ought to be separate, distinct, and discrete points. Overall the outline should follow some meaningful sequence such as those identified above.

Transitions help clarify the organization of messages. Unlike written communication which offers to the reader a variety of visual cues regarding structure, oral communication requires the use of oral signposts. In writing we use paragraphing, topic sentences, headings, italics, and the like to provide structure and emphasis. None of these tools are available to the oral communicator. Instead he or she must use oral means of accomplishing the same purposes. Especially important to the task of giving structure to the oral presentation of messages is the use of oral transitions. "My first contention is...," "A main idea to keep in mind is…," and "Here is the central point…" are all examples of transitions which serve to signify that a major or the main point is about to be articulated. "Why do I say this?" and "Here are some reasons for believing that…" are examples of transitions which serve to signify that the speaker is moving from a main point to a subordinate point. "Here is an example…" and "Let's look at the facts…" are transitions that signify that the speaker is going to present supporting material. Similar oral signposts serve to guide the listeners from one coordinate point to the next. Internal summaries serve not only to reinforce points of the message by repetition but also to signify the conclusion of a unit of the message and hence transition to another unit.

Several experimental studies have asked the most basic question of all about message organization, namely, "Is organization essential to retention and persuasion?" Summarizing earlier studies Smith observes, "Evidence has been gradually accumulating to indicate that speech organization, so far as its effect on the audience is concerned, is unimportant for many if not all speeches, both for amount of information remembered and persuasive effect" (1958, pp. 106-7). Yet, he conjectures that "audiences will be unable to remember the main ideas of long speeches unless the organization and transitions are clear. Likewise, unless such relationships are clear, difficult material will not be grasped." Cronkhite, in considering these and later studies, concludes that "while the question is still open, the speaker seems well advised against random reordering the material within his speech. That conclusion will surprise only those who have read or heard of a few early studies which failed to detect differences in attitude change due to random reordering" (1969, p. 192). We strongly encourage careful attention to message arrangement.

Language. All communication is in part a process of stirring up meanings in the mind of a receiver that as closely as possible approximate those meanings in the mind of the sender. One way of communicating meaning is through the use of verbal symbols, words. The process is imperfect. By vocalizing a particular word we have no assurance of conveying a meaning that has a one-to-one correspondence between speaker and listener. Meanings are in people rather than in words. Word meanings vary from person to person— always a little, sometimes a lot. Since being understood is prerequisite to persuasion, we examine first the nature of verbal language.

What is the nature of the language? How can we use it to better assure mutual understanding? General semanticists supply some insights into these questions. (1) Language is something more than a dictionary definition. A dictionary can give us spelling, general meanings, pronunciation, and the like. But a dictionary cannot give an entirely up-to-date definition, all shades of meaning, or our interpretation of a word. People mean rather than words. Some semanticists have called it a "container myth" that words contain meaning when actually people mean. This observation suggests fundamentally that we ought to be audience oriented and centered in our selection of words and consider how audience members came to possess their word meanings. Thus, a second observation: (2) Language meanings are determined by a person's past experience, age, geographic origins, sex, and culture or sub-culture. Consider a few examples. "Dog" means "my dog" first and foremost to a dog owner. "War" means World War II to a person of draft age in 1941 and Vietnam to a person of draft age in 1968. "Bubbler" means an object from which to get a drink of water in Milwaukee and probably nothing at all to a New Englander. "Chairman" may mean sex discrimination to a libber. And "crib" may mean home for an inner city black. (3) Language is abstract. Words stand in abstract relationship to the things they represent. The language is not the thing in the same way that a map is not the territory. Particularly to assure common understanding of highly abstract words such as freedom, honor, democracy, and socialism it is useful to provide definitions, concrete examples, illustrations, synonyms, or comparisons. (4) Language tends to classify that which is unique. A word for everything would yield an infinitely complex language. Our categorizing, therefore, is essential to education and communication, but classifying is arbitrary, hides individual uniqueness determined by purpose, and focuses on one aspect, ignoring others. This tendency leads to such problems as stereotyping and can be mitigated by the use of limiting and qualifying words. (5) Language tends to ignore change. Names of people, for example, remain the same while the people themselves change. Thus, we should date and specify. (6) Language tends to dichotomize. We frequently talk of right or wrong, good and bad, rich or poor, ignoring the points along the continuum between these extremes. (7) We sometimes tend to ignore different uses of language: to express ideas, to create harmony and disharmony, to entertain, to clarify, to report reality, to command, to arouse emotion, and so on. The speaker, for example, may intend irony or satire but be taken literally by the listener. We stress again the importance of making sure as speakers that listeners understand clearly the purpose of the persuasive message.

Style is one of the classical canons of rhetoric. Style has to do with the use of language in setting out and personalizing ideas of the message. Aristotle says of style, "For it is not enough to know *what* we ought to say; we must also say it *as* we ought; much help is thus afforded towards producing the right impression of a speech" (1954, p. 164). The traditional approach to the teaching of style in rhetoric has been to set out criteria for good speech style. Brigance (1952) cites as criteria (1) clarity and accuracy and (2) good taste. Bryant and Wallace (1969) cite (1) clearness, (2) appropriateness, and (3) interest and attractiveness. Sarett and Foster (1946) cite (1) accuracy, (2) force,

(3) suggestiveness, and (4) ease. It is clear that these criteria are very similar, appropriate that the speaker should consider them, and interesting to listeners if they do.

A last word about style in the persuasive message is to encourage an oral versus a written style. Wilson and Arnold recall the observation of James A. Winans, "A speech is not an essay on its hind legs," and summarize from research and their own observations some characteristics of oral style in contrast to written style. Oral style uses: (1) more personal pronouns, (2) more variety in kinds of sentences, (3) more variety in sentence lengths, (4) more simple sentences, (5) more sentence fragments, (6) many more rhetorical questions, (7) more repetition of words, phrases, and sentences, (8) more monosyllabic than polysyllabic words, (9) more contractions, (10) more interjections, (11) more indigenous language, (12) more connotative than denotative words, (13) more euphony, (14) more figurative language, (15) more direct quotation, and (16) more familiar words" (1968, p. 393).

Nonverbal Cues. Another way of communicating meaning is through the use of nonverbal cues. Brooks (1974, pp. 176-8) in synthesizing nonverbal research identifies three principles of nonverbal communication. First, "one cannot *not* communicate." All behavior communicates meaning whether intentionally or unintentionally. Second, "nonverbal channels are especially effective in communicating feelings, attitudes, and relationships." And third, "involuntary nonverbal messages often are of high validity." This last conclusion implies that listeners have a valuable means of checking the consistency of verbal and nonverbal cues. This conclusion should assure the sincere and committed persuader and strike some fear in the charlatan.

Body language constitutes a major category of nonverbal communication. Body language includes cues provided by eyes, facial expression, gestures, gross movements of the body, and positioning of the body or posture. Paralanguage is a term to describe nonverbal but vocal cues which accompany verbal speech. Voice quality, pitch, rate, and articulation are examples. So are vocalizations such as laughing, moaning, "uh-huhing," and "ah-hahing." Object language includes all artifacts manipulated by persons which convey meaning such as clothing, eyeglasses, and cosmetics. Touching is another category which includes such actions as shaking hands in greeting or placing one's arms over another's shoulder to express sympathy, support, or friendship. Physical characteristics, such as height, weight, hair, and general attractiveness, communicate too. Finally, speakers and listeners communicate through use of space and time. For example, a speaker may move closer to his audience to reinforce an important point with the intensity of his presence. Even a pause can be meaningful. Again we call your attention to the fuller treatment of the topic of nonverbal communication in chapter three.

Key Variables in the Environment of the Persuasive Process

Persuasion takes place within a social setting. A persuasive communication event can be viewed as a temporal event, an event with a past, a present, and future implications. The individuals involved in

the process are the products of their culture. Efforts at persuasion take place in a given time and place, and a person's goals and expectations tend to shape that person's responses to the here and now. Since both senders and receivers in the process of persuasive communication are influenced by their culture, we begin with an attempt to define culture and describe its impact on persuasion. In turn, we will consider the types of audiences that may confront the persuader or of which the receiver may be a part, the influence of group pressure on the individual audience member, and specific audience characteristics, and finally, the elements of the immediate occasion which may have impact on persuasion.

Cultural Considerations. What is culture? The word often connotes the height of artistic accomplishment of a civilization, but it is not in this sense that we refer to culture. Culture is rather a composite or totality of the thought and behavior patterns of a definable community or population. When we speak of American, Chinese, Afro-American, or Navaho culture, we imply their familial, educational, social, political, economic, religious, artistic, and linguistic structures and characteristics.

The individual learns elements of culture by coping with the environment and interacting with the significant others on whom his or her social needs depend. Accordingly such cultural learning shapes our perception, our self-concept, our attitudes and values, and our notion of acceptable and appropriate roles and behaviors. Ultimately, and this is most significant to communication, cultural learning shapes the meanings we attach to verbal and nonverbal symbols.

Cultural difference contributes to salient "we-they" feelings which stand as barriers to communication and understanding. Any person who has attempted to communicate with another who speaks an unfamiliar language has experienced this feeling. "We-they" feelings even manifest themselves in culture simulation as Schnapper reports of Canadians preparing to go abroad as teachers and technical advisors. Such persons along with their families were grouped into units of twelve to fifteen and asked to simulate a situation where they had crash-landed in a new environment and were forced to evolve a new culture to cope with a new situation and each other. After three days of developing their own culture, each group was brought into contact with another group which had evolved a different culture to cope with a different environment. "Most participants were shocked at their own reactions. They felt, and later came to appreciate, that strong feelings of ethnocentricity could be formed in three days" (Schnapper, 1973, p. 5).

What, then, are the implications of these observations about culture for the persuasive process? First, the social perceptions and meanings of source and receiver are largely culturally determined and likely to be strongly held. Second, cultural differences create special barriers to communication which require sympathetic understanding to surmount. This implication looms larger as the world shrinks and we increasingly recognize our interdependence. Archie Bunker and Fred Sanford are not alone in frequently confronting intercultural communication situations. Finally, cultural analysis constitutes a gross form of speaker-audience analysis. Minnick observes that audience analysis means "the application of all that is known about human behavior in general to a specific audience in order to anticipate or evaluate its response to a particular persuasive communication" (Minnick, 1968, p. 253). If we become familiar with the cultural characteristics of a particular audience, we are in a position to infer some of the probable responses of that audience to a given persuasive message.

Cultural analysis is an exceptionally difficult undertaking, requiring vast knowledge and rare insight and understanding. Outstanding efforts at cultural analysis of the American experience lie in the writing of historians Frederick Jackson Turner and Charles A. Beard, the *Main Currents in American Thought* series by Vernon L. Parrington, and *The Americans* series by Daniel J. Boorstin. Studies like these are obviously a macroscopic way of viewing speakers and audiences of a particular culture, but they help us meet the high demands and comprehensive standards of the Minnick prescription for audience analysis or the Platonic stricture that the noble rhetorician must be able to discern the nature of the soul of the person he would presume to teach or persuade. In the context of an overview of intercultural communication Porter provides us with something of a framework for cultural analysis when he describes eight variables which "have the ability to influence our perceptions and to affect the meaning we assign to communicative acts." These variables are (1) attitudes, (2) social organization, (3) patterns of thought, (4) roles and role prescriptions, (5) language, (6) use and organization of space, (7) time conceptualization, and (8) nonverbal expression (Porter, 1972, p. 5).

Audience Types and Characteristics. Persuasive communication can take place in a variety of arenas. One such setting we call diadic, because two persons are involved. One college roommate urging another to go to a particular movie on Saturday would serve as an example. Another setting we call small group. An example would be one member of a family arguing for a family vacation in the mountains. Still another setting we call one-to-many or a public speaking arena. A politician pleading for votes in a shopping center is an example. Finally, a mass communication setting implies a mediated form of communication such as mass mailings, flyers, billboards, magazines, radio, or television. We find everything from soap to automobiles advertised through mass communication. All of these settings involve an audience, requiring adaptation of the persuasive message to that audience's characteristics. Let us describe, then, some types of audiences, identifying a few of the adaptations possibly made with each of them.

Hollingworth audience types help us visualize one dimension of audiences. Hollingworth describes six different types of audiences according to their degree of orientation to the speaker or their degree of attention to the speaker and interest in his proposal (Hollingworth, 1935, pp. 19-32). He labeled these six types: (1) the pedestrian audience, (2) the discussion group and passive audience, (3) the selected audience, (4) the concerted audience, (5) the organized audience, and (6) the absent audience. The pedestrian audience is one with the lowest degree of orientation toward the speaker. Hollingworth gave us an example "pedestrians on a busy street, before whom the street-corner orator sets up his box." The relationship between a freeway commuter and a billboard or the television viewer of Sunday football and a cat food commercial would be parallel, except that such individuals have little or no interaction with other viewers. The passive audience voluntarily enters into the speaker-audience relationship, but has a low degree of interest in the speaker's message. The selected audience comes together "for some common purpose of a more active sort," but individuals in such an audience have varying sympathies with one another and the speaker's view. Hollingworth cited a labor union meeting and a jury as examples. The concerted audience "assembles with a concerted, active purpose, with sympathetic interest in a mutual enterprise, but with no clear division of labor or rigid organization of authority." The organized audience has all of the characteristics of a concerted audience, except that it does have a rigid division of labor and authority. A military unit or an athletic team are examples. Finally, Hollingworth calls our attention to another use of the word "audience" to refer to absent and isolated individuals who perceive the works of writer, publisher, or artist. However, he does not dwell on this sort of audience because individuals have little opportunity to interact directly with other "audience" members or the speaker.

In considering techniques to be used by the persuader in adapting to these audience types, Hollingworth identifies five fundamental tasks: (1) to capture attention, (2) to build interest, (3) to impress the audience with significant details, (4) to convince the audience of the wisdom or desirability of the proposition, and (5) to direct the actions of the audience (1935, pp. 12-13). With the pedestrian audience it is necessary for the persuader to begin with the first of these five tasks and accomplish each in turn. With the passive audience attention has already been gained, and it remains for the speaker to carry out the remaining four tasks. The selected audience requires only that the speaker perform the last three tasks; the concerted audience demands only the last two tasks; and the organized audience needs only direction. Thus, Hollingworth schematically outlines the task demands of specified audiences (1935, p. 25).

Pedestrian Audience	Discussion and Passive Audience	Selected	Concerted	Organized
Attention	. . . .	. . . .	. . . .	. . . .
Interest	Interest	. . . .	. . . .	. . . .
Impression	Impression	Impression	. . . .	. . . .
Conviction	Conviction	Conviction	Conviction	. . . .
Direction	Direction	Direction	Direction	Direction

The *influence of group pressure* on individuals is present in audiences. The stress Hollingworth places on the importance of interaction among audience members stems from a long standing controversy over what constitutes a psychological crowd and how individuals are influenced by others in a crowd, group, or audience situation. French sociologist Gustav LeBon writes of the crowd as having a magnetic or hypnotizing influence over the individuals who compose it. To LeBon the crowd is not merely a casual gathering of people but individuals commonly attending to something of great importance to the whole group. Perhaps "mob" would be a better word, for LeBon characterizes crowd behavior as erratic, irrational, and impulsive. Persons in such a crowd lose their individuality, behave as they would not behave alone, and submit to a "crowd mind." This perspective might seem a convenient and an appealing way to explain such despicable acts as a lynch mob or a revolutionary throng might commit, but LeBon has been largely discounted in emphasizing crowd behavior as something essentially different from individual behavior.

Allport's notion of "social facilitation" is far more realistic. Allport argues that individuals in crowds respond essentially as they would as individuals — only more so. That is to say, the presence of others and the individual's awareness of their responses facilitates or heightens the individual's response. Visualize yourself at home alone watching your favorite comedian on television. The comedian tells an hilarious story. What is likely to be your response? You enjoy the story; you smile widely; you may chuckle. But now visualize yourself in the same situation except with a group of your best friends who also like this comedian. The same story is told. What are likely to be the responses this time? All smile; someone chuckles; another laughs heartily; and soon knees are being slapped and tears of laughter are in several eyes. This group reaction is social facilitation, and that is why, incidentally, mediated comedy shows use "canned" laughter or "live" audiences. The implications of the social facilitation phenomenon to persuasive communication are obvious. Individuals react not only to persuasive speakers and persuasive messages but also to the responses of others in the audience.

Hostile or believing audiences are next considered. In order to conduct research into the persuasive demands of various speaker-audience relationships, a number of audience characteristics have been identified. One important characteristic label is "hostile or believing." A hostile audience is one which holds attitudes which are at variance to one degree or another with the attitudes held by the speaker or the proposition the speaker is advancing. An advocate of legalizing abortion speaking to a "right to lifer" or a supporter of sex education in the schools addressing members of the John Birch Society represent extreme examples of a hostile speaker-audience relationship. Sherif, Sherif, and Nebergall (1965) conceive that individual attitudes toward a class of objects or positions on an issue can be placed on a continuum, so that we may measure and speak of the discrepancy between the attitudes held by a receiver and the attitudes expressed in a persuasive message.

When the individual evaluates a message as not widely discrepant from his or her own attitude, the message falls within a range or latitude of acceptance. If the message is highly discrepant, it falls beyond the range of acceptance into a range of rejection. Between or related to the ranges of acceptance and rejection Sherif, Sherif, and Nebergall speak of a latitude of noncommitment. They stress that "the probability of receiver attitude change toward an advocated position is greater when the number of feasible alternative interpretations of the topic is great, when the individual is somewhat unfamiliar and is not highly involved with the topic, and when the source and communicator have high prestige" (1965, p. 44).

The following questions underscore the relevance of audience analysis by the persuader, critic, or researcher: What are the attitudes of the receiver relating to the speaker's message? What is the degree of familiarity and involvement and, therefore, commitment that the receiver has with the topic? How objective is the structure of the object or topic? What degree of prestige, standing, or credibility does the source have with the receiver?

Homogeneous or heterogeneous audiences are labels for another audience characteristic. An homogeneous audience is one in which individuals who comprise it share a number of specific characteristics relevant to the persuasive situation, such as intelligence and age level, knowledge of and attitudes toward the topic or proposition, sex, open and closed-mindedness, and group identification. An audience which is homogeneous in nature is easier to analyze than one which is heterogeneous in nature, and the persuasive demands of the situation are more clear-cut. This is not to say that the persuader is more likely to be successful in accomplishing his or her aims with a homogeneous audience, for such an audience may be uniform in its hostility toward speaker and message. Rather, it is simpler for the speaker to identify the adaptations he or she must make to enhance persuasiveness with a particular homogeneous audience. For example, if speakers know they have low credibility or only moderate credibility with the bulk of an audience, they should use no or low-fear appeals and lots of evidence and opinions from sources that are highly credible to audience members. The more heterogeneous the audience, the more the speaker must make appeals general and abstract in order to hope for wide agreement.

Specific audience characteristics relevant to the situations mentioned above are discussed next. First, intelligence and age level need to be determined. No communicator wishes to aim over the head of listeners or, on the other hand, to insult the intelligence of listeners by seeming to talk down. Assessment of intelligence and age level can instruct the speaker on the kind of vocabulary that should be used. In general, speaking, writing, and reading or listening vocabularies are successively larger for each individual. While the range of an individual's vocabulary depends substantially upon cultural, familial, and educational background, intelligence and especially age provide a convenient index for assessment of vocabulary range and level. Age, too, may account for differences in connotative meanings assigned to given words. Just as the "peace" sign for the Vietnam generation was a "victory" sign for the World War II generation, so generational differences are manifestly apparent in the slang words of the young. Insofar as the speaker seeks to select supporting materials aimed at the first-hand and immediate experiences of the audience, listener age is important. Teachers sometimes joke (?) that their students get younger each year, and age is a concern for every speaker to keep in mind in selecting examples, illustrations, and the like.

Audience analysis should further consist in assessing the knowledge of and attitudes toward the speaker's topic or proposition. If you will recall our discussion of the Aristotelian enthymeme, you will appreciate that audience members are inclined to respond to what a speaker is saying by adding or filling in from their own experience. The speaker, for example, may merely assert a generalization and listeners affirm the generalization by recalling supporting instances they have witnessed, heard, or read about. The speaker who strives to establish common ground with his audience is seeking to capitalize on this inclination. The speaker who asks a rhetorical question, a question to which he expects a silent or covert answer, depends upon this same inclination. To anticipate correctly the ways in which receivers will add to or fill in a message, the sender must know something of their background and experience with the topic or proposition.

Frequently the persuader anticipates from analyzing audience knowledge of the topic that his listeners have little personal experience that relates to the proposition. In this kind of situation the communicator must realize that he can rely very little on audience participation in the filling-in process. Here the speaker must do the filling in. Here the speaker must create a vicarious experience for the listener. Here the persuader must offer ample concrete supporting material — definitions, real and hypothetical examples, illustrations, facts, opinions, statistics, narratives, and the like. In so doing the speaker should also strive, whenever possible, to relate his forms of support to experiences shared by sender and receiver. Metaphor, analogy, and other forms of comparison are means of establishing this relationship. For example, the words "suck," "squeeze," "pop," and "phooey" can aid the uninitiated in coming to understand the workings of the four-cycle, internal combustion engine. "Suck" — fuel and oxygen are drawn into the descending piston's open chamber; "squeeze" — the ascending piston compresses the mixture in the now closed chamber; "pop" — the spark plug ignites the explosive mixture, driving the piston downward and providing power; "phooey" — the exhaust is forced from the re-opened chamber by the re-ascending piston.

Analysis of audience attitudes related to the topic or proposition is helpful in evaluating an appropriate strategy to gain acceptance for the persuader's proposition. We have discussed above that some audiences are hostile, some are believing, and some are neutral with respect to a given proposition. Of course, these listener postures are determined through such analysis. But sender and receiver are rarely uniformly consonant, neutral, or hostile on all possible attitude scales. Nor are all attitude scales unrelated. Thus, a speaker is generally able to associate his proposition with listener needs, wants, desires, or values which are supportive of that proposition, to dissociate his proposition with those which are not supportive, or both. Gun control legislation, for example, may run contrary to the self-preservation instincts of an individual, but the same individual may value the prevention of accidental injury or death more than he fears armed robbery.

A considerable amount of experimental research has endeavored to discover whether or not there are kinds of people or types of personalities more prone to be persuaded than others. The susceptibility of an individual to persuasion, apart from the influence of proposition, source, or message, is usually called persuasibility. This research tends toward the conclusion that some persons are more persuasible than others. Specifically, authoritarian, closed-minded, or dogmatic individuals are generally more susceptible to persuasion than their opposites. Individuals who are low in self-esteem and less aggressive are inclined to be more easily persuaded than persons who are dominant, aggressive, and high in self-esteem. Women have generally been found to be more persuasible than men, and younger persons more persuasible than older persons (Cronkhite, 1969, pp. 130-39). Such information may be useful to the critic in partially explaining the response of an audience to a particular persuasive event, and it may be useful to the speaker in assessing the difficulty of the persuasive task that confronts him or her. However, viewed from the standpoint of the speaker, there is little the speaker can do to manipulate these audience variables, and it may be difficult even to identify some of them. The speaker could, of course, seek out only young audiences, avoid male audiences, and ask those with high self-esteem to leave the room; but that approach would pretty effectively limit the converts. Moreover, McGuire, like Cronkhite, cautions about overgeneralizing.

> If it is safe to make any simple generalization about personality-influencing relations, it is that no simple generalizations are valid ....There are few, if any, simple personality-influenceability relations that are valid over a wide range of conditions....Any valid theory of personality-influenceability relations must, therefore, hypothesize relations that are complex and situational-interacting or else must be of very narrow generalizability (McGuire, 1968, p. 1172).

A final observation to be made about audience members is that they tend to conform to the norms and standards of the groups to which they belong or with which they identify. Again we observe that humans are social and gregarious. Reasons for group membership or identification may range from simple interpersonal attraction to group members to conviction on the part of the individual that important goals and tasks can only be realized and carried out through group effort. Some of the factors which determine the importance the group holds for the individual are the degree of (1) interpersonal attraction, (2) coincidence of group and individual goals, (3) salience or importance to the individual of group goals, (4) dependence of the individual upon the group for rewards and satisfaction, (5) continuing individual involvement with the group, (6) status of the individual within the group, and (7) cohesiveness of the group. These factors lead to two important conclusions on the persuasive process. First, the expressed and observed attitudes and opinions of groups to which the individual belongs or with which the individual identifies provide an index to the individual's opinions and attitudes. This conclusion underscores the relevance and importance for audience analysis of assessing a listener's group associations. Second, majority opinion has great persuasive potential.

Occasion.

Having considered culture and audience elements in the environment of the persuasive process, we focus now on the element of occasion. By occasion we mean the time, place, and physical circumstances in which speaking takes place. Consider the celebration of a special event such as a birthday or a wedding. The celebration is likely to bring family, friends, or both together on a given day in a special location. There is likely to be eating, singing, dancing, and gift-giving. Symbols of the occasion abound. All of these elements conspire to focus attention on the guest or guests of honor and the event remembered; they heighten the joy of the celebration. Elements in the speaking occasion similarly can contribute to focusing listener attention on speaker and message and heighten listener response. Consider a national political nominating convention. Ultimately the purpose is to select a candidate and launch a party campaign. Outwardly, at least, the culminating event, the acceptance speech, is trapped with symbols appropriate to the purpose. All eyes and ears including those of television and radio are trained on the candidate. The time has come to join battle. The hall is decked with symbols of country, states, party, and leader. Thousands present stir to music and light. In their homes millions more are caught up by the occasion.

The relevance of time to the persuasive environment may be conceived broadly or narrowly. In a broader sense the persuader should be alert to the stage of development of audience thinking to his topic or proposition. What is the "gut" issue for the audience? For example, the world today is faced with a population explosion that severely taxes human ability to produce and supply millions with the essentials of existence. However, for some of the world's peoples, the question is not how to control population but why control it. After the 1929 stock market crash in the United States the question was not "Has economic disaster befallen us?" but rather "How do we cope with the depression?" After Pearl Harbor in 1941 the question was not "Do the Axis powers pose a threat to the U.S.?" but rather "How do we win a war against them?" On the other hand, people like Rachel Carson (Silent Spring) and Alvin Toffler (Future Shock) have primarily attempted to warn us about the existence or potential of problems, the dangers of pesticides on animal life and the threats to psychological well-being of information overload. Thus, the time may be ripe for one audience on a given topic to explore a problem, and the speaker should concentrate his energies and the direction of his analysis on that problem. On the other hand, the time may be ripe for the speaker to address another audience on possible solutions. For the speaker in the latter case to devote his attention to the needs or problems would be unnecessary at best and counterproductive at worst.

In a narrower sense there may be more immediate time considerations bearing on the persuasive situation. Some questions relevant to these time considerations are as follows: (1) How much time does the speaker have to prepare for the speech? Can certain supporting materials such as factual information or visual aids be acquired or prepared in the time available? Adjustments in the speech plan need to be made accordingly. (2) How much time does the persuader have available to present the message? Sometimes a time allotment is assigned a speaker. Program format or cost may limit the length of a radio or television statement. The platform speaker may find himself a part of a larger program and thus required to proportion his comments appropriately, to the larger purpose of the gathering. The estimated attention span of the audience will also place time limits on the speaker. A pedestrian audience, for example, is likely to have a very brief attention span unless the persuader can very quickly build interest; a concerted audience is generally more willing to attend over a longer time period. (3) how much time does the audience have to consider and act upon the speaker's proposal? Much has been written and spoken about the political candidate who started his or her campaign too soon and peaked out too early or about the one who started too late and failed to peak in time for the election. Persuaders interested in distant future action should bear in mind the frailties of the human memory.

Besides time considerations, place or the physical location of a communication event can influence source, message, and receiver. A classroom, a factory gate, a church or synagogue, the site of an historical event, a home, and a corporate board room are widely disparate environments for persuasion. The ordinarily business-suited campaigner is well-advised, if not naturally moved, to meet workers on their ground at the factory gate in shirt sleeves. The level of style, of language usage, appropriately varies with the formality or informality of the setting and reason for coming together. The listeners' mood may be inspired simply by their presence in an historic building, a magnificent auditorium, or a scenic outdoor amphitheatre.

Many of the physical circumstances of the public speaking setting can be controlled to facilitate communication. Seating, heating, lighting, ventilation, and other creature comforts are usually manipulable. Thought given to means of sound amplification, forms of decoration, and preparation of audio-visual aids may contribute greatly to the focusing of audience attention. Consideration of these physical elements should be part of the speaker's or critic's analysis of occasion and overall analysis of the persuasive environment.

In sum, this section has stressed the bearing on persuasion of culture, audience factors, and occasion. Some of the specific elements we have discussed are within the control of the persuader to manipulate; others are given to which the speaker must adapt. All of these elements should be included in the overall analysis of the environment of a particular persuasive situation. The aim of such analysis is to provide guidance in making choices or evaluating choices made in the persuasive message.

Theories Which Bind These Variables

Learning Theory. Learning theory is one approach to understanding the overall nature of the persuasive communication process. Representatives of this approach are Hovland, Janis, and Kelley who describe their perspective as follows: "We assume that opinions, like other habits, will tend to persist unless the individual undergoes some new learning experiences. Exposure to a persuasive communication which successfully induces the individual to accept a new opinion constitutes a learning experience in which a new verbal habit is acquired. That is to say, when presented with a given question, the individual now thinks of and prefers the new answer suggested by the communication to the old one held prior to exposure to the communication" (1953, pp. 10-12). They view persuasive stimuli as consisting of observable characteristics of the perceived source of communication;" "...the setting in which the person is exposed to communication, including, for example, the way in which other members of the audience respond during the presentation;" and "...content elements, referred to as 'arguments' and 'appeals'." These stimuli lead individuals "...to react with at least two distinct responses. He thinks of his own answer to the question, and also of the answer suggested by the communication." Finally, Hovland, Janis, and Kelley assume that acceptance of a new opinion "...is contingent upon *incentives*, and that in order to change an opinion it is necessary to create a greater incentive for making the new implicit response than for making the old one." The bases of acceptance, then, lie in a combination of arguments or reasons and "...other special incentives involving anticipated rewards and punishments which motivate the individual to accept or reject a given opinion...." (1953, pp. 10-12).

Perception Theory. Perception theory is another approach to understanding the nature of the persuasive communication process. "Perception," according to Minnick, "may be defined as the assigning of immediate meaning to sensory data by the central nervous system. By swiftly classifying incoming sensory data, a person is able to evaluate its relationship to his goals and to respond accordingly" (1968, pp. 34-5). The social judgment-involvement approach of Sherif, Sherif, and Nebergall is representative of perception based theories. They explain their perspective of attitude change as follows: "Stripped to its bare essential, the problem of attitude change is the problem of the degree of discrepancy from communication and the felt necessity of coping with the discrepancy. The discrepancy in question is the degree of divergence between the position advocated in a communication or message and the own position of the subject exposed to it. Of course, psychologically, the discrepancy in question is the divergence experienced or felt by the individual between the position he upholds and the position to which he is exposed" (1965,

p. 225). They further explain that "The attitude of a person represents a range of acceptances and a range of rejections for a class of objects or positions on an issue, and it may include positions toward which he is noncommittal." Based on these assumptions, Sherif, Sherif, and Nebergall predict that "If a message or communication does not fall appreciably beyond the range of acceptances, the discrepancy will be minimized in placing the communication. Hence, the communication is likely to be *assimilated* into his range of acceptances." On the other hand, "If the message falls well beyond the range of acceptances, the individual will appraise it as more discrepant than it actually is. Its position will be displaced away from his acceptable range, and the extent of the *contrast effect* will be in proportion to the divergence of the communication from his acceptable range." Also, they predict, "The greater the commitment or dedication of an individual to his stand on an issue, the greater the displacement of a discrepant message away from the bounds of his acceptance" (1965, p. 226).

Function Theory. Function theory is still another approach to understanding the nature of the persuasive communication process. Representative of this approach is Katz who discusses his persepective as "The Functional Approach to the Study of Attitudes" (1960, pp. 163-204). In Katz's view there are four functions that attitudes perform for the personality which provide a basis for motivation. The first of these he calls the adjustment function. "Essentially this function is a recognition of the fact that people strive to maximize the rewards in their external environment and to minimize the penalties." A second is the ego-defensive function. "People not only seek to make the most of their external world and what it offers, but they also expend a great deal of their energy on living with themselves. The mechanisms by which the individual protects his ego from his own unacceptable impulses and from the knowledge of threatening forces from without, and the methods by which he reduces his anxieties created by such problems, are known as the mechanisms of ego defense." The third is the value-expressive function. "While many attitudes have the function of preventing the individual from revealing himself and others his true nature, other attitudes have the function of giving positive expression to his central values and to the type of person he conceives himself to be." And the fourth is the knowledge function. "Individuals not only acquire beliefs in the interest of satisfying various specific needs, they also seek knowledge to give meaning to what would otherwise be an unorganized chaotic universe." Of attitude arousal and change Katz observes, "The most general statement upon the excitation of some need in the individual, or some relevant cure in the environment.... The most general statement that can be made about the conditions conducive to attitude change is that the expression of the old attitude or its anticipated expression no longer gives satisfaction to its related need state" (1960, pp. 163-204).

Consistency Theory. Consistency theory is a final approach to understanding the nature of persuasive communication which we shall discuss. Zajonc (1960, pp. 280-96) has summarized related concepts which subsumes under the label of consistency, namely, balance, congruity, and dissonance. "Common to the concepts of balance, congruity, and dissonance is the notion that thoughts, beliefs, attitudes, and behavior tend to organize themselves in meaningful and sensible ways." Balance theory is attributed to Heider (1946, pp. 107-112). "The consistencies in which Heider was interested were those to be found in the ways people view their relations with other people and with the environment. The analysis was limited to two persons, labeled P and O, with P as the focus of the analysis and with O representing some other person, and to one impersonal entity, which could be a physical object, an idea, an event, or the like, labeled X....Heider proposed that the person's (P's) cognitive structure representing relations among P, O, and X are either what he termed 'balanced' or 'imbalanced'....Thus a balanced state is obtained when, for instance, P likes O, P likes X, and O likes X....The fundamental assumption of balance theory is that an unbalanced state produces tension and generates forces to restore balance" (1960, pp. 280-96). Graphically balanced states can be visualized as follows:

Likewise imbalanced states which will cause P to reevaluate his or her attitude toward O or X can be visualized as follows:

  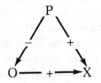

The principle of congruity, which is in fact a special case of balance, was advanced by Osgood and Tannenbaum in 1955 (1955, pp. 42-55). It deals specifically with the problem of *direction* of attitude change....the principle of congruity holds that when change in evaluation or attitude occurs it always occurs in the direction of increased congruity with the prevailing form of reference. The paradigm of congruity is that of an individual who is confronted with an assertion regarding a particular matter about which he believes and feels in a certain way, made by a person toward whom he also has some attitude....When the attitudes toward the person and the assertion are incongruent, there will be a tendency to change the attitudes toward the person and the object of the assertion in the direction of increased congruity....A further derivation of the congruity principle is that incongruity does not invariably produce attitude change, but that it may at times lead to incredulity on the part of the individual....Osgood and Tannenbaum have formulated the principle of congruity in quantitative terms allowing for precise predictions regarding the extent and direction of attitude change in predictions which in their studies were fairly well confirmed" (1960, pp. 280-96).

Festinger's (1957) theory of cognitive dissonance has been summarized by Cronkhite (1969) as well as Zajonc (1960).

> Festinger points out that it is possible for "cognitions" (by which he apparently means anything which can be known, including beliefs and attitudes) to be irrelevant, consonant, or dissonant relations to one another.... He then lists a number of situations which, as he puts it, "imply dissonance." The first of these is the situation in which a choice has been made between two or more alternatives.... Typically, an individual who has made an irrevocable choice will reduce dissonance by seeking evidence that his choice was the correct one, by maximizing the advantages and minimizing the disadvantages of the chosen alternative.... A second situation which "implies dissonance" might really be considered a subcategory of the first: 'Dissonance almost always exists after an attempt has been made, by offering rewards or threatening punishment, to elicit behavior that is at variance with private opinion."... If the individual performs the behavior, he will seek to reduce dissonance by minimizing the importance of the belief, changing the belief, and by maximizing his perception of the threatened punishment or offered reward. If he does not perform the behavior, he will reduce dissonance by minimizing his perception of the lost reward or the impending punishment.... A third situation which Festinger lists as dissonance is that in which an individual is exposed to information which contradicts beliefs he holds.... Actually, this third type of dissonant situation probably can be most profitably discussed in relation to the fourth: that in which an individual encounters someone who disagrees with him.... Dissonance will be reduced by attempting to convert the other person, by changing one's attitude toward the other person, by minimizing the importance or extent of the disagreement, by seeking new and consonant information, including others who agree with one's own view or, if none of these means are available, by changing one's own view or, if none of these means are available, by changing one's own belief or attitude (Cronkhite, 1969, pp. 56-60).

Dramatistic Approach to Persuasion

The rationalistic approach to persuasion assumes that people are motivated to act out of good reasons. The psychological approach to persuasion assumes that people are motivated to act out of attitudes, beliefs, or values held or needs felt. In contrast the dramatistic approach to persuasion assumes that people are motivated to act by language itself. Kenneth Burke (whose method of analysis of human motivation he labeled "dramatism") describes the realistic function of rhetoric as follows: *"For rhetoric as such is not rooted in any past condition of human society. It is rooted in an essential function of language itself, a function that is wholly realistic, and is continually born anew; the use of language as a symbolic means of inducing cooperation in beings that by nature respond to symbols"* (1962, p. 567).

Ernest Bormann, after studying the behavior of people in small groups, concluded that small work groups get caught up in fantasies that transport them out of the "here-and-now" reality of their jobs into a symbolic world that is highly dramatic. Once the group culture is created, it in turn serves to control behavior and is a powerful source that can be drawn upon for the purpose of persuasion by a speaker who is familiar with the group's fantasies. Bormann argues that just as in small groups, large collections of people get caught up in societal fantasies that are based on here-and-now facts and the two together form what Bormann calls a public or rhetorical vision (Bormann, 1972, pp. 398-407).

Probably the easiest way to spot an ongoing rhetorical vision is by looking for the shorthand or dramatic one-liners that refer to them. These dramatic lines are repeated and repeated in the media and in various speeches until finally their mere reference chains out the whole drama. For example, see if a whole drama, complete with heroes and villains, a dramatic scene and a plotline, does not come before your mind's eye when the following one-liners are read: "Ask not what your country can do for you, ask what you can do for your country;" "By God, if one of those long-haired hippies lays down in front of my car, it will be the last car he lays down in front of;" "I have a dream...we shall overcome;" "Are you, the silent majority, going to allow the vocal minority...;" and "There is a light at the end of the tunnel." These one-liners do not form rational arguments, yet they contain rich imagery that, when invoked by a skillful speaker, can and have produced tremendous responses from audiences.

Sometimes a rhetorical drama is used by a company as a means of selling their product. Advertising agencies often develop a series of commercials that attach a product to an ongoing drama. The 7-Up commercials of the late 1960's are good examples. Remember 7-Up became the "Un-Cola" and the commercial came to you from the "underground," sometimes with gurus delivering the message. Recall that Coca-Cola responded by identifying with established americana and thus it was the "Real Thing." The attempts of 7-Up to fit its product into the counter-culture drama were blatant, yet the strategy sent sales of 7-Up soaring. Another obvious example is the Virginia Slims commercials. These ads clearly "tap into" the women's liberation drama. How powerful is this approach? Well, can you picture John Wayne or Walter Cronkite smoking Virginia Slims? And, on the other hand, would they smoke Camels and Marlboros? Why? Clearly, the explanations lie outside of our rational models of persuasion.

In message construction, you should examine your materials with an eye for dramatic imagery. If you need to develop a heroic character, say for example, a liberated woman in the 80's, you might construct your heroine by contrasting her with the dramatic form that is found under the label, "Women's Libber," or you might trace her development historically. However you "rationally" structure your speech, there should be in addition to your rational arguments an image of what the heroine looks like, how she dresses, what she says, and most importantly, how she will act (motive). If you were making this speech, you would probably not depict her with a bottle of Ripple in one hand, a basket of laundry in the other, a clothespin in her mouth, and three children in diapers crying at her feet. Yet you will describe her, and this dramatizing may well chain out a vision of your heroic woman to your audience.

Dramatic forms adhere to human speech-making. However, when there is too much dramatizing in a speech, it becomes melodramatic. When there is too little, the speaker appears static and non-human. The right blend of here-and-now events, rational arguments, and dramatizations produce an effective message. Depending on your purpose, you will be embellishing the hero character, castigating a villain, unfolding a scenario, describing a dramatic setting, or drawing upon dramatic one-liners to give power to your speeches.

References

Allport, F.H. *Social Psychology*. Boston: Houghton-Mifflin, 1924.

Andersen, K. *Persuasion: Theory and Practice*. Boston: Allyn and Bacon, 1971.

Aristotle. *The Rhetoric*. W. Rhys Roberts, trans. New York: Random House, 1954.

Berlo, D.K., Lemert, J.B., and Mertz, R.J. "Dimensions for Evaluating the Acceptability of Message Sources," Research Monograph, Department of Communication, Michigan State University, 1966.

Bormann, E.G. "Fantasy and Rhetorical Vision: The Rhetorical Criticism of Social Reality," *Quarterly Journal of Speech*, 58 (1972).

Brigance, W.N. *Speech: Its Techniques and Disciplines in a Free Society*. New York: Appleton-Century-Crofts, 1952.

Brinton, C. *The Shaping of the Modern Mind.* New York: New American Library, 1958.

Brooks, W.D. *Speech Communication* (2nd ed.) Dubuque, Iowa: Brown, 1974.

Bruner, J.S., Goodnow, J.J., and Austin, G.A. *A Study of Thinking.* New York: Wiley, 1956.

Bryant, D.C. and Wallace, K.R. *Fundamentals of Public Speaking* (4th ed.). New York: Appleton-Century-Crofts, 1969.

Burke, K. *A Grammar of Motives, and A Rhetoric of Motives.* New York: The World Publishing Company, 1962.

Cronkhite, G. *Persuasion: Speech and Behavioral Change.* New York: Bobbs-Merrill, 1969.

Dewey, J. *Democracy and Education.* New York: Macmillan, 1916.

_____. *How We Think.* Boston: D.C. Heath, 1910.

Ehninger, D., Monroe, A., and Gronbeck, B. *Principles and Types of Speech Communication* (8th ed.). Glenview, Illinois: Scott, Foresman and Company, 1978.

Eisenson, J., Auer, J.J., and Irwin, J.V. *The Psychology of Communication.* New York: Appleton-Century-Crofts, 1963.

Festinger, L. *A Theory of Cognitive Dissonance.* Evanston, Illinois: Row, Peterson, 1957.

Fishbein, M. *Readings in Attitude Theory and Measurement.* New York: Wiley, 1967.

Fotheringham, W.C. *Perspectives on Persuasion.* Boston: Allyn and Bacon, 1966.

Hayakawa, S.I. *Language in Thought and Action* (4th ed.). New York: Harcourt Brace Jovanovich, Inc., 1978.

Heider, F. "Attitudes and Cognitive Organization," *Journal of Psychology,* 21 (1946).

Hollingworth, H.L. *The Psychology of the Audience.* New York: American, 1935.

Hovland, C.I., Janis, I.L., and Kelley, H.H. *Communications and Persuasion.* New Haven: Yale, 1953.

Hovland, C.I., Lumsdaine, A.A., and Sheffield, F.D. *Experiments on Mass Communication.* Princeton: Princeton University Press, 1949.

Hultzen, L.S. "Status in Deliberative Analysis," in *The Rhetorical Idiom.* D.C. Bryant, ed. Ithaca, New York: Cornell, 1958.

Katz, D. "The Functional Approach to the Study of Attitudes," *Public Opinion Quarterly,* 24 (1960).

Kennedy, G. *The Art of Persuasion in Greece.* Princeton: Princeton, 1963.

LeBon, G. *The Crowd: A Study of the Popular Mind.* London: Unwin, 1925.

McBurney, J.H., and Mills, G.E. *Argumentation and Debate: Techniques of a Free Society* (2nd ed.). New York: Macmillan, 1964.

McGuire, W.J. "Personality and Susceptability to Social Influence" in *Handbook of Personality Theory and Research.* E.G. Borgatta and W.W. Lambert, eds. Chicago: Rand-McNally, 1968.

_____, and Papageorgis, D. "Effectiveness of Forewarning in Developing Resistance to Persuasion," *Public Opinion Quarterly*, 26 (1962).

Maslow, A.H. *Toward a Psychology of Being.* Princeton: Van Nostrand, 1968.

Minnick, W. *The Art of Persuasion* (2nd ed.). Boston: Houghton Mifflin, 1968.

Osgood, C.E., and Tannenbaum, P.H. "The Principle of Congruity in the Prediction of Attitude Change," *Psychological Review*, 62 (1955).

Perelman, C., and Olbrechts-Tyteca, L. *The New Rhetoric: A Treatise on Argumentation.* J. Wilkinson and P. Weaver, trans. Notre Dame: Notre Dame, 1969.

Plato. *Phaedrus* in *The Dialogues of Plato.* B. Jowett, trans. New York: Random House, 1937.

Porter, R.E. "An Overview of Intercultural Communication" in *Intercultural Communication: A Reader.* L.A. Samovar and R.E. Porter, eds. Belmont, California: Wadsworth, 1972.

Randall, J.H. *The Making of the Modern Mind* (rev. ed.) Boston: Houghton Mifflin, 1940.

Rieke, R.D., and Sillars, M.O. *Argumentation and the Decision Making Process.* New York: Wiley, 1975.

Sarett, L., and Foster, W.T. *Basic Principles of Speech.* Boston: Houghton Mifflin, 1946.

Schnapper, M. "Culture Simulation As a Training Tool," *International Development Review*, 15 (1973).

Sherif, C.W., Sherif, M., and Nebergall, R.E. *Attitude and Attitude Change: The Social Judgment-Involvement Approach.* Philadelphia: W.E. Saunders Co., 1965.

Simons, H. *Persuasion: Understanding, Practice, and Analysis.* Reading, Massachusetts: Addison-Wesley Publishing Company, 1976.

Smith, R.B. *Principles of Public Speaking.* New York: Ronald, 1958.

Wilson, J.F., and Arnold, C.C. *Public Speaking As a Liberal Art* (2nd ed.). Boston: Allyn and Bacon, 1968.

Winans, J.A. *Public Speaking.* New York: Century, 1917.

Zajonc R. "The Concepts of Balance, Congruity, and Dissonance," *Public Opinion Quarterly*, 24 (1960).

Ziegelmueller, G.W., and Dause, C.A. *Argumentation: Inquiry and Advocacy.* Englewood Cliffs, N.J.: Prentice-Hall, 1975.

8

Conflict Resolving Communication

William D. Semlak

Conflict is a growing part of our culture. Increasingly, individuals, groups, and even large sections of our society are involved in arguments, disagreements, and other forms of conflict. This chapter will focus on the role communication plays in the resolution of conflict.

Conflict resolving communication differs from the other forms of communication discussed in this book. Conflict resolving communication is employed in situations in which the parties involved in a dispute have both a *motive to compete* and a *motive to cooperate*. For example, conflict resolving communication cannot work in a situation in which one of the parties in the conflict withdraws from the situation and refuses to talk about the problem. Both parties must be motivated by a desire to cooperate toward a solution.

This chapter will examine communication in the conflict process by exploring the historical background of the study of communication in conflict and then examining how you can improve your communication in a variety of conflict situations.

Historical Background

Communication in conflict situations has been examined by researchers in a number of the social sciences. The following section of this chapter will briefly overview the contributions made by a number of disciplines to the understanding of communication in the conflict process.

Speech Communication

Classical rhetorical theory contributes much to our understanding of the role of communication in the conflict resolution process. In his *Rhetoric* Aristotle outlined the role of public speaking in classical Greek life. Two types of public speaking noted by Aristotle involved conflict resolution. The first—often called *forensic* speaking—involved speaking in the courts. When conflicts over such things as property rights arose, Greek citizens were called on to present their cases to the courts. The courts would listen to the arguments presented by all the parties in the dispute and then make a decision based on the strength of the case.

A second role of public speaking related to conflict resolution outlined by Aristotle has been labeled *deliberative* speaking. Greek political issues were settled by open citizen participation in a democratic form of decision making. Conflict over issues of public policy were settled by citizen debate over the merit of the issues with the eventual policy being selected by voting. Although forensic and deliberative speaking are usually studied under the topic of persuasion, it is important to consider them under a study of conflict resolution. For example, it is clear that early Greek tradition established a principle of conflict resolution being a rational process. Both forensic and deliberative speaking emphasize the use of rational argument and logic as tools in resolving conflict. It is also clear that the early Greeks viewed the resolution of conflict as an adversary relationship.

This focus provided the dominant contribution of the Speech tradition to conflict resolution throughout most of the present century. The belief was that knowledge of logic and good reasoning and the ability to communicate one's positions in a logical, well-supported manner would provide each individual with the tools necessary to resolve conflict.

During the 1940's and 1950's the Speech tradition started to consider resolving conflict from a discussion perspective. The discussion perspective suggested that groups of individuals discovered the answers to problems that created conflict through the systematic group investigation of a problem. Using a systematic method of inquiry, often the reflective thinking process of John Dewey, individuals would objectively sit down and discuss common problems and come to a solution acceptable to all parties through consensus. Although the deliberative and forensics traditions mentioned above stressed individuals resolving conflict by convincing others of the correctness of their position, the discussion . tradition emphasized individuals resolving problems through give-and-take and the discovery of solutions acceptable to all parties in the conflict.

More recently, during the 1960's, a third tradition in the field of Speech has contributed to our understanding of conflict resolution. Concern about communication and its impact on the relationship between the parties in communication was discussed by many authors. Watzlowick, Beavin and Jackson (1967) argued that any communication included two elements: *content* and *relationship*. This means that in communication "what is said," "how something is said," or "what something that is said actually means" is very much influenced by the relationship between the participants in the communication. This concern about relationship in communication is very much at the heart of interpersonal communication as discussed elsewhere in this book. The importance of this tradition to conflict resolution rests in the growth of concern for interpersonal climate in conflict resolution. Such variables as trust, willingness to communicate, and communication style were found to be important in the development of conflict resolution effectiveness. For example, in some conflict situations a low level of trust among the parties involved in the conflict results in a very slow disclosing of information. The communication climate in such a conflict is very different from the climate found in relationship building communications discussed elsewhere in this book.

Later in this chapter we will see how the three traditions mentioned above are central to our understanding of the three levels of conflict resolution discussed in this book. Much of our knowledge about *bargaining* and *negotiation* comes from research in *interpersonal communication, discussion* and *group communication*. In addition, what we know about *mediation* is very much influenced by research in *group decisionmaking*, especially in the area of consensus. *Arbitration*, on the other hand, draws heavily from the *classical tradition* of *deliberative* and *forensic speaking*.

Communication and Conflict Resolution

Americans have responded to conflict in society with the belief that communication is a critical tool for resolving conflict. During the post-revolutionary period, Americans developed a sense of pride and respect for the idea that the "American way" of resolving political conflict utilized discussion and debate of the issues rather than the use of force. Historians point to the role of the Henry-Madison debates over ratification of the Constitution, the Webster-Clay debates over slavery, and the Lincoln-Douglas Senate campaign debates as examples of the American commitment to rational discussion of conflict and resolution of such conflict through communication.

Unfortunately, such a view does not provide the complete answer for conflict resolution. The Civil War is only one example of historical inability to use communication to resolve conflict. Today is the age of the "communication breakdown." At every level of human interaction communication breakdowns exacerbate conflict. The Arabs cannot communicate with the Israelis, the Irish Catholics cannot communicate with the Irish Protestants, the old cannot communicate with the young. Parents and children, brothers and sisters, teachers and students, faculty and administrators, all are purported to experience communication breakdowns from time to time. Communication, which to many represents the solution to conflict, in such an age becomes a barrier to conflict resolution. Today, many problems escape resolution because people cannot communicate.

Experience demonstrates that for anyone to become an effective agent of conflict resolution, he or she must develop the proper attitude toward resolving conflict. Historically three personal factors seem essential to resolving conflict. To become an effective conflict resolution agent, one must recognize these personal factors. First, the persons must be willing to work hard to overcome conflict. Very often conflict is not resolved because the involved individuals fail to try hard enough to overcome communication breakdowns. How many times have you failed to patch up a disagreement with someone because you were unwilling to communicate with the other person? Conflict will not solve itself. Individuals must view themselves as active communicating agents when they are involved in conflict and take active roles in trying to overcome conflict by overcoming the communication breakdown fostering it. Conflict resolution requires *active communication*.

A special responsibility for conflict resolution rests on the shoulders of those trained in communication. As you finish your study of communication you should realize that you have gained special insight into the problems of communication. In your everyday interactions you will encounter people who do not understand how their communication contributes to the conflicts in which they are involved. As you deal with these people you should assume the role of a conflict resolution clinician. You should develop the ability to apply your skills in communication to conflict situations in ways that will help those lacking communication skills resolve their conflict. Later in life you might find yourself in a civic group attempting to deal with a government agency. A conflict over the future location of a highway may have generated considerable conflict. Your skills as a negotiator may be critical to resolution of the conflict. At the same time you may have to teach each member of your bargaining team about communication so that they may effectively contribute to the deliberation without jeopardizing the negotiations. Perhaps you may find yourself in a management position in which you have to teach your employees to develop a communication style that will help them avoid constant bickering. In such a situation

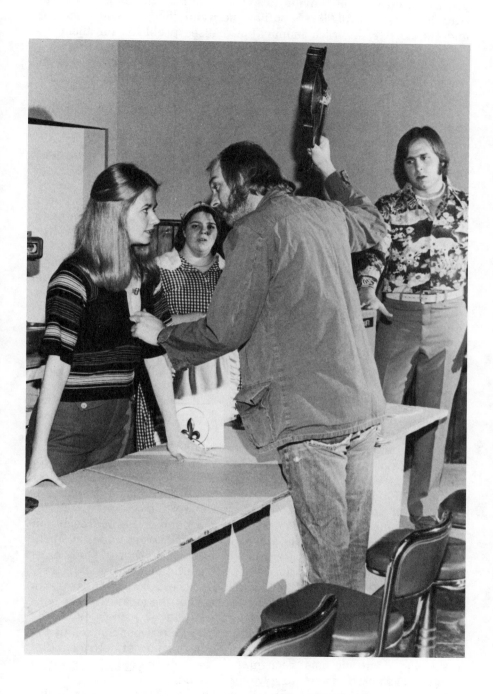

you may find yourself having to apply your communication skills to situations which involve conflict between people who do not understand why their communication causes problems for them. In such a role you will have to act as a communication clinician teaching your workers how to communicate with each other. Your skill in communication will become a valuable commodity which you must share with others to resolve conflict.

A second personal factor essential to your becoming an effective conflict resolution agent is a recognition that you may need to modify your personal communicative behavior to be effective. People have a tendency to blame the other parties in conflict for all the communication breakdowns that occur. How many times have you felt that your problem could be solved if only the other person would listen, or not be so irrational, or would compromise. Most people tend to view their own behavior as acceptable and try to blame the other party's failure to adapt for their own failure to communicate. Everyone has to realize that before someone can become part of the solution, he must recognize he is part of the problem. Conflict resolution demands that each individual reexamine his communication and determine what it contributes to the conflict. Once the individual makes that determination he must be willing to modify his communication. He must be willing to admit that his past communicative behavior may have been a cause of the problem and must adjust his communication accordingly. This is very difficult. Communication is a very important part of self-image. Often it is very difficult for an individual to recognize that something that he or she does when he or she communicates contributes to conflict and communication breakdown. Yet everyone must make this adaptation to effectively resolve conflict. Conflict resolution requires adaptive communication.

A third personal factor essential to becoming an effective conflict resolution agent is the recognition that *conflict resolution is a delicate social science which can be learned.* For the past several years scholars in communication, psychology, political science, economics, and related fields have attempted to formulate the scientific study of conflict resolution. These scholars have approached conflict resolution from a variety of perspectives and conducted numerous experiments to determine the principles that reduce conflict. The years of study have demonstrated that conflict resolution is a multidimensional, extremely complex process. We have observed that certain principles seem useful in resolving conflict and that in general the most useful way to overcome conflict is a systematic application of principles to the problem. This book as well as others in the field reports much of the systematic base of conflict resolution. To become an effective conflict resolution agent you must recognize that effective conflict resolution requires systematic efforts to solve the problem.

The systematic concept becomes especially important later in this chapter when considering arbitration. For arbitration to be successful the parties involved have to establish procedures as well as systematic argument to maximize their position. The Toulmin Model of argument will be suggested as a specific method of systematic argument.

Communication Style and Conflict

Individuals seeking to improve their communication in conflict situations often find the recognition of diverse communication styles a useful tool. Not only does each person engage in a pattern of communication that reflects a certain style but the various individuals with whom one comes into conflict may have very different communication styles. As one becomes experienced in conflict resolution one realizes that certain styles are highly compatible and individuals using them find conflict resolution easy while other styles are often somewhat incompatible and individuals using them have difficulty solving their problems.

Although many different characteristics make up a total communication style, two elements are important when considering an individual's conflict resolution style. Individuals differ in their *assertiveness* and *cooperativeness* levels. By assertiveness we mean the willingness of an individual to emphasize the satisfying of his/her own needs while recognizing the rights and needs of others while communicating. An individual is said to be *nonassertive in conflict* situations if he or she adopts a passive communication style that does not communicate his or her needs or feelings to the other parties in the conflict. Nonassertive individuals often are shy and passive and face problems by hoping that they correct themselves. The non-assertive individual has little self-confidence and often finds it difficult to gain the respect of others. An *assertive* individual, on the other hand, is able to handle conflict by the skillful expression of his or her personal needs, wants, and desires but without attacking others or dictating a solution. Assertive individuals usually are confident and have the respect of others.

Cooperativeness, on the other hand, reflects the extent to which an individual attempts to satisfy the concerns of the other parties in the conflict. Uncooperative individuals often adopt *aggressive* postures by either overtly or covertly working to hurt, humiliate or threaten the other individual. Aggressive persons are highly insensitive to the feelings and needs of other participants in the conflict. Their actions usually provoke resentment in others.

Assertiveness and cooperativeness combine to form five different communication styles (Kilmann and Thomas, 1975). Each style contains different attitudes toward conflict and as a result different responses in a conflict situation. Figure 1 represents the five communication styles identified by Kilmann and Thomas.

Figure 1
Summary of Kilmann and Thomas' Communication Styles

Style	Characteristics
Competing Style	High Assertive Low Cooperation
Accommodating Style	Low Assertive High Cooperation
Avoiding Style	Low Assertive Low Cooperation
Collaborating	High Assertive High Cooperation
Compromising	Moderate Assertive Moderate Cooperation

A *competing* style is often employed by a person who is assertive but uncooperative. Such a person pursues his or her own objectives at the expense of others. A competing individual employs power-oriented strategies to achieve an objective. Such strategies include the ability to argue, the use of status and position, or the use of threats. Individuals who tend to compete generally perceive that they are standing up for their rights, defending what is right, or trying to win.

An individual who is unassertive and cooperative is said to be employing an *accommodating* style. The accommodating style is the opposite of a competing style in that an individual neglects his or her own concerns in an attempt to meet the concerns of the other individuals in the conflict. A person who chooses to use an accommodating style tends to avoid conflict situations when possible but once he or she becomes involved accommodating manifests itself in self-sacrifice, obeying orders he or she would prefer to disobey, or yielding to a point of view he or she does not hold.

The *avoiding* style includes unassertive and uncooperative characteristics. The avoiding individual does not immediately pursue either his or her concerns or the concerns of others. Rather, he or she does not address the conflict, often pretending it is not there. An avoider might sidestep the controversy, attempt to postpone treatment of the issue, or actually withdraw from the situation.

Opposite of the avoiding style is the *collaborating* style, which includes both assertive and cooperative elements. A collaborating individual attempts to work with others until a solution is discovered that fully satisfies the needs of all concerned parties. For a collaborating style to be effective the individuals in the conflict have to identify their underlying concerns and explore alternatives that are compatible. Collaboration requires a willingness of the individuals in the conflict to disclose considerable information and a high level of trust between the conflicting parties. Collaboration may include analysis of the disagreement to learn from each other's insights and trying to find creative solutions which eliminate the basic source of the problem.

A *compromising* style includes a mix of assertiveness and cooperativeness. Compromising individuals attempt to find practical, expedient, mutually acceptable solutions. The compromising style includes elements of the four styles above. A compromising individual gives up more than a competing individual but less than an accommodating person. In addition a compromiser addresses issues more directly than an avoider but not in as much depth as a collaborator. Many would argue that the compromising style is the best communication style in a conflict resolution situation because an individual maximizes his or her ability to find the solution best for all parties involved in the conflict.

Conflict Situations

Individuals use their differing communication styles with differing degrees of success depending on the type of conflict situation in which they find themselves. This chapter will focus on communication strategies which are useful for conflict resolution in three situations: bargaining, mediation and arbitration.

The Bargaining Situation

Often the communicative behavior of the parties involved in conflict attempts to resolve the situation through achievement of a mutually acceptable arrangement. This strategy involves an attempt to achieve consensus or negotiate a position acceptable to all parties involved. Inherent within such a strategy is an assumption that all parties will approach the conflict willing to bargain. In other words, each party approaches the bargaining table with the recognition that they will have to give up part of their original demand in order to achieve a settlement. At the same time they recognize that the other party will be in the same position and that the final outcome will be somewhere between the two initial positions. Such a situation should produce an atmosphere in which risk to parties is minimized because the outcome produces no absolute winners or losers. For example, in labor relations management and labor both approach the bargaining table with a series of positions. Each recognizes it is unlikely that the final outcome will represent either of the initial positions. Rather, both sides recognize the final outcome will reflect a position that will emerge during mutual give and take. This type of communicative behavior falls into the broad category of bargaining.

One of the most important points to recognize here is that bargaining is a rather informal method of conflict resolution. On a day-to-day level each one of us is constantly bargaining to resolve conflict. You want to buy a stereo from your friend. He wants $100.00 but you do not think it is worth that much. You point out to him that the system is seven years old, that the components are tube rather than solid state, that it is not compatible with most new equipment. You then offer him $75.00.

You get a test back. It is graded "D." You feel that the grade is not indicative of your understanding of the subject matter. You go in to see the instructor. She says she is sorry that you did not do better on the test but there is nothing she can do for you. That is your cue to start bargaining. You suggest that perhaps you could do extra work? Perhaps you could take the test over? Perhaps you could count the next test double? You pose as many alternatives as you can and hope to work out a better grade. Your strategy is designed to make the instructor feel that she is being unreasonable if she does not accept one of your options. Here you appear to be reasonable—willing to accept any option. Your strategy should encourage her to bend and accept one of the options.

Bargaining in such situations is largely a matter of interpersonal communication strategy. You put yourself on the line. You initiate the communication, you suggest the options, you take the risk, you force the other party to act. You shift guilt to the other party if bargaining breaks down. More important you often attempt to appeal to personal prestige and honor to achieve a settlement. You promise to do better on the next test, to come to class more often in the future, to study harder, all to impress your opponent with your bargaining sincerity.

The above example represents only one of the simplest examples of bargaining in a dyad. Only two factions are represented and one member has very little at stake. The outcome will depend largely on the student's shifting a sense of guilt to the instructor and encouraging her to adopt a more flexible policy. On occasions the number of actions involved in the interchange are not so simple. In such cases the process may be inadequate to resolve the conflict and the employment of a different form of conflict resolution may be necessary.

The Mediation Situation

At times individuals are not able to resolve their conflicts through bargaining. For example, professional athletes are unable to negotiate contract arrangements. Despite considerable efforts, for one reason or another, the parties involved cannot reach a common solution. One or more parties in the conflict may believe they have reached their minimum acceptable positions. One party involved may be reluctant to continue bargaining because he or she believes the other party is not bargaining in good faith. Regardless of the reason, a bargaining impasse precludes settlement.

When a conflict reaches this stage it is often resolved through a form of third party conflict resolution called mediation. In mediation, a person removed from the conflict attempts to assist the conflicting parties to reach a settlement by attempting to use persuasion, argument and reasoning to help move them toward a solution. A small claims court referee often functions in this fashion. The referee's duty is to mediate disagreements by convincing the parties involved to compromise toward a common settlement. Often squabbles between children are mediated by the parents. The department chairperson in a university might find it necessary to mediate a conflict between factions of the faculty. The boss at work mediates an argument over who will take their vacations during June. Throughout society, within a wide range of situations, various individuals are required to mediate conflict. In all of these instances the mediator tries to facilitate the resolution of conflict by bringing the parties together. The role of the mediator is essentially that of a persuader. Mediation is an important skill in business and professional life. Increasingly, large corporations and industries experience internal conflict. Any management-level position requires mediation abilities to bring competing factions together.

The Arbitration Situation

If a third party is unable to bring conflicting parties together, arbitration may become necessary. Arbitration involves granting the power to a third party to study the conflict and reach a solution which is binding on all involved parties. Civil matters are usually resolved in this fashion. If two businesses are in conflict over a contract, for example, they will probably attempt to resolve the conflict by trying to negotiate a mutually acceptable solution. If that fails they may call in a third party to act as a mediator, to advise them. If that fails they may take the issue to court. In court all the facts would be presented and the judge or jury would render a decision binding all parties to a solution.

Three important assumptions underlie any arbitration situation. The first is an assumption of rational judgment based on the facts of the case. In arbitration, custom dictates that all sides present all material relevant to the case and the third party then renders a decision. Court proceedings, for example, often settle conflicts. During the proceedings the opposing lawyers present their material in the form of rational, logical arguments based on as much evidence as possible. This procedure assumes that a rational judge or jury will sort out all the material and render a decision on the facts of the case. Second, arbitration assumes that procedures and rules of conduct are worked out and agreed to by both sides. Usually arbitration is employed in a situation which could not be resolved through a more informal conflict resolution technique. Often channels of communication between the various parties are completely closed. Divorce cases offer an example of the need for clear procedural standards in arbitration. Some divorce cases involve two parties so bitter toward each other that they are unable to sit down and talk calmly about anything. Only by presenting their cases in court and letting the judge establish the arrangements of the divorce can anything be worked out. Usually in such instances previous attempts to settle the conflict through negotiation or mediation failed. Only because the arbitration process involves clear procedural standards accepted by both parties and their spokespersons is it able to succeed. A third assumption important to arbitration is the importance of the parties involved accepting the decision of the arbitrator. In some instances legal requirements mandate acceptance of the decision. Court decisions are binding. Often, however, the parties involved in conflict recognize that the only way to overcome their problem is to turn the decision over to an arbitrator and then abide by the decision. On the interpersonal level we often take such action to settle conflict. How many times when you were involved in a struggle with a friend over a course of action do you remember asking a third person to decide for you? Often, fighting lovers, partners, or friends write ''Dear Abby'' asking her to render a final answer. In such instances both parties usually recognize that no solution can be generated on a face-to-face level so they appeal to a respected higher source of wisdom or objectivity for a decision. Due to mutual respect and trust of the arbitrator both parties agree to accept the solution.

Arbitration, then, is a useful tool for resolving conflict. It may vary to a considerable degree in formality and structure. Interpersonal conflict between friends often only asks a third party to decide if the dance or the game will be the night's entertainment. In such informal situations rules are largely unstated and tacit agreement exists to accept the third party outcome. Yet at times arbitration deals with multi-million dollar labor/management settlements in which teams of lawyers present voluminous briefs to a panel of expert arbitrators. In such a climate numerous rules exist to govern the proceedings.

Communication in Negotiation and Bargaining

In bargaining and negotiation situations the optimum communication style is that of compromise. Since all parties in the process have to realize that a certain amount of give and take is necessary, a willingness to modify position through pragmatic decisions is necessary. To do this several communicative techniques are important. When you present your position it is important that _you describe your needs_. This will help show the other parties why you are taking your positions. This often motivates other parties in the conflict to try to help you solve your needs. In addition the information about your needs provides the other parties in the conflict situation information about your positions that may encourage suggestions of alternative ways to meet your needs while resolving the conflict. For example, a couple may be arguing about their plans for an evening. he wants to go to the ball game and she wants to go to a movie. She hates sports and he does not want to spend money. If she says she wants to go to the movie because she doesn't understand football and he says he wants to go to the football game because it is free, they may have an easy time thinking of alternatives that she understands and are free.

After the needs of individuals in the conflict have been described, _brainstorming possible solutions_ is an appropriate strategy. In the above example the couple may suggest such solutions as watching television, going for a walk, and studying together. In doing this the conflict parties should be sensitive to the needs described by the other party in the conflict.

Once most of the possible solutions have been brainstormed, the participants should _choose the best alternative_. Ideally the best solution will emerge but you may have to reject some of the solutions. When evaluating solutions that are unacceptable it is best to provide your reason for rejection.

Overall, individuals in a bargaining situation find that two sets of communication skills enhance their effectiveness. The first set of skills relates to treating the parties in the conflict as rational individuals and consists of using argumentation skills to present your position. These skills include _planning and selecting_ the best arguments in favor of your position, _organizing_ your case in a reasonable way, providing _evidence_ when needed and _evaluating_ all arguments so that you may give in when superior positions have been established by the other parties in the conflict.

A second set of communication skills necessary in bargaining includes personal skills related to ability to deal with other people. Such skills include _asking_ critical _questions_ and _listening_ to the other party's position carefully, keeping the channels of communication open through an *assertive* as opposed to an aggressive style, maintaining a certain degree of trust in others and using interpersonal *influence* when appropriate.

Characteristics of Other Bargainers

Reseachers have attempted to determine if certain demographic, psychological or motivational characteristics influence the general approach an individual takes to bargaining. Rubin and Brown (1975) summarized research in this area and identified several characteristics one should consider. In terms of age, young children tend to use a competitive bargaining style. As they grow older and reach college age, they tend to develop more accommodating, collaborating or compromising styles. Individuals of the same race tend to bargain more cooperatively than individuals of different races.

A considerable amount of conflicting research has been conducted in an attempt to discover any common bargaining characteristics of either sex. The commonly held assumption is that males tend to bargain more competitively while females tend to bargain more cooperatively. However, research demonstrates that both males and females vary their bargaining styles to a considerable extent. Females tend to bargain more cooperatively with other females than with males. In addition, females are more likely than males to vary their bargaining type depending on the attractiveness of the person with whom they are bargaining.

Individuals who tend to be able to think in abstract terms have a better ability to approach bargaining with a cooperative style. Such individuals appear to tend to see the value of maintaining interpersonal climate while bargaining and thus tend to be more considerate of others. Individuals with a high need for affiliation also tend to value the quality of the interpersonal climate in bargaining situations and thus adopt a more cooperative or collaborating communication style.

When engaged in bargaining certain types of strategic communications may be important. A systematic approach to conflict resolution is useful in maximizing the effectiveness of one's efforts. The following communication strategies seem to have potential to improve one's bargaining ability.

Sincere Communication

The most essential preliminary communicative behavior that a bargainer should master is sincere presentation. Sincere communication involves two dimensions: bargaining in "good faith" and an impression of bargaining in "good faith." A bargainer must bargain in good faith to be viable. This requires absolute willingness to fulfill all terms of the solution.

As important as bargaining in good faith is the perception in the minds of the other parties that the bargaining is in good faith. A negotiator who has a record of over-extending bargaining authority is of little value because the parties in the negotiations may perceive him or her as nontrustworthy. Certain ritual behaviors are useful in giving the impression that bargaining is in good faith. Early in the negotiations bargainers may take extreme positions from which they can back down quickly and move toward middle positions. They may take breaks to consult with other members of the negotiating team or with the principals they represent. One stylistic characteristic of a bargainer who is establishing a perception of bargaining in good faith is the use of tentative language. Try to avoid talking in absolutes when "probably" and "possibly" may be used. Then only after the position is firmed up should you take a definite position. The appearance of good faith negotiation is essential for a bargaining agent.

Nonpolarizing Communication

As mentioned earlier in this chapter the bargaining situation is one in which the parties involved reach a settlement in which all maximize

their position within a framework of a solution acceptable to the other parties. Polarization communication is an impediment to such a goal. Polarization communication is communication which portrays the issue at hand in a win-lose situation. Such communication portrays the various positions as miles apart and suggests that any settlement will be at the expense of one party's central issues. Much of the current controversy in Ireland is magnified by the polarizing nature of the communication. Both involved parties talk in terms of any settlement requiring complete control of policies for their side. Such communication increases bargaining tension. When such tension exists parties do not enter into open bargaining. They perceive the risk as too high and often engage in what we will classify later as avoidance communication. When polarization communication takes place early in the bargaining process it is essential that a new bargaining agent be found or that the present agent be encouraged to modify his or her rhetoric. If the polarization is caused by factors other than the bargaining agent it is incumbent on the bargainer to reduce tension by reassuring the other party that no position the other side perceives as a loss is essential to the settlement. Polarization communication violates the principles of limited risk and mutually acceptable solutions essential to the negotiation process.

Signposting Communication

To avoid high risk induced bargaining tension, custom dictates bargaining signposts. Bargaining signposts are communications which establish the parameters in which a negotiation can take place. Early in the negotiations each faction should establish signposts which identify high risk bargaining tension areas. For example, one non-negotiable demand of a student radical group may be amnesty for the participants in a demonstration. The group may have held a demonstration primarily to draw attention to their position and feel that at present they may negotiate any of the initial issues which led to the demonstration. However, they may believe their future success in involving non-members in demonstrations rests on gaining amnesty for demonstrators. During negotiations in such a situation the bargainers would signpost such a position by threatening to leave the bargaining table and resume demonstrations every time the administrators question the amnesty issue. The administrators would soon realize the student faction perceived refusal to grant amnesty in a win/loss perspective. The students would signpost this area as a high risk bargain tension raising issue. The administrators are not required to give in to the amnesty demand, but they are warned of a source of high risk bargaining tension by the students' effective signpost communication. Arguing couples often employ a similar strategy with statements like "I can tolerate anything but visiting your mother" or "I won't object to anything that costs less than $50."

Flexible Communication

An effective bargainer develops a flexible communication strategy before entering the negotiation. First, he or she will establish his or her "musts." He or she will determine the minimum compromise that can be accepted. Then he or she will determine what the bargaining issues are and which issues are least important. These become the "give" points. Flexible bargaining requires a careful weighing of "give" points. At the same time the bargainer will learn as much as possible about the opponents' position. During the negotiation he or she will have to trade "give points with the opposition. Care must be taken not to give too easily to opponents' points. At the same time the bargainer has to know what the "musts" are and gain as many as possible. American foreign policy negotiations often display considerable art in trading "give" points. While negotiating a settlement to the war in Vietnam the release of the American prisoners of war was a "must" for the American delegation. Since the representatives of the Republic of North Vietnam recognized this fact they were able to trade almost all their "give" points for that "must" point. On the domestic level, divorce settlement often involves such "must" points as possession of the house, car or children, and such "give" points as paying for the child's education, paying the life insurance premium or taking possession of the pet goldfish.

An effective bargainer also maintains a flexible bargaining style. The communication approach should vary to fit the presentation. At times the bargainer must demonstrate a firm temperament. At times a conciliatory approach is best. Some circumstances demand a hostile approach to shake the opponent or to get a vital message across.

Avoidance Communication

Resolving conflict requires that all parties involved recognize that conflict exists, and communication must take place to resolve it. On occasion parties involved in conflict choose to retreat from communication by avoiding the issue. Sometimes parties in the conflict refuse to confront the other parties but instead complain about their working conditions to fellow workers. For one reason or another they feel that they have been treated unfairly or that they did not get the raise they deserved. The problem becomes so serious as far as they are concerned that their work is affected. Yet these same individuals when confronted by their superior say that everything is all right. This situation illustrates how status may become a deterrent to open communication. Rather than discussing the issue the party avoids communication on the topic.

Such a condition aggravates the conflict and hinders the resolution of the problem. A closely related situation involves the parties who encourage conflict by telling others about their dissatisfaction but denying that a problem exists when confronted by the factions involved. Sometimes individuals within businesses use such strategies to jockey for position within the power structure. Conflict within such a context has little possibility of being resolved. Avoidance communication precludes the solving of conflict because both parties do not accept the underlying assumption of bargaining that a mutual solution can be achieved.

Often when an attempt to resolve conflict is in progress another type of avoidance communicative behavior appears when a party in the conflict attempts to change the subject. Sometimes as the conversation reaches the most sensitive part of the conflict one or more parties try to shift the focus to another subject. Effective bargaining requires overcoming all forms of avoidance communication. Individuals have to force others to come to grips with the sensitive area of discussion.

Misdirected Communication

Another kind of communication which hinders effective bargaining is misdirected communication. This involves a variety of strategies which attempt to focus attention off the point of conflict and onto other issues. One type of misdirected communication attempts to make the other parties in the conflict feel guilty for their role in the conflict. This is a typical situation observed in interpersonal conflict. Often a lover's quarrel over an issue boils down to one side trying to get the other party to admit the problem was all his or her fault and take the entire initiative in making up. While this can be an effective strategy if one party accepts the entire blame for the situation it will more likely exacerbate the conflict.

This type of communication is also often observed in situations involving individuals with role differences. Parents often try to convince their children that the problem is all their fault. Such situations often do include successful examples of making one party in the conflict assume the entire blame but often the outcome is the other party taking even more rigid positions.

A much better approach would have the parties involved in the bargaining attribute blame for the problem to inevitable circumstances, some unnamed third party, mutual misunderstanding, or something of this nature. The "guiltless crisis" is easier for both parties to solve. When neither party is blamed for the conflict neither has to respond in a defensive way.

An additional example of misdirected communication is communication which focuses on aspects of the opponents' lives irrelevant to the conflict at hand. Perhaps two years ago the parties had a conflict over another matter. References to such a conflict only increase bargaining tension and do nothing to improve the current situation. Often misdirected communication involves random attacks on the past life of the parties involved in bargaining. Such a communication strategy only increases the rigidness of the attacked parties' positions and does little to promote bargaining.

Sometimes misdirected communication takes the form of a trap. One party in the bargaining process may say, "Let's be totally honest with each other." After the other parties in the bargaining process lay their cards on the table not only does the trapper refuse to lay out his or her position but he or she attacks the other positions as totally unacceptable. Avoiding the trap situation is especially critical during bargaining. Information should always be revealed gradually and positions modified incrementally.

Misdirected communication often takes the form of character analysis during the bargaining process. After someone expresses a feeling or opinion such misdirected communication will attempt to tell everyone how the person "really feels" by interpreting what was said in a different way. Inherent in character analysis is an attempt to undermine the credibility of a bargaining opponent by casting doubt on his or her sincerity, credibility, motivation, or on some other factor.

Inflated Communication

Bargaining requires that communication related to the issue under consideration be realistic. Often persons engaged in bargaining feel that a strategic advantage may be gained by overstating the facts of the case. Exaggeration, fictitious examples, actual lies, are all examples of types of communication which attempt to inflate a position through deception. Once the actual position becomes known the deceiver is forced to retreat from his position without the other party giving ground *but also* with a considerable loss of personal credibility and face.

A second type of inflated communication involves the piling up of small gripes and issues tangentially related to the issue being discussed. By including every possible problem regardless of its actual relationship to the principal position this strategy hopes to overwhelm the opposition by sheer weight of material. While this strategy has some merit in an arbitration situation where the conflict will be resolved by a third party, in a bargaining situation it is much less effective. Because the opponent in bargaining is closely associated with the facts of the case he is quick to recognize the peripheral nature of the small problems. His or her most natural response to such a strategy is to discount the importance of such issues and to question the bargaining sincerity of the party who introduced them.

Personal Communication

When bargaining, not everyone approaches the bargaining table with the same interpersonal skills. Certain personal behavior inhibits bargaining. The participants must have a sense of the appropriate communication at all times during bargaining. For example, a sense of humor and wit are useful tools in reducing bargaining tension. However, they must be employed at the correct moment. Just as a bargaining opponent is making a serious point a joke is not in order. Bargaining should include the perceptive sense of humor.

A person engaging in bargaining also needs to refrain from overpersonalizing in the bargaining process. Often there is a tendency to perceive the opponent's attack on positions as a personal attack. Individuals who are too ego-involved with positions make poor bargaining agents since they interpret attacks against positions as attacks against themselves. They become defensive and emotional. Rather than evaluating the substance of the opponent's position they respond with rigid, aggressive, defensive arguments. The effective bargainer has the ability to remove himself or herself from personal involvement with the issues.

The good bargainer also develops critical listening skills. Listening in a bargaining situation requires remembering what has been said and using that information effectively. When appropriate, a good bargainer takes notes. In formal bargaining situations both sides often tape-record bargaining sessions and study the verbal interaction. When several parties form a bargaining team members often pool their mental notes after each session to maximize their picture of what occurred.

Numerous suggestions are advanced to aid listening effectiveness. Such common advice as listening for main ideas, concentrating on the subject at hand, compensating for issues to which you react emotionally, maintaining a relaxed physical position, taking breaks to avoid overload, all contribute to an effective personal listening style.

Bargaining agents must also learn to recognize the meaning of nonverbal cues during discussion. Facial expressions, body tension, hand movements, eye contact, posture, vocalic features, all potentially communicate important information. An effective bargainer must be able to determine when he or she has gained all he or she can on an issue; when he or she is on a sensitive issue; when his or her ideas are perceived as acceptable. Interpreting nonverbal communication may be the most important factor in making such assessments. The effective bargainer must also learn how to control nonverbal cues. Generally the best bargaining style will sort out as many unintentional nonverbal cues as possible.

In general, personal communication skills such as tact, common sense, and courtesy contribute to the effectiveness of bargaining. However, attempts to be overly cooperative or friendly often are interpreted by others in bargaining as rhetorical ploys. One should always recognize that bargaining is essentially a confrontation situation in which both parties, through give and take, attempt to resolve a conflict. Parties in conflict quickly recognize the reality of the situation and are not victimized by overly submissive role portrayals.

Negotiation is a highly complex communication encounter. While we often negotiate in a largely informal setting, negotiation also includes some highly formal communication. As you can see from this chapter your ability to bargain is determined by a wide variety of communication skills.

Mediation

A second situation in which communication plays a critical role in resolving conflict is mediation. Individuals constantly find themselves in positions in which they have to assist other parties in resolving conflict. Two friends who are bickering should be brought together, your brother and sister who are fighting should be reconciled — just to mention two common examples of conflict which require mediation. Mediation is an important skill in business and professional life. Increasingly large corporations and industries experience internal conflict. Any management level position requires mediation abilities to bring competing factions together. The following communication variables are important to mediation.

An Effective Mediator Has High Credibility

Credibility is usually defined as the perceived image of a person in terms of trustworthiness and expertise. That is, someone who is said to have high credibility is perceived as both knowledgeable and reliable. These are both essential characteristics for mediation. For example, a fraternity president might be called upon to settle a dispute between the pledge chairperson and the treasurer. His or her status as president often gives him or her the position from which to be a credible mediator.

An *Effective Mediator is Neutral*

Often you will find your friends involved in disputes. Your ability to mediate the conflict will be predicated on your being perceived as neutral. To be an acceptable mediator you should refuse to become ego involved with either position. You should not make any statements which could be interpreted as taking a position on the issue. If either party has any reason to believe that your sympathy lies with the other party, your ability to mediate will be reduced. Marriage conflicts often demonstrate this point. Often troubled parties confide in their friends and seek advice. Sometimes a well-meaning but inept friend tries to bring the two parties together by mediating the conflict. Unless the friend carefully maintains an absolute aura of neutrality—very difficult since a friend is usually closer to one marriage partner than to the other—his or her efforts are usually worthless or even harmful. All kinds of behavior may contribute to this failure. Even minor things which happened several years ago may cast doubt on his or her neutrality. This suggests a reason why trained marriage counselors are effective. Not only are they well schooled in common marriage problems but they can easily establish themselves as neutral third parties. Often a zero history mediator—one with no previous relationship with either party—has the best chance to be perceived as neutral.

An *Effective Mediator Manages Conflict Between Parties*

Mediators are often called in because the parties involved are unable to achieve anything constructive through face-to-face communication. The parties may be hostile toward each other and personal contact may increase the hostility. A mediator must be able to sense when face-to-face contact is desirable and when it should be avoided. Sometimes it is useful to call a meeting between the involved parties early in the mediation process. At such a meeting each side should be instructed to present their positions. Such a meeting is useful for the mediator to assess the level of disagreement and the actual positions. The meeting also gives the mediator useful indications of the amount of future contact between factions that he or she should arrange. The mediator may observe that the parties involved are receptive to listening to the other side and determine that contact will facilitate understanding. On the other hand, the mediator may conclude that significant private sessions are necessary before the factions can gain anything through face-to-face communication. Often lawyers working on out-of-court settlements never bring the parties together when mediating a settlement because the hostility between factions is so intense progress would actually be retarded.

Flexibility is the key to party contact management in mediation. No rigid formula offers the answer. Often preliminary interviews with the factions give sufficient insight to determine the amount of contact desirable. On other occasions only actual contact gives the mediator the insight necessary to gauge the amount of future contact which will facilitate resolution of the conflict.

An Effective Mediator Manages Rumor

Those who mediate conflict, especially in large institutional settings, recognize that one of the biggest barriers to conflict resolution is rumor. Rumor may be generated and transmitted by both parties involved in the conflict and by parties not involved at all. An effective mediator always develops channels to monitor rumor so that he or she is aware of it. He or she will try to find noninvolved parties in key locations who will inform him or her of any rumors which may be operating against resolutions of the conflict. An alert mediator will also develop communication strategies to counter rumor. He or she will flood the system with counterevidence when necessary to disprove rumor; he or she will consult with the parties involved to dispel rumor; he will discredit the rumor source to stop rumor. Often the presence of rumor will require the mediator to bring the parties together to dispel it. Actual face-to-face presentation of issues sometimes is the only effective tool a mediator has to counter rumor. Such a situation sometimes can have a highly positive effect on the mediation. If considerable tension between sides was built up by rumor, the effect of breaking down the rumor often operates as a threshold which encourages future mediation. A very skilled mediator can use rumor to his or her advantage but the risk is high. If rumor cannot be dispelled it often exacerbates the conflict.

An Effective Mediator Knows When to Listen

Usually a mediator is brought into a conflict that is well developed. Before the mediator can be effective he must understand every aspect of the conflict. He or she will encourage all parties to tell him or her the whole story in private sessions. Often minor facts which neither party mentions are important to the conflict. To be effective the mediator must discover these facts. In listening the mediator often functions as a tension reliever. Often talking to the mediator gives the parties in the conflict a chance to ventilate their hostilities. Once such hostilities are out in the open the mediator can help each party overcome feelings which must be modified to resolve the conflict. Such an internal tension reducing process may be the prime agent of conflict resolution.

The mediator also listens to get the facts straight. He or she sorts out those things on which both sides can agree. He listens for any hint of common ground. He or she tries to determine what rumors have contributed to the conflict. He or she tries to determine what are the maximum acceptable positions of both parties. He or she determines who are the leaders of both factions who might possibly be most susceptible to changing their opinion, and who might work as opinion leaders for him later in the process. In short the mediator listens for anything and everything essential to solve the conflict.

An Effective Mediator Conveys Information

Often while meeting separately with the parties the mediator will discover information which should be conveyed to the other side. An effective mediator, however, is very strategic about what information he or she conveys and the manner in which it is presented. In a hostile situation a mediator will often temper the remarks conveyed so that the intent of the message remains intact but the emotional connotations are removed. Information which one side wants conveyed to the other side but the mediator feels could inhibit the conflict resolution process is often suppressed. A skilled mediator conveys information very selectively. He or she will carefully evaluate everything and pick key phrases, ideas, and concepts and present them to the other side. Items which could form the basis of a breakthrough on an important issue are *highlighted* in the presentation of information. Overstatement is avoided at all costs and material is presented tentatively rather than absolutely. The mediator tries to convey material in a way which maintains communication flexibility and position flexibility for both sides.

An Effective Mediator Promotes Internal Inquiry

Mediation requires considerable effort to get parties in conflict to modify their positions. An effective mediator will encourage the parties to reevaluate their positions constantly. He or she will encourage the participants to try to separate complex issues and consider them in smaller units. He or she will probe their positions with them searching for points of potential compromise. Often the mediator plays devil's advocate presenting various alternatives, some of which are obviously unreasonable, in an attempt to place an issue in perspective or show the number of options available. The mediator in this respect functions as a resource person offering the parties in the conflict information and ideas to promote inquiry.

An Effective Mediator Uses Allies

Within any faction many perspectives exist. Often the mediator identifies members of the factions inclined to adopt middle ground positions and encourages them to rally the support of the other members. Sometimes the allies are not members of the faction but interested bystanders who can easily influence the members. Recently a university committee mediating a dispute between warring departments encouraged the president of the university to send each department a letter encouraging them to accept the compromise worked out by the committee. Upon receiving the letter, each department somewhat reluctantly moved toward the compromise position. This demonstrates the extent to which some mediating agencies go to gain ally support for their settlement. One coed who was trying to mediate a lovers' quarrel convinced the boy's roommate to pressure his buddy to apologize in return for a date.

Within the factions in conflict certain parties are more prone to change than others. In addition, some parties serve as opinion leaders within the faction and wield a powerful influence over the rest of the members. Often mediators approach such members and sell them on helping solve the problem. Such a strategy requires the mediator to shift from his or her mediator role and approach the individual on the interpersonal level. Often mediators use their personal prestige to convince such members to serve as their agents. Often they suggest rewards to the individuals such as "you can take credit for the idea" to enlist their support. Business managers often find the best way to mediate conflict within an organization is to decide themselves how to resolve the conflict and, to insure that the conflicting parties accept the compromise, heap lavish praise on the parties involved for their efficient settlement of the conflict. The surprised parties quickly support the compromise which they received acclaim for establishing. Mediators often find the use of interpersonal influences essential to success. Statements such as "I've worked hard for months, and I'm afraid it will have been for nothing unless you can help me out," "If you could just see yourself clear to accept this I'll buy the beers" or "If you could do me one small favor" are all approaches to using interpersonal influences in mediation.

An Effective Mediator Minimizes Risk

Conflict resolution involves bringing parties together in such a way that various factions give up something that they want in the settlement process. Within this process there is inherent risk that a side will perceive it is losing too much. Effective mediators attempt to convince the parties involved that they can shift their positions without losing face. In addition the mediator attempts to convince each party that they are not losing significant ground and reminds the parties of the ground the other factions are giving up.

Mediation then may be described as the "art of persuasion." We advanced the above hints as general strategies to employ in mediation. Be sure to remember that most of the concepts designed to help you bargain more effectively are also useful in mediation. It is also important to recognize that mediation involves a more risky conflict resolution situation for the participants. In negotiation it is often quite possible to develop a solution that is perceived as acceptable by all parties involved. However, in mediation the risk to the involved parties is increased because it is more likely that an acceptable solution to the other parties in the conflict will require an individual "giving up" important points. Thus an effective mediator needs to convince the involved parties to modify their positions. This may be achieved by showing how the other side is giving up points to be reasonable; by telling a faction that they can gain strategic advantage by giving up a position; by asking a party in the conflict to look at his/her own position because you think it might need to be modified. In short a good mediator is often forced to persuade the conflicting parties to move closer so that the final solution does not seem to be one in which only they are giving up important issues.

Arbitration

So far this chapter has examined face-to-face bargaining during which the conflicting parties have been able to resolve their differences, and mediation through which third parties have been able to assist conflicting individuals or groups to resolve their conflict. Often conflict situations reach a point where neither bargaining nor mediation are capable of resolving the differences and in such a case often arbitration results. Arbitration involves both parties in the conflict situation presenting their positions to a third party who decides which side has the best case and then selects a decision that is binding on all parties. For example, in a university it is possible that both the History and the Philosophy departments want to offer a course entitled "History of Philosophy." University policy might preclude two departments offering the same course so the departments attempt to resolve their conflict. First the chairpersons meet and try to solve the problem through bargaining but they are unsuccessful. Next the chairperson of the college curriculum committee might attempt to mediate the conflict by talking with both parties and arranging meetings between the two departments but, again, the conflict remains unresolved. Finally both parties take their case to the Dean, who has the power to arbitrate the situation and make a decision binding on both parties. The Dean, for example, might decide the History department will offer the course; he might decide both departments will cross-list the course and teach it alternate semesters; or he might decide neither department should offer the course until new faculty resources become available to teach it.

Situations such as the one above happen in everyday life more than you might think. Parents arbitrate conflicts between children, fraternity officers arbitrate conflicts between members, and small claims referees arbitrate conflicts between citizens. More and more positions of management require skill at both presenting cases during conflict and resolving conflict based on the cases presented by conflicting parties. In the courtroom juries and judges listen to both sides of cases and then make decisions, thus arbitrating such conflicts as civil suits and divorce settlements.

The central thrust of this treatment of arbitration will be on the development of the skills necessary to make one's case and present it to an arbitrator. Parties in arbitration situations soon learn that they have a burden of proof. The burden of proof is essentially the responsibility of each party to assemble the arguments and evidence necessary to convince the arbitrator that their position is correct.

When you have a conflict with another party and you wish to settle it through arbitration you operate much like a lawyer in a trial or a college debater. You assemble all the facts and arguments that you can marshal together and attempt to convince a third party arbitrator of the wisdom of your position. You will employ evidence in such a way as to construct arguments which you believe cannot be countered by the opposition. To accomplish this you need an understanding of proper argument, reasoning and evidence.

Argument is usually referred to as the inferring of conclusions from data. Perhaps the most useful way of looking at argument is the Toulmin Model of Argument. The Toulmin model of argument includes six parts which combine to form a complete argument. The model is divided into two parts: the essential and the secondary. The three essential parts of the model exist in any argument. Even the simplest argument you and a friend present when you ask another friend to decide if you should go to the movies or the ball game requires three components. The three essential parts of the Toulmin model of argument are data, warrant and claim.

> *Data* is the evidence you use in the argument. It includes the facts, opinions, statistics, examples and testimony that are employed.

> *Warrant* is the mental leap which enables you to infer the claim from the data.

> *Claim* is the position you are supporting. It is the conclusion that you want the third party to reach.

The following hypothetical example should clarify the essential parts of the Toulmin argument. Suppose ballplayer Tom Smith is presenting his case to an arbitrator. He may be arguing that he deserves a 25% pay increase. When he presents his case he points out to the arbitrator that last season he played in 25% more games, hit 25% more home runs, stole 25% more bases and made 25% fewer errors. He then argues that since he improved his contribution to the team by 25%, he ought to get a 25% pay increase. The argument would be diagrammed on the Toulmin model as follows:

Figure 2
Toulmin Model

Data	Warrant	Claim
Tom Smith	A 25% improvement	Mr. Smith
1. Played in 25% more games	in play deserves a 25% increase in pay	deserves a 25% pay increase
2. Hit 25% more home runs		
3. Stole 25% more bases		
4. Made 25% fewer errors		

According to Brockriede and Ehninger (1960), two leading scholars on the Toulmin model, the warrant of a substantive argument may be one of six types. These six types of warrant provide us with six types of argument which are useful in conflict resolution. One example is argument from *cause*. In an argument from cause the warrant takes the data presented and attributes to it a creative or generating power and specifies the nature of the effects that it will produce in the form — the claim. The following example illustrates the point:

Figure 3
Toulmin Model: Causal Warrant

Data	Warrant	Claim
Ballplayer X: 1. Practiced batting 25% more this spring 2. Practiced fielding 25% more this spring 3. Reported to training 25% earlier this spring	Practice in playing ball will cause an improvement in actual play	Ballplayer X will improve 25% this year

The above example of a warrant of cause is just one example of the various types of warrants in argument. While detailed examination of each type of warrant is beyond the scope of this work, arbitration situations often find considerable use of all types of warrants when the various factions present their cases.

The data presented in the argument should conform to the rules of good evidence usually studied in persuasion and debate. This is especially critical to arbitration because the arbitrator is usually skilled in the art of argument and likely to spot weak or insufficient evidence. In court procedures judges often rule evidence inadmissable for a variety of reasons and skilled labor/management arbitrators can spot specious evidence easily and ignore it in their decisions.

Data may include a variety of types. Examples, illustrations, analogies, testimony, and statistics are typical of the material used as data. When employing examples, one should remember that a sufficient number of representative examples is needed to prove a point. Analogies should include comparisons of items that are similar in all essential ways. Testimony should include statements from objective experts in the area of their expertise. Statistics can be misunderstood or misapplied easily unless the user of the statistic understands what the statistic really represents.

The three essential elements of the Toulmin model—data, warrant, and claim—often are sufficient by themselves to make an argument. However, as arguments become more sophisticated, three secondary elements come into play. They include backing, reservation, and qualifier.

> *Backing* is support for your warrant. At times a warrant requires additional support for the audience to make the mental leap from the data to the claim. This support is called backing.

> *Reservation* is the statement of conditions under which your claim is not true. Perhaps the position you are arguing is true under certain conditions. The reservation allows you to specify the conditions under which it is not true.

> *Qualifier* is the measure of force behind your claim. Qualifiers include statements such as probably, possible, certainly, etc.

These three secondary elements add the following dimensions to the diagram previously presented:

Figure 4
Toulmin Model: Complete Diagram

Qualifier
1. Mr. Smith might
   deserve...
2. Mr. Smith probably
   deserves...

Data Tom Smith	Warrant	Claim Tom Smith
1. Played in 25% more games 2. Hit 25% more home runs 3. Stole 25% more bases 4. Made 25% fewer errors	A 25% improvement in play deserves a 25% increase in pay	deserves a 25% pay increase

Backing

1. Past player settlements have often been based on percentage increases in performance

2. Mr. Jones improved his performance 25% and received a 25% increase

Reservation

1. Mr. Smith was hurt in the last game of the season and it is doubtful whether he can play

2. The team's attendance was down 50% last year and management may not have any extra money

In an arbitration situation the complete argument would be presented in this way:

Distinguished Arbitrators: Last year my client Mr. Smith played in 25% more games; he hit 25% more home runs; he stole 25% more bases; his fielding improved 25%. I believe that this performance deserves a 25% increase in pay for Mr. Smith. Now I think you will remember that last year

Mr. Jones received a 25% increase in pay when his performance improved in a similar way. In addition, every other player on the team received a salary adjustment based on the percentage change in his performance. I can see where this position would not be justified if there was some doubt about Smith's health but he is well. I understand that if the team did not have the money this might seem too high, but they have sufficient funds. Therefore, I certainly believe you must award Mr. Smith a 25% increase in salary.

Of course both sides would present their best arguments and the arbitrator would decide on the merits of the case.

Conclusion

Thus the communication tradition provides considerable insight into the improvement of conflict resolution skills. Once an individual orients him or herself toward a positive attitude toward conflict it is possible to use skills from such diverse traditions as interpersonal communications and forensics rhetoric to communicate more effectively.

When attempting to resolve conflict, it is necessary to recognize that a conflict resolution agent must engage in *active* and *adaptive* communication and approach the problem in a *systematic* way. Also an appropriate conflict resolution style often combines *assertiveness* and *cooperativeness* and is labeled a *compromising style of communication*.

The three major conflict situations include *bargaining, mediation,* and *arbitration.* Bargaining includes face-to-face interaction between two parties involved in a conflict, while mediation brings a third party into the conflict who helps the conflicting parties move toward a solution. In arbitration a third party is called in to settle the conflict by providing a solution that is binding on both parties.

When engaging in bargaining it is important to describe your needs, brainstorm possible solutions and then choose the best alternative. Skills of planning, selecting, organizing, providing evidence, evaluating, asking, listening, maintaining an assertive style, and using appropriate influence all contribute to effective bargaining. Good bargainers use sincere communication, non-polarizing communication, signpost communication, and flexible communication, and they do not rely on avoidance communication, misdirected communication, or over-personalized communication.

During the process of mediation, effective communicators use credibility, remain neutral, manage conflict and rumor, know when to listen, how to convey information, when to promote inquiry and how to use allies and avoid risk.

In arbitration situations effective communicators make use of argumentation skills. The Toulmin model of argument is a useful tool for understanding how data, warrant and claim combine with backing, reservation, and qualifier to make an effective arbitration argument.

Overall, conflict resolution is an important aspect of communication and the skills focused on in this chapter should assist you in improving your communication.

References

Adler, R.B. *Confidence in communication: a guide to assertive social skills.* New York: Holt, Rinehart and Winston, 1977.

Brockriede, W. and Ehninger, D. Toulmin on argument: an interpretation and application. *Quarterly Journal of Speech,* 1960, 46, 44-53.

Frost, J.H., and Wilmont, W.W. *Interpersonal conflict.* Dubuque, Iowa: W.C. Brown, 1978.

Jandt, F.E. *Conflict resolution through communication.* New York: Harper and Row, 1973.

Keltner, J.W. *Elements of interpersonal communication.* Belmont, California: Wadsworth Publishing, 1973.

Kilmann, R. and Thomas, K. Interpersonal conflict-handling behavior as reflections of jungion personality dimensions. *Psychological Reports,* 1975, 37, 971-980.

Nye, R.D. *Conflict among humans.* New York: Springer Publishing Company, Inc., 1973.

Rubin, J.Z. and Brown, B.C. *The social psychology of bargaining and negotiation.* New York: Academic Press, 1975.

Schelling, T.C. *The strategy of conflict.* New York: Oxford University Press, 1971.

Semlak, W.D. and Jackson, T.R. *Conflict resolving communication.* In Illinois State University series in Speech Communication, J.F. Cragan (Ed.), Dubuque, Iowa: Kendall/Hunt, 1975.

Smith, C.G. (Ed.). *Conflict resolution: contributions of the behavioral sciences.* South Bend, Indiana: Notre Dame University, 1971.

Toulmin, S. *The uses of argument.* Cambridge, England: Cambridge University Press, 1958.

Villard, K.L. and Whipple, L.J. *Beginnings in relational communication.* New York: John Wiley and Sons, Inc. 1976.

Watzlowick, P.J., Beavin, J., and Jackson, D. *Pragmatics of human communication.* New York: W.W. Norton and Company, 1967.

9

Mass Communication

Ralph L. Smith
Wenmouth Williams, Jr.

Introduction

Perhaps the most common simile used to describe the contemporary
person's involvement with mass communication is that of "immersion".
Each of us is figuratively bathed (some critics cry, "Drowned!") in a
sea of symbols, of messages gushing from a variety of media channels.
The purpose of this chapter is to analyze the nature of the mass
communication environment and to study some effects of our
immersion. It would not be inappropriate to stretch the simile a little
further. The twentieth century has been called the electronic era — a
time characterized by rapidly successive inventions exploiting the
unique characteristics of electro-magnetic forces. With the arrival of
the telegraph, radio, wire-photo, television, computers and satellites,
an increasing flood of electronic messages has changed the chemical
composition of the communications sea. Each human being is an
element suspended in a communications bath with the ensuing electrol-
ysis altering the self through mediators which "extend the human
capacity to share and process information in the form of data, images,
ideas, and even feelings (Real, 1977, p. 10)."

As we examine the historical development, the nature, and the
techniques of these mediators in the next several pages, we will be

ing a background for considering in the last part of the chapter
what the functions of mass communication are, what they do for and to
our society. If, indeed, the mass media change our very selves as they
extend our communicative capacities, then it is imperative that we
become informed critics, capable of influencing the direction of the
changes being wrought in us.

Historical Development

Looking back in time, even comparatively recent time, may seem
irrelevant to persons accustomed to the speed of the electronic present
and the promise of an even more accelerated future. So, let us ease into
history by acknowledging the impact of media on our lives in the here
and now and by taking a brief look at what lies ahead. It is morning in
any college town U.S.A. Check the daily array of media contacts. The
clock radio jolts us awake with a dash of wiry rock and roll. A
succession of brisk voices helps us select clothes appropriate for the
weather, adopt a mood suitable to the sports results of the previous
night and the current new scandals, and propel us toward a fast food
restaurant whose virtues are trumpeted in a brassy jingle. Whether we
jog or bike to class, we are apt to clap on our radio ear muffs to
maintain a rhythmic pace. Often our first conversations of the day
include comments about a TV show or movie from the night before,
and, if we have been skillful at manipulating our class schedules, we
can slip off at mid-morning to continue our addictive involvement in
lives which are wobbling as the world turns. We may assuage the
boredom of a lecture by scanning a folded newspaper and willingly
suffer the boredom of a block long box-office queue to spend a sizeable
sum for tickets to a concert by Emerson, Lake and Palmer or the
Grateful Dead. Then it's back to the room for a session with the
textbooks, punctuated, we must admit, by the latest stereo "dolbyized"
sounds from our personal pop music center. Mass mediated audio,
visual and print stimuli fill our waking hours, guide much of our
behavior, dictate our fashions, shape our tastes and attitudes.

Understandably, for many college students, mass communication is
more than a consumer interest; it is a career interest as well. The
astounding enrollment in journalism programs is a good example of
such interest. It is partly traceable to journalistic results of the U.S.
media event of this century—the uncovering of the Watergate
scandals by two reporters for a major newspaper, the compilation of
their adventures into a best selling book, and the adaptation of that
book into a successful film, *All the President's Men*. Woodward and
Bernstein alias Redford and Hoffman have motivated the journalistic
careers of thousands of young people who were inspired by their
toppling of a corrupt administration. Statistics for 1977 show 64,502

journalism majors in colleges and universities as against 11,000 in 1960, with the big boom starting in 1971 and 1972 (Carmody, 1972). From consumer involvement to professional involvement, college youth are media youth. Current media history is your history, and the future story of mass communication will be your story as well.

Consider briefly technological innovations which are just around the corner. Persistent attempts to achieve recorded musical sounds which are more and more faithful to the live event may make quadraphonic broadcasting more than an experimental experience, just as AM stereo promises to replicate the musical superiority of FM sound. Two-

way television, with home viewers being able to press response buttons in answer to queries from a studio, is now in use on a cable TV channel in Columbus, Ohio. Its "fun and games" application is merely a harbinger of more serious educational, medical, and financial transactions which may some day be available. If the enormous costs can be met, home computer terminals, linked by cable to a variety of institutions, could deliver newsprint as well as TV screen images. Further, home video cassette recorders will enable us to compile individual informational and entertainment libraries supplemented by personally designed and produced programs. As Alvin Toffler (1978) has said, "The tape recorder makes each of us a broadcaster, or more accurately, a narrow-caster. (It and other technological advances represent) the ultimate de-massification of the mass media [p. D-20]." The laser beam, both military threat and communications blessing, will multiply communication channels and create the excitement of holographic television pictures which are startingly three dimensional. And satellites, those transmitter/receivers suspended thousands of miles out in space, will increasingly free our present communications systems from the bonds of land lines and micro-wave towers, permitting cross cultural message sharing on an undreamed of global scale.

Whether or not Toffler's prediction of "de-massification" will actually come to pass, there is no question that the technological whirlwind is reshaping the structures of our mass media. But even as they twist and turn to accommodate new forces, the many among us who want to be intelligent consumers of media and the additional few who seek a professional media relationship need to examine the outlines of structures we have generally taken for granted. We need to study particularly their *business* oriented foundations, and, if you will, engage in the new, TV generated national pastime of tracing our media "Roots."

The Daily Press

A few years ago the publisher of an evening paper in a medium sized, mid-western city invested well over a million dollars in automated equipment which would allow reporters to compose their stories on cathode ray tube terminals and store them in a computer memory bank for later electronic editing. In some plants "papers coming from the presses are stacked, wrapped, tied, and conveyed by computer directed trays into designated slots in delivery trucks for shipment to readers" (Bloomington, Il. *Daily Pantagraph*, June 16, 1974, p. A-5). Why the adoption of expensive, computer technology by a publishing company which enjoyed monopoly status as the only paper in town? The aim was to shave one-half hour from delivery time so the evening newspaper would hit the front porches before the townspeople switched on a television newscast. Electronic competition compelled a counter electronic strategy. Eventually, of course, newspaper content may be delivered via cable directly to a home printer making obsolete the paper boy, if not the front porch.

This switch to computers emphasizes the historical dependence of all mass media on developing technology. In fact, mass communication by definition has meant machine-produced and distributed communication. It was almost a century ago in 1886 that Ottmar Mergenthaler introduced a machine which could set 7,000 characters of type in an hour. Fifty years before that the invention of a steam driven rotary press made possible the printing of 1500 complete papers an hour and heralded the birth of the mass newspaper. Swift distribution of the urban newspaper to a readership far beyond the city came with the extension of the railroads, and the even swifter assemblage of news items from distant points followed the creation of the first telegraph news network (later to be named the Associated Press) in 1848 only four years after the inauguration of the basic device by Samuel Morse. From a score or so of daily papers in the major east coast cities of the 1830's, the newspaper industry increased its output to approximately 500 dailies in 1870 (Emery, 1962, p. 345) and then to a peak of approximately 2500 in 1910. A decline at the early part of this century levelled off, and, for several years now, the number of dailies has remained at approximately 1800 (Sterling & Haight, 1978, p. 20).

The increasingly large sums necessary to take advantage of production efficiencies available in press invention require financially sound operations, and most newspapers are well-run businesses. Despite higher newsprint costs, labor costs and the rivalry of radio/television, newspapers on the whole in this latter part of the twentieth century, remain a very profitable medium. For example, in 1976 data on the major publicly owned newspapers indicate that pre-tax income varied as a percent of revenue from 5.4 to 38.3 percent (Sterling & Haight, 1978, p. 165). Certainly, such respectable profits do not rest on the reader's purchase price. For almost a century and a half, since the appearance in 1833 of Benjamin Day's penny paper, the New York Sun publishers have depended on the rest of the business world to support them by utilizing their pages for advertisements. By 1880, fifty percent of a newspaper's revenue came from advertising (Emery, 1962, p. 398). For the last several years, advertising income has provided about 73% of a newspaper's revenue, and even in these days of high inflation the purchaser pays on average only 15 cents for the paper (Sterling & Haight, 1978, pp. 158, 169).

No astute businessman is going to advertise in a newspaper unless he knows his message will be seen by a vast public. The inducement for the public to read the paper, of course, lies in the content which surrounds the ads. And so, lively reading matter is the catalyst which brings together machines, advertising money and audiences to create the mass media newspaper. First credit must go to those innovative publisher-editors like the aforementioned Benjamin Day, James Gordon Bennett (New York Herald, 1835), and Horace Greeley (New York Tribune, 1851), who retained some of the sober political base of earlier colonial newspapers but added the human interest base of crime reporting, titillating tales of sin in high and low places, and descriptions of unusual events which redefined the concept of "news" from that time forward. These early publishers demanded topics and styles of writing which could attract and hold the attention of thousands of recipients of the new and plain but seviceable common school education.

Lively journalism spawned a style of sheer sensationalism by the end of the nineteenth century, with papers goaded into news excesses at the urging of daring circulation builders like Joseph Pulitzer (New York World, 1883) and William Randolph Hearst (New York Morning Journal, 1895). The successful publisher of one paper soon established another until the pattern of newspaper chains or groups has become the dominant mode of press operation in our time, with over 70 percent of circulation controlled by chains (Sterling & Haight, 1978, p. 83). However, the responsibility of presiding over the complex activities of a modern newspaper group has necessitated a shift from the flamboyant leadership of an earlier day to management specialists with much the same orientation as other industrialists.

The Broadcasting Press

The ominous ticking of a huge stop watch seen in close-up on the television screen is the regular Sunday night reminder in seventeen million American homes (Chagall, 1978) that for the next 60 *Minutes* they will be sharing vicariously experiences from the real world brought to them by a top-flight team of seasoned, investigative journalists. Using the early '50s as the start of a national television system, it took about twenty-five years for a TV news series to more than comfortably hold its own in the frenetic competition of the Sunday evening entertainment schedule. But, for those ancients who can recall the intricate adjustment of dials necessary to generate scratchy voices from an early radio horn, the current mass interest in electronic news comes as no surprise. After all, it was the announcement of President Harding's election in November, 1920 via the wireless facilities of KDKA in Pittsburgh which triggered the birth of *audience* broadcasting in the United States. Telegraphic communication without wires had, of course, been in use ever since Marconi had demonstrated the practicality of harnessing electromagnetic energy in 1895. Improvements before the First World War permitted voice communication, and the radio telephone had become an accepted instrument for business and military transactions over vast distances. But immediately after the war, the sale of radio parts to amateur broadcasters and of complete receiving sets to those not technically inclined created a large group of listeners eagerly awaiting whatever might emanate from transmitting towers being erected in major urban areas. Whether it was the election returns, the voice of our national leader at the White House, or the shouts of the crowd from a live pick-up at a boxing match, early listeners were fascinated by radio's ability to bring them events as they happened. The new medium was a natural channel for the transmission of news as well as music and all the other entertainment forms devised in the late 20's and early 30's.

It was also a natural focal point for confrontation with the newspaper industry. There were two sensitive issues: 1) in the traditional race to deliver stories to the public in the fastest possible time, a radio wave would always beat a rotary press, 2) in terms of financial support, the new industry had settled for advertising as its sole source of income, thus threatening the newspapers' relationship with long-time clients. Some astute publishers joined the enemy and started their own radio stations. Others pressured their wire services to limit the sale of news to broadcasters. The youthful but rapidly growing radio networks were denied wire service news outright. The National Broadcasting Company (NBC) and the Columbia Broadcasting System (CBS) countered by organizing news departments in 1933 (Barnouw, 1968, p. 19). Within four or five years it became apparent that radio bulletins were not enough to satisfy audience news needs. Listeners wanted amplification of what they had heard and continued to buy papers for additional information. And although advertisers were now splitting their budgets between media, more new advertisers were joining the ranks, and in general the financial machinery of the print and electronic presses continued to be well-oiled.

In the end, the economic pressures which brought on the press war and resulted in the creation of major network news departments benefitted our nation as it plunged into World War II. Coverage of that cataclysmic event compelled the assignment world-wide of reporters who could deliver their stories live over an electronic network managed with split-second timing. It motivated the development of audio recorders from which came new techniques of editing and new forms like the documentary. It generated enough advertising money to finance experimentation with television news and to provide an initial foundation for the kind of visual pioneering of the 50's which resulted in TV series like Edward R. Murrow's *See It Now* and Walter Cronkite's *Twentieth Century*. The prestige of network news and public affairs efforts over the years has, in addition, stimulated the development of strong news departments at the local TV station level. American audiences now consume electronic news with the same avidity accorded the daily press. This increasingly high interest in news has begun to turn a traditional red-ink aspect of broadcasting into a marginal profit factor. For example, between the years 1972-76, network news operations which had been losing $16,635,000 a year were steadily able to increase advertising rates on news shows until the latest statement indicated a profit of $21,560,000 (Michie, 1977). A similar healthy financial situation exists at local television stations. By contrast with the evolution of the daily newspaper from a flamboyant, turn of the century adventurer into a more sober-suited compendium of information, the broadcast press may still seem like a brash upstart. But both media continue to meet the demands of readers, listeners and viewers for knowledge of what is taking place in the world around them.

Prime Time Entertainment

The pervasive availability of hard news, much of it bad, exacts a toll from society. The cynicism, the anxiety, the apathetic response are symptoms of our general malaise with regard to the ill winds which blow around us. However, a palliative for this condition is produced by the very same media. Bad news on the tube at six drives us to "Happy Days" on the tube at seven when the fictional world of prime time takes over from the real world of crime time. And when we tire of television, we turn to the soothing or at least distracting sounds of pop music.

Just as the mass media historically have depended on technology for their development, so have they depended on entertaining content for their continued existence. The roots of electronic entertainment lie in comedy often associated with an array of light-hearted diversions collectively known as "sit-coms". It is not difficult to see in Fonzie and friends a relationship to the youthful Henry Aldrich, high school prankster in the hey-day of network radio, nor to discern a similarity between *Welcome Back, Kotter* and *Our Miss Brooks* who made an easy transition from radio to television in the 1950's. The indestructible Bob Hope typifies variety show entertainers who have descended directly from the song, dance and patter artists, first of British music hall days before the turn of the century, and then from the flourishing vaudeville circuits 1900-1925.

These two forms—situation comedy and variety—were the major program types which attracted national advertising money in large enough amounts even at the start of the depression to assure the financial success of NBC (founded 1926) and CBS (founded 1928). Local radio stations were anxious to contract for telephone line connections with networks, since these program suppliers not only filled many hours, particularly the prime listening time between 7 p.m. and 10 p.m. (C.S.T.), with highly polished entertainment, but they also returned to the station a portion of the national sponsor's payment. So successful were the chain broadcasting systems that network revenue from the sale of advertising grew from $63,000,000 in 1935 to $99,000,000 five years later (Sterling & Haight, 1978, p. 122). By the end of World War II, radio had achieved, as we have seen, enormous prestige for its coverage of news and public affairs and also enormous wealth as the largest purveyor of popular entertainment. In the process, the radio industry had relinquished to advertising agencies its control over program creation.

Within a few years all had changed. Coast to coast television networking was completed by 1951. NBC, CBS, and the step child ABC were regaining program control in the new medium, since national advertisers were wary of television's cost and effectiveness. Radio, deprived of its prime time entertainment role, was learning to attract enough local advertisers so that the number of AM stations more than doubled between 1946 and 1951 (Sterling & Haight, 1978, p. 43). Even FM radio, successfully tested in 1934 then placed in storage, slowly became accepted as an alternative source for discriminating music fans. Radio is now a specialized music and local news service, similar in function to the specialized magazines.

The rest is the recent history of a nation still trying to come to grips with the economic, cultural, and political colossus which television has become. The networks, which also own five TV stations each, are now so wealthy that, like many newspaper chains, they invest in a great many other businesses. This, some critics believe, is to the detriment of a more sharply focused concern for their major function of broadcast communications. For example, CBS manufactures musical instruments and children's toys (Creative Playthings). It owns a chain of stereo stores and publishes Women's Day magazine as well as a massive line of paper-back books (CBS Annual Report, 1977, p. 7). The roots of broadcast entertainment touch many aspects of the business world, and they are finally beginning to intertwine more closely with that most glamorous of "show biz" activities, the big screen whose directors, actors, and actresses have always been larger than life.

The Movies

The creators of America's commercially packaged dreams have become flexible businessmen and artists moving from one entertainment medium to the other. As one example, John Dykstra, producer of ABC's 1978 television series *Galactica*, devised the special effects for the Twentieth Century-Fox film *Star Wars* (TV Guide, September 9, 1978, p. 31). And for several years now, Universal Studios, a major force in the Hollywood film industry, has also been the largest producer of network television programs. Other famous studios, like Paramount, Columbia, and Warner Brothers, are busy with television series and with acting as financiers and distributors for independent film producers with whom they contract on a picture to picture basis.

The financial machinations of movie making are particularly complex, since films are paid for not by commercials but by extremely unpredictable ticket sales. The average film has a $5.3 million budget (up 178% from 1974-1978). The risk that millions may be lost on a picture with a poor box-office is still offset however by the lure of riches such as those generated by *Star Wars* which resulted in Twentieth Century-Fox reporting "record earnings of $50.8 million for 1977—an astonishing 474 percent increase over 1976" (*Newsweek*, February 13, 1978, p. 73.) Hollywood may be ailing but it has definitely exorcised the specter of cavernous, empty sound stages which haunted the visions of its movie moguls during the 50's as television was staking out its audience claims. Film's initial working arrangement with TV came in the mid-60's with a decision on the part of Hollywood executives to finally release to the networks hours of superb dramatic and comedy fare stored in their vaults.

Many of these executives had learned to change tack several times before. During the 30's and 40's, eight major studios controlled almost all film production in the United States. They owned both production facilities and theaters and gave steady employment to hundreds of writers, stars and supporting players. However, in 1948 they were forced by a Supreme Court, anti-monopoly decision to divest themselves of their movie house chains. The exhibition of films now had to be negotiated separately for each picture made. Theater owners could no longer be forced to take a string of mediocre releases in order to qualify for showing first-rate films. In 1927, these same companies at tremendous cost had to retool their equipment and find new, vocally adept stars who could accommodate themselves to the arrival of "sound" movies. Even earlier than that, business entrepreneurs closely allied with the banking industry had garnered control of the production/distribution process and had seen the one reeler's of 1905 expand to full length features and move out of tiny store front theaters into larger, garrishly designed palaces. The flickering 1889 invention of Thomas Edison and George Dickson had become during the first half of this century the regular "evening out" for thousands and then millions of Americans. "By 1947, 87 million people were going to the movies every week" (Pember, 1977, p. 249). Even though the crowds have fallen off, preferring to remain glued to the tiny screen, a night at the movies still retains some of the old excitement, and Hollywood, embracing as it does film and television, is still the mass media entertainment capital of the world.

Media Regulatory Roots

No human enterprise runs trouble free, and one devoted to the creation and dissemination of communication messages varying from investigative news stories to passionate love scenes is bound to have its conflicts with the public or its representatives. Social control of the mass media is a persistent problem. Take the case of the Stanford Daily, an independent student newspaper at Stanford University. On April 12, 1971, four law enforcement officers with a search warrant entered the newsroom seeking photographic evidence for the prosecution of persons who had injured some police in a sit-in demonstration at Stanford Hospital several days earlier. The newspaper had published pictures of the dispersing of the demonstration, and the authorities wanted to identify additional law-breakers. After an examination of files, drawers, and wastebaskets they found nothing. The "Daily" took the case to court claiming illegal search of an innocent third party and violation of First Amendment rights as a member of the press.

Lower courts upheld the newspaper indicating that a subpoena (which can be resisted in court) requiring the staff to submit specific materials would have been more appropriate than the much looser device of a search warrant which could destroy reporter/source confidentiality and threaten the press's newsgathering ability. But, seven years later in May 1978, the U.S. Supreme Court issued a stunning (5-3) reversal stating that, First Amendment or no, when it came to possession of evidence of criminal activity, the press had no special privileges. The minority court opinion held that, under the First Amendment, our Constitution explictly protects the freedome of the press. Many newspersons now feel that, in the future, hastily issued warrants will result in a continuing open hunting season on journalists (Czerniejewski, 1978), although California, itself, rapidly passed a law effective January 1, 1979, protecting reporters with the subpoena restriction, and the Carter Administration has asked for similar national protection.

The "Stanford decision" exemplifies our society's constant need to weigh conflicting considerations — in this case support of a criminal investigation by the police versus support of unhampered news gathering. In the weighing of such issues, reference is invariably made to that first regulatory principle enunciated in the Bill of Rights 187 years ago by revolutionaries who had suffered for their ideas in print at the hands of an angry crown. But, as we have just seen, press freedom need not be interpreted as absolute, even if it rests on many revered historical documents stretching back through distant centuries to pronouncements on liberty of thought and the dependence of truth on a free marketplace of ideas. In fact, the tap root of the First Amendment, helpful though it has been in assuring the dissemination of a riotous profusion of viewpoints, runs parallel to other devices used to prune and shape mass communication efforts into socially responsible paths.

Despite occasional reversals, the print media in the United States have been legally free (libel being the major exception) to do essentially as they please. Not so with broadcasting. Except for a few years at the beginning, broadcasters have had to procure a license from the federal government, promising to operate their stations in the public interest, convenience and necessity. The Communications Act of 1934 declares that the air waves are owned by all the people and that no user can have a perpetual license. Owners of stations must request renewal every three years, and their operations are reviewed at that time. To be sure, the act includes a free speech provision consonant with the First Amendment. It even includes a doctrine which attempts to define how a broadcaster is to be fair in allowing divergent viewpoints to be aired. But the rules and regulations emanating from the FCC (Federal Communications Commission) over the last 44 years leave no question that the broadcaster must follow a complex array of guidelines.

Why a plethora of mandatory rules for broadcast media and not for the media of print and film? Partly because the original legislation of the 20's and 30's reflects the state of electronic technology at that time. Radio receivers lacked proper circuitry to prevent the overlap of signals on nearby frequencies and transmitters were not designed to hold to a constant frequency. With more and more stations taking to the air, the only quick way to prevent a deteriorating service was to limit licenses and define each transmitter operating at an assigned frequency in a certain geographical area as a monopoly subject to the kind of public interest concerns historically demanded in earlier public utility legislation. Broadcast regulations also reflect the uniqueness of radio and television as family media which, because they so easily enter the home, can more appropriately be held to account than other media.

However, technology (and permissive entertainment, it would seem) moves inexorably along, and just about the time the Supreme Court was reminding newspaper publishers that their First Amendment rights could be controlled, the Congress in June 1978 received for consideration a bill which would radically decontrol broadcasting. The architects of the proposed law argue that the public utility concept applied to radio and television has encouraged the dominance of our entire broadcasting system by three major networks. The bill would substitute "a free and open market where all the existing (as well as the newer media of cable, satellites, laser transmission would)" compete relatively unobstructed by the Federal Government. Broadcast licenses would become permanent, with the stations required only to present some news and local programming each day (Brown, 1978, p. D-41)." In exchange for essentially unfettered operation, a single commercial broadcaster would be more severely limited in the number of stations he could own (down from 21 to 10), and he would have to pay a substantial, annual "spectrum use" fee for each station. The fees, estimated to total $350 million/year, would meet the operational expenses of a new regulatory commission and help subsidize public, non-profit television and radio stations. These two examples of governmental concern, varying all the way from court restrictions on the press to a proposal for laissez faire regulation of electronic media, highlight the continuing dilemma of devising rules to insure the free and diverse but responsible operation of mass media in a democracy.

Nor has industry self-regulation resulted in any more thoroughly satisfactory solutions to widespread public irritations with mass media for such grievances as biased reporting, an inordinate emphasis on sex and violence, and harmful advertising. Newspapers have had an ethical code for journalists since 1923. Hollywood has experimented for decades with several different film content evaluation systems, the latest being a picture rating system (G, PG, R, X) adopted in 1968. And broadcasters, through their national association, voluntarily subscribe to several pages of rules (first adopted in 1927) regarding such items as appropriate plots, language, costumes, and product announcements.

Nevertheless, the tempers of all sorts of critics remain short, and many of them are banding together, searching out ingenious strategies for expressing their displeasure even to the point of causing governmental agencies like the FCC, FDA (Food and Drug Administration), FTC (Federal Trade Commission) to demonstrate anew concerns which have all but lain dormant for decades. For example, ACT (Action for Children's Television), a consumer group founded in 1968 and dedicated to reducing commercial abuses in children's programming, has pressured the Federal Trade Commission to start hearings in early 1979 on proposed rules to ban all television advertising directed to children under eight and, in the interests of dental health, to restrict children's commercials for sugared products (Re:Act, Fall 1978).

Other complaints involve issues which cut across different media and are directed at the limited access which most people have to the varied communications enterprises supposedly operating in their interest. A landmark decision by a U.S. Court of Appeals in 1969, allowed the black community of Jackson, Mississippi, supported by the Office of Communication of the United Church of Christ, to intervene directly in challenging the license renewal of WLBT-TV on the basis that the station was not meeting its needs (Parker, 1972). The challenge eventually led to a citizen's group becoming the licensee and creating new TV programs for the city. Numerous renewal cases in other communities followed, some resulting in new ownership and others in concessions made particularly in the area of minority employment and programming. Such agitation had indirect repercussions for the newspaper industry which over the years had invested heavily in

broadcasting properties, frequently resulting in media monopolies in many communities. Although a Supreme Court ruling in 1978 has preserved many existing joint ownerships, 16 crossownerships must be dissolved, and the FCC is authorized to block future crossownerships (*Quill*, July/August, 1978, pp. 7,8).

Society's ambivalent concerns about matters such as free speech, station licensing, harmful media content, and concentrations of ownership have resulted in a complex tangle of governmental and private regulatory maneuvers. Historically, the fear was that dissenting voices would be quashed by central authority. Hence, a constitutional guarantee of press freedom. However, as mass media have developed, a new fear has arisen. Giant combinations of newspaper, film and broadcasting interests, heavily supported by businesses needing to sell goods and services, are seen as another kind of concentrated authority frequently unresponsive to enhancing citizen access to media and to meeting constructive informational and entertainment needs of the people. Hence, continuing and often contradictory demands for new tools of media regulation.

The Nature of Mass Communication

Describing American mass communication is not an easy task. But, the very word "mass" provides an inevitable starting point. We can always measure the size of the various components and their audiences, and that we propose to do first. Then we will examine some basic characteristics of mass communication as they pertain to the audience, the communicative experience, and the communicator.

The Extent of Media Systems

Certain statistics have already been cited as evidence of the amazing growth of mass media as the nation itself moved through the stages of westward expansion and industrial revolution into the present period of high technology. But now we must examine our "incredible communications hulk" in greater statistical detail. It is not enough to mention that our media system includes 1811 daily newspapers (Sterling & Haight, 1978, p. 20), 8346 radio stations, 967 television stations (*Broadcasting*, May 8, 1978, p. 76), 15,969 movie theaters (Sterling & Haight, 1978, p. 36), and that almost 19 billion dollars were spent by advertisers in placing commercial messages with the print and electronic media in 1976 (Sterling & Haight, 1978, p. 129). Some indication of the news/editorial, program, and film activity in these highly competitive media factories can be seen in the following production approximations:

1. The average daily newspaper consists of about 56 pages, with perhaps 21 pages being devoted to editorial copy (news and features) and 35 to advertising (Hiebert, Ungurait & Bone, 1974, p. 237).

2. The average radio station broadcasts music about 18 hours a day. A 1977 survey in the top 25 markets reported that "contemporary," "middle-of-the-road," and "good" music are the most-listened to formats (Clift & Greer, 1978, p. 125).

3. The average television station broadcasts a wide variety of program types 18 hours a day. An analysis of network

programming which accounts for as much as two-thirds of a local station's air-time, reveals that light entertainment consumes about 75% of the evening hours and about 60% of the daytime schedule (figures extrapolated from Sterling & Haight, 1978, p. 316). This does not include sports and station purchased syndicated entertainment. News, public affairs, and miscellaneous other program types complete the television offerings.

4. By contrast with the thousands of hours of programs produced by the television industry each year, the feature films released to movie houses by the eight major distribution companies, in 1976 for example, totaled only 92 (Sterling & Haight, 1978, p. 31).

Considering the prominence which the press, broadcasting, and films have in our society, and in light of their high productive output, employment in these fields is not massive. The Bureau of Labor Statistics tells us that in March 1977 approximately 383,000 persons were employed by newspapers, 202,000 by the motion-picture industry, and 157,000 by radio and television companies (Sterling & Haight, 1978, p. 219.) In comparison, the telephone segment of the communications industry alone employs almost one-million persons.

But, of course, the social impact made by mass media institutions is not a function of the size of the employee roster. These are highly visible enterprises because the people in our society pay them so much attention. And that attention has been measured, dissected, and analyzed from almost every conceivable angle. We know, for example, that 61 million newspapers are bought every day, that 71.5 million homes (97.9% of all homes) have television sets and that those sets are in use about 6.5 hours each day. We also know that 44 million people went to the movies during an average week in 1965 (Sterling & Haight, 1978, pp. 333-374). This last bit of dated information may reflect the film industry's embarrassment at releasing figures to a public which has transferred big screen loyalty to the little screen.

So it goes. Simple nose counting has expanded over the years into marketing research, with skilled professionals charting not only demographic items like audience age, sex, income, and education, but also attitudes and emotional reactions to material, even to measuring the dilation of eyes (pupilometrics) and the sweating of fingers (galvanic skin testing).

Such meticulous probing is done by many of the 6,000 advertising agencies, by departments within the mass communication industry, and by special research firms like the A.C. Nielsen Company, compiler of the notorious Nielsen Rating Index which spells life or death for network television programs. The index is so well-known and exemplifies so clearly, the utter financial dependency of a giant communications industry on a slim sample of audience feedback, that it will be worthwhile to comment specifically on the system and in the commenting to reveal yet another aspect of mass media's nature.

For all its power, the basic Nielsen procedure is a simple tallying of the number of television receivers tuned to the various TV stations in a carefully selected nationwide, cross-section of American homes. Twelve-hundred locations form the reporting group, and their program choices are charted electronically through audimeters connecting the TV sets to a computer center in Florida. Periodically, during the broadcast schedule the sets are "called" automatically over special phone lines and the data is processed. Television personnel from network executives, to local station managers, from west coast producers to nervous writers and actors anxiously await two numerical results. The first is the "rating" figure for a show. It indicates what percentage of the nation's 71.5 million television homes are watching that program. The second figure is the "share"—a comparative percentage which indicates what proportion of all home sets turned on are actually watching that program and what percentage are tuned to other shows.

A few seasons back, ABC's *Roots* became the most watched entertainment television program in history, and its Nielsen report will clarify the process. For example, on Sunday evening, January 30, 1977, the *Roots* episode garnered a 51.1 rating (over half of all the TV homes in the nation were tuned into the drama) and a 71 share. The latter figure means that of homes with sets turned on, 71% of them were watching the ABC network, leaving CBS, and NBC, to split up the remaining 29% of the audience between themselves [Clift & Geer, 1978, p. 48]. Quite an evening for ABC, and quite a disappointment for the others, because ratings and shares translate directly into the dollars which network broadcasters can charge national advertisers and which local stations can charge hometown merchants. "A commercial minute on a top-rated show like 'Three's Company' costs an advertiser $147,000 compared with a charge of $60,000 or even less for shows low in the rankings (Chagall, 1978, p. 4)." And, averaged out over an entire season, dips of one or even a few tenths of a rating point can result in millions of dollars lost to a network which must adjust its advertising rates downward.

It once again becomes clear why the mass media, broadcasting quite obviously and newspapers somewhat less so, have as a basic part of their natures, a constant nagging concern for what will please rather than serve the largest audiences, for what will attract advertisers rather than meet community needs, for what creative writers and other artists must do rather than want to do. Radio and television, in particular, have always been so bound by the numbers game, that box scores remain the sole determinants of program schedules.

It makes little difference that there has been serious criticism of the Nielsen formula which produces ratings statistically accurate only two out of three times. Dr. James H. Myers, research consultant to large corporations, has said of the Nielsen procedure, "I've never seen any reputable firm using such a low level of confidence. If I were advising any business firm using their data, I would tell them caveat emptor—let the buyer beware [Chagall, 1978, p. 8]." Sponsors and broadcasters have heard this kind of warning for years, but they are not interested in paying any more money for a large sample and better maintenance of an expensive system. After all, a large advertising agency may already be paying the Nielsen Company $300,000 a year for its services [Chagall, 1978, p. 3]. Further, one could argue that the audimeter tally is still more constant and less subject to error than having to rely on phone calls and diaries and audience memories. Thus, the tyranny of numbers. What should be only one guideline to programming decisions, ends up as the master of the broadcasting industry.

Basic Characteristics of Mass Communication

As we consider additional aspects of mass communication, sociologist Charles R. Wright would remind us not to mistake the technology for the process. Mass communication is a special kind of social intercourse involving three factors: the nature of the audience, the nature of the communication experience, and the nature of the communicator. Further, he suggests that each of these factors includes a number of specific characteristics (Wright, 1975).

Newspaper readers, television viewers, film goers share some common qualities at least with respect to the initiators of communication messages. All three audiences are large in the sense that there is no possibility for an intimate, face-to-face relationship between the sender and the receiver of a message. The message flows only one way. Consequently, immediate feedback and the useful interchange which promotes clearer understanding gives way to such devices as "letters-to-the-editor" columns and the kinds of audience research alluded to earlier. Further, mass communication audiences are heterogenous—a mix of ages, sexes, economic and educational backgrounds. This tends to force message content into stylistic molds emphasizing easy vocabulary levels and easily recognizable structures. Efforts to create messages for more narrowly defined groups continue with obvious success in the magazine world, and with growing sophistication in the world of FM radio. Even television, realizing that essentially everyone is addicted, still hammers out its prime-time schedule each year with a greedy ratings eye on the purchasing power of couples between the ages of 18 and 39. Finally, media audiences are anonymous. But inventive entrepreneurs have devised numerous strategies for fans to at least recognize each other. We may not yet have followed Howard

Beale's wild exhortation in the film *Network* to throw open our windows and shout, but t-shirts, bumper stickers, posters, rallies and conventions occasionally draw us from the normal isolation cells of our mass communication environment.

Audience members may be private and anonymous, but the messages in the mass communication experience are so intensely public that various forms of censorship or at least control are frequently called into play. For example, in 1973 the Supreme Court reassured citizens concerned about obscenity that contemporary community standards should prevail in reaching decisions about media content. In addition to their public nature, mass communication messages share two other characteristics: rapidity and transiency. Items of national policy such as the recognition of the People's Republic of China which, a century ago, would have taken months to reach the level of community debate can now be announced on the radio at noon, refined in the local newspaper at five, and analyzed in a network TV public affairs program at ten-thirty the same night. Further, through proper orchestration of media deadlines, a small, impoverished, but determined group can make its cause an item for national policy by taking similar advantage of the sweep and speed of mass communication.

Media channels, crowded with brief messages, squeezed in and around advertisements, dictate against thoughtful, patient presentation. All too often the emphasis is on timeliness, superficiality, and sensation. This element of transiency is a particular characteristic of the electronic media, many of whose messages are designed to be heard or seen once and then disappear into nothingness. The ephemeral nature of electronic entertainment may be of small consequence. But, as main instruments of public enlightenment, literary critic Northrup Frye (1970) reminds us that radio and television's transiency is a danger. "...the written or printed record," he says, "makes it possible to return to the experience. ...The document is also the focus of a community...it is only writing that makes democracy technically possible. It is significant that our symbolic form for a tyrant is 'dictator': that is an uninterrupted speaker [p. 35]."

Charles Wright's third factor in the mass communication process is the nature of the communicator. A visitor walking into a newsroom, a television control room or a film studio for the first time is frequently bewildered by the seeming confusion. How can a reporter, let alone an editor, organize a clear sequence of thought amid the constant ringing of the phone and the bustle of other workers? How can a director compose all the sources of picture and sound into a smoothly flowing, split-second segment of television when five monitor screens, headphone commands, and engineers' comments all vie for attention? How can an actress used to building a characterization in a quiet, darkened theater perform short scenes requiring instant concentration while keeping an eye out for microphone position, floor cables, and unwanted shadows? The mass media communicator is merely one professional among many. Media messages are produced in a complex, tightly organized setting involving a high degree of specialization and obviously an enormous budget. For example, in 1976 newsprint and ink alone consumed thirty percent of a large city newspaper's income of $31,000,000 a year (Sterling & Haight, 1978, p. 166). During the period 1950 to 1974, the cost for one episode of a typical half hour, network drama rose from $12,910 to $100,515. Of course, the earlier drama would have been a live performance, but most of the production elements would have been similar (Sterling & Haight, 1978, p. 214). And we have already mentioned the average production cost of $5,300,000 for a feature film (see p. 12). This intricate, mass communications world of productivity by committee and of high finance has the practical effect of removing the creative artist (the initial writer and idea person) several stages away from decisions about and responsibility for the final product. Further, the cost factor makes it almost impossible for modestly financed groups to start a newspaper or for unknown persons with valid, worthwhile ideas and skills to get a hearing before media program planners. Meanwhile, the harried, talented professionals, already overburdened by work, perform in an atmosphere of speed and intense competition which can become exhausting to creativity.

The institutions of mass communication can partly be described by referring to their size and the extent of their operations and partly by explaining how they differ in several ways from other forms of communication. But obviously some comments about media content are in order. Since details are impossible in a brief space, some general points about mass media technique must suffice.

Media Content

The basic intention of all communication is the generation of a response to a received message. In the one-way flow of mass communication, responses may be varied and delayed, but the clearest, most satisfying response of all, as far as media managers are concerned, is the return of the audience for more. When circulation goes up, the publisher is happy. The long line at the cinema box-office is as much a cause for joy among movie moguls as an upward swing of households using television is for broadcast executives. And the advertisers are equally gleeful when the cost per thousand of impressions (an impression occurs when an individual sees or hears a commercial) seems justified by the immense size of an audience.

It would seem that the whole trick lies in seizing and holding the attention of the receiver and then providing enough satisfaction to insure a return visit. How do artisans of the mass media do it? Obviously, there is no single answer, but among the welter of exhibits to which we are all exposed we should be able to detect a few significant techniques. Three will be briefly described and analyzed not only with regard to their efficacy but also with regard to their weakness.

Message Simplicity

Theodore Peterson (1963) claims that the mass media have followed the path of other mass-production industries. In the change from personal craft industries, they have become impersonal and standardized, adjusting their content to a "common denominator of taste, interest, and capability [p. 420]." A common denominator implies common expectations on the part of the media audience and common perceptions of the audience on the part of the craftsman. The result is message composition according to fairly rigid formulas which stress simplicity and repetition in structure, in theme, in language. To be sure, production factors, at least in press and broadcasting, also mandate the simple formula technique. The frantic pace of media output does not provide time for finesse. Nor does the space allotted to news stories as contrasted with advertising space allow room for background detail. A similar situation exists in radio and television, with commercial announcements regulating the amount of time available for program content.

The formulas bring us information and entertainment in short, uncomplicated bursts. A reporter must learn to compress the major aspects of an event into the initial paragraphs, since busy people and those for whom reading is a chore will turn to something else long before the end of the story. This so called "inverted pyramid" style is also helpful to editors who can more easily meet production deadlines and the shifting limits of space by scratching chunks of writing without damaging the basic facts of an item. If deletions are a frequent practice at newspapers, they are an absolute necessity in broadcast news where twenty stories each scarcely twenty seconds long comprise a TV station's look at the day's events (Townley, 1974). All too often the announcement "Headline News" has become just that in radio and television — headlines and no more.

Situation comedies and mystery/adventure shows are the best examples of formula entertainment. If our television diet seems bland and unexciting season after season, blame it on the fact that these twenty-six or fifty-two minute slices of processed life have become totally predictable. Despite exceptions like *All in the Family* or *M*A*S*H* or *The Mary Tyler Moore Show*, where characters sometimes grow and develop. The basic process that Harold Mehling (1962) described with a good measure of cynicism still obtains:

> The series formula locks the writer into a carefully padded cell. ...He cannot endow them (the characters) with personalities he would like to explore; their personalities were molded long ago by the studio, the network, and the sponsor and are not, of course, subject to change from week to week. And he cannot violate the laws that closely govern their existence on television: he must dramatize this week's problem quickly, allow for a commercial interruption, thicken the plot with familiar acceptable misadventures, allow for a second commercial, solve the problem in a familiar, acceptable way, allow for a third commercial, and exit with a bit of familiar banter or homily. If he violates these rigid laws, he does not have a show, and if his violations are chronic, he does not have a career [p. 158].

Notice Mr. Mehling's use of the word "familiar" as part of the concept of the formula show. Just as readers have come to expect the meat of the news in the first paragraph and listeners have been trained to flip the radio on at the top of the hour for instant headlines, so audiences expect to see the same old television friends going through essentially the same old paces week after week. The familiar, the repetitious, is an aspect of message simplicity which media managers recognize as being essential to audience acceptance. Even films, which have more time and more opportunity to present plots with complicated twists and turns and to explore character in greater detail, often settle for an *Airport II* or *Star Wars II* or the casting of a new talent in a succession of stories which simply emphasize one set of characteristics already thoroughly exploited in a TV sitcom. John Travolta is the predictable, sensitive "macho" in *Saturday Night Fever*, *Grease*, and *Moment by Moment*.

Simplicity pervades the choice of symbols comprising the various language elements (verbal, pictorial, musical) of media messages. Certainly, much mass media material is written for people on the run. There is no time to muse over the meaning of a complex sentence while being jostled in the subway. And the drive-time news must be crystal clear for the harried motorist whose mind is everywhere. Lean, pithy language requires craftsmanship of a high order, and media information frequently displays such craftsmanship. The risk, however, lies in the narrow context into which the description of events must be forced. The audience for the day's intelligence comes away thinking it is literate and knowledgeable when it is still illiterate and uninformed about issues. In one sense the on-the-spot film clip has given them the picture, but in another the swift dissolve into the next stream of images still leaves them blind.

The simplified symbols in media fiction permit instant identification and the comfort and satisfaction that comes from knowing the score. By dress, by vocal mannerisms, by closeups on a straightforward or shifty gaze, by an ominous or peaceful musical progression, we know the good guys from the bad guys. Three minutes into a series segment we can predict, with a fair amount of accuracy, further revelations and the final resolution of the story. We have become as scene-wise as the talented artists responsible for the message.

Again, the satisfactions that derive from such awareness and recognition are not to be decried. But, we would probably agree with Abraham Kaplan (1967) that "the world of popular art is bounded by the limited horizons of what we think we know already; it is two-dimensional because we are determined to view it without budging a step from where we stand [p. 32]." Audiences tend not to look for new experiences in the mass media, but for a repetition and even an affirmation of their old experiences.

Message Intimacy

For all its eventual impact, the actual process of communicating with a "mass" is flat and unreal. The communicator is writing or talking or acting to the unknown. Consequently, media professionals have worked hard to analyze their audiences and to try to devise techniques which will draw the reader, the listener, the viewer into as close a psychic bond as possible considering the total absence of physical ties. To some extent the attempt to involve the reader more deeply in the pages of the newspaper is contradictory to the more austere assumption of the press that its job is to present events with stringent objectivity. But there is no denying the recent influence of a reportorial style loosely called the new journalism. Stemming from the middle 60's work of Tom Wolfe, Jimmy Breslin, Gay Talese, Truman Capote and others, the thesis is that the real world is internal and that the reporter's task is not merely to give readers facts but to help them "walk in the shoes" of the principals in an event, to draw them into sharing the experience. Such writers have illuminated traditional news items like political campaigns, murder trials, military strikes, by substituting scene by scene structure for the inverted pyramid style, by stressing dialogue instead of prose narration, by including references to props and costumes. The result is often closer to a short story than a news article. The reader is indeed brought into more intimate contact with human experience.

Even papers which frown on adopting the new journalism style for their news pages have been adding more personal departments to the traditional horoscope and *Dear Abby* columns. The emphasis in features seems to be on you and me as consumers, investors, and Mr.

Fix-its around the house. If we have psychological hurts and physical pains, the newspaper will provide a confidante who will share our difficulties. And if that isn't enough, we can compare our sufferings to the problems of jet-setters and other "newsworthy" people whose most private lives are revealed in ever more daring gossip columns. Newspapers are reaching out to touch us and draw us into a more intimate and involved relationship.

What are the techniques of the electronic communicator who is trying to establish a one-to-one rapport with the unseen audience? Obviously verbal style is important. In the days of old time radio, Arthur Godfrey was one of the first station hosts to move away from the meticulous, formal style deemed appropriate for announcers. He talked with his listeners in a casual manner, like a guy in the corner bar. He even laughed at the exaggerated claims he was supposed to read for his sponsor's products, and audiences loved him as a friend and neighbor. The new, intimate style was only slightly altered in terms of energy and pace as radio became a young person's medium and a performer called a disc jockey chattered his way into the lead position. To listen to John Landeker of big-time rock station WLS in Chicago, is to listen to a talented conversationalist, hugging the microphone, able to convince high-schoolers and other youth that he cares about their interests, that he is their friend.

In television, it's not only the comfortable personality of old buddy Johnny Carson that helps us in the lonely night hours, it's the camera technique as well. We catch his intimate, knowing wink because it's intended for us alone as he looks directly into the close-up lens. Even as he keeps the conversational ball bouncing between one or two guests, his is the dominant presence. He relates to us because his microphone is always closer to his lips than is the boom microphone to the other performers. And the camera shots of Johnny during interviews are always more numerous than the shots of the guests. From emcee to anchor person to weather reporter to the nervous, one-time political candidate, anyone in a television studio tries to master the skill of talking through the teleprompter and through the lens to engage the viewer as in real-life contact.

Tony Schwartz, radio documentarist and creator of hundreds of commercial announcements and political ads for radio and television, is an informal researcher who propounds a theory of communication closely related to this matter of message intimacy (Schwartz, 1974). For him the key word in the design of successful media messages is "resonance", a term he borrows from the acoustic laboratory where physicists have studied the way in which a small amount of sound energy can become greatly magnified when it is set to reverberating in a properly tuned chamber. Turning to radio and television, Schwartz believes that resonance occurs when the stimuli in an electronic message evoke meaning in a listener or viewer. He states the receiver brings far more information to the communication event than the communicator can put into his program or commercial. It is the job of the communicator to understand the kinds of information and experiences stored in the audience memory and then to marshall appropriate words, music, pictures, and sound effects to trigger these stored experiences. The idea is not to try to direct information into an audience but to evoke stored information out of them in a patterned way. Schwartz cites as an example a TV anti-smoking spot announcement he designed for the American Cancer Society. Rather than give the viewers death statistics, he drew on viewer experience and showed two children dressing up in their parents' clothes. "At the very end, a voice-over announcer says very calmly, 'Children love to imitate their parents....Children learn by imitating their parents. Do you smoke cigarettes?' The American Cancer Society said it was the most successful spot they ever ran....The anti-smoking message was not in the words or visual of the commercial but in the feelings evoked by the commercial stimuli [p. 55]." The evocation of feeling, the responsive chord struck between the writer, the radio or television personality, the film star and his audience depends a great deal on the sensitive probing into audience experience. This intimate alliance between the unseen communicator and the unknown receiver is a remarkable aspect of message design.

Message Vividness

The one aspect of media messages it is hard to escape is their vividness, their presence, their basic impact on the senses. The print media of course have type size as the main attention getter, with striking photos as the second stimulus. In addition, the contrast of dark copy set within a generous field of white space arouses the reader's awareness of the message. Today, elaborate color-photo processing is available, and lush newsprint pictures greatly enhance the attractiveness of the paper. In recent years, editors have spent more and more time reducing the cluttered appearance of a news page by extending column widths and grouping stories so that many articles are now contained on one page only. All of these efforts contribute to newspapers which command attention, look interesting and are more convenient to read.

Hollywood, even with its financial ups and downs, has not forgotten how to produce vivid celluloid dreams. The movie industry is the unchallenged leader in spectacle. Television may try, but massive effects and vast panoramas lose detail when shrunk to the living room screen. Consider the sensory impact of *Earthquake* with throbbing sound machines that made the very theater walls shake as the skyline of San Francisco tottered then crashed. Consider the multi-million dollar mechanical sharks which loomed on cinema screens and literally drove people off the sunny beaches of America. And finally, consider *Star Wars*, the fairy tale to end all fairy tales, or *Close Encounters of the Third Kind* with its awesome space ship hovering above the earth, drawing the smiling, appointed ones like a magnet into its mysteries. These films were mass communication marvels of special computerized photographic effects and electronic music, certainly contrived as dramatic literature but splendid examples of message vividness.

Of all the media, the most fluent exponents of attention commanding messages are radio and television. The majority of radio programs strive for a total flow of sound and no dead air. Frenetic music is

matched with breathless announcing, punchy delivery of a newscast, and high decibel commercials. The musical line not only ties it all together but wraps itself around the listener, who is surrounded in turn by his stereo speakers. Tempo is characterized as "fast and upbeat" in marked contrast to a few FM stations which are "mellow and laid back" in style or even fewer classical music stations totally indifferent to the lure of pop vividness.

An interesting professional scientist has entered the radio scene to help rock station managers select music which will "send" their teen age audiences. Psychologist Dr. Thomas Turicchi of Houston will, for a fee, attach willing young people to his psychographic equipment and measure their heart beats, respiration rates and sweating palms while listening to new records. The music responses thus computed emerge as play lists for stations which can then take listeners on an emotional trip (Lenehan, 1974). This is vividness with a vengeance.

We finally come to American television which, without a doubt, is tops in the world in the production of slickly written, superbly edited, lively, light theater pieces. From the opening titles — swift collages of still photos, action shots and pungent music — to the fadeout at the end, we are treated to high and vivid segments of comedy, adventure, and drama. The attention of millions is seized and held for three hours each night by the breathtaking squeal of tires on a steep narrow San Francisco hill or by an equally compelling riotous bit of slapstick in *Laverne and Shirley*. Notice the staccato tempo of comic lines and the energetic facial mugging in *Different Strokes* and the rapid camera cutting in most of the major shows. The programs themselves, of course, are more than matched by the bursts of color, action, and sound in the thirty second plugs for products.

Message simplicity, intimacy, and vividness, then, are the means by which the mass communicators compel our attention. That they have been undeniably successful in that task there is no doubt. But an interesting and troubling issue remains. The competitive drive for audience attention seems to force all of the media into strategies of the theater, into "show biz tactics" as *Variety*, the Bible of the entertainment world, might phrase it. Of course, show biz is what it's all about in feature films, in prime time television and rock 'n roll radio, and in the cacaphonous world of ad agency pitchmen; but what of the solid, respectable world of newspapers and the serious corridors of electronic journalism?

Should the citizens of the world's greatest democracy have their daily print journals of fact and opinion about the crises and issues facing society become light-weight compendia of personal care techniques, sports trivia, bright gossip, and guides to the materialistic good life? Should the news of significant events be submerged by the attention paid to bizarre crimes of sex and passion? This trend toward more dramatic and entertaining copy which sells can be seen in the flamboyant press of Rupert Murdoch and in other less garish big city and suburban papers which have almost become daily magazines.

Australian press tycoon Murdoch, known as "the dirty digger" in London (He owns papers on three continents.), has been acquiring large U.S. city dailies for several years. After a successful 1973 subscription war in San Antonio in which his *News* cut into the dominant Hearst *Light* by "front-paging," so the competition charged, "some sex crime or other for twenty-two straight days (Waters & Dotson, 1975, p. 53]." Murdoch bought the prestigious *New York Post* in 1976 and proceeded to bring his blood-and-guts journalism to the big town. Despite the outrage of many journalists who feel standards are being lowered, one of Murdoch's Texas editors shrugs, "The cemetary is full of well-edited, well researched publications. But not enough people read them (Waters & Dotson, 1975, p. 53]."

Broadcast journalism can be even more susceptible to being caught up in the theatrical spirit. Somber Edward R. Murrow, CBS Olympian Newsman for a generation, sensed the danger as early as 1958 and stated the issue bluntly: "If radio news is to be regarded as a commodity, only acceptable when salable, then I don't care what you call it—I say it isn't news (Bliss, 1975, p. 20]." One wonders what Murrow would call the present concept of stars and staging so eagerly sought by broadcast managers that about ten firms now act as full-time consultants to local TV and radio news departments. Although companies like Frank N. Magid Associates assert that they are increasing visual sophistication and improving reporting techniques, many journalists complain of appalling results which they have pejoratively labelled "happy talk" and tabloid news. Magid rests his case by reminding critics that more than half of his client stations have moved into the number one rating positions in their respective markets. His firm earns its substantial fees by providing a station with a detailed survey of audience viewing traits, by recommending changes in personnel and in the packaging and presentation of stories, and by monitoring and critiquing news program video tapes. A study of consultant recommendations revealed emphasis on such items as increasing film stories, cutting back on city hall and political news, strengthening visuals, stressing the importance of on-air conversation, and redesigning news sets [*Broadcasting,* September 9, 1974, pp. 22-23].

Although the networks have largely resisted the extreme cosmetic tampering with newscasts which is engaged in by their affiliated stations, the solid journalism of CBS' *60 Minutes* show and NBC's razzle-dazzle *Weekend* still reflect the trend toward surrounding ever shorter segments of informational material with ever more sprightly "show biz" trappings. Whether serious messages designed by proponents of the entertainment school will continue to serve society with a tough-minded, thorough, responsible exploration of public affairs remains to be seen.

Since all of the mass media inevitably affect each other's techniques, the overwhelming emphasis on light entertainment cannot help but be a major influence in the coloration of non-entertainment fare. Further, the subsidization of most American mass communications systems by advertisers who demand large audiences seems only to sharpen such influence.

Now that we have traced the history and development of press, broadcasting and film, and analyzed some of their particular communications characteristics, techniques, and problems, it is time to turn to an exploration of the effects these inescapable forces have on society.

Media Effects

You might conclude from the preceeding discussion that the media have a tremendous effect on us. They are powerful. This notion of a powerful media was first realized in the 1930's. After television was introduced, mass media researchers found that the media effects are determined by specific situations, needs and desires of their respective audiences. Finally, we have returned, in the 1960's, to the belief that the media are powerful. However, this power is somehow affected by audience needs. We will begin the study of media effects by turning to the 1930's.

The Powerful Media

As our country developed, so did the roles performed by the mass media. During the early part of the twentieth century, the media were primarily responsible for shaping perceptions of how people thought about their environment. As American society became more developed, so did needs for information about the institutions constantly being developed to serve the populace. As these institutions became more complex, people became more dependent on the mass media for information about them. For example, we no longer could visit Washington, D.C. to learn everything about the federal government; government bureaucracies grew and produced more information. As we became involved in World War I, this need for information about our government increased; we needed information about how our troops were doing in Europe and the media provided this information (DeFleur & Ball-Rokeach, 1975).

However, the media were more than just a source of information during this period of history. They, especially motion pictures, were also used as a propaganda tool by the federal government to boost our spirits — national pride was necessary for a successful war movement. The media performed this propaganda function well. Almost too well. The result of this success was the popular notion that the media were all powerful, controlled by all powerful persons, which led researchers to conclude that, if you provide an audience with a stimulus, you will automatically get the desired response in return. Using this line of reasoning, if I produce a commercial for a popular brand of toothpaste and broadcast it on your local television station, you would purchase the product on your next visit to the grocery store. DeFleur and Ball-Rokeach (1975) label this process the "instinctive S-R theory" or the "hypodermic needle theory". You inject a message, the stimulus, and produce the desired response.

However, it was not until World War II that the "hypodermic needle theory" was put to its ultimate test. The 1930's, as you will recall, saw the growth of radio as the first real *mass medium*. For the first time, producers of a message could reach a national audience and receive the first mass response. Techniques developed from World War I films were even more successful when tried on radio. One of the most successful propaganda programs involved radio personalities, such as singer Kate Smith, selling war bonds. The success of these campaigns was based, for the most part, on persuasion research. One study, conducted by Cartwright (1949), suggested that persuasion campaigns should focus on three basic processes: (1) creating a particular cognitive structure (relate the message to the audience member's perceptions); (2) accepting the message into this structure (activate the necessary processes within the audience member's structure); and (3) creating the necessary behavioral structure (tell the audience what behaviors are desired). If these steps were followed, desired mass effects could result because media audiences could be grouped based on their cognitive structures or how they "saw their environment".

This mass behavior was no more evident than when Orson Welles broadcast his 1938 Halloween spoof reporting an invasion from Mars. "War of the Worlds" was presented as a news event. The realism of Welles' program, which produced great panic across the country, was studied by Cantril, Gaudet and Herzog. They divided the mass audience into four categories based on their responses to the program. Cantril, et. al. found that behaviors ranged from checking the validity of the broadcast with the newspaper program listings to believing the information presented by Welles because of the tensions and conflicts occurring in Europe at the time. Similar to the Cartwright study, Cantril, et. al. found that audiences could be categorized by groups based on certain mass effects produced by the media (Cantril, 1971).

The "hypodermic needle theory" eventually lost favor among media researchers as they began to realize that, even though mass audiences did interrelate with one another and could be cognitively grouped, they were still comprised of individuals with independent sets of needs, wants and desires. The primary stimulus for this line of reasoning was provided by Berelson (1948) who said, "some kinds of communication on some kinds of issues, brought to the attention of some kinds of people, under some kinds of conditions, have some kinds of effects". Based on this notion, media researchers saw the media not as all powerful, but only influential on their audiences.

The Influential Media

The late 1940's marked the beginning of the minimal effects notion that the media were mildly influential in our daily lives. Berelson first argued, in a discussion of media effects on public opinion, that the media affect us only under certain conditions; whereas, the previous notion of the all powerful media assumed that messages always produced the desired effects. Berelson argued that direct effects were impossible because public opinion also affects communication. This idea makes sense when we consider that the mass media, as we know them, exist because they can attract audiences of sufficient size to sell time or space to advertisers. If these audiences were not reading the newspaper or watching television, the media would not exist as they do today. To attract these audiences, the media must present programs or information that basically agrees with substantial numbers of readers, viewers or listeners. Readers select newspapers, in part, based on their philosophy; television audiences watch programs that conform to their value system; radio audiences determine the type of music broadcast by listening to the station that best reflects their musical tastes.

The second part of Berelson's discussion involved the effect public opinion has on communication. Certain types of communication are more successful in reaching specific goals. For example, interpersonal communication is more effective in changing attitudes. Radio was more effective in political campaigns than newspapers during the Franklin Roosevelt years. Television, today, is more effective in reaching the apathetic, unconcerned voter.

Berelson's third point is that the ability of the media to affect public opinion involves the kinds of issues with which the media happen to be dealing. The media seem to be most powerful in creating opinions on new issues. For example, the media were fairly influential in creating public opinion on the Equal Rights Amendment, but fairly ineffectual in affecting more deep-seated attitudes toward types of birth control. Further, the media are more likely to affect opinions concerning what may seem to be unimportant issues. Again, with regard to birth control, the media have more effects on Protestants than on Catholics.

Kinds of people also determine the effect the media have on public opinion. Different people rely on different media for information. The audience that relies on newspapers for its information rarely watches television news specifically for information on important issues. Further, people with strong opinions concerning specific issues are least likely to be affected by the media. First, they are likely to ignore information contrary to their opinions. Second, they are likely to misinterpret information to fit these opinions. This process is called selective perception. Basically, we agree with information that agrees with our perceptions and attitudes.

The conditions under which information is presented also affects how the media change or create public opinion. If a form of communication enjoys a monopoly over information in a specific location, it can have more of an effect than if there are competing sources of information. For example, a politically conservative newspaper will have more of an effect on liberals if there are no available liberal-oriented media.

The final determiner of media influence, according to Berelson, is kinds of effects. Berelson argues that the presentation of certain issues by the media can have two effects. First, audiences agree that a given issue is important because the media discuss it. Second, the regular presentation of this issue can eventually lead to apathy because learning about an issue can be substituted, within one's cognitive structure, for a solution. Apathy can also result from the presentation of so many issues that the audience "gives up" in frustration. The more we try to understand the important issues, the more we realize that real understanding is impossible. There simply are too many issues and not enough time available to learn about them. The apathy and other effects are conditional. The conditions under which these effects are found have received much research. Studies in this area designed to identify conditions under which specific effects result have been called the uses and gratifications approach.

One of the first studies in this area, conducted by Arnheim (1944), was designed to identify character types in daytime, radio soap operas. He found that most of these programs: were set in smaller towns, had characters in middle class occupations, were concerned with personal relationships, and had both "weak" characters who created their own problems and "bad" characters who created problems for others. Interestingly, males were most likely to be weak characters; ideal women were most likely to be eligible for marriage or already a wife.

The Arnheim study suggests some uses and gratifications for these early radio soap opera. First, the good or strong character was female. The primary audiences for these programs were female. Second, many people watch soap operas to solve their problems and to find that other people have problems similar to their own. The majority of daytime serial programs deal with problems common to their audiences.

A second early study using what we now call the uses and gratifications approach compared the credibility of radio before and after World War II. In 1945, radio was most credible when compared to other social institutions such as government, schools, churches and newspapers for the performance of their socially prescribed tasks. Radio ranked second in its ability to perform its tasks in 1947 — after the war. Lazarsfeld and Kendall (1948) suggested that the change in ranking was due primarily to the decreased need for rapid information from overseas after the war. However, radio was consistently more credible for the more frequent listeners (over three hours per day).

Education and social class were related to program preferences in a third early radio study. The more educated person favored serious music and public affairs programs; the less educated preferred "hillbilly" music and religious programs. Preferences for the general audience included news, sports and popular music. Age was also related to program preferences. The older listener liked religious, serious and classical music programs. The younger audience listened to dance music. Finally, females were less interested in current affairs than males (Lazarsfeld & Kendall, 1948). These findings suggest that different programs satisfy different needs for different radio listeners.

Program preferences and demographic variables such as education and age were not related when soap operas were considered in a study conducted by Herzog (1950). She found few demographic differences between soap opera listeners and non-listeners. The primary audience for these programs still consisted of females. However, program preferences such as the ones studied by Herzog were undergoing a dramatic change in the early 1950's. Whan (1948; 1949; 1950; 1951) found that drama and variety programs for both men and women decreased in popularity; popular music and news were the favored programs. These changes in program preferences suggest that television was "taking over" the functions formerly performed by radio prior to and during World War II. Television had begun to program soap operas, copying formats used on radio. Audiences, preferring to see rather than just listen to these programs, switched their allegiance to television. Radio programmers, finding it difficult to maintain audiences large enough to attract advertisers, tried other types of programs not likely to be used on television — popular music.

The growing popularity of television also had a dramatic effect on radio research. Radio was now used, by its audiences, as a background medium and was therefore almost ignored by media researchers. Research turned to the discovery of media effects in terms of their functions. The person partially responsible for this popularity was a sociologist named Charles Wright (1959). Based on the work of Lasswell, Wright developed a category system of functions describing how people used the media. The four basic functions were: surveillance, cultural transmission, entertainment and correlation.

Surveillance involves the collection and transmission of information about the environment or society. The two beneficial effects, according to Wright, are the ability of the media to: warn us about possible dangers such as tornadoes or war and inform us about the environment in terms of how our society affects us. These effects might be classified as either manifest (intended effects) or latent (unintended effects). A manifest function would be to inform the public about an issue; a latent function might include the prestige people get from their friends and others because they are informed about current events. Dysfunctions (negative effects) associated with the surveillance function include panic that might result from false warnings such as the one given by Orson Welles described earlier. A second dysfunction might be caused by uncensored news that allows the audience to compare their conditions to other segments of society. For example, ghetto blacks received television exposure to white, middle-class comforts which was partially responsible for the racial riots in the 1960's.

Cultural transmission is a function which assists in the socialization of media audiences. We learn many social norms from television, radio, films and newspapers. For example, most of us have never been subpoenaed to appear in court. Yet, "Perry Mason" has told us what to expect. Further, even though most television programmers do not intentionally socialize us, one latent function is the unification of social norms. Such unification may be either functional or dysfunctional. Functionally, we may share cultural norms which would make for better communication throughout society. Whites may better understand blacks by watching "Roots". Dysfunctionally, the universal transmission of norms may eliminate subcultural differences that we all proudly identify as our heritage.

Both the functions and dysfunctions of cultural transmission can result from the third function identified by Wright, entertainment. Television is probably the most influential socializer for all audiences, regardless of age. For example, children will probably watch more television before they enter school than they will later spend in a college classroom earning a bachelor's degree. Much of what the child learns about society is learned during the pre-school television viewing period. Older adults also rely on the media, especially radio and television, to "pass the time away" or for companionship during periods of loneliness.

The last function discussed by Wright is correlation. The media generally attempt to interpret information gathered from our environment, especially during newscasts. For example, editorial comments on television news attempt to interpret events important to the audience. The editorial page in the newspaper also fulfills this function. Films can often be discussed as the filmmaker's interpretation of an event in history or predictions for the future.

"Saturday Night Fever" is an example of an interpretation of history.

The interpretation function can be helpful by preventing over-stimulation of the audience through information transmitted by the media. For example, reports about a tornado might result in panic. However, careful interpretation of the event might prevent such a reaction. Dysfunctionally, the media, by incorrectly interpreting an event, might slow necessary social change. Interpretations that civil unrest is unimportant has slowed change in this area of social reform.

Wright's functions provided the stimulus for much research into what the media did for their audiences. The result of these studies was the eventual discarding of the "hypodermic needle theory" of media effects. Researchers now believe that the media affect us differently depending on what DeFleur (1970) called our social category. Social categories are comprised of people with similar demographics such as age, education, sex, race, etc. Category membership was important in media research because it determined, in part, what functions were most important for segments of the mass audience. For example, the more educated television news viewer received more prestige from knowing about current events. The less educated viewer was more interested in watching the news for its entertainment value.

An example of the importance of education in media research was documented in a study conducted by Lazarsfeld, Berelson and Gaudet (1948). While studying the 1940 political campaign in Erie County, Ohio, the researchers found that the media most affected what were later identified as opinion leaders. These opinion leaders, characterized as more educated than the general electorate, then communicated campaign information to their less educated followers. The result of this finding was the development of the two step flow of communication theory.

Education and social class were also important in a campaign study conducted by Berelson, Lazarsfeld and McPhee (1948). They found that the more educated voter collected the most political information and was most interested in the campaign compared to the less educated voter. Further, this interest and information collection was true regardless of political party; Republicans who gathered much information about Dewey (the Republican) also gathered much information about the democractic candidate for president (Truman) than uneducated Republicans.

Whereas Berelson, et. al. found that education did determine the media functions performed during this campaign, they did not find them having much effect on behavior and opinions concerning the candidates. The results of this and other similar studies convinced researchers that the media were only capable of minimal effects; they could communicate information, but had few other effects. Further, the media functions performed were determined by one's social category. This notion was "short-lived," however, with the introduction of television in the early 1950's. Researchers still believed that the media performed different functions for people in different social categories, but that the effects on these people were much more pronounced than they first thought. As the media performed their four functions (surveillance, correlation, cultural transmission and entertainment) they became powerful forces in the socialization of their respective audiences. Consequently, from the late 1950's to the present, researchers returned to the notion of the powerful media.

The Powerful Media: A Reconsideration

Because the powerful media affect us differently depending on the functions they are performing, the typology discussed by Wright (1975) will be used to organize the following presentation on current media research. The four functions are: surveillance, correlation, cultural transmission and entertainment.

Surveillance

Surveillance is the news function performed by the media. Manifest functions include: warnings, information transmission, status conferral, public opinion management and cultural contact. The warnings function can best be described in terms of a study, conducted by Peled and Katz (1974), to determine what mass media were best for informing, for understanding and for relieving tensions during the 1973 Yom Kippur war. They found that the more educated Israeli depended on radio for information, radio and newspapers for understanding and interpersonal communication for tension relief. The less educated depended on television for information and interpersonal communication for both understanding and tension relief. The fairly-well educated person depended on television solely for tension relief. Radio was the most important medium for information when considering the population as a whole; almost seventy percent of the Israelis listened to the radio all day for news bulletins. Finally, television was viewed by most of the population for tension relief. Education was most important in determining how Israelis used the media during this time period.

Information transmission was also found to be affected by education in research reported by Robinson (1972). The most frequent users of the print media generally were better informed than infrequent or non-users. The more frequent users were also the more educated. Education also played an important role in information gain from the media. For example, the more educated person knew more about the Far East than the less educated person. Based on these two results,

Robinson (1972) concluded that the more educated are generally more informed about world events because they make more serious use of the media for this purpose. Also, they are more able to use the print media because of their education. However, these differences, due primarily to differences in education levels, can be reduced by any person paying careful attention to the media for information. For example, another study reported by Robinson (1972) suggested that differences in information gain can be reduced for topics like foreign affairs and national politics by regular use of any of the media, if they are used for information and not just entertainment. Since the more educated person generally makes a conscientious attempt to be informed, and usually turns to the print media for this information, Robinson concludes that there is a "knowledge gap" between socio-economic classes of people that results from differences in education. This gap increases when the less educated are not regular users of the print media, but decreases when the issues in question are widely publicized or when the less educated are regular users of the print media.

A specific example of education's role in information gain can be found in research about political campaigns. The more educated voter tends to seek information about candidates early in the campaign.

They purposively seek information about the issues and then select a candidate that best fits their perceptions of the issues. These voters, about one third of the electorate, along with those who vote for candidates based on their political party affiliation, are called "early deciders" and usually select their candidate prior to the party conventions (Kraus & Davis, 1976). Voters who decide later in the campaign generally are less educated than the "early deciders." "Late deciders" rely more on television and sources of information other than the print media for political information. These voters focus on candidate image rather than stands on issues.

Political effects of the media are not just limited to assisting the electorate in its voting decisions. The media also have more general effects when performing the surveillance function. McCombs (1967) suggests that the media provide a "frame of reference" for the voter. The television news commentator, by reporting on relevant political issues, suggests which ones are most important in a given campaign. The voter then uses these issues to judge potential political leaders.

The television anchorman is not the only way a voter can determine the important political issues. A recent development in national politics, the televised debates, provides a second source of information. Many studies, conducted after the Kennedy-Nixon debates, found these programs had few effects, in terms of voting decisions, on the "early deciders." In fact, the results of this research show that the programs actually crystallized support for both candidates. However, the debates did help Kennedy persuade the undecided or "late deciders" toward him. A similar effect was found after the Carter-Ford debates in 1976; undecided voters used information provided in these programs to make voting decisions (Chaffee, 1978).

A third source of information during campaigns is the paid political advertisement. Prior to the election of Dwight Eisenhower in 1952, the primary methods of advertising political candidates were the newspaper, film trailers (shown after a feature film) and leaflets. All forms of ads were somewhat influential in persuading people to vote for selected candidates. Eisenhower was the first presidential candidate to use television ads during prime time. These advertisements, aimed primarily at the "late deciders," were fairly successful for reaching the less educated voter (Kraus & Davis, 1976).

The basic conclusion from the preceding discussion of the surveillance function is that the ability of the media to inform their audiences is dependent on one's social category. Specifically, information transmission is most successful for the more educated audience member in the upper to middle socioeconomic classes. The communication of this information is also dependent on the selection of events to transmit via the media. This selection process is the correlation function.

Correlation

Interpretation of events by the news media is labelled by Wright (1975) as the correlation function. The most common method of interpretation involves selecting information for news programs and articles. The process, known as gatekeeping, involves many people, ranging from the television or newspaper photographer to the news editor. It is very complex. All these people make important decisions which affect what we learn about our environment. For this reason, the gatekeeping process has received considerable research over the years. One of the first studies, by White (1950), involved the investigation of one gatekeeper called "Mr. Gates." White found that this person, a newspaper.editor, used personal opinions, space in the newspaper, the time a story was received, writing style and story type to select 1297 column inches to print from 12,400 available inches of news copy. Seventeen years later, Snider (1967) studied "Mr. Gates" again and still found him using his own opinions to make news decisions. However, he was using more of the available news stories to fill his newspaper.

Fortunately, most gatekeeping decisions are based on more objective criteria. Buckalew (1969; 1974a; 1974b; Clyde & Buckalew, 1969), after interviewing several journalists and journalism instructors, found five important variables were used in defining news. These variables were: significance (presence of conflict), visuals, timeliness, prominence (story about someone known) and proximity (distance from the station or newspaper). These variables were used in all the media studied by Buckalew including newspapers, television and radio; the more variables a story had, the more likely it was to be used by the gatekeeper.

The gatekeeping process is not the only topic receiving attention by media researchers studying the correlation function. One such area of study has involved the agenda setting function of the media. Essentially, the news media present us with an agenda of stories that we perceive as important just because we see it on television. Because we have few personal experiences with issues on this agenda, the media are able to present us with issues to think about. However, the media, while objectively reporting the news, do not attempt to tell us what to think about these issues (Cohen, 1963). Agenda setting has usually been studied in political settings. The first published study, conducted by McCombs and Shaw (1972), found that the media were able to set the agenda of undecided voters during the 1968 presidential campaign. A study of the 1972 election by McLeod, Becker and Byrnes (1974) found newspaper agenda to be similar to the agenda of older voters with weak party affiliation.

Television news also has an agenda setting effect during political campaigns. Shaw and Clemmer (1977) found that television had a short term impact on the electorate's agenda, especially for frequent viewers. Compared to newspapers, television's agenda setting effect is minimal (Williams & Semlak, 1978). However, the ability of television to set the political agenda increases as election day approaches. This result can be traced back to the uses of these two media in political campaigns discussed earlier. Television is generally used by the low-involvement, "late deciders"; newspapers are used by the high-involvement, "early deciders." Unfortunately for the "late deciders," television tells us little about campaign issues, stressing the candidates' image and the campaign itself. Therefore, these "late deciders" tend to make their voting decisions based on how they "feel" about a candidate and not his/her stand on the issues (Patterson & McClure, 1976; Williams & Semlak, 1978).

Agenda setting is not only an effect found in political campaigns. According to a study by Williams and Larsen (1977), the media can set our agenda of national and local issues during off-election years. Newspapers again were best able to set these agenda, followed by network television and radio newscasts. However, these findings differ depending on what medium people choose for their information. For example, television was best able to set the agenda of viewers preferring it for information on their perceived most important issue.

Based on the agenda setting research, the media influence not only what we know about our environment, but also the importance we assign to this information. In other words, the media, while performing the correlation function, socialize us in terms of knowledge about society and its institutions. We are also socialized by the media when they attempt to transmit our culture, the third of Wright's four functions.

Cultural Transmission

We learn about our culture from various places. First, and potentially most important, we learn cultural values from our parents. The role parents play in the family, the rules they establish and the examples they set affect how we learn socially acceptable behavior. A second source of information about cultural values is the school. Our teachers help us learn socially acceptable behavior through example and the discipline they mandate in the classroom. Also, the various subjects we study have an enduring effect on how we perceive our world and our culture. The third most influential source of cultural information is the mass media. We start absorbing various messages, very early in life, by spending many hours watching television. We learn that the world is full of violence and that violence is a way of solving most of our important problems. Violence is a cultural value learned through characters such as Spiderman and Wonderwoman.

Television also teaches us how to dress, how to relate to other people, and how various social institutions affect our lives. Lessons learned from television say that: medical doctors can spend many hours with their patients, lawyers only handle one case at a time, and a policeman's life is full of danger and adventure. Much research has been conducted to determine how effectively these lessons are learned from the media.

One of the first studies in the area of cultural transmission was conducted by Himmelweit, Oppenheim and Vince (1958). They compared English children from two neighborhoods. One neighborhood had television available to its residents, the other did not. Children in the television neighborhood spent more time watching the medium than interacting with their friends. Females in the television homes were more likely to desire marriage and a family life; males were more ambitious and anticipated good jobs in the future. Children in the non-television homes did not exhibit these attitudes.

Probably the greatest concern of researchers such as Himmelwait, et. al. is the effect televised violence has on perceptions of such violence and its likelihood of being copied by children. Many of these studies, sponsored by the U.S. government, have found that watching violence does lead to some violent behavior. Specifically, these studies indicate: children who like violent programs are more likely to be violent when compared to children who dislike these programs; children who consistently watch televised violence are more likely to perceive violence as an acceptable behavior; and children who watch substantial amounts of violence are more likely to be violent (Liebert, Neale & Davidson, 1973). Despite these conclusions, we can not say that watching televised violence directly *causes* violent behavior because there are many other reasons why people are violent. For example, children from violent homes are more likely to be violent than children from non-violent homes. The findings do indicate that children can *learn* violence from television, especially if their viewing is unsupervised by an adult. (Parents and other adults are more influential on their children's behavior than even television.) Violence is a learned cultural value from television.

The learning of cultural values from television is not limited to children. The constant viewing of violence can even affect adult perceptions of reality. A study of the 1977 television season found that violence occurred in at least two thirds of all prime time programs. (The overall amount of violence did decrease from the 1976 season.) The analysis of specific television violence found the male characters most likely to be involved in an aggressive act were: "bad," foreign and in lower socio-economic classes. Violent women were: "bad," low class and single. Television programs were dominated by violent young, white, middle class men who victimized the other characters. Most of the television characters who killed were "good" males. This presentation of a violent world has numerous effects on adult perceptions. Previous studies have found that heavy television viewers (watch more than average amounts of television) were more likely to: think they would be involved in violence and register more feelings of mistrust than infrequent viewers. This effect was not minimized by education. Further, children, who were heavy television viewers, were more likely to approve of physical violence as a solution to problems than lighter viewers (Gerbner, Gross, Jackson-Beeck, Jeffries-Fox & Signorielli, 1978).

To this point in the discussion of cultural transmission, the media have been characterized as having only negative or antisocial effects on their audiences, especially children. Television and the other media can also communicate positive cultural values to the younger viewers. For example, in a study conducted by Stein and Friedrich (1972), viewers of "Mister Rogers' Neighborhood," a prosocial children's program, were markedly less violent than children who watched "Superman" and "Batman" — two violent cartoons. Also, children who watched "Mister Rogers' Neighborhood" exhibited more prosocial behavior such as helping.

In terms of prosocial and antisocial behavior, television has been found to be a powerful transmitter of cultural values. With these results in mind, researchers have begun to investigate how the media transmit other values to its viewers. Much of this research has involved the study of how women are portrayed in the media. Courtney and Whipple (1974) reviewed four of these studies and found that television women were most likely in the home doing "housework;" men were outside the home earning a living for the family. Commercials for home-related products such as laundry detergent and bathroom products were advertised by more women than men. The only conclusion possible from this review and many other studies in this area is that women portrayed on television are not much like women in the "real world."

The women's movement and other concerned groups have sought to change this unrealistic portrayal of women in the media for fear that such portrayals are the only source of information concerning the females' role in society. This fear is especially felt for children. Research has found that stereotypes are even more pronounced in programs aimed at the younger audience (Miller & Reeves, 1976). The potential effect of showing unrealistic women in programs designed for children is that these cultural values will be learned and internalized by both boys and girls. One such effect has been tentatively identified by Olsen (1978). This result, coupled with past studies such as the one conducted by Himmelwait, et. al. shows that cultural values, realistic or unrealistic, are learned from television by children. The primary source of this information is entertainment programs which represents the fourth function of the media discussed by Wright (1975).

Entertainment

The entertainment and cultural transmission functions are almost inseparable in terms of categorizing media effects. Most of the effects discussed under cultural transmission could also be presented as a result of watching entertainment programs. Effects stressed in this section, however, will include more general applications of the violence research presented earlier and the effects of pornography.

Traditionally, the effects of television violence have been categorized in terms of three theories; social learning, frustration-aggression and catharsis. The social learning theory, based on the work of Bandura and other social psychologists, explains the influence of presenting televised novel, aggressive acts on children's modelling behaviors. The initial study to test this relationship showed novel, aggressive acts being performed on a Bobo doll. These presentations differed in that one was a televised cartoon, one used a real-life situation and one was a film. The fourth group saw nothing. The groups viewing the novel behaviors (groups one through three) were more likely to model or copy the behaviors in a later play situation with the doll. The results of this study indicate that children can learn and then imitate novel aggressive behaviors shown to them in many forms (Bandura, Ross & Ross, 1963).

A second study testing the social learning theory found that the presence of an adult, who gave reinforcement (positive comments) for good behavior and negative comments for undesirable behavior while the child viewed the violent film, dramatically reduced the amount of violence performed by the child. Still another study found that children watching the aggressor being punished for acting violently toward the Bobo doll will be less likely to act violently in subsequent play situations (Liebert, et al, 1973). However, none of these studies suggest that the learning of violence will necessarily lead to violent behavior, only that it can be copied.

The frustration-aggression or disinhibition theory is based on the work of Berkowitz. Using the classical approach developed by Freud and other psychologists that frustration leads to aggression, Berkowitz suggested that television can be the source of frustration and can teach aggressive responses to frustrations encountered in daily life. The key to this approach is the eliciting cue — a similarity between a viewed television situation (with an aggressive solution to a problem) and a real situation. A study conducted by Berkowitz (1965) shows how the eliciting cue works. College students were met by the experimenter and his assistant in a laboratory. The assistant was introduced as either a speech major or a college boxer and then insulted the college student subject after the experimenter left the room. The subject then viewed a portion of the film *The Champion* (a violent boxing match) or saw no film. The subject was then asked to grade a theme supposedly written by the experimenter's assistant. Subjects who viewed the film gave more shocks or lower grades to the assistant posing as the college boxer than the other subjects insulted by the speech major. According to Berkowitz, the boxing scene acted as an eliciting cue for the later acts of aggression toward the assistant posing as the boxer. By extending this finding, and the results of other research in this area, it is possible to conclude that a person, confronted with a frustrating situation similar to one viewed on television, will most likely react aggressively to reduce the level of frustration.

The catharsis theory suggests opposite results than those found by Berkowitz. Based on the work of Feshbach and his associates, watching violence on television, in an aroused (frustrated) state, will vicariously or indirectly reduce the likelihood of violent behavior. To test this assumption, Feshbach and Singer (1971), compared two groups of boys in two different environments: a private junior high school and a boys' home. Boys in both environments were divided into two groups. One group in each environment saw only violent programs; the second group saw only non-violent programs. Behaviors of boys in all four groups were compared for violent behavior before and after watching these programs. Subjects in the boys' home, who viewed the violent programs, were least likely to act violently when compared to their peers who saw non-violent programs. There were no differences between the two groups in the private junior high school. In fact, subjects viewing violence in the junior high school were more violent. Feshbach argues that the subjects in the boys' home were aroused by being detained against their will, and watching television violence reduced their likelihood of acting violently. Unfortunately, many problems have been found with this study by other media researchers. These problems were so severe that this theory has been discarded when explaining the effects of televised violence.

A fairly recent line of research, partially using the three preceding theories, has developed to explain the effects of watching televised violence. Based on the work of Zillman (1971), these studies have led to the arousal theory or the excitation transfer model. This theory or model suggests that not only the effects of television violence, but also all arousing communication are additive. In terms of television violence, two effects are possible. First, television produces a cognitive effect—it affects what we know. A second effect is affective—the medium also affects our emotional levels. The cognitive effect is short-term. We easily forget violent programs almost as soon as we are through watching them. However, our bodies do not physically forget the arousal produced by watching these programs. Our affective responses are reduced or extinguished more slowly than are the cognitive effects. For this reason, affective effects can build upon one another because each televised program has residual emotional arousal left over after its conclusion. For this reason, violent programs can additively affect our arousal levels. The residual affective effect of watching an episode of "Charlies' Angels" is added to the immediate affective effect of violence viewed on "Starsky and Hutch." The result is that people who watch consecutive violent programs will be more violent than people who watch one violent program. The former viewer has the additive effects on arousal resulting from many exposures to arousal-producing messages. The testing of the arousal theory involves three steps. First, the subject is angered by receiving electrical shocks of unpleasant, high-pitched noises. The second phase involves some exposure to a violent program or film. The third phase is the subject's response in reaction to the person administering the shock or noise in phase one. One study using this procedure was discussed by Tannenbaum and Zillman (1975). First, the subjects were angered and then exposed to one of three videotapes that contained one of three levels of violence. Subjects who viewed the most aggressive program content produced the most aggressive behaviors in the response phase; subjects viewing the least aggressive content responded less violently than subjects in the other two groups. These responses could only be produced by the levels of violence in the exposure phase as the angering was the same for all subjects. The explanation, according to the arousal theory, is that the emotional arousal, produced by the initial angering phase, was added to the arousal produced by exposure to the very violent program sequences, resulting in more violent responses by the subjects. The arousal transferred from the angering phase to the exposure phase and was observed in the response phase.

A second study testing the arousal theory, conducted by Zillman, Hoyt and Day (1974) compared affective responses to both violent and pornographic materials. All subjects received unpleasant, high-pitched noises in the angering phase. Affective arousal was measured by the subjects' heart rate. Each subject then viewed one of the following four films: *Marco Polo's Travels* (neutral condition), *The Champion* (agressive condition), *Wild Bunch* (very violent condition or mildly erotic scenes (pornographic condition). Each subject then viewed a short film called *Rivers* to determine if the affective responses produced by the angering and exposure phases could be reduced by a non-involving film. The subject was then allowed to return the unpleasant noise to the person who delivered it in the angering phase. Only responses produced by subjects viewing the erotic film were different from responses from subjects viewing the neutral film. This finding was expected because the heart rate produced by the erotic film was higher when compared to the other three groups. These findings supported the arousal theory because the communication producing the highest affective response also produced the most retaliation.

The value of the arousal theory is its ability to explain the results obtained from research testing the other three violence theories. The frustration-aggression theory explains the effects of television violence in terms of eliciting cues. Zillman (1971) argues that aggressive responses occur when the affective arousal produced by some angering agent (a television program with an eliciting cue), transfers to an aggressive communication experience. Behaviors that result from the transfer of these arousal levels will be heightened by repeated exposure to such messages.

The arousal theory can also be used to explain results obtained from the social learning theory. Imitative learning will occur, as a response to aggressive programs, when the arousal produced by such programs exceed arousal present in previous situations. These behaviors result regardless of the content of the television program. Imitative learning should not occur if transferring of arousal levels is absent. Conversely, catharsis will result when the communication situation following an arousal producing situation is less arousing than the preceding confrontation. An example of this effect was found in the Zillman et. al. study. The non-involving film *Rivers* effectively reduced the arousal produced by the transfer of excitation between the angering and exposure phases for subjects viewing the aggressive and violent films.

The generality of the arousal theory is not limited to explaining the effects of viewing televised violence. It also can be used in other communication situations. Arousal can be transferred from situation to situation, regardless of the content or sources of the message. For example, repeated arguments can transfer arousal that may result in a person being physically violent when that person is not normally inclined toward physical violence.

The effects of televised violence, as well as the other issues discussed to this point, all result from the four functions performed by the mass media. These effects can be described as either manifest or latent functions or dysfunctions resulting from how we use the media and the functions we demand of them. Our motives or reasons for using the mass media as well as our social category also determine the effects the media will have on us. The following section details these motives.

Explanations of Media Effects

The basic concern of most media researchers has been the identification of effects produced by the media. One conclusion they and you should have formed by now is that there are no simple explanations of media effects. In fact, Berelson's early suggestion that the effects of the media are conditional (kinds of messages, kinds of people, etc.) is probably the most accurate, but least specific to date. However, researchers have been in the process of determining under what conditions certain effects can be expected. The preceding discussion should give you some insight into these conditions as they relate to functions performed by the media. If we expect to be entertained, we do not want to watch a documentary on current social problems. Conversely, if we want information on daily events, we do not expect to be entertained. We all have certain expectations of the media — functions they are expected to perform. Closely related to these functions are the uses we make of the media. Functions are intended or unintended by the communicator; uses are the functions we, as audience members, expect the communicators (like the television networks) to provide for us. These uses are then expected to provide some gratification or reward. If we want to use the newspaper for information about a problem we view as important, we expect the information use (surveillance function) to be provided. We are gratified if we find information on the problem; we are not gratified if we do not find the item. Research on the uses and gratifications, discussed in the section on early radio research, seeks to discover specific conditions under which we make certain uses and what specific gratifications we receive. The early studies suggest some uses and resulting gratifications produced by radio.

Current research on the uses and gratifications approach, discussed by Blumler and Katz (1974), identify four elements crucial to this method. First, use of the mass media is goal directed. We all have reasons for using the mass media; there is no idle, unreasoned use of the media. For example, we often watch television to pass the time. The second element involves relating media use and gratifications. We all have our own reasons for watching specific programs or reading specific portions of the newspaper. We may watch "Three's Company" to look at Suzanne Somers. Third, the media must compete with other methods of attaining specific gratifications. For example, the need to be entertained may be satisfied by watching television or reading a book. Fourth, the individual is at least subconsciously aware of their uses and can express them.

The uses and gratifications approach, then, assumes an active audience. The application of this approach to the study of the mass media is designed to determine how the media are used by this active audience. The functions suggested by Wright (1975) are an attempt to determine some of these uses and their effects. The audience might be described by what functions the media perform for it. For example, the media provide gratification for the information need when functioning as surveillance. These functions might also provide social connections for media audiences. Katz, Blumler, and Gurevitch (1974) suggest that the media provide many such connections, depending on one's needs. Watching Walter Cronkite might provide connections between a person and his/her peers when discussing current events. Without the information provided by Cronkite, the person could not enter current events discussions — there would be no connection. Unfortunately, the list of various needs necessary for these connections is complex and incomplete. A person might watch Walter Cronkite one night for information on current events, the next night for entertainment, and the third night for companionship. One program can satisfy different needs for the same person depending on his/her motives.

Further, different media may satisfy the same needs for different people. We can learn about current events from watching network, television news or reading the newspaper. Television may be better at satisfying the need for information for the less educated; newspapers may satisfy this need for the more educated person. Each mass medium has its own "grammar" that allows it to meet these needs for different people depending, in part, on their social category (Katz, Blumler & Gurevitch, 1974). These attributes make some media better able to serve needs for some people, but unsuccessful for others. Newspapers may be able to satisfy the need for information, but not the need for entertainment.

Determining the various functions performed by the media and needs served by them is only part of the problem of determining how and why people turn to the media. More basic to the problem is where these needs originate. Katz et. al. suggest some of these need sources might come from everyday experiences and tensions. Tension relief can be the result of using the media. A second source of needs might come from society. Our social system is dependent upon the reinforcement of its cultural values such as obeying the law. The media can satisfy this need. A third source might also be the family. Certainly family environments and expectations produce specific needs for individuals. For example, people from more educated families might have more of an information need than a person from a less educated family. The former person would be more dependent on the mass media for information because of his/her social category.

Identifying sources for our needs and how we satisfy them can lead to some insight into how the media affect us. However, this process, known as the uses and gratifications approach, is very complex. A pictorial representation, the Media Effects Diagram, should help to understand this process. First, the entire process occurs in social reality. Messages are constructed and effects happen within the social context in which we live. The source of these messages can be a variety of people or social institutions, ranging from the federal government giving us information on foreign affairs to programmers developing a show for prime time television. The source communicates its information to the mass media. In the case of the federal government, all the major news organizations would be given the information, process it and decide whether to send it to its audience. The information then goes through the cultural values screen. Values and other elements that make us individuals affect how we perceive and process information. These cultural values are outside the individual

Media Effects Diagram

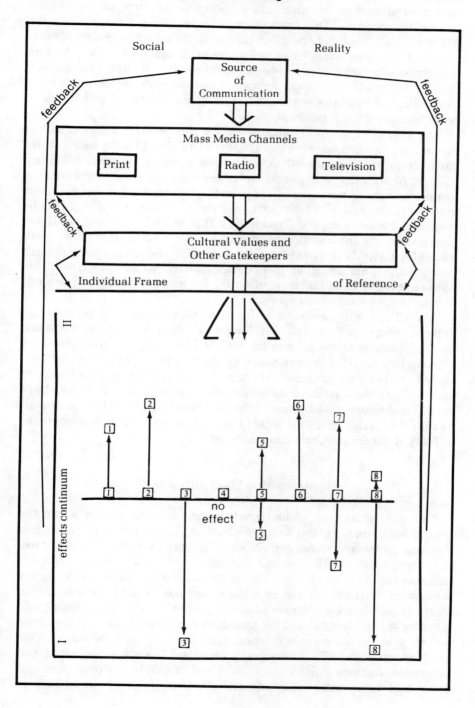

and are communicated by parents, schools or the media. The values are internalized by us, the media audience, to form our individual frame of reference. This frame of reference filters out some types of information (selective perception) and assists in the processing of other types of information. For example, research has shown that the best predictor of voting behavior is our parent's political party affiliation. If we are Republican and receive negative information about a Republican candidate, we are likely to avoid the message because it violates our frame of reference.

The frame of reference determines how the media can then affect us because it dictates our needs that must be satisfied by the media. If we come from an environment that stresses learning and education, we will probably value and purposively seek information. More educated people generally turn to newspapers for information. Therefore, our need for information, a function of our environment, will most likely be satisfied by newspapers. Translating this information to the effects continuum, the information produced by the federal government will probably have its greatest impact on the more educated person, such as #6 in the diagram, when it is communicated by the newspaper. This same information will be most effective for the less educated person if it is communicated on television.

A similar result might occur for television violence. A person may have a need to act aggressively. The need was probably learned from his/her environment and can be satisfied by watching a violent television program. If these programs are less arousing than this person's arousal level, the program will function to reduce the likelihood of aggressive behaviors such as person #3. This same program may have no effect on person #4 because it did not satisfy a need. The end result is that the media affect all of us in specific situations. However, these effects, if not desired, can be minimized.

Minimizing Media Effects

One overriding conclusion from the preceding discussion is that the media have the potential to harm all of us. The question is: what can be done to prevent unwanted effects? The easiest answer is to not use the media to satisfy needs. However, this solution is probably unacceptable for most of us. The only way we can still use the media and avoid detrimental effects is to change the content. As was shown earlier, just being educated about negative effects is not enough to prevent them. One method for changing media content is to join civic action groups that have organized campaigns against the media. One such group is the PTA. They are determined to reduce the amount of television violence during prime time and in children's programs and have had some interesting effects. For one, Sears has refused to advertise on excessively violent programs. Other advertisers have followed. The PTA is currently organizing a campaign to make other advertisers refuse to sponsor violent programs. They could be successful.

Another way to affect television is to petition the FCC to deny stations their licenses. Such petitions demand legal services and could be very expensive if attempted without an organized group. Such petitions have been successful for violations of equal opportunity hiring and might succeed in decreasing violence on the media.

Affecting newspapers and other print media is even more difficult for the media audience. Newspapers are not answerable to any government body as long as they obey the law. Again, the only real method to change newspapers is through their advertisers. Some newspapers have ombudsmen, reporters assigned to critique the newspaper or operate action line columns to solve readers' complaints. Writing to a paper's ombudsman might produce desired effects. Finally, newspapers in some communities have agreed to discuss their operations with press councils. Again, however, these alternatives are only successful when the editor listens to them.

Summary

The preceding review suggests that the media can have many effects on their audiences. These effects are affected by a very complex process that differs depending on the individual, message, channel and various conditions. These differences might be explained by the various functions performed by the media. For example, the media have special effects that occur when the surveillance function is performed. The effects of television violence prevail when the media perform the entertainment function. Identifying functions such as these may lead to some explanation as to how the media affect us. We all use the media to serve our needs. If we have a need for relaxation, we may turn on the television or the radio. The behavior, in turn, may lead to a variety of effects.

The most powerful effect the media can have is their ability to socialize us or teach cultural values. Much of what we learn about our society comes from television and the other mass media. Since much of what the media communicate is unrealistic, we can have very distorted views of our culture and society. Fortunately, other socializers, the family and schools, often minimize these socialization effects. We, too, can minimize these effects by attempting to change the media. Education, though not a cure-all for these maladies, can lead us to a more realistic picture of our world and how we can make it a better place in which to live.

References

Apropos the FTC. *Re: Act.* Fall. 1978, *8*, 1-3.

Arnheim, R. The world of the daytime serial. In P. Lazarsfeld & F. Stanton (eds.), *Radio Research 1942-1943.* New York: Duell, Sloan and Pearce, 1944.

Bandura, A., Ross, D., & Ross, S.A. Imitation of film-mediated aggressive models. *Journal of Abnormal and Social Psychology,* 1963, *67*, 527-534.

Berelson, B. Communications and public opinion. In E.E. Dennis, A.H. Ismach, & D. Gillmor (eds.), *Enduring issues in mass communication.* St. Paul: West, 1978.

Berelson, B., Lazarsfeld, P., & McPhee, W. Political processes: The role of the mass media. In W. Schramm and D. Roberts (eds.), *The process and effects of mass communication* (Rev. Ed.). Urbana: University of Illinois Press, 1971.

Berkowitz, R. Aggression: *A social psychological analysis.* New York: McGraw-Hill, 1962.

Bliss, E. Remembering Edward R. Murrow. *Saturday Review,* May 1975, *31*, 20.

Blumler, J.G., & Katz, E. (eds.), *The uses of mass communications: Current perspectives in gratifications research.* Beverly Hills: Sage, 1974.

Brown, L. Should broadcasters be freed from federal controls. *New York Times,* November 1978, *12*, D-41.

Buckalew, J.K. News elements and selection by television news editors. *Journalism Quarterly,* 1969/1970, *14*, 47-54.

Buckalew, J.K. The local radio news editor as a gatekeeper. *Journal of Broadcasting,* 1974, *18*, 211-221(a).

Buckalew, J.K. The radio news gatekeeper and his sources. *Journalism Quarterly,* 1974, *51*, 602-606(b).

Cantril, H. The invasion from Mars. In W. Schramm and D. Roberts (eds.), *The process and effects of mass communication* (Rev. Ed.). Urbana: University of Illinois Press, 1971.

Carmody, D. These are boom times in schools of journalism. *New York Times,* March, 1977, *6*, E-8.

Cartwright, D. Some principles of mass persuasion: Selected findings of research on the sale of U.S. war bonds. In W. Schramm and D. Roberts (eds.), *The process and effects of mass communication* (Rev. Ed.), Urbana: University of Illinois Press, 1971.

Chaffee, S.H. Presidential debates — are they helpful to voters? *Communication Monographs,* 1978, *45*, 330-346.

Chagall, D. Can you believe the ratings? *TV Guide,* June 1978, *26*, 2-13.

Clark, W.C. The impact of mass communications in America. In E.E. Dennis, A. H. Ismach & D. Gillmor (eds.), *Enduring issues in mass communication research.* St. Paul: West, 1978.

Clift, C. III, & Greer, A. (eds.). *Broadcast Programming* (4th ed.), Washington, D.C.: University Press of America, 1978.

Clyde, R.W., & Buckalew, J.K. Inter-media standardization: A Q analysis of news editors. *Journalism Quarterly,* 1969, *46*, 349-351.

Cohen, B.C. *The press and foreign policy.* Princeton: Princeton University Press, 1963.

Courtney, A.E., & Whipple, T.E. Women in TV commercials. *Journal of Communication,* 1975, *25,* 56-65.

Czerniejewski, H. Your newsroom may be searched. *Quill,* July/August 1978, 66 (7), 21-25.

Daily newspapers alive, changing. *Bloomington Illinois Daily Pantagraph,* June 1974, *16,* A-5.

DeFleur, M. *Theories of mass communication* (2nd ed.), New York: McKay, 1970.

DeFleur, M.L., & Ball-Rokeach. *Theories of mass communication* (3rd ed.). New York: David McKay Co., Inc., 1975.

Dennis, E.E., Ismach, A.H. & Gillmor, D. (eds.). *Enduring issues in mass communication.* St. Paul: West Publishing Co., 1978.

Emery, E. *The Press and America.* Englewood Cliffs, N.J.: Prentice-Hall, 1962.

Fall pre-view. *TV Guide,* September 1978, 9, 26, 31.

Feshbach, S. & Singer, R.D. *Television and aggression.* San Francisco: Jossey-Bass, 1971.

Gerbner, G., Gross, L., Jackson-Beeck, M., Jeffries-Fox, S., & Signorelli, N. Cultural indicators: Violence profile, No. 9, *Journal of Communication,* 1978, 28, 176-207.

Herzog, H. What do we really know about day-time serial listeners? In B. Berelson and M. Janowitz (eds.), *Reader in public opinion and communication.* Glencoe: Free Press, 1950.

Hiebert, R., Ungurait, D., & Bohn, T. *Mass media.* New York: David McKay, 1974.

Himmelweit, H., Oppenheim, A. N., & Vince, P. *Television and the child: An empirical study of effects of television on the young.* London: Oxford University Press, 1958.

Inside Hollywood. *Newsweek,* February 1978, *13,* p. 73.

Kaplan, A. The aesthetics of the popular arts. In I. Deer & H. Deer (eds.), *The popular arts.* New York: Charles Scribner's and Sons, 1967.

Katz, E., Blumler, J.G. & Gurevitch, M. Utilization of mass communication by the individual. In J.G. Blumler & E. Katz (eds.), *The uses of mass communications: Current perspectives in gratifications research.* Beverly Hills: Sage, 1974.

Kraus, S. & Davis, D. *The effects of mass communication on political behavior.* University Park: Pennsylvania State University Press, 1976.

Lazarsfeld, P., Berelson, B., & Gaudet, H. *The people's choice.* New York: Columbia University Press, 1948.

Lazarsfeld, P., & Kendall, P. *Radio listening in America.* New York: Prentice-Hall, 1948.

Lenehan, M. Avoid the dread tune-out! *Chicagoan,* February 1974, *1,* 82-87.

Liebert, R.M., Neale, J.M., & Davidson, E.S. *The early window: Effects of television on children and youth.* New York: Pergamon Press, 1973.

McLeod, J.M., Becker, L.B., & Byrnes, J.E. Another look at the agenda-setting function of the press. *Communication Research*, 1974, 1, 131-166.

McCombs, M.F., & Shaw, D.L. The agenda setting function of the mass media. *Public Opinion Quarterly*, 1972, 36, 176-187.

Mehling, H. *The great time-killer.* New York: World Publishing Company, 1962.

Michie, L. New money maker. *Variety*, April 1977, 27, 39.

Miller, M.L. & Reeves, B. Dramatic TV content and children's sex-role stereotypes. *Journal of Broadcasting*, 1976, 20, 40-51.

News doctors: Taking over journalism. *Broadcasting Magazine*, September 1974, 9, 21-28.

1977 Annual Report to the shareholders of CBS, Inc. New York: CBS, 1977.

Northrup, F. Communications. *Listener*, July 1970, 9, 33-35.

Olsen, J.E. The relationship between sex-role stereotyping in TV programming and children's autonomy. Master's thesis. Illinois State University, 1978.

Parker, E. In the public interest, convenience, and necessity...*Civil Rights Digest*, October 1972, 5, 6-11.

Patterson, T.E., & McClure, R.D. *The unseeing eye: The myth of televison power in national elections.* New York: Putnam, 1976.

Peled, T., & Katz, E. Media functions in wartime: The Israel home front in October 1973. In J. Blumler and E. Katz (eds.), *The uses of mass communications: Current perspectives on gratifications research.* Beverly Hills: Sage, 1974.

Pember, D. *Mass media in America* (2nd ed.), Chicago: Science Research Associates, 1977.

Peterson T. Why the mass media are that way. *Antioch Review*, Winter 1963-64, 23, 405-424.

Real, M. *Mass mediated culture.* Englewood Cliffs, N.J.: Prentice-Hall, 1977.

Record. *Quill*, July/August 1978, 66 (7), 7-8.

Robinson, J. Mass Communication and information diffusions. In F.G. Kline and P. Tichener (eds.), *Current perspectives in mass communication research.* Beverly Hills: Sage Publications, 1972.

Schwartz, T. *The responsive chord.* New York: Anchor Books, 1974.

Shaw, D.L., & Clemmer, C.L. News and the public response. In D.L. Shaw & M.E. McCombs, (eds.), *The emergence of American political issues: The agenda setting function of the press.* St. Paul: West Publishing, 1977.

Snider, P.B. "Mr. Gates" revisited: A 1966 version of the 1949 case study. *Journalism Quarterly*, 1967, 44, 419-427.

Stein, A.H., & Friedrich, L.K. Television content and young children's behavior. In J.P. Murray, E.A. Rubinstein, & G.A. Comstock (eds.), *Television and social behavior, Vol. II: Television and social learning.* Washington, D.C.: GPO, 1972.

Sterling, C., & Haight, T. *The mass media: Aspen Institute guide to communication industry trends.* New York: Praeger Publishers, 1978.

Summary of broadcasting. *Broadcasting Magazine*, May 1978, 8, 76.

Tannenbaum, P.H., & Zillman, D. Emotional arousal in the facilitation of aggression through communication. In L. Berkowitz (ed.), *Advances in experimental social psychology* (Vol. 8). New York: Academic Press, 1975.

Toffler, A. Signs that mass media are in death throes. *Bloomington, Illinois Daily Pantagraph*, 30 April 1978, D-20.

Townley, R. The news merchants. *TV Guide*, March 1974, 9, 22, 6-11.

Waters, H. & Dotson, J. Shoot-out in San Antonio. *Newsweek*, July 1975, 14, 53.

Whan, F.L. *Iowa audience radio survey*. DesMoines: Central Broadcasting Co., 1948-1951.

White, D.M. The "gatekeeper": A case study in the selection of news. *Journalism Quarterly*, 1950, 27, 383-390.

Williams, W. & Larsen, D.C. Agenda-setting in an off-election year. *Journalism Quarterly*, 1977, 54, 744-749.

Williams, W., & Semlak, W.D. Campaign '76: Agenda setting during the New Hampshire primary. *Journal of Broadcasting*, 1978, 22, 531-540.

Wright, C.R. *Mass communication: A sociological perspective*. New York: Random House, 1959.

Wright, C. *Mass communication: A sociological perspective* (2nd ed.), New York: Random House, 1975.

Zillman, C. Excitation transfer in communication-mediated aggressive behavior. *Journal of Experimental Social Psychology*, 1971, 7, 419-434.

Zillman, D., Hoyt, J.L., & Day, K.D. Strength and duration of the effect of aggressive, violent and erotic communications on subsequent aggressive behavior. *Communication Research*, 1974, 1, 286-306.

IV

Public Communication

10

How to Prepare and Deliver Speeches

Herb Jackson

Most students who enroll in a basic speech communication course anticipate at least a portion of the course will be devoted to acquiring practical oral communication skills. Many immediately associate learning to prepare and deliver speeches with such a course. Indeed, most basic speech communication courses are, at least in part, devoted to the acquisition of public speaking skills. Why? It is an important question; it deserves more than a perfunctory response. We believe part of the answer lies in the *foundational nature* of presentational or public speaking skills.

Most of us who teach and do research in this field tend to consider the abilities and confidence often acquired through actually preparing and presenting speeches as being fundamental or *foundational* to other forms of communication. Acquiring the kinds of creative, analytical, organizational, and language skills basic to effective public speaking frequently appears to serve students well in a variety of communication encounters, be they interpersonal or small group in nature.

Our next question, then, becomes this: What sort of *foundational skills* appear important to adequately preparing for and presenting an effective and communicative public speech? Hopefully, the content of this final section will provide some practical, concrete answers. The

following pages describe, in step-by-step fashion, a series of essential considerations typically associated with most any speech. Nevertheless, the applications we make are specifically appropriate for speeches that possess either an *informative* or a *persuasive* intent, or both. We have chosen to focus on these two types of speeches because they appear to be the kind people are most frequently called upon to present in their professional and social lives. We also feel the following chapter offers some sound, practical advice on how to prepare and deliver these kinds of public speeches. We believe this is the case because much of the advice given is truly time-honored, more importantly, *time-tested* in nature. Offering students sound, time-tested prescriptions on public speaking is one of the things we're supposed to do. It's a product of a tradition of the field that stretches back for centuries.

In reading this section and following the guidelines it contains, keep in mind your ultimate purpose with respect to presentational or public communication. While a "how to do it" approach to such an endeavor may reflect for you the immediate goal of classroom success (i.e., "If I make a good speech I will get a high grade."), your long-range goal should be one of personally mastering effective oral communication skills for future application as well. We cannot stress strongly enough the value of acquiring such skills — for future application in the public marketplace of information and ideas, in personal relationships, indeed, in every realm of human activity. Be evermindful of the fact that ultimately, textbooks, guidelines for skill-acquisition, and classroom practice merely provide an immediate means with which to prepare for future human enterprises.

Insuring Productive Effort

When we talk of constructing or composing a speech, the sort of speech we naturally have in mind is the truly successful or effective one, the one that achieves the purpose for which it was intended. An achievement of this sort is usually preceded by a period of time devoted to careful planning and analysis, to flexing one's "analytical muscles" as it were. Also, such an accomplishment often results from having previously invested no small degree of care and attention in the speech's organization, content, wording, and so on. The point is obvious: Like so many other achievements in life, speaking success is often highly dependent on an investment of *productive effort* prior to the actual presentation, prior to ascending the podium. Notice we qualify such effort as "productive."

Suppose you're about to give a speech, and just before it comes time for you to stand up and face your audience, you take a last-minute glance at your notes. Suppose, also, that while thumbing through those notes you say to yourself, "Wow, I sure did put a lot of hours into this speech!" Whereupon you begin recalling how those many hours of preparation were actually spent and in your review, you come to realize that much of the time invested was actually spent procrastinating, waiting for some blazing inspiration to strike—the one that never seemed to come. Then there was all that time you spent groping through the library, wandering aimlessly through issues of news magazines and other handy sources, drafting sheeves of disjuncted notes, false starts, and paragraphs that never seemed to hang together—all culminating with a frenzied, last-ditch effort at putting something together the night before. And, worst of all, your eleventh-hour panic resulted in copying words and thoughts not even your own. Suddenly, you find you're less confident, less assured that this speech of yours is going to get you through the next few minutes. Small wonder.

Suppose, on the other hand, you have glanced through your notes with the honest conviction that they are the result of time invested in productive effort, in work guided and organized by a rational, practical plan or design. Such a plan or design may have involved following a series of interdependent steps, laid out in logical sequence with each making some contribution to the production of a well-honed, effective, communicative presentation. Knowing this you will, no doubt, approach the podium with heightened confidence or conviction in your message. Time and work guided by a practical, logical plan or design, then, is what we would call *productive effort* with respect to message composition. It is the converse of the disorganized, ineffectual, or unproductive effort described in the preceding paragraph.

An important pre-construction consideration then, is knowing roughly how much and what sort of effort is required for the task ahead. And, knowing whether or not this work can indeed be organized in some efficient and productive way is another. We therefore consider it appropriate to present the "blueprints" of a twelve step plan for speech construction and delivery before launching immediately into a detailed discussion of the first step. This way you can form an overall impression of the merits of the plan and the work it entails.

Twelve Steps in Preparing and Delivering an Oral Presentation

Based in part on what our lengthy heritage tells us, what others in the field tell us*, and years of personal experience in instructing others on speech-making, we have derived a step-by-step process, a sequential series of guidelines or principles one can follow when drawing up an informative or persuasive presentation. While we feel our plan incorporates prescriptions that appear applicable to practically any instance of message preparation, we know they are particularly appropriate to the task of constructing and presenting informative and/or persuasive messages.

The plan's impetus is, candidly, a mixture of practicality and idealism. We are convinced the plan is both workable and time-tested in character. In addition, while endeavoring to design a practical work scheme for speech-making, we have also been ever-mindful that following such a plan or scheme should result in a quality product.

Table 1

Twelve Steps in Preparing and Delivering an Informative or Persuasive Speech

Step   1: Deal with the preliminaries
       A. Determine the purpose(s) of the speech
       B. Analyze the prospective audience
       C. Choose a general subject area appropriate to the purpose
          and audience

*We especially wish to thank Ms. Gail Lovinger, a professional speech writer for the American Hospital Association and Dr. Catherine Konsky, a faculty member in the Department of Information Sciences, Illinois State University, for their assistance with the present chapter.

Step   2: Define the specific topic
      A. Limit the subject area to a manageable topic
      B. Determine a central idea or thesis

Step   3: Perform general, preliminary research on the topic
      A. Generate a personal "diary" on the topic
      B. Compile a bibliography on the topic
      C. Survey other, non-print sources

Step   4: Compose a tentative outline
      A. Perform initial analysis of your topic
      B. Organize your thoughts

Step   5: Perform more focused research
      A. Examine printed sources identified earlier
      B. Explore non-printed sources discovered earlier

Step   6: Compose a detailed, well-organized outline
      A. Select a pattern of arrangement
      B. Support major statements

Step   7: Attend to stylistic considerations
      A. Focus on word choice
      B. Attend to features of oral composition

Step   8: Prepare visual and/or audio support
      A. Select the right media aids
      B. Learn to use media aids effectively

Step   9: Write an introduction

Step 10: Write a conclusion

Step 11: Practice the speech
      A. Focus on content
      B. Attend to length and delivery

Step 12: Deliver the speech
      A. Attend to audience feedback
      B. Self-critique

If you have examined the plan carefully, you may have noticed that it does not direct the speaker to dash off immediately to the library. The important considerations outlined under Steps 1 and 2 should be dealt with prior to initiating any library research. Having done so will help make what research you may need to do far more efficient and productive. You may have also noticed that following the plan requires that you postpone writing an introduction for your speech (Step 9) until you have completed the preceding steps. The main portion or body of the presentation is developed first. It strikes us as abundantly sensible to compose and arrange what you intend to say before attempting to introduce it. Postponing composing a conclusion to Step 10 appears equally sensible. It makes little sense for you to try writing a conclusion before you have a firm notion of what you are concluding. There is also some practical wisdom in writing a conclusion after having developed the introduction of the speech as well as the body. This way the speaker can both summarize the major points presented in the body and tie back to what was said at the beginning.

Finally, you may have noticed that we include practicing the speech (Step 11) as part of the plan. It is important that the preceding ten steps be completed far enough in advance of the speech's actual delivery (Step 12) in order to allow ample time for practice. We have found that sufficient, guided practice heightens both the speaker's confidence and the effectiveness of the presentation.

Let's suppose you have been asked to make a speech. Like anyone else, you would probably like to put together and present your speech with as little trauma and as much success as possible. We believe that following the twelve-step plan outlined in Table 1 will certainly help in achieving such a goal. This is not to say, however, that your speech will come together with little effort. Composing and delivering a truly effective, communicative presentation is rarely a simple and easy task. Nevertheless, faithfully adhering to the step-by-step plan outlined and illustrated in this chapter will help assure productive effort on your part and effective, communicative presentations can be the result as well.

Step 1: Deal with the Preliminaries

In discussing the first step of the plan, our attention will focus on three general but important factors: (1) the primary purpose of the presentation, (2) general features of the prospective audience and setting, and (3) the general subject area. In other words, preliminary to drawing up any presentational message is anwering the question: "On what do I wish to speak to this audience, in this setting, and why?" The pains you take in deriving a complete, precise response will pay dividends throughout your preparation, or, as you encounter subsequent steps in the plan. This becomes evident very quickly; when it comes time to go to step number two (i.e., defining the specific speech topic), for example, you will discover how helpful it was to have previously defined a general subject area.

Determine the Main Purpose of the Speech

Most of us like to think of ourselves as doing things for a reason. As a rule we are all in the habit of attributing certain motives or a sense of purpose to our own behavior as well as the behavior of others. Presumably, then, people speak to one another, whether in a face-to-face, group, or more public situation, because they have a purpose or goal in mind, because they seek a certain response from those they address. According to Brooks (1978), the general purpose of any communication is simply "to win a response" (p. 311). The response we usually seek, however, is not a highly overt one; first and foremost we want our auditors to understand or comprehend our message — a decidedly mental or cognitive response. When this does occur, we can say we have been successful at presenting a *communicative* message. Yet, it should be emphasized that both speaker and listener, both source and receiver, actively participate in the achievement. It usually takes care and hard work to construct a well-organized, easy-to-follow, comprehendable message and comprehending or understanding the message often requires concentration, attention, or what is often called "active listening," on the receiver's part.

As we have stated, however, instances of public communication are usually prompted by a purpose, or by purposes beyond the simple goal of message comprehension. Speakers typically want their audiences to comprehend or understand the things they talk about *in a certain way.* Perhaps we can best represent this notion graphically:

Speaker's Purpose:	**Audience Response Sought by the Speaker:**
To Inform	Grasp an idea, a concept, a process; comprehend, retain the information presented and perceive it as useful, interesting.
To Entertain	Understand or perceive something as humorous, whimsical, ironic, etc.
To Persuade	Understand or perceive something as acceptable, sensible, beneficial, good, etc.

When, for example, you identify persuasion as your primary purpose, you are naturally seeking a specific kind of audience response. If you are able to construct and present a message that prompts or wins the specific response you seek, then you may characterize the enterprise as an *effective* one. Defining your purpose, then, can prove to be an initial step toward achieving it.

The purpose of one speech may be largely informative whereas the intent of another may be persuasive. Certain presentations may carry an imperative or command intention while others are strictly for purposes of entertainment. The Sunday sermon, the commencement address, the campaign speech or the eulogy accompanying a funeral or memorial service each possess different purposes. This is not to say, however, that all speeches must possess but *one* purpose; a speaker may set out to achieve any number of ends or fulfill any combination of purposes. While a sales presentation may generally possess a persuasive intent, it may also be informative with respect to what the product does, how it can be used, and so on. Such a presentation could even be amusing or entertaining at times. Yet, a sales presentation, like most presentations possessing multiple purposes, typically sets out to achieve one, primary end; whatever else it achieves along the way is usually auxiliary or supportive with respect to this primary purpose.

Isolating and defining the *main* purpose of the speech and classifying appropriate others as auxiliary or *supportive* is often very helpful. What is most important is that you keep the primary and auxiliary nature of the purposes you have so designated in mind throughout the preparatory stages of your presentation. Take, for example, the speaker who set out to persuade an audience to adopt caring for houseplants as a hobby. To persuade, then, became the primary purpose of the presentation. The speaker also had an informative purpose in mind and rightfully so. After all, people cannot be expected to want to do something they know nothing about. An auxiliary purpose of the presentation, then, was to inform. However, the speaker subsequently prepared and delivered a seven-minute presentation with the first six minutes being devoted to displaying varieties of houseplants, explaining how to care for them, and so on; the remaining minute was thus all the speaker had left to explain why the audience should seriously consider houseplants as a hobby. In this case, the speaker was unable to achieve the overriding purpose of the presentation because the respective primary and supportive roles of the two purposes, to persuade and to inform, were not maintained or kept in mind throughout the preparatory stages. They somehow became reversed in the actual presentation. The speech was not effective because it failed to achieve the main purpose intended or what the speaker set out to accomplish in the first place.

Defining the purpose or purposes behind a presentation and, in the case of multiple purposes, classifying them as "main" and "supportive" thus become important to completing Step 1. And, as will become clear, defining one's purpose or purposes in this way will prove helpful in terms of audience analysis as well.

Analyze the Prospective Audience

While we would certainly be reluctant to consider the houseplant speech described earlier as *effective*, in the sense we use the term, it could conceivably have been a highly communicative one. Audience members may have received and understood lots of new and useful information on, say, the proper care of houseplants. Suppose, on the other hand, the audience was primarily made up of horticulturists or houseplant enthusiasts. Such an audience might find the presentation repetitive of what they already knew and were convinced of; they may even have become inattentive and bored after the first few minutes of the speech. And, when the crucial final minutes of the presentation did arrive, perhaps few were listening with any attention at all. The presentation could not even be considered communicative if such were actually the case — all of which serves to emphasize the importance of including audience analysis as a preliminary consideration in message preparation.

In practice, however, it may not be efficient or necessary to attempt to discover *everything* possible about a given audience. For example, the usefulness of determining whether or not audience members hold to certain humanitarian beliefs or values would be limited indeed if one were merely wishing to inform them on how to change a tire, winterize an automobile, or bake a cake. The point is this: the usefulness of what one can learn about a prospective audience, to a great extent, is determined by the purpose of the presentation.

Purpose and audience analysis. Let us say that persuasion is the main purpose of the presentation you are preparing, or perhaps your primary intention is the dissemination of information. Correspondingly, what would be useful information with respect to your prospective audience given either one, or both, of these purposes? If persuasion is your purpose, you would probably want to focus your analysis on the audience's attitudes, beliefs, or perceptions with respect to (1) you, that is your credibility, and (2) your subject once you have defined it. If, on the other hand, your purpose is an informative one, you will want to know (1) what sort of information your audience would find interesting and/or useful and (2) what they already know with respect to your subject once you have defined it. If you have both an informative and a persuasive purpose in mind, then you will need to know all of the above. Notice that keeping your audience in mind is also important when selecting a subject, the third and final preliminary consideration listed under Step 1 of the plan.

Choose a General But Appropriate Subject Area

We intend the term *subject area* to designate a fairly broad and sweeping category, one which could conceivably include a variety of more specific *topics*. A subject area like "inflation" could, for example, include such topics as "soaring energy costs" or "your shrinking food dollar." A subject area is considered *appropriate* for speaking purposes when it appears salient to the interests or predispositions of audience members, and when it seems right for the speaker and the purpose s/he has in mind.

Selecting a subject area, like choosing practically anything, requires that you exercise some judgement. But, like so many important decisions, choosing an appropriate subject area is rarely a product of whim or caprice. Rather, informed, reasoned, and qualified or criteria-bound judgment is what typically leads to an appropriate choice. To assist you in selecting an appropriate subject area we have therefore compiled a list of criteria in the form of questions you might take to practically any subject area (see Table 2). To make the best use of this list, however, we suggest you do two things. Begin by compiling a list of as many potential subject areas as you can. You may even try applying the "brainstorming" techniques discussed in Chapter V to your efforts at generating such a list. Then, examine each item on your list of potential subject areas according to the criteria given in Table 2.

Table 2

Criteria for Subject Area Selection

Speaker:

1. Are you personally interested in this subject area?
2. Are you knowledgeable about this subject area (through readings, experience, research, occupations, travel, etc)?
3. Will you be able to adequately research this subject area?

Audience & Purpose (To Inform):

4. Will the audience find this subject area interesting or timely?
5. Do members of the audience already know something about this subject area?
6. Can relevant information be made useful to audience members?

Audience & Purpose (To Persuade):

7. Will audience members find this subject area salient to their needs or interests?
8. Do audience members already hold an attitude, either pro or con, on this subject?
9. Do audience members feel one way or another with respect to related subjects, topics, or issues?

Setting:

> 10. Can this subject be adequately treated in the time allotted?
> 11. Is this subject appropriate for the occasion?
> 12. Is this subject suitable for the physical setting of the speech?

Step 2: Define the Topic

As compared to Step #1, completing the second step of the plan will probably require far less time. The principal goal of this step is to limit the subject area you have chosen to a manageable topic. A topic is "manageable" when it can be adequately researched and when it can be adequately treated in the time allotted your presentation. By "topic" we mean a precise statement of the central, but specific, idea you wish to express. In the case of a persuasive presentation, "topic" refers to the specific position your speech will take, the thesis it will advance and defend.

Completing Step #1 should result in your selecting a subject area; further, it should be one that is appropriate to you, your purpose, and the prospective audience. Still, you are not quite ready to start drafting the content of your presentation. Having landed on a subject area means you have a *general* idea of what you are going to talk about, but you have not yet decided on the *specifics*, i.e., on the exact information you will convey, the issues you will address, the direction you will take, and so on.

For purposes of illustration, let's say you have decided that "self-disclosure" is an appropriate subject area. Like practically any subject area, "self-disclosure" is very broad, very indefinite. What specific aspects of self-disclosure will you cover? How will you develop the content? Do you want to address self-disclosure within the content of relationships? If so, what kind of relationships? Friends? Family? Spouse? Co-workers? Is there a general lack of self-disclosure in our society? What dangers, if any, are attached to too much self-disclosure? What does current research have to say on the subject? Based on what we already know, the knowledge we currently possess on the subject, we are thus able to generate quite a number of appropriate approaches to the subject area, "self-disclosure." In other words, our task now becomes one of limiting our subject area to a specific topic. Failure to limit a subject area can result in a highly unfocused presentation, i.e., one that says a little bit about a lot of things but fails to develop an important thought or idea fully, adequately. Presenting such an undirected, sweeping, or disjuncted speech provides audience members very little from which to draw a clear, precise sense of what the message said or intended.

Focusing the content of a message is not only beneficial from the audience's point of view, but from your own as well. Typically, there are time limits associated with preparing for and delivering any presentation. One could not adequately address *all* the issues and questions we raised earlier in regard to "self-disclosure" in, say, five to eight minutes. And, considering the volume of research devoted to this subject, it could take a good many hours simply to gather and digest the necessary information. How many additional hours might be required to organize, arrange, illustrate, amplify, and practice the presentation?

The Topic Sentence or Thesis Statement

While you may be convinced by now that narrowing a general subject area to a specific topic is a good idea, you may not yet have a concrete notion of how to go about doing it. We suggest you begin by constructing a single *topic sentence*, one that does at least two things for you.

First, and foremost, a useful topic sentence is one that further delimits the subject area you have selected. Given the present example, we might select "self-disclosure *in relationships*." Second, a truly useful topic sentence is one that encapsulates the main thought or *states the central idea* you want to communicate to your audience. This is certainly the case if your purpose is to inform. If, on the other hand, you are wanting to persuade or convince your audience of something with respect to the topic you have selected, then your topic sentence should serve as a *thesis statement* or proposition as well. We will illustrate with a few examples.

With self-disclosure as a subject area and an *informative* purpose in mind, we can derive the following topic sentence: "Self-disclosure appears to be important in a number of different human relationships." Notice that the sentence reports the central theme or idea we want to convey; we want to inform our audience on self-disclosing within the context of specific human relationships. Our presentation could, conceivably, inform audience members of how self-disclosure appears important in (a) friendships, (b) courtships, and (c) marriages.*

You may have noticed a second feature of our informative topic sentence. In a certain sense it can be characterized as a "factual statement" because it states or asserts something to be a fact. Topic sentences for informative speeches usually take the form of factual statements. The thrust of the presentation, then is to establish *why* the statement is true or accurate, i.e., to present factual, concrete, or

---

*Each of the relationships we have identified here may easily become major headings when outlining the speech (steps 4 and 6 below).

practical information on the topic.

A topic sentence for a persuasive presentation, on the other hand, differs markedly in that it often carries overtones of decision-making that go beyond accepting or rejecting a statement of fact.

With self-disclosure as a subject area and a *persuasive* purpose in mind, we can point to at least three topic sentences or thesis statements (or propositions) as appropriate:

1. Self-disclosure should be an integral part of marriage relationships.

2. It is better to self-disclose with friends than with mere acquaintances.

3. Practicing appropriate self-disclosure during courtship can lead to a stronger relationship between spouses.

Notice the words "should be," "is better," and "can lead" in the three respective examples. Our intent is not merely to ask audience members to accept the information we present or report as factual. Rather, we are asking them to exercise their judgment, to draw a specific conclusion, to make a specific kind of decision.

The first thesis statement or proposition, "self-disclosure should be an integral part of marriage relationships," is intended to prompt what amounts to a policy decision. It asserts that something *should* happen. We will, therefore, call this first type of thesis statement a *proposition of policy* and label any other thesis statement or proposition that asserts "something should happen" as such. With the second thesis statement, "it is better to self-disclose with friends than with mere acquaintances," we are asking our audience to accept the idea that behaving in a certain way is *better* done with certain people than with others. In short, we are asking them to make a value judgment, to choose between two specified alternatives. Any thesis statement, therefore, which purports that "something is better than something else" we will call a *value proposition*. The third thesis statement above asserts that a cause-to-effect relationship exists between "appropriate self-disclosure" and "a stronger relationship between spouses." This, and any similar statement, we will label as a *causal proposition* because it maintains that "something causes, or will cause, something else."

By completing Step 2 of the plan, then, you will have accomplished a number of tasks important to composing an effective speech. You will have both limited the subject area selected earlier to a manageable topic and derived a precise statement of the thought, idea, or proposal central to your speech as well. And, as will become evident, casting a topic sentence with an eye for the characteristics associated with the four types of statements outlined in Table 3 will help you greatly in pursuing subsequent analysis and composition.

Table 3

The Form and Types of Topic Sentences

Speech Purpose	Example	Form	Type of Statement
To Inform	Self disclosure appears to be important in a number of different human relationships.	Something did occur or is occurring.	Statement of fact
To Persuade	Self-disclosure should be an integral part of marriage relationships.	Something should happen	Proposition of policy
	It is better to self-disclose with friends than with mere acquaintances.	Something is better than something else.	Value proposition
	Practicing appropriate self-disclosure can lead to a stronger relationship between spouses.	Something causes or will cause something else.	Causal proposition

Step Three: Perform General, Preliminary Research on the Topic

It might be useful to think of Step 3 as an exercise in preliminary intelligence- or information-gathering. Surveying available print and non-print sources of information before launching into a jungle of data, arming yourself with a sure sense of "what's out there" and where things are located could prove highly productive and efficient. The idea behind Step 3 is to gather enough general information to be able to sketch-out a tentative outline of your speech (Step 4). And, you may think of the tentative outline as a rough, but invaluable topical map, one that will certainly help you to pursue a more intensive exploration (Step 5) of the jungle of information that may surround your topic.

We suggest, therefore, that you keep the future utility of what you discover in mind as you generate the materials resulting from your preliminary, general research: (1) a "diary" of what you already know about your topic, (2) a bibliography of relevant, printed materials, and (3) a survey of other, appropriate, non-printed sources.

Produce a "Diary" on Your Topic

We stressed earlier that personal knowledge and experience are important when selecting a subject area; they can be equally important when researching your topic. Monroe and Ehninger (1974), for example, suggest that a good way to *begin* your search for speech material is "to jot down on a piece of paper everything you already know [about your topic] as a result of personal experience or observation" (p. 288). Following this advice could produce something that resembles a personal accounting or "diary" of the knowledge or information you already possess on your topic.

Prior to seeking information from other sources, we suggest you write your topic sentence or thesis statement across the top of a page of notebook paper and try to produce a diary of what you know about your topic. You may also discover that a diary generated in the "brainstorming" spirit will require more than a single piece of paper. Jot things down as they occur to you; don't worry about the overall structure or order of your diary. You can impose some order on these notes at a later stage of your preparation. Try to get down everything you can think of that relates to your topic sentence. You may find it advisable to exercise at least some care, however, when recording what occurs to you. Your diary will be of little assistance if your jottings are so cryptic that you cannot decipher them.

While Monroe and Ehninger (1974) recommend augmenting the information recorded in this fashion with "further observation and/or personal experimentation" (p. 288), an idea we would certainly support, we can think of two immediate, practical uses for your diary as it now exists. Relating a personal observation or anecdote is often a good way to illustrate a point. A vividly described personal experience or even a humorous anecdote frequently helps audience members to identify with or in other ways attend to features of your message in a receptive way. Your diary may, therefore, prove a handy source for this kind of speech material. It can also serve another useful purpose. If you have compiled your diary with care and have thereby produced a complete picture of what you already know about your topic, it can serve as an indicator of what you *don't* know as well. In other words, examining your diary with an eye for those areas of informatin that appear incomplete and need fleshing-out can provide a concrete notion of what you will need to look for when exploring other sources of information, principally the library.

Compile a Bibliography

There are, of course, a whole host of topics that may require little additional research on your part. For example, you may already know enough about transplanting houseplants, changing a tire, or finding the best places to snow ski to enable you to put together an effective presentation on any one of those topics. If this is the case, you may not need to explore sources of information outside yourself, your diary. More typically, however, having to speak knowledgeably, or convincingly, on a selected topic demands that you augment what you may already know. What Oliver and Cortright said years ago (1961) still holds today: "Every speech is likely to be a challenge to broaden or to sharpen your knowledge of the topic selected" (p. 205). Surveying available *printed* materials for information relevant to your topic is an important step toward amassing the additional data you require. Undoubtedly, the best source for this printed information (and even some non-printed materials like records, films, and tapes) is the library.

If a visit to the library is required at this point, we see no need for it to become an extended stay. It probably would not be necessary to arrange for a friend to bring you sandwiches. Remember, one of the purposes of Step 3 is initial intelligence-gathering. We therefore recommend that you devote your initial trip to the library to compiling as complete a list of relevant printed sources, i.e., as complete a *bibliography* on your topic, as you can. Postpone the actual withdrawal and examination of the sources on your list until later, when completing Step 5 to be exact. At that point your bibliography can become a useful guide for "what's out there" and "where to find it."

Compiling a bibliography does require the ability to use a library, some knowledge of how·certain materials are organized there and how they are referenced or catalogued for ease of location. If you feel your library research skills are not quite up to the task, or you need a brief refresher on how to use a library, you will find the instructions contained in any one of the following sources useful:

> Ella V. Aldrich, *Using Books and Libraries*, 5th ed. (Englewood Cliffs, N.J.: Prentice-Hall, 1967).
>
> Jacques Barzun and Henry P. Graff, *The Modern Researcher* (New York: Harcourt Brace Jovanovich, 1957); see especially, Chapter IV, "Finding the Facts," pp. 61-87.
>
> Douglas Ehninger and Wayne Brockriede, *Decision by Debate* (New York: Dodd, Mead & Co., 1963); see, Chapter V, "Obtaining Information: Printed Sources," pp. 42-59.
>
> James D. Lester, *Writing Research Papers, A Complete Guide* (Glenview, Ill.: Scott, Foresman, 1967; see, Chapter III, "The Library," pp. 15-34.

It is obvious that providing the above list of practical guides to library research will be of little help to someone who does not know how to locate them in the library. You can find any one of the references given above in the same way we did, that is, by consulting the library's card catalogue. For those who are unfamiliar with such an initial step, we will explain how to use the card catalogue and some other handy indexes as well. We will also attempt to provide assistance in dealing with the basic problem facing any library user: Once inside the doors, where does one go to get needed information.

The card catalogue. The card catalogue is the starting point for finding books related to your topic. It is like an inventory list of all the books (and in some instances, the phono-discs, tapes, films, microforms, and archives as well) in the building. On alphabetically arranged cards, with a separate card for each item, the catalogue is able to index each book or item three different ways: (1) by author, (2) by title, and (3) by subject. This triple listing method should enable you to find material on your topic. If you do not know any specific book related to the topic, for instance, simply consult the *subject* listings given alphabetically in the card catalogue (see Figure 1). Once you have found a relevant book or source in the card catalogue, you will need to jot down the author or authors, the title, and, above, all, the *call number* given on the card.

Figure 1: Entry Card for a Book

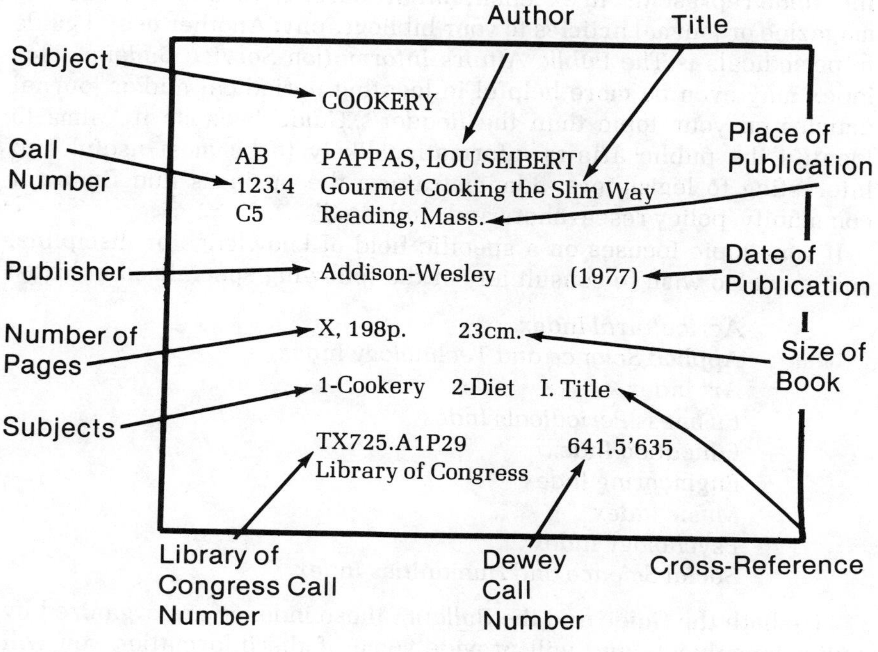

The call number indicates where the book is located in the library. If you feel you will need some assistance later, when trying to find the books you have call numbers for, then consult a librarian.

In order to compile a working bibliography on your topic, you will need to know how to use some additional indexes also available in the library. In addition to the card catalogue, many libraries stock the *Cumulative Book Index* (formerly the *U.S. Catalog*), which also lists published books by title, author, and subject. The card catalogue, however, remains the best reference to those publications the library actually holds.

Periodicals. Most libraries, especially college libraries stock both popular and scholarly periodicals and journals. Publications of this sort provide more timely information and more concise commentaries than that usually found in hardbound references. The problem, of course, is finding the journal and/or magazine articles that best serve your informational needs. Literally hundreds of periodicals are published every month, and, when they are combined with back issues, your library may actually hold thousands of articles on a wide spectrum of topics. Perhaps the most efficient method for finding specific articles on your speech topic is to turn, again, to available indexes compiled for that purpose.

The most frequently used index to popular periodical material is the *Reader's Guide to Periodical Literature*, a cumulative author and subject index published monthly. Indexing more than 160 publications, the *Guide* represents an excellent initial source to turn to when adding magazine or journal articles to your bibliography. Another useful guide to periodicals is *The Public Affairs Information Service Bulletin*. This index may even be more helpful in locating periodical and/or journal articles on your topic than the *Reader's Guide* because it "aims to identify the public affairs information likely to be most useful and interesting to legislators, administrators, the business and financial community, policy researchers and students."

If your topic focuses on a specific field of knowledge or discipline, you may also wish to consult any of the following specialized indexes:

> *Agricultural Index*
> *Applied Science and Technology Index*
> *Art Index*
> *Business Periodicals Index*
> *Education Index*
> *Engineering Index*
> *Music Index*
> *Psychology Index*
> *Social Science and Humanities Index*

Like both the *Guide* and the *Bulletin*, these indexes are organized by topics or subjects and will provide some of the information you will need to locate given articles in the library: the title of an article; author's name, if known; the name of the journal or magazine in which the article was published; the appropriate volume and year of publication; and the article's pages. Be certain to record all this when including a relevant article in your bibliography.

Your library probably does not subscribe to nor hold *all* the issues of all the magazines and journals indexed. You will need to ascertain what periodicals are actually available in the library and where they are located in the building. Looking for the titles of the periodicals listed on your bibliography in the card catalogue should provide you with the call number you will need to find those journals or magazines (see Figure 2). Some larger libraries maintain a separate card catalogue that exclusively lists periodicals and their call numbers. In any event, you must be certain to indicate (with appropriate call numbers) where the periodicals, in fact where all the items on your bibliography can be found in the library. Doing so will make your job much easier when you will need to trace-down and examine crucial items on your bibliography (i.e., when completing Step #5).

Figure 2

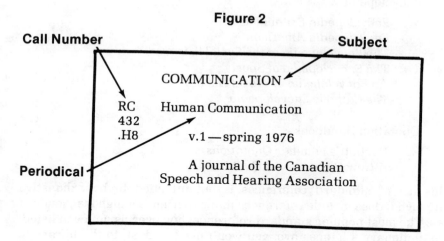

Standard reference works. Perhaps the best source to turn to for definitions of key concepts or technical terms, or for general background information on your topic is one of the standard reference works. Many researchers *begin* their library work with an examination of such standard reference works as an unabridged dictionary and a set of encyclopedias. Typically, such references are shelved in a separate section of the library for easy access. You may find one or any of the following standard references of some help:

Atlases:

>   *Rand McNally Commercial Atlas*
>   *Encyclopedia Britannica World Atlas*

Biographies:

>   *Who's Who in America*
>   *Current Biography*
>   *The Directory of American Scholars*
>   *International Who's Who*
>   *American Authors*
>   *Dictionary of National Biography*
>   *Biography Index*

Almanacs:

>   *Information Please Almanac*
>   *The Statesman's Yearbook*
>   *World Almanac*
>   *Statistical Abstract of the U.S.*

Encyclopedias:

>   *Encyclopedia Britannica*
>   *Encyclopedia American*
>   *The Encyclopedia of the Social Sciences*
>   *The Encyclopedia of Sports*
>   *An Encyclopedia of World History*
>   *The Catholic Encyclopedia*

Quotation Handbooks:

>   Bartlett's *Familiar Quotations*
>   *A New Dictionary of Quotations*

This list of standard references is not intended to be exhaustive although it does include references that experience a high frequency of use. The most popular standard reference, however, is not even listed: the dictionary. Chances are, you won't need to dash to the library to find one. But, if you are looking for the *best* dictionary, *Webster's Unabridged Dictionary* can usually be found in any library.

Newspapers. News stories, book reviews, and feature articles represent additional printed sources of value to many speakers. *The New York Times Index* is an alphabetical and chronological guide to information contained in the daily issues of that newspaper. Since news articles of more than local interest usually appear on the same dates in various papers, the *Times Index* can provide a guide to other newspapers as well. However, you may wish to check the *Newspaper Index*, a monthly publication that indexes the following newspapers:

Chicago Tribune
Los Angeles Times
New Orleans Times-Picayune
Washington Post

In addition to these newspapers, those that also enjoy a fairly good reputation for objective reporting are: *Wall Street Journal, Washington Star, Manchester Guardian, Atlanta Constitution,* and the *L.A. Times.*

If your topic is a fairly timely one, you should not overlook newspapers as a source of facts and interpretations on contemporary issues and problems. If, on the other hand, you are searching for a point-of-view not typically found in large daily newspapers, then you may want to examine the *Alternative Press Index,* an irregularly published subject index of many alternative or underground publications. Due to their limited circulation, however, actually locating an issue of an indexed publication may prove very difficult.

Government publications. A valuable source for speech materials on a wide spectrum of topics, and one that is frequently overlooked, is the publications of the federal government. If your topic falls within such subject areas as education, law enforcement, labor relations, business, transportation, agriculture, foreign trade, national defense, home economics, science and technology, medicine, ecology, recreation, and energy, among others, then you can be assured that the Government Printing Office has published something on it. Many fail to explore the wealth of information available through government publications because they do not know how to search for it.

The first and most comprehensive source of information on government publications usually available is the *United States Government Publications Monthly Catalog.* It is often referred to as the *Monthly Catalog.* This index may be considered the government publications' counter-part to the *Reader's Guide to Periodical Literature;* it is alphabetized according to subjects and the governmental agencies from which publications have emanated. One section of the *Monthly Catalog* indexes current publications and assigns an "entry number" to each item or publication. Then, you simply turn to another section which lists current publications by issuing agencies, look for the entry number under the appropriate agency, and find a description of that publication (see Figure 3). Actually locating the publication might not be quite so quick and easy however.

As was the case with periodicals indexed in the *Guide,* your library probably does not hold more than a fraction of the government publications listed in the *Monthly Catalog.* Usually, they must be acquired directly from the issuing agency or department, by writing to one's Congressman, or by submitting an order to the Superintendent of Documents, Government Printing Office, Washington, D.C. 20402. For precise ordering instructions, see the "General Information" section of

Figure 3

Sample Index and Sample Entry, the *United States Government Publications Monthly Catalog*

Index Page:

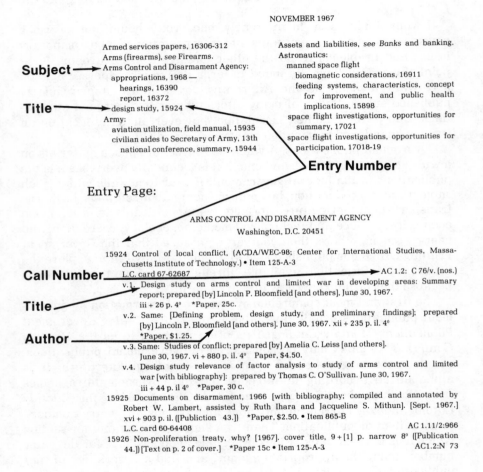

NOVEMBER 1967

Subject → Arms Control and Disarmament Agency:

Armed services papers, 16306-312
Arms (firearms), see Firearms.
Arms Control and Disarmament Agency:
  appropriations, 1968 —
    hearings, 16390
    report, 16372
Title → design study, 15924
Army:
  aviation utilization, field manual, 15935
  civilian aides to Secretary of Army, 13th
  national conference, summary, 15944

Assets and liabilities, see *Banks* and banking.
Astronautics:
  manned space flight
    biomagnetic considerations, 16911
    feeding systems, characteristics, concept
    for improvement, and public health
    implications, 15898
  space flight investigations, opportunities for
    summary, 17021
  space flight investigations, opportunities for
    participation, 17018-19

Entry Number

Entry Page:

ARMS CONTROL AND DISARMAMENT AGENCY
Washington, D.C. 20451

15924 Control of local conflict, (ACDA/WEC-98; Center for International Studies, Massachusetts Institute of Technology.) • Item 125-A-3
Call Number L.C. card 67-62687   AC 1.2: C 76/v. (nos.)
  v.1. Design study on arms control and limited war in developing areas: Summary report; prepared [by] Lincoln P. Bloomfield [and others], June 30, 1967.
    iii + 26 p. 4° *Paper, 25c.
Title   v.2. Same: [Defining problem, design study, and preliminary findings]; prepared [by] Lincoln P. Bloomfield [and others]. June 30, 1967. xii + 235 p. il. 4°
    *Paper, $1.25.
Author v.3. Same: Studies of conflict; prepared [by] Amelia C. Leiss [and others].
    June 30, 1967. vi + 880 p. il. 4° Paper, $4.50.
  v.4. Design study relevance of factor analysis to study of arms control and limited war [with bibliography]: prepared by Thomas C. O'Sullivan. June 30, 1967.
    iii + 44 p. il 4° *Paper, 30 c.
15925 Documents on disarmament, 1966 [with bibliography; compiled and annotated by Robert W. Lambert, assisted by Ruth Ihara and Jacqueline S. Mithun]. [Sept. 1967.] xvi + 903 p. il. ([Publiction 43.]) *Paper, $2.50. • Item 865-B
  L.C. card 60-64408   AC 1.11/2:966
15926 Non-proliferation treaty, why? [1967]. cover title, 9 + [1] p. narrow 8° ([Publication 44.]) [Text on p. 2 of cover.] *Paper 15c • Item 125-A-3   AC1.2:N 73

the *Monthly Catalog.*

Although not every bibliography need contain book, periodical, standard reference, newspaper, and government-printed sources, you should attempt to survey and record those sources that appear most useful and relevant to your topic. Remember, the idea is not only to compile a complete bibliography but one that will also serve you later, when seeking-out specific sources in the library. Having thus compiled a working list of viable *printed* sources, you may want to give some thought to pursuing certain additional *non-printed* sources as well.

Survey Other, Non-printed Sources

Conceivably, with some topics, an extensive search for printed sources may prove unnecessary, perhaps even futile, whereas, with others, it becomes necessary to glean information from a combination of sources. With most topics, however, at least some library research is absolutely crucial. If your topic touches on the national crime rate, for example, then relevant information is best gotten in the library. If, on the other hand, you are also interested in the crime rate in your community, then you would be well advised to supplement the time you spend surveying local newspaper sources in the library with an interview with a representative of the local police department, the sheriff's office, the prosecuting attorney's office, and so on. Before outlining a presentation on women's inter-collegiate athletics, perhaps you should talk with an appropriate person in your athletic department; before taking a position on alternative energy sources, you might find it helpful to seek out authoritative sources in the physics department, the geology department, or the agricultural department. If you merely want an opinion then you can ask practically anyone. Our point is this: Some kinds of information are best obtained through library research; other kinds are better gotten by asking the right questions of the right people. Careful library research can yield invaluable factual data; but interpretations, commentaries, opinions, impressions, predictions, and the like are often best obtained through face-to-face interactions with appropriate experts. The degree of validity one can associate with the latter information is, however, dependent on the perceived credibility of the source, the person you talk with.

It would certainly be in keeping with the purpose of Step 3 to begin giving some serious thought to the possibility of your gathering some relevant information through interview. However, now is not the time to actually arrange, plan, and conduct an interview with a carefully selected, authoritative source. For an interview to be maximally productive you will need to have done more than the sweeping, general sort of research described so far. Nevertheless, drawing up a tentative list of appropriate experts, members of both the campus and local community, may provide you with a valuable reference later.

Another source of non-printed information—other than direct interviewing—is that made available through mass media and various forms of public communication. There are numerous network news specials, PBS programs, televised panel discussions or interviews, and radio broadcasts of the "face the nation" variety that are often available to those seeking information on timely, local, national, or

international issues. Beyond these, there is an added source of information readily available to members of many campus communities. It's a rare college or university that does not have an active program of lecturers and speakers visiting the campus throughout the academic year. These speakers often possess national reputations, special insights on specific features of the contemporary scene, or information on topics of concern to thinking persons generally.

In addition to hosting individual speakers, many campuses, college groups, organizations, certain affiliated professional or service associations, as well as some local groups frequently organize and conduct on-campus forums, symposia, conferences, workshops, panel discussions, and the like on a variety of topics. Typically, these events are open to the general public as well as to members of the sponsoring group or organization.

Survey the local radio and TV listings for future programming of special significance to your topic; examine campus and/or local newspapers for coming lectures or programs that appear relevant. Jot down the time and place of any future instance of public communication germane to your topic and plan to attend if at all possible. As a student of speech, attending any form of public communication out of a need for specific information can pay double dividends. Hopefully, you will not only be able to gather the information you seek, but also have an opportunity to observe an effective speaker at work.

Completing Step 3 should result in your having generated a variety of materials as they appear necessary and useful: (1) a diary summarizing or listing the knowledge, information, insights, observations, and so on that you currently hold with respect to your topic, (2) a thorough bibliography on relevant printed sources, and/or (3) a survey of other, non-printed sources which may include a list of potential, qualified interviewees or available experts who can comment on your topic and/or (4) a tabulation of future instances of media or public communication that appear germane. Hopefully, the research activities associated with Step 3 and the materials they produce will facilitate your completing the next two steps in the plan.

Step Four: Write a Tentative Outline

This step is very important. It could be considered one of the more crucial steps toward your developing an intelligible message, a truly communicative presentation. Also, it is, at least in part, a culminating step in terms of what you have done to this point.

The preliminary analysis of purpose, audience, and subject that you performed in completing Step 1 hopefully lead you to derive a correspondingly appropriate and precisely stated topic sentence (Step 2) and the content of that sentence provided a basis for and helped direct the general, preliminary research you performed when completing Step 3. To complete Step 4 adequately you will need to exercise or develop two important skills. First, you will need to *analyze* carefully the content and implications of your topic sentence as well as that of some of the research materials you have generated so far — and do so while keeping your purpose and audience in mind. Then, you will need to *organize* the thoughts, information, and ideas that come out of your analysis into a comprehendable, useful, albeit tentative, pattern or outline.

Topic Analysis

We suggest that, before trying to organize any speech outline you focus your analytical abilities on the topic sentence you constructed earlier and on some of the research materials you have generated thus far. It has also been our experience that truly efficient and productive analysis is typically guided by purpose and a sense of audience. In practical terms this means you will need to examine your topic sentence and such materials as your diary and, if you compiled one, your bibliography, while keeping the specific audience response you desire, the goal you wish to achieve, constantly in mind.

Your topic sentence is the first and most important object of analysis. If you constructed your topic sentence as we suggested in Step 2, then it represents a statement of the central idea or concept you wish to convey. Also, following our guidelines should have resulted in a topic sentence that is phrased according to purpose or intent. For example, we framed the following statement to illustrate a topic sentence with an informative purpose: "Self-disclosure appears to be important in a number of different human relationships." As with any informative presentation, the degree to which audience members are able to comprehend the information we convey, to grasp our central concept (i.e., self-disclosure), is highly dependent on how well we explain, illustrate, or support the statement we have made. Our ultimate success or effectiveness, therefore, is a direct product of our having presented information in an orderly, systematic, easy-to-follow way. Our first analytical task, then, is to break down the concept to be explained, the ideas to be presented, into their respective parts so that the whole may be understood. Good information results from the intelligent separation of a concept, idea, or process into parts and then clearly treating each in a logical sequence.

Analytical Strategies

In analyzing either an informative topic, such as the one given above, or a thesis statement that embodies a more persuasive intent, you may find it helpful to employ any one, or a combination of the five analytical strategies that have served speakers well in this regard for many generations.

Definition. Defining something is often an initial step in coming to understand it. For purposes of illustration suppose we begin with the topic·sentence we isolated earlier: "Self-disclosure appears to be important in a number of different human relationships." In this case we would probably begin our analysis with a definition of the important concept, "self-disclosure." Then, defining or in the other ways describing precisely what is meant, important to the present discussion, etc., would be in order.

Your diary or one of the standard references listed on your bibliography may prove helpful in defining the concepts that appear central to your topic.

Classification. By applying this analytical strategy we can systematically group things according to some characteristic or determining principle. With the present example, the obvious candidate for analysis through classification is "human relationships." The characteristic of interest is "self-disclosure." We may, then, attempt to classify a number of human relationships (e.g., friendships, courtships, and marriages) according to the relative degree of self-disclosure that occurs within each.

Exemplification. This analytical strategy translates the abstract and the general into the concrete and the specific. We can analyze and explain important but abstract notions, concepts, etc., such as self-disclosure, with appropriate, vivid examples, illustrations, descriptions. Often a definition is too abstract for quick comprehension; thinking of illustrative and appropriate examples helps to make things more concrete, more easily understood.

Causation. Applying the strategy of causation means looking for apparent causal links between events, forces, or other phenomena. Analysis through causation represents an attempt to answer the question: "How?" For purposes of our present analysis, an important question would be: "How does self-disclosure affect certain human relationships?"

Motivation. This analytical strategy is most appropriate for persuasive topics and is embodied in attempting to answer the question: "Why?" It represents an initial analysis of why one might agree or disagree with the policy you advocate or the value judgment you advance. The strategy of motivation may also be applied to certain informative topics. For example, exploring possible motivations behind "self-disclosure" could prove a useful exercise.

Whatever analytical strategy is brought to bear, an important axiom appears to be that sound, well-organized presentations usually stem from the speaker having invested his or her efforts in a period of analysis and self-questioning, an internal dialectic, analyzing relevant information, issues, and reasoning, long before attempting to inform or persuade others.

Applying Analysis to Organization: The Tentative Outline

A speaker's initial attempt to organize a presentation is often a natural consequence of having engaged in some prior analysis of the topic. For example, can you see how the following tentative outline grows from our having applied four of the five analytical strategies discussed above to the topic sentence, "Self-disclosure appears to be important in a number of different human relationships."?

While the outline given in Figure 4 serves as an excellent illustration of the close link that often exists between topic analysis and initially structuring or outlining a speech, it also provides a basis for discussing two characteristics common to tentative outlines.

First, you will notice that the outline in Figure 4 is incomplete. While the use of relevant examples or illustrations is indicated, specific instances are not given. Hopefully, additional research will provide the examples called for in the outline. If not, we may be forced to re-draft certain portions of the outline. Also, while a definition for self-disclosure is provided, we may have been similarly forced to postpone formulating such a definition, until an acceptable one surfaced through subsequent research. Like most tentative outlines, then, this one is but a sketch, a framework we can build upon. We can certainly add detail to our sketch later, or, if the need arises, we can alter the framework.

There is a second feature of the outline that is also common to outlines of this sort. Although it is a product of some care and thought, it need not be invested with a high degree of permanence. In other words, it is subject to refinement, elaboration, or change. It should hardly be treated as *the definitive outline* on the topic at hand. There probably is no such thing as the singularly correct tentative outline. Pursuing the same four patterns of analysis on the same topic sentence, perhaps you could derive an altogether different tentative outline than the one we present in Figure 4.

Pursuing a careful and thoughtful analysis of your topic typically leads to producing a useful tentative outline. The usefulness of such an outline often becomes especially apparent while engaging in the more focused research associated with Step 5.

Figure 4
A Tentative Outline

Purpose: To Inform

Topic Sentence: Self-disclosure appears to be important in a number of different human relationships.

(definition)   I. Self-disclosure defined: The honest, intelligent, and benign disclosure of feelings, thoughts, beliefs, and so on, while intending positive, constructive relational consequences.

(classification)   II. The relative degree of self-disclosure (as defined) that typically occurs within certain human relationships

A. Friendships

    1. example

B. Courtships

    1. example   } (exemplification)

C. Marriages

    1. example

(causation)   III. How self-disclosure (as defined) affects certain human relationships.

A. Friendships

    1. example

B. Courtships

    1. example   } (exemplification)

C. Marriages

    1. example

Step Five: Perform More Focused Research

With the completion of Step 4, the body of your speech should be starting to take shape. By the time you have finished with a subsequent step, Step 6, it will have taken its final form. Thus, Step 5, our present concern, represents an important intervening step in the development of your presentation. Completing this step requires that you (1) build upon or extend what has been accomplished thus far in terms of research, analysis, and organization and (2) provide the substance or materials needed to complete Step 6, that is, construct a more detailed, well-supported outline.

Examine Printed Sources Identified Earlier

The printed sources you identified earlier, while compiling your bibliography, now become important sources for the more specific information and support you will need to produce a more detailed outline. Specifically, you will need to turn to the bibliography you compiled in Step 3 and seek out those books, periodicals, standard references, newspapers, or government-printed sources that appear to have special relevance to your topic and examine each carefully. Having already taken the time to record accurately such information as the call numbers, your search for needed bibliographical items should go fairly quickly. Much of the time and effort you invest in research may, therefore, be devoted to actually examining these materials. As you turn to each item, keep your tentative outline in mind. Be particularly alert for the following types of materials:

1. Statements which clarify your own ideas.
2. Illustrations and examples of what you have in mind.
3. Facts and evidence which test or support the validity of your own ideas.
4. Testimony and opinions of authorities concerning your views.

Explore Non-printed Sources Discovered Earlier

As you may recall, the general or preliminary research we described earlier included drafting a list of possible non-printed sources; namely, persons who, due to their special training or experience, represent potentially valuable sources of specific information relevant to your topic. If you feel that a personal interview with one or more of these expert sources is indeed viable, now is the time to arrange for and conduct one.

A haphazard, ill-planned, and poorly conducted interview is not likely to produce the desired results however. A successful interview, i.e., one that produces the information you seek, is often a consequence

of having followed a few simple guidelines.

Select your source carefully. Selecting your source — the person you wish to seek information from — may at first appear to be a simple matter; this is not always the case. Keep the apparent credibility and objectivity of your source in mind. This is especially important if you intend to take a position on a controversial topic. If you are seeking authoritative comments or factual information, then the source or sources you select need to possess sufficient expertise on the topic. The special training or experience, the credentials or degrees a source may possess and, above, all, the reputation he or she has established, are all important factors to consider when selecting an interviewee.

Once you have selected a source, you will need to obtain his or her cooperation. Interviewing a busy person may require some time and tenacity on your part. Get in touch with your intended source as far in advance of your deadline as possible and be certain to explain why you are seeking the interview, why you think he or she can provide the information you need. If you intend to tape all or part of the interview, you must obtain your source's permission to do so in advance.

Do your homework. Presumably, after you have selected the right source, you will want to ask the right questions. Like other important speech interactions, an interview requires planning and preparation. Your preparation should focus both on the topic and on your interviewee. You will need to know enough about the topic to be able to ask relevant and provocative questions. Also, your ability to frame pertinent and penetrating questions is, in part, dependent on knowing what your source has already stated publically or in print (e.g., in books, articles, newsprint, speeches, etc.).

Prior to the interview, establish in your own mind the specific purpose you wish to achieve as a result of the interview. Then carefully construct a series of questions that best achieve that purpose.

Conduct a smooth, nonconfrontive interview. While you may come to the interview with a prepared sequence of questions, you may find it necessary, or even desirable, to veer from your plotted course. Deal with issues or sub-issues as they arise; but avoid highly tangential questions if at all possible.

Interpret, evaluate interview results. Your job is not done until you have carefully reviewed your interview notes and/or tapes. Make an accurate determination of what your source said during the interview and interpret its meaning or value with respect to your purpose.

For additional guidelines on interviewing strategies and techniques, you may wish to examine any of the following references:

Raymond L. Gordon, *Interviewing: Strategy, Techniques, and Tactics* (Homewood, Ill.: Dorsey Press, 1969); see: Chapter IV, "Interviewing Strategy," Chapter V, "Techniques in Interviewing," and Chapter VI, "Tactics in the Interview."

Stephen A. Richardson, Barbara S. Dohrenwend, and David Klein, *Interviewing: Its Forms and Functions* (New York: Basic Books, 1965); see: Part III, "The Question-Answer Process."

Charles J. Stewart and William B. Cash, *Interviewing: Principles and Practices*, 2nd ed. (Dubuque: Wm. C. Brown, 1978).

Finally, we would suggest that if you do intend to take advantage of the informational resources also available through mass media or various forms of public communication, you endeavor to provide yourself with an accurate, useful set of notes. When conducting an interview, you are often very much in control of the content and direction of the interaction. This is not the case with, say, a T.V. broadcast or a lecture. Chances are, for example, Ralph Nader will not be invited to speak on your campus so that you may personally "pick his brain" with respect to your topic. Through attentive, active listening and judicious note-taking, however, you might be able to pick up and record relevant information, opinions, or arguments as a result of attending his lecture.

When your research of available printed and/or non-printed sources has provided sufficient detailed or supportive material to flesh out your tentative outline, it is time to proceed to the next step, to perform the additional analysis and selection and impose the necessary order required to produce a detailed outline of the body of your speech.

Step Six: Compose a Well-organized Detailed Outline

When data is organized, when ideas are carefully orchestrated, when thoughts are marshalled in a sensible way, better comprehension and understanding usually results. If you completed Step 4 as we suggested, then you have already imposed at least a rudimentary order on your thoughts and ideas; and, the analytical and organizational effort necessary to completing Step 4 no doubt facilitated the research necessary to completing Step 5. To complete the present step, Step 6, you must bring certain analytical and organizational skills to bear once again. Your goal becomes one of producing a complete, well-organized, and adequately supported outline of the *body*, the large and important middle section of the speech. To accomplish this you will need to: (1) select an appropriate pattern of arrangement for the important statements you wish to make, (2) develop, support those statements with the factual or explanatory material made available through previous research endeavors, and, in the case of a persuasive presentation, (3) support important statements with material that helps justify the claims they make. In the process of composing the body of the speech in this way, you may want to employ some of the important techniques of outlining as well as apply a fundamental principle of speech composition, namely, *make a statement and then support it*. Our first topic of discussion, then, becomes the task of selecting a pattern of arrangement.

Selecting a Pattern of Arrangement

Ordering, partitioning, or placing speech materials into some pattern of arrangement is both a practical necessity and a natural outcome of discerning analysis and research. We have already demonstrated how our initial topic analysis and general research lead to creating the embryonic outline necessary to complete Step 4. Such a tentative sketch, along with the more specific research findings that should have resulted from completing Step 5 combine to provide some of the raw materials for a finished speech. But, like an exquisite Swiss watch, a finished speech is more than a random collection of pieces, a sum of raw materials; it is an organization, a patterning of various parts in an interrelated way. Mills (1972) put it more concretely: "After a speaker has completed his analysis and research, he needs to partition and organize his materials. Accomplished speakers and writers know that this task is made easier by dividing the materials according to a consistent method, principle, or viewpoint..." (pp. 23-24). We can identify a number of conventional *patterns of*

arrangement frequently used to provide the "consistent method, principle, or viewpoint" that Mills speaks of. The ten patterns of arrangement often used to serve this function are:

1. The orientation-to-conclusion pattern
2. The topical pattern
3. The spacial or geographical pattern
4. The chronological pattern
5. The sequential pattern
6. The causal pattern
7. The simple-to-complex or familiar-to-unfamiliar pattern
8. The problem-solution pattern
9. The comparative analysis or pro-and-con pattern
10. The motivated sequence

Selecting an appropriate pattern from among those on this list or, perhaps, combining a couple of these patterns in a sensible way, is usually a matter of careful judgment. Attention to the purpose of the presentation, the nature of the material, and to some of the constraints present in the speaking situation usually leads to making the best choice or choices in this regard.

The orientation-to-conclusion pattern. This is the basic, straightforward plan that characterizes any speech organized according to the tripartite scheme of introduction, body, and conclusion. This pattern of arrangement best illustrates the long-standing maxim that a speaker should "tell them what he's going to tell them, tell them, and then tell them what he told them." First, the introduction *orients* listeners to the central idea, the major points, or the important issues to be discussed. Then, the central idea is developed, the major points or issues are treated in the order forecast, and finally, the speech ends with a *conclusion*, or summary, or recap of what was said concerning each point in the body of the presentation.

I. Introduction: Orientation to central idea and listing of points

II. Body: Development of each point

III. Conclusion: Summary or recap

The orientation-to-conclusion pattern is especially appropriate when dealing with a familiar or much-discussed topic of some controversy. Also, this pattern is general enough to work well in combination with other patterns of arrangement. For that matter, eight of the nine remaining patterns may be used in conjunction with this one as a means of organizing the *body* of the speech.

The topical pattern. The topical organizational pattern is also a fairly straight-forward development. Based on the association of ideas, it sets out or divides a topic according to categories or sub-topics. Breaking down a news story according to the "who-what-when-where-why-how" pattern familiar to journalists is an instance of using a topical approach to organization.

Many subjects or topics seem to lend themselves naturally to a topical pattern of arrangement. For example, it seems very natural to discuss features of government according to the categories *local, state,* and *national,* to arrange a financial report by *income* and *expenditures.* We can illustrate uses of the topical pattern with two additional examples that strike us as breaking into natural sub-topics:

    II. Body: Governmental remedies for inflation
        A. Monetary policies
        B. Fiscal policies

    II. Body: Features of college life
        A. Intellectual
        B. Social
        C. Recreational

When speech material seems to fall into natural or conventional categories like this, then a topical arrangement is the best plan. Chances are, if your material lends itself to widely accepted categories, then your listeners will find it familiar and easy to follow. The probability of your delivering a communicative presentation is thereby increased.

The chronological pattern. This pattern of arrangement organizes material according to a progression in time (either forward or backward). Organizing things according to "past-present-future" is a familiar example of using a chronological pattern. Discussions of the development of certain contemporary social phenomena, like modes of dress or fashion, popular music, entertainment, media, etc., could be organized in chronological order. Like so many features of contemporary life, they are products of past changes or evolutionary processes.

Organizing material in chronological order is particularly useful when it is important for your listeners to perceive and clearly understand certain time relationships. If, for example, you wish to take or defend a position on an issue of some controversy, you might find it helpful to outline the chronological events that contributed to the development of the issue.

The sequential pattern. The sequential pattern is actually a variant of the chronological pattern. While the underlying organizational principle of the chronological order is *change,* or events unfolding over time, the sequential pattern carries the added notion that these events occur due to an overall plan or design. We can often discern functionally ordered steps in the completion of many tasks, from changing a tire, transplanting flowers, and brewing beer, to filing a tax return or preparing a speech.

II. Body: There are four simple steps in finishing wood furniture.
  A. Prepare the wood
  B. Stain the wood
  C. Apply sanding sealer
  D. Apply a liberal coat of finish

Thus, when treating certain subjects or topics through a "how-to-do-it" approach, using a sequential pattern that outlines the interrelated steps involved in completing the task seems to be a natural organizational scheme. You can understand, then, why we instinctively turned to the sequential pattern when organizing this discussion on how to prepare a speech.

The causal pattern. Because any cause-to-effect relationship is inherently one of antecedent leading to consequence, the causal pattern is also a variant of the time or chronological pattern of arrangement. Causes must precede effects in time.

In using a causal pattern of arrangement, a speaker may demonstrate how present conditions represent antecedent causes for future effects. For example:

II. Body: When city zoning is ineffectual, family housing suffers.
  A. This community's zoning ordinances are outmoded and inconsistently applied.
  B. A proliferation of fast food establishments, gas stations, and liquor stores in prime residential areas will result.

Or, the speaker may discuss present conditions or effects in terms of the past causes which appear to have produced them:

II. Body: There seem to be three causes of the inflationary spiral that marks the contemporary American economy.
  A. Big corporations controlling prices.
  B. Strong unions controlling wages.
  C. Wide-spread government spending.

Not surprisingly, the causal pattern of arrangement is best suited for persuasive presentations built around a causal proposition.

The Simple-to-Complex or Familiar-to-Unfamiliar Pattern. The underlying organizational principle of this pattern of arrangement is one of *increasing complexity or difficulty* and is most useful with informative messages on complex or unfamiliar topics. Because it could prove counter-productive to immediately launch into the intricacies of certain highly complex topics like the tax code, inflation, microwave communications, or the use of the breeder reactor in the production of nuclear energy—because there is the risk of discouraging or confusing audience members with complex or unfamiliar material—the speaker should begin where his or her listeners are in terms of knowledge or interest. Notice, for example, how the following presentation on logarithms begins with the familiar sub-topic of fractions.

    II. Body. Performing logarithmic functions
       A. Fractions
       B. Proportions
       C. Progressions
       D. Logarithms

A crucial thing to remember when using this pattern of arrangement is to be certain that what you identify as *simple* or *familiar* is truly so from your audience's perspective. Also, you will need to exercise some care when developing the material you intend to use transitionally. Be certain that in moving from the familiar to the unfamiliar, from the simple to the complex, that you make sense along the way.

The problem-solution pattern. While the problem-solution approach is a logical one for persuasive speeches, it can be a useful organizational pattern for informative speeches as well. Nevertheless, it is most frequently used in conjunction with propositions of policy. Consider the following propositions or thesis sentences:

1. Due to the energy shortage, the federal government should ration gasoline.

2. Because of the severity of last winter, the state should initiate an extensive roads and highway repair program.

3. The cost of medical care in this country should be reduced.

4. Careful planning and preparation should precede your job search.

Each of these statements suggests a problem and offers a solution. The obvious intent behind the first three propositions is persuasion, but the fourth could easily pass as a topic sentence for an informative presentation as well. In any event, a presentation on any of the four can be divided into two major parts: a perceived problem and a recommended solution. Often the problem portion of this pattern is developed in an effect-to-cause manner; the recommended solution or solutions then prompt a corresponding policy decision of some sort. For example, a presentation on the first proposition above can be organized as follows:

    II. Body: Due to the energy shortage, the federal government should ration gasoline.
       A. An effect of finite quantities of crude oil world-wide is a shortage of petroleum energy.
       B. The federal government should control the consumption and conservation of gasoline in this country through an equitable rationing system.

The chief concern in using a problem-solution pattern is that of propor-tion. While you will certainly need to spend some time establishing that a problem does exist as you perceive it, proposed solutions, which are typically less familiar and often controversial, deserve the major portion of your presentational time. If, on the other hand, you perceive your audience as not realizing a serious need for action, then you would be well-advised to devote a larger portion of time to the problem you identify — but certainly not more than one-half.

The Comparative Analysis or Pro-and-Con Pattern. We stated earlier that most value propositions assert that "something is *better* than something else." In supporting such a proposition, a speaker is usually asking audience members to make a judgment, to choose one of two alternatives. The comparative analysis pattern of arrangement, therefore, lends itself very well to a presentation of this sort.

We can characterize the underlying principle of this pattern as embodied in the familiar cliche, "there's no such thing as a free lunch." In other words, it's a rare choice that doesn't carry a few costs, disadvantages, or negative consequences along with the benefits. To be certain, there are times when we are confronted with choosing between obviously positive and negative alternatives. But such clear-cut choices, especially with issues of any consequence, are more the exception than the rule. More often than not, available options carry *both* positive and negative consequences. As rational decision-makers, we usually try to go with the option that appears more comparatively advantageous; we try to opt for situations in which the benefits outweigh the costs, the pro's outweigh the con's.

The comparative analysis pattern consists of listing and examining each of the options that appear important, outlining the pro's and con's associated with each, and then indicating why one option appears comparatively positive or advantageous, i.e., *better.* To illustrate:

II. Body: Going to college is better than entering the work force directly out of high school.
   A. The pro's and con's of going to college
   B. The pro's and con's of entering the work force right after high school
   C. Of the two, going to college is better

The truly crucial feature of this pattern is embodied in the key term "better." You need to establish how you are using or applying such a relative concept as grounds for important decision-making. In other words, indicate the *criteria* by which you have chosen to apply the term. Stipulating these criteria is important not only when supporting the eventual choice you advocate but also when discussing the pro's and con's relevant to each option. For example, attending college may require living away from home. This may be considered an advantage or disadvantage, depending on how it is viewed, depending on what criteria are brought to bear.

The motivated sequence. As a pattern of arrangement, the motivated sequence (Monroe and Ehninger, 1974) is particularly well-suited for persuasive presentations that call for a specified action stemming from a policy decision. It also incorporates features of other patterns of arrangement, most obvious among them being the orientation-to-conclusion pattern and the problem-solution pattern.

The underlying principle of the motivated sequence is *need satisfaction*. By following a sequence of five, interdependent steps, the speaker is able to demonstrate how some degree of satisfaction can be achieved with respect to a felt or generated need. These five steps and the function each is intended to perform are presented directly below.

Step	Function
1. Attention Step.	Get listener's attention.
2. Need Step.	Establish the need; describe the problem.
3. Satisfaction Step.	Satisfy the need; present solution(s) to the problem
4. Visualization Step.	Visualize the desired condition which the solution will create.
5. Action Step.	Call for specific action or belief leading to desired condition.

*Based on Monroe & Ehninger, 1974, p. 362.

The functions of steps three and four in this sequence are identical to those of the problem-solution pattern described earlier, and the organizational development of the entire sequence, i.e., steps one through five, corresponds with the overall plan of the orientation-to-conclusion pattern, the first pattern of arrangement we discussed. Perhaps this will become apparent through illustration. The five steps of the complete motivated sequence are illustrated in the following outline of a speech on smoke detectors.

Attention Step   I. Introduction: Did you know that oil soaked rags left in a storage closet could burst into flames spontaneously?

                         II. Body: You should purchase and install a home smoke detector (proposition of policy).

Need Step	A.	*Problem*: Few homes are completely free from dangerous fire hazards.
Satisfaction Step	B.	*Solution:* To help protect your home and loved ones, purchase and install a home smoke detector.
Visualization Step	C.	You will enjoy a sense of security, the peace of mind that comes from knowing you and your loved ones are protected.
Action Step	III.	Conclusion: Buy and install a home smoke detector now.

The usefulness of the motivated sequence as a pattern for arranging the major points of a persuasive presentation should be fairly apparent. It also bears utility for speeches to inform; but, completing the first three steps in the sequence is all that is required.

Step	Function
1. Attention Step.	Get listener's attention.
2. Need Step.	Demonstrate the need to know the information to be presented.
3. Satisfaction Step.	Present the information itself.

*Based on Monroe & Ehninger, 1974, p. 364.

Having thus become familiar with the ten most commonly used patterns of arrangement, the task of organizing the major headings of your detailed outline may not appear quite so formidable. Selecting an appropriate pattern, or combination of patterns, does, however, require careful thought and informed judgment.

Support Major Statements

Having selected an appropriate pattern of arrangement (or combination of patterns) can serve to help organize the major points of your speech; doing so results in constructing a needed framework or skeleton for the body of your speech. Yet, you can quickly see that merely enumerating the main points or the major headings of your outline to an audience could prove to be a wholly unsatisfactory attempt at communication. Try picturing yourself standing before an audience armed only with the partial outline we used earlier to illustrate the sequential pattern of arrangement:

II. Body: There are four simple steps in finishing wood furniture.
   A. Prepare the wood
   B. Stain the wood
   C. Apply sanding sealer
   D. Apply a liberal coat of finish

What does "prepare the wood" mean? How is it done? What tools and materials are required for the task? How long will it take? Will it require a lot of effort? As for staining the wood...As you can see, there is a definite need for elaboration here.

Although, selecting a pattern of arrangement and applying it to the major points or statements you wish to make has the result of lending an overall order to your speech, it is, nevertheless, incomplete. While possessing form, your speech lacks substance. Providing this substance, or what is generally called *supporting material,* is usually a matter of following a fundamental principle of speech composition: *Make a statement and then support it.* Here, the word "support" means providing the additional information or evidence often required to make a statement more understandable or acceptable to the audience.

The Mechanics of Support: Outlining

Translating the fundamental principle of speech composition into practice, that is, supporting the major points or statements you have so carefully patterned, usually means writing the necessary supporting material in an outline format, one that may include: (1) secondary speech points, (2) specific speech details, and (3) supplementary speech details. Visually, such a format appears as follows:

I. Introduction

II. Body
   A. Major point
      1. Secondary point
        a. Specific detail
          (1) Supplementary detail

Supporting Material {

   B. Major point
      1. Secondary point
        a. Specific detail
          (1) Supplementary detail

Supporting Material {

III. Conclusion

Notice that the secondary points are subsumed under and are supportive of the main headings of the outline, that the specific details support these secondary points, and that the supplementary details, in turn, support these specific details.

The Substance of Support: Supporting Material

Like so many of the other aspects of speech composition, what is actually said, in the way of support, is largely dependent upon the overall purpose of the speech. In other words, a speaker will better achieve an informative end if the supportive material s/he selects is *material that explains*; a speech will be more persuasive if the important points it advances are supported with *material that justifies*. Also, as you may suspect, there may be certain instances in which a persuasive presentation will need to contain both material that explains and material that justifies in order to adequately support the major points or contentions it contains.

Under the term "material that justifies" we are subsuming the various forms of reasoning and tests of evidence previously discussed in Chapter VII. Should you feel the need, review relevant sections of that chapter with an eye for what can be effectively used to support important statements as you have them arranged in the body of your speech. What we are calling "material that explains," on the other hand, has not been discussed with any specificity so far in the text.

Material that explains. This type of supporting material may be generally defined as statements that help make other statements clear, comprehendable, or concrete. Put another way, material that explains helps to bring the meaning of a statement within the experience of the hearer. There appear to be a number of different devices that effective speakers frequently rely on to make their statements clear, comprehendable, or concrete, namely, the use of (1) definitions, (2) factual information or statistics, (3) similarities or differences, and (4) examples and illustrations. Perhaps it would prove helpful if we were to examine each of these devices with an eye for their explanatory value.

Definitions. Sometimes, when expressing a major point, it becomes necessary for a speaker to use a word or phrase which is unfamiliar to audience members or subject to different interpretations. In these instances some degree of clarity and, consequently, comprehension or understanding can be achieved through the use of suitable definitions.

In many instances the simplest kind of definition is the best, that is, the sort of definition that merely declares the speaker's intention to use a word or phrase in a certain way, to give it a particular meaning. For the sake of convenience we shall call definitions of this sort *derived definitions*. For example, "We use the term 'derived definition' to refer to those definitions that are constructed by the speaker and not quoted directly from a dictionary or other source." It is usually best to state such a definition in a way that shows it is the speaker's own definition and may not, therefore, be treated as universally accepted. Phrases like "I use...," "I define...," "By this I mean...," and so on, are useful in designating a definition of this sort. Introducing or designating a derived definition in such a way is very important. Doing so helps distinguish it from an *authoritative definition*, or one extracted from a dictionary, an encyclopedia, or an established textbook, and indicates a less than universally applied usage. Designating derived definitions this way emphasizes that, unlike authoritative definitions, their meaning should not be taken to apply beyond the immediate context or speaking situation. In other words, although simple, straight-forward derived definitions may help establish some clarity or specificity in meaning, they should not be treated as if they carried universal application—a characteristic of those broad and sweeping definitions one usually finds in dictionaries.

While usually intended to enhance comprehension or understanding, a definition that is not selected with care and judgment may produce the opposite effect. This is especially the case when derived definitions include emotionally charged words or phrases. For example, defining "national health insurance" as "creeping communism" tends to confuse concepts which most sophisticated listeners hold as distinct.

Factual information or statistics. A factual statement is one that reports something in an empirical way; it is verifiable through direct experience, through our five senses.

This is not to say that a factual statement, merely because it is a factual statement, is necessarily a true or accurate one. "There are 2,000 students taking courses at this university" is a factual statement in the sense that it quantifies something, students in this case, and reports a situation that is verifiable. Nevertheless, such a statement may be incorrect—especially if practically any state-supported university in this country were the institution in question. Our point is this: Establishing the veracity of one factual statement often requires support in the form of other factual statements. For example:

It costs less to buy pizza at "Bonzo's"

1. An 18" cheese pizza purchased at establishment A costs $3.25.
2. The same pizza costs $3.45 at establishment B.
3. At "Bonzo's," an 18" cheese pizza costs only $2.95.

Notice how the use of supporting factual material helps explain the initial statement, how it helps to establish the veracity of the statement, to make it clear or concrete, and bring its meaning into the experience of its auditors.

Statistics, on the other hand, are used so frequently that many people forget that they are very abstract summaries of complex facts. Because they represent a tidy way of bundling up and presenting complex factual information, however, statistics are of some value and are often effectively used as supportive speech material.

Nevertheless, statistics can be very difficult to grasp when presented orally and should be used sparingly. To illustrate, try reading this passage, taken from a student's speech, aloud to a friend and see how much of the information it contains is actually comprehended or retained, even briefly:

> How much have food prices gone up? In February 1975, food prices averaged 93% higher than in 1974. In 1975 alone, they went up 7%. This figure includes food purchased for home use and meals eaten out. In 1955, $11 billion was spent on eating out — this averages out to $74 per person. In 1975, $27 billion was spent on eating out — this is an average of $128 per person. This represents a 73% increase, and the total spending on food increased by 131% between 1955 and 1975. During 1975, the average person spent ten cents more a day on food than in 1974. One half of the food dollar is spent for meat. Beef consumption per person has gone from 47 pounds per year in 1935, to 62 pounds per year in 1955 (an increase of 32%), to 116 pounds per year in 1975 — an increase of an additional 87%.

We would be surprised if your listener's reaction differs from that experienced by the original author of this passage: initial attention followed by confusion or indifference. It is usually a good idea to avoid "statistical overkill" when using this form of supporting material.

This is not to say that a speaker needs to totally avoid the use of statistics as factual support. However, when statistics are required and presented orally, the speaker needs to help make them as comprehensible as possible. For example, a speaker can often simplify complex numbers and still convey the same information; .739875 can become "about three-fourths" and 20,858 can be expressed as "nearly twenty-one thousand." Also, statistical data is often best understood when it is presented visually as well as orally. While the principle, "information is more likely to be understood and retained when it is related visually" (Verderber, 1976, p. 104) applies to information generally, it is particularly appropriate in the case of statistical data. Not only are statistics particularly well suited to visual portrayal, but they are also more likely to make sense and be remembered when a speaker presents them visually as well as orally — something you might recall to mind later, when completing Step 8, "Prepare Visual and/or Audio Aids."

Another method of conveying statistical information in a

comprehendable way is to recast it in a different form. Rather than mechanically spouting bald statistical data, as did the speaker on the rising cost of food, try expressing the same information in a slightly different way, one that helps bring its meaning into the listener's experience. Beyond reporting that 20% of the population of the United States lives in poverty, for example, one could convey the *meaning* of such a statistic by casting it as the equivalent of five students in a class of twenty-five.

Similarities, comparisons and differences. Using supporting material in the form of a comparison—or its counterpart, a contrast or difference—often helps an audience to understand or relate to something that would otherwise remain unfamiliar, i.e., outside their realm of experience.

> There have been recorded instances of the great white shark attaining weights in access of 2,000 pounds. That's roughly equal to the weight of a medium-sized pick up truck or more than ten times the weight of any linebacker in pro football.

Here is an example of how using both a familiar comparison (equal to a pick up truck) and a familiar difference (more than a football linebacker) helped to convey a piece of information that is probably outside the direct experience of most of us, the size of a particular kind of shark.

Comparisons and differences help an audience to visualize things, to bring the information you present out of the vague realm of abstraction and make it real, concrete. Composing them is not difficult but can require careful thought on your part. Begin by isolating the information you wish to convey, the qualities you wish to emphasize, and then identify familiar objects which possess the same qualities in similar or different degrees. Of course, you are merely applying the principle, make a statement and then support it, but this time your support takes the form of a comparison or a difference, or both.

As with other forms of material that explains, however, using comparisons or differences may also cast potential pitfalls in your way. The vigilant and informed speaker knows to avoid comparisons or contrasts that fail to amplify or support and merely confuse the issue or detract from the thought presented. Obvious examples of this include an over-reliance on trite comparisons, e.g., "life is like a bowl of cherries," or, what's worse, drawing incomplete comparisons and/or differences.

Examples and illustrations. For purposes of this discussion, we define examples or illustrations as particular cases of general phenomena. Perhaps we should illustrate with a couple of concrete examples.

General Phenomenon: Textbooks are expensive

Particular Case: I spent $85.00 on textbooks for this semester alone.

General Phenomenon: Some U.S. Presidents have been accomplished public speakers.

Particular Case: Abraham Lincoln
John F. Kennedy

General Phenomenon: Material that explains

Particular Case: Examples or illustrations

No doubt, you can readily see a relationship between the general phenomena and the particular cases we cite.

Of the types of material discussed so far, examples and illustrations are probably the most widely used for purposes of support or development. For that reason they probably require little explanation. If we do little else, however, perhaps we should distinguish between examples and illustrations and then examine a few problems that can creep into their use.

The principal difference between examples and illustrations is merely one of length. Illustrations are very long examples. Sometimes a speaker will tell a story or relate an anecdote in order to illustrate a point. This is especially helpful and effective when the audience is relatively unfamiliar with the subject at hand. An obvious limitation to using lengthy illustrations is the amount of presentational time they require. Also, if they are too extensive, an audience's attention may drift from the point being illustrated.

Unlike illustrations, examples typically include only relevant details and are, therefore, shorter in length. In order for an example to be truly effective, however, the details or particular case cited should indeed exemplify or represent a specific instance of the general phenomenon it is supposed to explain. Finally, both the particular case and the general phenomenon should appear relatively familiar, that is, within the listener's general realm of experience.

On the other hand, there may be times when building an illustration around events that really happened or using an example that includes familiar people, places, or things seems next to impossible. If carefully done, using a *hypothetical* example or illustration can be the answer. While examples and illustrations are often more explicative when they include particular cases or events that have actually happened, a hypothetical construction, if vividly described, at least allows the audience to see themselves in a relevant situation which could or might happen.

Nevertheless, a counterproductive situation may arise if hypothetical examples or illustrations are misused. The speaker who repeatedly represents hypothetical constructions as if they were describing something real, actual, or true, can do severe damage to his or her own credibility. By simply introducing hypothetical examples and illustrations as unmistakably fictitious, however, a speaker can avoid the taint of deception. Useful phrases include, "Suppose you find yourself...," "Try to imagine that...," "Think what it would be like if...," and so on. While more attractive phrasing can be invented, introducing hypothetical constructions this way helps to make their fictitious nature obvious.

Here is how one speaker used a hypothetical illustration to help explain something as complex as world socio-economics and introduced it in an effective way:

> Let's imagine for a moment that, rather than living in a world filled with three billion people, we are actually living in a village of one thousand. What do we find when we look at the people in our village? First, we find that less than ten percent of them are North Americans and a little over half of those North Americans pledge allegiance to the good ol' stars and stripes. Among the remaining 900 or so people in our village we would find 50 South Americans, 210 Europeans, 85 Africans, and 565 Asians. About 300 people in our village are white and the remaining 700 are non-white. Now, here's the most interesting fact so far. A mere 6% of the people living in our village accrue almost one half of the total income available. They call themselves "U.S. Citizens."

Thus, material that explains, whether it takes the form of a definition, factual information or statistics, comparisons, differences, examples, or illustrations, represents one kind of supporting material. It is one that helps make important statements clear, comprehensive, or understandable. The acceptance of proposals or assertions which possess a persuasive intent, on the other hand, usually rests on the effective use of a second kind of supporting material, namely, material that justifies.

Completing Step 6 of the plan should result in a well-organized and well-supported outline of the *body* of your speech. Organizing the major points in your outline is simply a matter of employing an appropriate pattern of arrangement (or a workable combination of patterns) and each major point, in turn, should be supported with material that explains or justifies — or both. Completing the next step in the plan, Step 7, requires that you examine your newly organized and supported outline with an eye for certain stylistic considerations. And, once you've polished the body of your speech stylistically and organized the audio/visual aids that appear necessary (Step 8), you should be ready to construct an *introduction* and *conclusion* for your speech (Steps 9 & 10 respectively). Then, it's simply a matter of practicing (Step 11) and delivering (Step 12) your speech.

Step Seven: Attend to Stylistic Considerations

In everyday parlance the term "style" is frequently used to characterize a mode of dress, a manner of doing something, or a particular way of behaving; and, it usually carries a fairly positive connotation. We intend to use the term in a more specific way, but one that refers to a particular kind of behavior—the way we put thoughts into words, the way we use language. We also intend the term to be neutrally descriptive, that it carry neither a positive nor a negative connotation.

Having an effective *oral* style means using both the content and form of spoken language in a communicative way, in a way that helps convey what we intend to our listeners. Notice that we characterize both the *content* (i.e., *what* is said) and the *form* (i.e., the *way* it is said) of spoken language as important stylistic considerations. The former refers to vocabulary phrasing, or *word choice* and the latter subsumes structural features of *oral composition*, like the degree of coherence, unity, conciseness, or emphasis embodied in the entire piece.

Completing Step 7 of the plan means examining the body of your speech, the outline you constructed while completing Step 6, with an eye for possible revisions in the content and form of your oral style. The intention behind any revision you find necessary is, of course, the creation of a more communicative presentation. This certainly requires that you know what to look for.

Focus on Word Choice

Because word choice is also a choice of image or meaning, taking some care with the words and phrases you use will help convey the meaning you intend, what you have in mind. The qualities of a truly effective oral style are similar in this regard to those associated with effective prose writing. Use words and phrases that make it easy for your audience to grasp your meaning. Composing clear, vivid descriptions, using natural, nonpretentious, or unhackneyed phrases, and avoiding needless technical language or jargon contribute greatly to a quick and easy comprehension of your thought or meaning. To illustrate how excess verbage and pretentious phrasing can get in the way of easy comprehension, compare these two descriptions of the same accident.

1. When the secretary pushed the file drawer closed, her right thumb got caught in the drawer.

2. Failure of the clerical employee to accurately estimate file drawer closure speed prevented the timely removal of her digit.

Which did you find easiest to comprehend?

Perhaps one of the most obvious virtues of effective oral phrasing is a reliance on brief but concise sentences. Unlike written prose, which is often more formal, more complex in structure, an effective oral style seldom relys on highly convoluted sentences with multiple parathetical constructions or other complex forms of expression. Minnick (1979) explains the difference rather succinctly; "effective oral style is tuned to the ear rather than the eye" (p. 145). Thus, oral expression or phrasing contains more short, simple words, more contractions (e.g., let's, they're, I'm, etc.), more personal pronouns, and a greater reliance on direct address (e.g., "you should support this change because...."), than standard written prose (DeVito, 1970).

Examine the body of your speech as you composed it in Step 6 and check for possible revisions that reflect what you have thus far discovered about the content of an effective oral style. Then, focus on your outline with an eye for a second stylistic consideration, composition.

Attend to Features of Oral Composition

When examining the body of your speech for features of effective oral composition, keep three relevant virtues in mind: coherence, unity, and emphasis. In certain ways, each contributes to making an oral composition "tuned to the ear rather than the eye."

That prose writing is tuned to the eye is evident in the convention of paragraphing. By indenting a certain amount of space, the writer signals the beginning of a new paragraph; the reader is presented with a visual clue that a new, important statement or idea is going to be developed. This convention assists the reader somewhat in terms of comprehending the content of the writing or following the author's train of thought.

A speaker, on the other hand, does not have such a handy indicator at his or her disposal. It is, therefore, helpful to indicate verbally when attention needs to shift from one major thought or statement to the next. Two devices often used to achieve a degree of coherence in oral composition appear very useful in this regard.

Transitions and internal summaries. Internal summaries are especially helpful when a major thought or statement has required extensive supporting material. A concise summary of that material not only helps achieve comprehension or acceptance but also helps to establish closure or a sense of completeness with respect to the point you have made. This, in turn, tends to indicate that you have treated the point thoroughly and are ready to start afresh with a new or different thought. Perhaps quickly following a concise internal summary with a transitional phrase or sentence (e.g., "Now, let me move to my second point...") would be an effective strategy in such an instance. In any case, both transitions and internal summaries help to establish an overall sense of coherence or natural flow in the sequence of things.

A unity of composition. This is achieved through insuring each supporting sentence indeed contributes to the thought or statement it is intended to develop. Unlike other features of oral style, a degree of unity is a virtue of both effective written and oral composition.

Make certain the body of your speech possesses a degree of unity in thought. Examine the supporting material given in your outline and determine whether or not every statement contributes to the development of the thought or idea it is intended to support. If not, cross out each irrelevant comment. If something is related, but not clearly so, revise it to make the relationship clear.

Emphasis. Everything you say, every statement you include in your outline — from major point to the most specific supplementary speech detail — does not carry equal importance. Nor does the most important feature of your outline include only its major points. Your success at establishing a major point may, for example, wholly depend on a crucial piece of supporting material. For your listeners to comprehend the significance of a specific piece of information, they may need to carefully attend to a particular example, illustration, or body of statistical data. You can ensure this indeed occurs through emphasis.

If you were composing written prose, then you could use any of a number of conventional devices, like underlining, setting key terms in capital letters or alternate type, or using certain punctuation marks (like dashes and exclamation points), and thereby emphasize your statements visually.

A fairly common way to emphasize something orally is by repeating it or, more specifically, through the use of literal or synonymous restatements. A literal restatement is simply repeating a statement or phrase in exactly the same terms used initially. Here is an illustrative example extracted from one student's speech advocating the conservation of gasoline:

> The price of many consumer goods have steadily risen in recent years at an annual rate of five to seven percent. It's tough enough to see your clothing dollars buy less now than they did a year ago. But, the price of petroleum, and, naturally, certain petroleum-based products like paints, plastics, and petro-chemicals, have increased in cost by as much as a hundred percent. One hundred percent!

In this case you can see how the speaker's use of a literal restatement served to emphasize a fairly significant piece of factual support. Nevertheless, literal restatements often sound harshly mechanical, become tiring, and consequently fail to serve their intended purpose if used excessively. Perhaps effective emphasis is best achieved through a combination of literal and synonymous restatement.

A synonymous restatement, or casting the initial thought in slightly different language, offers the value of repetition for emphasis without the shortcomings of literal restatement. Because the English language affords a fairly rich, or at least abundant, vocabulary, it is possible to express a thought or idea several different ways. While the practical range of variations is, in part, limited by the functional vocabulary of both the speaker and the audience, the number of possible variations is almost endless in most cases. For example, all of the following phrases express about the same idea as "certain communication skills are essential for success":

...the ability to communicate effectively is the foundation of achievement.

...speaking ability is often required for professional success.

...interactional skills are crucial in most job situations.

...professional advancement often hinges on one's capacity to communicate.

We are certain that more could be added to the list (e.g., "...the articulate job candidate is often the first to get hired") but, we don't want to labor the point.

Either literal or synonymous restatements can provide the speaker with an effective means of emphasizing relatively important statements through repetition.

Once you have carefully composed an organized and well-supported outline of the body of your speech (Step 6) and included the stylistic revisions that appear necessary (Step 7), then you are ready to turn your attention to a few final considerations with respect to the body of your presentation. It's at this point that some important decisions need to be made concerning your use of visual and/or audio forms of support.

Step 8: Prepare Visual and/or Audio Aids

The decision to augment the verbal support you include in the body of your speech with such visual material as graphs, charts, diagrams, pictures, slides, or even audio material like tape recordings or records, rests on how you answer the following question: "Will I make my message more understandable or acceptable if I express certain parts of it through media or a medium other than the spoken word?" After all, there are times when words alone seem to be enough. Using a verbal medium alone is sometimes sufficient to generate thought, stir feelings, fire imaginations, perhaps even prompt action. Those of us who are old enough to remember radio drama at its best know this can be the case.

Yet, there are times when words alone are not enough. When poor reading or listening habits, poor audibility or visibility, physical discomfort, linguistic limitations, distractions, noise, preoccupations, or prejudices prevent adequate reception and comprehension, then, no matter how well expressed verbally, the message is lost. Appropriately used, audio-visual aids can help overcome these situational and personal obstacles to understanding. Nevertheless, success in this regard is closely linked to adequately performing two important tasks: selecting the kind of audio-visual aid that best serves the intended purpose and then presenting it in an effective way.

Selecting the Right Media Aid

The general purpose of any audio-visual aid is the same as the verbal supporting material we discussed earlier, namely, to help make important points or statements clear, concrete. Media aids are, therefore, intended to supplement a presentation, to help develop or enliven a message, and should not be used to overwhelm its content nor as a substitute for careful preparation.

Beyond this general purpose, various types of media aids appear differentially suited to fulfilling specific informational needs. While we agree with DiSalvo's general observation that highly complicated and potentially confusing information represents the most obvious candidate for visual as well as verbal supports (1977, p. 147), selecting media aids that fail to make a genuine contribution toward better understanding is little help indeed. If media aids are not selected and used with care and intelligence, they may simply add to the confusion. It is, therefore, to your advantage to be aware of the potential instructional value of various kinds of media aids.

Key word displays. If it is important for your listeners to perceive and retain a sequence of steps or follow along as you discuss selected subtopics within the context of your speech, then you may find using a key word or concept display very helpful. In figure 5, for example, certain key words telegraph the sequential pattern of arrangement used to organize the body of a presentation we sketched out earlier.

We could, conceivably, introduce our entire presentation with this display; it could also come in very handy when making transitions from one step to the next. And, if we wished to summarize the presentation by recapping the major points of the speech, then Figure 5 could become useful once again.

Notice that in using a key word display in the manner we describe, we are actually showing our audience the major points contained in the body of our speech. We have thereby made it possible for our listeners to see the overall structure of our presentation, to see the way we have organized the information it contains. This is fairly useful because we

Figure 5

> # Prepare the wood
> # Stain
> # Apply sealer
> # Apply finish

know that when information is perceived as sensibly organized, it is more likely to be received, understood, and retained (Verderber, 1976, pp. 105-106).

Object display. There may be times when it is important to show an audience the characteristics or special features of a particular object, like how it can be used, that it is indeed portable, lightweight, durable, well-constructed, and so on. This may be especially important when attempting to convince audience members to purchase or use a product or device of some sort. In cases such as these the object itself becomes the best visual aid to use.

Nevertheless, not all objects are easily suited to display. When an object is so small that it cannot be seen simultaneously by all audience members, then its use becomes impracticable. Some speakers, upon finding themselves in this situation, have tried passing the object around during the presentation and soon learn that doing so merely serves as a source for distraction; they often succeed only in damaging their own effectiveness. When the object itself is too small or too large to display effectively, a picture or diagram of it will usually prove a suitable substitute.

Pictures and diagrams. Obviously, any photograph, drawing, or sketch does not offer the features of realism, like size, true color, or fine detail, that make object displays so useful. Yet, pictures of various kinds are very portable and make it possible to emphasize key features of the subject or object at hand. In your selection, however, make certain the picture, drawing, or sketch is neither so plain nor intricately detailed that it obscures the central features you wish to emphasize. Three-dimensional, color photographs that are large enough to be seen are usually the best and often easily obtainable through magazine advertisements or other promotional materials.

Figure 6

TYPES OF TIRE CONSTRUCTION

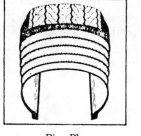 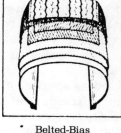 

Bias-Ply   Belted-Bias   Radial

Finally, a colored slide projection is the ideal way of displaying pictures. If this is not practical, however, at least mount your pictures on cardboard, posterboard, or the like.

Diagrams in the form of line drawings or three-dimensional drawings are often used in fairly specific ways. A three-dimensional diagram, such as a "cutaway" or an "exploded" view of something, serves to show the construction or internal workings of something. Figure 6, for example, shows the construction of different kinds of automobile tires through a cutaway view.

A line drawing diagram, on the other hand, is well suited to showing the organization of something, chains of command, or the sequential steps of a process. The line diagram given in Figure 7 illustrates the organization of a college department. A line diagram can also be used

Figure 7

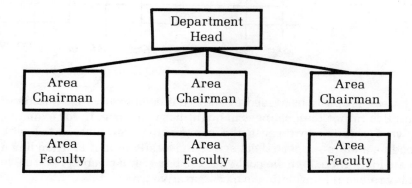

to show, for example, the various steps one must complete to register for classes, brew beer, or apply for a loan. Each step may be represented as a block in a flow chart. Or, to make the chart more eye-catching, each step may be illustrated with a picture or sketch rather than a lettered-in block.

Graphs and charts. Graphs and charts may be used to display comparisons or illustrate interrelationships by reducing numerical data or statistics to a form audience members can grasp at a glance. Either a line graph, bar graph, or pie chart may be used but each presents numerical information in a distinct way. Selecting and using the most appropriate chart or graph rests on knowing the potential informational value of each.

The *line graph* is best used as a means of displaying data so as to show development, change, or trends over time. In setting up a line graph, use the horizontal line to represent time (in hours, days, months, years, decades, etc.) and the vertical line to represent amounts of the measured quantity. Figure 8 illustrates how a trend becomes evident when statistical information is displayed in this manner.

Figure 8

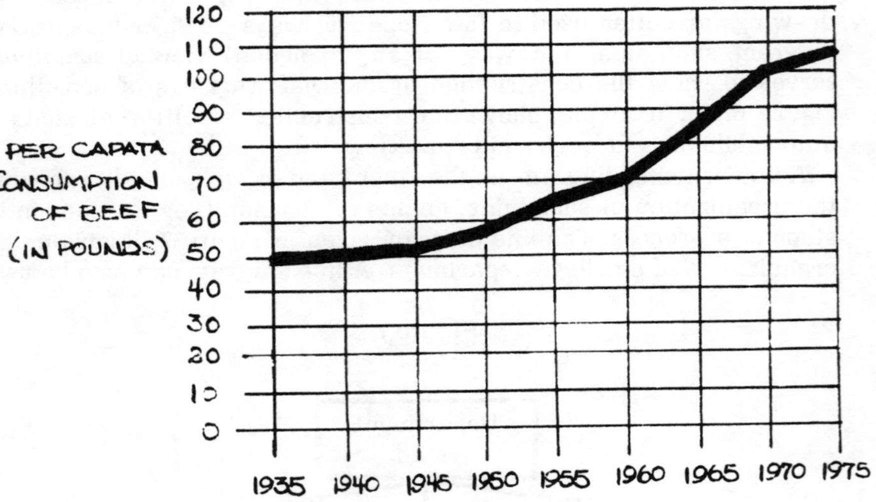

The *bar graph* is best used to show the comparative magnitude of quantities rather than changes in quantities over time. If, for example, we were wanting to discuss the comparative cost associated with attending a state-supported college or university to that of attending a private institution, then we could use the bar graph given in Figure 9 to display relevant information in a comparative way.

Figure 9

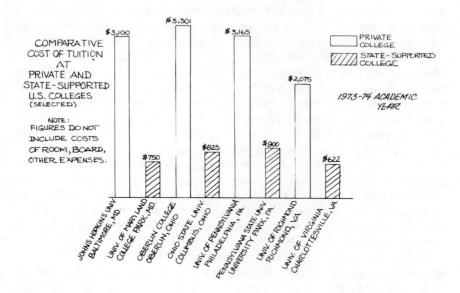

Should you need to show distribution or a proportional relationship between parts of a whole, a *pie chart* is the best visual aid to use. Figure 10, for example, provides a quick and easy way of showing differential government spending in combatting crime during the year of 1971. Notice that in slicing this pie, we cut it into pieces that correspond in area to the relative proportions of the thing being distributed — money, in this case.

Figure 10

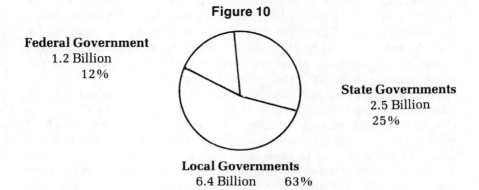

Audio aids. It would be impossible to show certain differences in styles of musical composition without a few illustrative selections. It would be fairly difficult to demonstrate the fundamentals of disco dancing without appropriate musical accompaniment. Hence, there may be times when a speaker needs to use such audio equipment as a tape recorder or record player. There are both advantages and disadvantages associated with each of these audio aids.

If fidelity of sound reproduction is crucial to the presentation, a clean record and a good quality phonograph is the best combination. But, many an otherwise well-paced, smoothly-run presentation has been marred by the speaker who fumbles with the phonograph player arm trying to cue up a specific album selection. In addition, phonographs are usually more bulky than a portable tape player-recorder and typically require external power. Consequently, finding an accessible electrical outlet or locating an extension cord become additional encumbrances associated with using a phonograph as an audio aid rather than a battery-powered tape player. But, the speaker who opts to use a portable tape player over a phonograph must realize that s/he is usually sacrificing some degree of sound fidelity for the sake of convenience.

Finally, because the manner in which media aids are actually used or presented is also important to a speech's effectivenesss, we feel we should include a few relevant guidelines in our discussion of step eight.

Guidelines in Using Media Aids

If you have determined that using certain media aids represents an opportunity to further clarify, illustrate, reinforce, summarize, or enliven the content of your speech, then you need to know there are a few techniques associated with their use that help insure their effectiveness.

Keep visuals simple, clear, and relevant. When a visual aid detracts from the content of a presentation or offers wholly irrelevant material, the effectiveness of both the visual aid and the speech suffers. Use bold, broad lines and bright colors to make your visual aids readily visible to all audience members. Omit unnecessary details and use more than one visual aid if the material is complicated.

The relevancy of visual aids is not only a matter of content, i.e., the information they present, but is also a matter of display. Visual aids should be displayed only as they become germane to the speech. If visuals are made visible when not in actual use, they become sources of distraction. Since this is especially true of material that is passed around the audience, you should totally avoid resorting to this strategy. Making certain that all your visual aids can be seen by all audience members will prevent you from having to pass anything around.

Media aids must be seen or heard. A chart or diagram that cannot be easily seen by everyone in the audience or a garbled, fuzzy, inaudible recording contributes little to a presentation. Display or project your visuals so they can be seen; use audio aids that are easily discernable aurally.

In practical terms this means not standing in front of a visual aid as you explain the material it contains. It means using the clearest recordings and volume and tone settings which reproduce that clarity best. It also means that in using a slide or overhead projector to display visuals like charts, graphs, or diagrams, you will need to dim or block out ambient lighting, guard against an inverted or out-of-focus projection, and not stand in front of projected images.

Prepare all media aids in advance. The effective use of any projection or sound equipment during a presentation requires attending to a few things in advance. Before delivering any presentation, make certain all necessary equipment is operational and ready to go. Little detracts more from a speaker's poise and confidence, and consequently, his or her message than a frantic, last-minute search for an extension cord or a functional projector bulb.

Drawing or writing on a chalkboard during a speech is rarely as effective as displaying well-prepared visual aids. Using a chalkboard not only consumes valuable speaking time but the visual information that results is rarely as clear or accurate as visuals prepared in advance.

Hopefully, our discussion of the considerations important to step eight has made it clear that if a speaker uses media aids at all, they should be selected with their differential informational value in mind and then carefully prepared and effectively presented before their real support or developmental value can be achieved.

Step Nine: Write an Introduction

Completing the preceding eight steps in the plan requires investing no small amount of time and effort in constructing the important middle section of your presentation, i.e., the body. Based primarily on the products of that effort, completing the next two steps, writing an introduction and then a conclusion, should be fairly quick and easy by comparison.

The most basic function of the introduction is to *provide entry into the body of the speech.* It is not simply one of "getting attention." On the other hand, if a speaker is at all successful in achieving the basic purpose we ascribe, and does so by applying the techniques we suggest, then gaining receptive attention on the part of audience members should be a positive by-product. The techniques we have in mind represent two different approaches to the task of providing entry into the body of the speech. First, there is the subtle, interest-generating methods of *foreshadowing* and second, there is the more straightforward *orienting* approach.

Foreshadowing

When an audience is perceived to be already interested in a topic or aware of the major issues under consideration, there is little to prevent the speaker from plunging directly into the topic at hand. A speaker we know, for example, recently introduced his speech before a group of college seniors with a single, brief sentence: "Let's talk about jobs." He saw little need to generate interest in an already-salient topic. Experienced speakers have, however, learned that it is sometimes necessary to introduce some topics in a way that churns up genuine interest or gains a degree of receptive attention. Effectively applying techniques like those we subsume under the term "foreshadowing" seems to work fairly well in this respect. The techniques we include generally perform the function of indicating what the speaker will talk about, and, thereby provide entry into the body of the speech, but do so in a fairly indirect way.

Identification. Using this technique requires an introduction that not only indicates what the speech is about but also helps to establish the speaker and audience as sharing a common ground, as possessing similar experiences, ideals, and so on. In showing that he or she can identify with the audience in relevant terms, the speaker is often granted an acceptance which grows from ingratiation. Notice how Dr. Simon Ramo, speaking on "The Coming Social-Industrial Complex" introduced his speech at the University of Houston in 1971 with a personal experience. In making reference to important features of the immediate occasion, he indicates having had experiences similar to those of his audience.

> When I was a student more than a third of a century ago there would occasionally be a guest lecturer on campus to impart wisdom on some important subject and connect my brain with the real world on the outside. I confess that I can recall neither any specific individual nor a single lecture subject. This was probably because something else was very much on my mind—this much I certainly remember. It was how in the world, and when, would I get a job after graduating;...*

A few sentences later, Dr. Ramo indicated how a scarcity of new jobs for graduates, both for him and his audience, related to the central issue of his speech, specifically, the economic and social implications of technological change. But, what is presently of interest is that in beginning his speech by describing a personal experience—especially one his audience could identify with easily—Dr. Ramo attained the receptive attention of his listeners and generally established himself as addressing an issue with the compassion and wisdom that is often born

---

Vital Speechs of the Day (November 15, 1971), p. 80

of experience.

Pertinent quotation. This technique, which is typically not quite as subtle as identification, also serves as a means of generating interest and foreshadowing the content of the speech. One student speaker, for example, introduced an informative presentation on "performance anxiety" with a pertinent quotation:

> As I stand here before you I'm reminded of something that Howard Goshorn once wrote. "The human brain is a wonderful thing. It operates from the moment you are born until the first time you get up to make a speech."

Since she chose to use this particular quotation, perhaps we should hold up this introduction as an example of using *identification* as well. In any event, we do want to point out that this speaker did not commit the error that many do when using a quotation as introductory material. Rather than assuming the relevance of the quotation she selected would appear immediately self-evident, she quickly tied it to the topic of her speech with a few brief explanatory remarks.

Rhetorical question. Another way of arousing interest and foreshadowing the content of the speech is for the speaker to put pertinent and challenging questions to the audience—without expecting immediate and direct answers. One or more rhetorical questions, especially if they are carefully worded and clearly related to your topic, often prompt listeners to examine the issues you present in their own minds and stimulate them to think about the matter you wish to address. Thus, in beginning a speech on the cost of higher education the speaker might ask, "How many qualified and capable high school graduates are prevented from attending college by the cost alone?"

Humorous anecdote. A frequently used, and too-frequently abused,introductory technique is telling a funny story or entertaining anecdote. Humor, to be an effective introductory device, needs to be appropriate to the audience and occasion, and, more importantly, it needs to be pertinent to the topic of the speech. It is humor with a purpose other than sheer entertainment. Using a witty turn of phrase or humorous anecdote that fails to make a relevant point is a bit like insisting that medical schools maintain entrance quotas for Christian Scientists. Polite indifference or a patronizing smile or two may be the only response generated.

Perhaps in no other kind of introduction is it more important to adapt a humorous story or anecdote to the audience and occasion. A subtle play on words may delight one listener and leave another suspicious of the speaker's condescending intellectualism. Relating one of the latest jokes may roll one audience in the aisles and send another to the nearest exit. And, as you have probably learned by experience, the same person may be responsive to humor one time and not even chuckle on another occasion. Those who have made a study of why people laugh appear to disagree on many things; but they do seem to concur on one point. The enjoyment of humor seems to depend upon the presence of a *playful spirit*. If an audience is tense or solemn, it rarely sees anything as funny.

If you inted to use an entertaining story — but one that illustrates a point important to your speech — as an introduction, you may want to keep a couple of points in mind. Never announce that you are going to say something witty or tell a funny story. Doing so puts your listeners on guard; laughter depends upon surprise. Also, if your listeners fail to see the humor in what you say, move quickly to the next idea. Explaining or repeating a joke or witticism rarely prompts laughter. What Eastman said many years ago (1936) still applys today: "You can learn to love — or so they say — but you laugh at first sight or not at all" (p. 27).

Real or hypothetical illustrations. Although a real or hypothetical illustration may be used to advantage at any time during a speech, starting with a vivid illustration which supports the central idea or thesis of your speech is often an effective way of providing entry into your message. Ernie Link, for example, introduced his speech on the Head Start program by relating a story about Tommy, a boyhood friend in the small Kansas town where he grew up. He began with a brief but vivid description of the condition of Tommy's house and the size of his family. he then recalled Tommy's first day of school.

> In the first grade almost everyone talked a lot, but Tommy didn't talk much the first day. Nor did he talk much the second day either. Sometimes our teacher would ask Tommy questions, but he would never answer them. He only shook his head and looked down at the top of his small, wooden desk. Tommy was different; he didn't speak well, and he couldn't express his thoughts to others.*

From his description of Tommy, he went on to discuss the problems of the disadvantaged child generally and how the Head Start problem can help in a number of ways.

Using any of the five devices we have discussed, identification, quotation, rhetorical questions, humor, or illustration, can serve to generate interest, suggest or prefigure the content of your speech, or help to earn the good will of your audience. All are subtle but effective ways of providing entry into the body of your speech. Some occasions, however, call for a more direct approach.

Orienting

In some instances the speaker may find it best to proceed directly, to use an introduction that simply reports what he or she is going to talk

*Ernie Link, "Come Take My Hand" in *A Time to Speak*, ed. Wil A. Linkugel and David M. Berg (Belmont, Calif.: Wadsworth, 1970), p. 139.

about. The orienting approach, that is, filling your audience in on what you are going to talk about before you talk about it, represents a fairly simple, straightforward, business-like way of introducing a speech. Zanes and Goldhaber define the orienting introduction as one that "may contain historical or other background information about your topic, definitions of important terminology, the boundaries of your speech (what it excludes as well as includes), and a preview (or presummary) of your central idea and main points" (1978, p. 134). We would point to the following introduction as one that performs at least the latter two functions Zanes and Goldhaber include in their definition:

> In my talk this morning I intend to outline a specific program designed to restore a favorable investment climate. This program is based on three important changes within the present tax system: One, a higher personal income tax; two, a lower capital gains tax; and three, broadening the use of special tax preferences. Now, let me present the logic that supports this tripartite program.

Whether you intend to use a straightforward, orienting approach or any of the foreshadowing techniques we described earlier, try to adapt your introduction to both the occasion and the audience's perceived predisposition toward you and your topic. An informative report or persuasive presentation introduced in the direct, orienting fashion, for example, is generally well received in most professional or job situations. If, on the other hand, your listeners do not appear to have a pre-established interest in your topic, it becomes necessary to begin your speech in a way that gains their receptive attention (using questions, pertinent quotations, illustrations). Moreover, if your audience appears hostile or seems to harbor negative feelings about your topic, you are well advised to invest a good deal of your initial speaking time gaining their good will, attempting to dispose them favorably to what you have to say (using identification, humor).

Step Ten: Write a Conclusion

An effective conclusion must do a number of things. It should bring together all the important thoughts, feelings, or ideas expressed in the speech. It should be a natural culmination of all that has been said. The closing words of a speech also represent the last opportunity a speaker has to emphasize or support the purpose, main idea, or thesis of the speech. An abrupt ending, or one characterized by a few weak, insipid remarks made as the speaker hesitantly leaves the podium, can obliterate the entire preceding message. In short, a speech needs to be brought to an effective close or ending and not simply stopped.

The important question at hand, then, is this: What factors appear important to an effective conclusion? In practically all instances, an effective conclusion is one that embodies at least one of three strategies. *Summarizing* the major points of the speech is a frequently used way of ending most informative presentations and giving the speech lasting *impact* or calling for a certain *action* on the part of audience members represent two, often effective ways of concluding persuasive speeches. We don't mean to insist, however, that the way a speech is concluded should be wholly dependent on its purpose. An informative speaker may want to show the potential utility of the information he or she has presented by demonstrating its application; doing so may amount to a call for action. But, the action specified would probably serve a utilitarian end rather than one pursued for purposes of policy change or decision-making. A persuasive speaker may, on the other hand, find a summary of major points to be a very effective conclusion. Our point is this: Of the three factors important to effective conclusions, *summary*, *impact*, and *action*, each appears differentially useful in terms of the two types of speeches we have been discussing all along. On the whole, however, a summarizing conclusion appears better suited to informative speeches and a conclusion that gives impact to the speech and/or calls for specified action seems well-fitted to most persuasive speaking situations.

Summary of Major Points

When a presentation is primarily intended to impart a good deal of information, summarizing or recapitulating the major points it contains offers a way of ensuring retention and possible use of the information it presents.

Remember the speech on finishing wood furniture we outlined earlier? We offer the following summary of the major points included in that presentation as an appropriate and effective way of concluding the speech:

> Let me try to recap the four steps in finishing wood furniture that I've discussed and demonstrated. First, it is often necessary to remove the old finish, unless, of course, you've purchased a piece at an unfinished furniture store. I have shown you how to apply and pretest the stain for tone and color. Third, once the stain is dry, apply a sanding sealer evenly and thoroughly using a clean brush or sponge. When that's dry, make the surface smooth again with fine sandpaper or number quadruple-zero steel wool. Finally, apply a coat of varnish or polyurethane — hard plastic — evenly, liberally, and thoroughly to give the piece a deep gloss, to en-

hance the natural beauty of the wood grain, and, of course, to protect it. Knowing how to follow these four steps, and some of the techniques they involve, may someday save you money, add beauty and a long, useful life to your wood furniture — and provide you with a sense of accomplishment and satisfaction to boot.

Notice how the conclusion summarizes the major points of the presentation with just a sentence or two devoted to each point. Notice also how the final sentence emphasizes the practical utility of the information presented, thereby giving the speech impact and possibly even prompting appropriate action on the part of some audience members.

A summarizing conclusion may also work well with a persuasive speech. To illustrate, we offer a conclusion taken from a student's speech advancing a proposition of policy:

> To be certain that we all understand my reasons for advocating the changes I've outlined, let me restate my main points. First, a world federation is the only type of government which might prevent the world's superpowers from destroying the earth through nuclear holocaust. Second, a world federation is the only type of government which is acceptable to the several nations, and third, a world federation represents the most democratic form of government that could possibly work on such a grand scale. It is for these reasons that I favor the establishment of a world government taking the form of a federation.

Giving the Speech Impact

Closing a speech with a striking but pertinent anecdote, quotation, or an epitomizing illustration of the central thesis or idea behind the speech often serves to give a speech impact. Again, we point to a conclusion extracted from a particularly well-composed speech delivered by one of our former students. This time, the speaker built her speech around a value proposition.

> I have been emphasizing the value of a liberal education by stressing the original meaning of the word "liberal" — freedom. I have characterized it as a learning experience that can help free the truly human qualities in each of us. I have also contrasted it with various forms of specialized training, training which may possess narrow and limited application, and often rapid obsolescence as well, in a contemporary labor market.
>
> Perhaps I can best emphasize the true potential of liberal education with a wonderful story once told by B.J. Chute, the writer. The story is about a small child who watched a sculp-

tor working on a slab of marble. Day after day, the child
watched and the sculptor chipped away at the stone.
Finally, one day the child's face lit up, she looked at the
sculptor in amazement and said, "But, how did you know
there was a lion in there?"

Unlike the sculptor's marble, we are not hard and inanimate
but made of hopes, ideals, and persistent inquiry. Nor are
we mere brutes. There is a humanness in each of us; with
skill and labor — and a liberal education — we can let it free.

As you can see, this conclusion actually represents an effective blend
of two different concluding strategies. Early in her conclusion, the
speaker summarizes the major points presented in her speech. She
then closes the speech and gives it impact by relating and commenting
on an epitomizing illustration of the speech's central thought or idea.

Call for Action

A call for action or an open appeal to believe or do what the speech
has advocated may be what is needed to clinch a persuasive speech.
This is an effective way of ending a speech when the overriding
purpose has been to stimulate or get action from the audience. It also
represents the prescribed conclusion for any presentation organized
according to the *motivated sequence* pattern of arrangement described
earlier.

For purposes of illustration we include the following hypothetical
conclusion:

Let us no longer sit here doing nothing while certain inept
and misguided politicians squander our tax dollars and drag
us to the brink of economic ruin. Let's go out and build a
better government. Let's do it tomorrow; it's election day
and our only hope.

Concluding a speech with a call for action is obviously the best strategy
when the speaker sets out to sell a product or service, to convince his
or her audience to donate money, give a pint of blood, vote for a
particular candidate — to actually *do* something.

Step Eleven: Practice the Speech

A source of much of the natural anxiety we all associate with
speaking in public is a lack of confidence in the content of our
messages. If you apply the advice and principles we have offered in
discussing the preceding ten steps, however, the result of your labors

should be a source of confidence rather than a cause for debilitating anxiety. But, the very thought of actually giving it a public hearing may still cause the butterflies to churn and flutter in your stomach. It's a natural reaction and one that is not unfamiliar to even the most experienced speakers. Experienced speakers have learned, however, that getting to know the content of a speech, becoming very familiar with the major points, their sequence and supporting material, certainly helps to minimize their anxiety. Learning the content of your speech and then honing features of your delivery through practice should, at a minimum, get the butterflies to "fly in formation" when it comes time to actually present the speech.

There does not appear to be one, single, always correct way to practice a speech. Nevertheless, for many speakers the most productive and efficient way appears to be one of proceeding in two phases with each possessing a distinct purpose. In phase one the speaker concentrates on the content of the speech and, in phase two, he or she attends to features of delivery and the time constraints associated with the speech.

Focus on Content

A poor presentation often reflects a lack of practice. A speaker cannot effectively communicate what he or she does not know well. When you appear unfamiliar with your own material your perceived credibility and the apparent value of your message will diminish significantly. The well practiced speech, on the other hand, manifests a certain conviction on the speaker's part that often moves audience members to want to listen, to attend to the information and ideas it presents. It is vital for the speaker to appear confident in his or her message right from the very start. We therefore suggest that you begin the first phase of your practice by concentrating on the content of the speech's introduction.

Practicing the introduction. While you may have carefully composed an introduction that is designed to establish rapport with or gain the good will of your audience, it will fail miserably in this regard if it is delivered in a hesitant, timid way or simply read, word-for-word, from a note card or outline.

Having the first things you intend to say firmly set to mind will not only increase your own confidence, lessen your anxiety, but it will also improve your effectiveness as a speaker and prompt receptive attention on the part of your listeners. Repeatedly going over the introduction you have so carefully composed, even changing some of the phrasing if it seems unnatural to you when spoken aloud, until you have it firmly committed to memory will pay you multiple dividends when it comes time to actually get up and talk.

Draw up a practice outline. If the outline of the body of your speech is very detailed at all, it will probably not fit on one or two pieces of paper. Experienced speakers have found that trying to speak from pages and pages of notes can be very distracting and may even cause the speaker to occasionally get lost. When the speaker is forced to fumble through sheaves of paper, or flip through a bundle of note cards in order to put or keep his or her thoughts on track, the speaker is courting danger. Little is more unnerving than frantically searching through a stack of notes for the next thing to say. This is why we suggest that you go to the podium, if at all possible, with but a single piece of paper.

But, putting your entire outline, along with the conclusion of your speech on a single piece of paper may cause you to write so small it becomes impossible to discern its content and, therefore, highly impractical as a speaking aid. We suggest you do two things. First, draw up a practice outline, one that includes only the major points presented in the body of the speech, with their supporting material expressed as key words or triggering phrases, and the conclusion of the speech. As we said earlier, the introduction should be committed to memory. Having drawn up such an outline, you may then concentrate on the task of setting the content of the body and conclusion of your speech firmly in your mind. The best way to do this is to place both the brief practicing outline and the more detailed version side by side. Go over both repeatedly until you feel you can present the content of your speech without glancing at your detailed outline, by consulting the practicing outline alone. When you have accomplished this, you need only rely on a single piece of paper for the remainder of your practice and your actual presentation as well.

Attend to Length and Delivery

Once you become confident in the verbal or content features of your message, your practice should then revolve around the nonverbal aspects of oral delivery.

Having a well-composed message firmly set in your mind will not automatically guarantee an effective oral presentation. Experience teaches most of us that the real effect of the spoken word is rarely a product of content alone, i.e., *what* is actually said. The particular *way* we say things also plays a significant role in the meaning ascribed to our messages. For a public speaker, three features of delivery appear to have major significance in terms of presenting an effective, communicative speech: rate, audibility, and eye contact. Beyond these features of delivery there is a fourth, important consideration the practicing speaker should keep in mind, the time limit associated with the speaking situation.

Speaking rate. Speaking too slowly often has a lullabying effect on audience members. On the other hand, the speaker who races through the presentation can generate a good deal of frustration among his or her listeners. They are not given the time it usually takes to digest the information or analyze the speaker's arguments. Beginning speakers, more often than not, err in the latter respect. Principally due to anxiety, the beginning speaker naturally wants to have the speech completed and be able to return to the relative unobtrusiveness of a seat in the audience as quickly as possible. Also, there is the added fear that "if I don't hurry up and get it out, I'll forget it."

We suspect that while some anxiety is only natural in a performance situation, much of it is a product of inadequate practice. By concentrating on your rate of delivery while practicing your speech aloud, then, you are not only contributing to lessening your anxiety but helping to assure your message will be adequately heard as well. When practicing your speech aloud, be certain to say things at your normal conversational rate. Also, you may find that building certain strategic pauses into your delivery will enhance the effect of what you say.

Audibility. As we use the term, the audibility of an oral presentation is not only a function of volume but articulation as well.

Having to strain to hear the speaker is as frustrating as having to listen to a speaker shout throughout the speech. While the size of the room, the number of people in the audience, and the availablity of a public address system are all situational factors that may have an effect on the audibility of your presentation, there are also a few relevant considerations you might keep in mind while practicing your speech aloud. Many of us have a natural tendency to increase our speaking volume when we get excited; also, for a good many people speaking in a relatively loud voice is an acquired habit and they may even do it in everyday conversations. Still others possess a fairly soft speaking voice and, for them, any increase in volume seems strained and laborious. Knowing what your natural volume is and making necessary adjustments up or down when practicing your delivery aloud help to assure your speech will be adequately or comfortably heard.

As we said, articulation is also a function of audibility. Your speaking rate and the pitch or volume of your voice may be conducive to hearing and understanding the things you say but, if you are in the habit of slurring or mis-pronouncing some of the words you use, then much of your work at establishing an effective rate and pitch will have been in vain. Determine whether or not you habitually mispronounce certain "everyday words" (like say "flustrate" for "frustrate" or "ax" for "ask") and concentrate on pronouncing them correctly. Then, be certain that you are correctly pronouncing any technical terms or unordinary words contained in your speech. It is often very difficult to correct a mispronunciation later, once it becomes habitual with repeated practice. Correctly pronouncing key terms during actual delivery is very important; much of your perceived expertise or credibility is at stake.

Finally, whether or not audience members will be able to comprehend your message adequately is also a function of the degree of precision or crispness manifested in your speaking. Slurring, mumbling, and dropping (i.e., not pronouncing) either the final or middle syllables from the words you use diminishes your effectiveness as a speaker. Practicing your speech by recording it on audio tape and then listening to your recorded speech can help you to detect and correct problems in articulation.

Eye contact. The speaker who is too dependent on his or her notes, who looks around the room, at the ceiling, the floor, the back wall, and so on does little to give the impression he or she truly wishes to communicate with the audience. By contrast, the speaker who establishes and maintains eye contact, i.e., looks *at* audience members rather than above, around, or through them, establishes rapport and encourages receptive attention to his or her ideas.

Actually, by having the full content of the introduction to your speech committed to memory, you should feel little need to look at your notes and can, therefore, establish eye contact at the very outset. Practice delivering your introduction with this in mind. The same holds true for the body and conclusion of your speech. Once you have established eye contact it becomes important to maintain it.

Traditional public speaking texts suggest practicing eye contact in front of a mirror and this is not a bad idea. At first, actually talking to yourself in a mirror may feel a bit awkward but it soon becomes more natural and often quite instructive. Can you remember the first time you heard a tape recording of your voice? Your reactions to viewing your own appearance during practice speaking sessions will become less discomforting as you do it with greater frequency.

Also, it might prove helpful to make a practice delivery in front of a friend or two. Ask for honest, constructive criticism not only with respect to your delivery but the content of your presentation as well.

Time constraints. Will the length of your speech fall within the time limits you are allotted? In most speaking situations, the speaker must abide by ordained time limits. This is true not only in the classroom but in business, professional, and political arenas as well.

Practice helps the speaker guage how long his or her presentation will take. Adhering to prescribed time limits sometimes makes it necessary to lengthen or shorten the speech. If it appears necessary to lengthen your speech somewhat, we suggest you first entertain adding additional supporting material for the major points already included before trying to include too many additional major points. Should it appear necessary to shorten your speech, which is more often the case than not, you must determine what material needs to be eliminated.

Perhaps you might be able to shorten an argument, example, illustration, or quotation a bit and still preserve the supporting value of the material. You can occasionally save some time by presenting certain information visually rather than orally. Look for opportunities to use additional media aids, therefore. If the speech appears to be grossly over time, then you will need to consider eliminating an entire section or two, that is, cutting out a major point or two along with accompanying supporting material.

Practicing your speech as we suggest means preparing for its actual delivery in two phases. First, concentrate on the content of your speech. Then, attend both to features of delivery, like rate, audibility, and eye contact, and to the situational factor of time. Hopefully, preparing this way will heighten your confidence in the message and your ability to deliver it. But, perhaps we should share a few thoughts on the topic of anxiety before discussing the final step in our plan.

Speech Anxiety

As we mentioned earlier, virtually every speaker or, for that matter, anyone who performs in some way before an audience (e.g., athletes, musicians, actors, dancers, teachers) experiences some degree of anxiety before and often during his or her performance. As we also suggested earlier, this anxiety is a natural, normal psychological reaction which frequently accompanies the need to perform in a situation perceived as highly significant. The physiological reactions or symptoms vary in accordance with the degree of significance attached to the situation and they appear to vary from person to person. These symptoms include: an increase in blood pressure, heart rate, the flow of adrenaline and burning more blood sugar than normal. These symptoms are reflexive or automatic and not, therefore, turned off and on at will. And, in combination, they account for the "butterflies" feeling in the stomach, muscular tension, "goose bumps," red blotches on the surface of the skin, and so on.

While these symptoms are typically experienced to varying degrees when confronting a situation perceived as highly significant, they are often made worse when the situation appears *threatening* as well. The threat or insecurity many speakers feel is often a result of a perceived *lack of control* over the speaking situation. This is particularly understandable when we consider that public speaking is something most people rarely do (unless they are in fields like teaching, politics, etc.). Also, for some people, facing practically any kind of performance situation triggers an impending sense of doom; they anticipate almost certain personal or emotional damage should the speech fail in any way.

Everyone does not experience speech anxiety in the same way or for the same reasons but increasing your sense of control over the speaking situation will help considerably. By completing the preceding eleven steps we described, and doing so with the best effort you can bring to the task, you will have accomplished much toward developing a sense of control over the speaking situation. This becomes evident when we examine some of the fairly specific advice offered by Zannes and Goldhaber (1978):

> Among the typical long-range solutions to stage fright [speech anxiety] are: Build a positive attitude [sense of control] or get more experience. Among the short range solutions are: Do a thorough audience analysis (to give you information to reduce your uncertainty and increase your control); be well prepared (know your speech, rehearse it, etc.); take several deep breaths (immediately before speaking); place your speech in its proper perspective (how important is it really going to be to your career and welfare?); ....(p. 26).

Step Twelve: Deliver the Presentation

A decade or so ago, it was not unusual to find practically any textbook on speech or public speaking devoting an entire chapter or more to advice on speech delivery (e.g., Anderson, Lewis, and Murray, 1964, Chapters 10 and 11; Soper, 1963, Chapter 2). They included advice on how to walk to the podium, how to stand, move, gesture, and use certain vocal devices (rate, pitch, variety, etc.).

While it can be argued that, for many speakers, knowing how to stand, gesture, and so forth may contribute to their developing a sense of control, our experience leads us to conclude that heaping too many prescriptions of this sort onto a beginning speaker can have the opposite effect. Worry about gesturing "correctly," for example, can make the speaker unnecessarily self-conscious, thereby increasing his or her speech anxiety. Our advice with respect to delivery, therefore, can be summed up in a single, very brief sentence: Be natural, spontaneous. Nevertheless, we do advocate exercising informed judgment in this regard. This means attending to certain features of your own nonverbal projection.

As listeners and perceivers, we simultaneously attend to both verbal and nonverbal features of the speaking situation. We may even consciously or purposely look for certain nonverbal cues or indicators in order to form an impression of the speaker, to invest meaning in what the speaker says. As a speaker, therefore, you need to be certain your nonverbal behavior is not at cross-purposes with either the intent or content of your message. For example, suppose the content of a particular speech is advocating and supporting a certain solution to a serious or dangerous problem as viable. If, on the other hand, the speaker's vocal delivery is dull, monotonous, inaudible, or generally lacks indicators of conviction, and his posture, facial expressions, manner of dress, and so on tend to reveal a general lack of concern, then how do you suppose audience members will construe the speech? Would you characterize the speech as an effective one in this case?

While audience members may be attending to features of the speaker's nonverbal behavior, either consciously or otherwise, the speaker may also be looking to his or her audience for certain nonverbal information or "feedback."

Attend to Feedback

Maintaining eye contact with an audience is important not only in establishing rapport but also in making it possible to receive visual feedback from audience members. Your listeners will sometimes provide obvious indicators, like holding a cupped hand next to an ear, that can prove useful in adjusting your volume and/or rate of speech in an accomodative way. An occasional frown, grimmace, or chuckle may also serve as more subtle indicators as to how your message is being received. Should the available cues appear to indicate a wholly unsympathetic or even negative reaction to your speech, however, we do not advocate you perform massive, on-the-spot surgery on your message. But, an objective self-critique of your presentation after it is over might prove very instructive and excellent preparation for your next speaking experience.

Self-critique

Once you have delivered your speech, be it a classroom presentation or a business report, it is generally helpful to engage in some post-analysis. As we said very early in this chapter, speaking seeks a response; specific goals or purposes usually provide impetus to speech. The most obvious question you need to ask once your speech is over, then, is: Was it effective in achieving its underlying purpose?

Summary

With this, our final chapter we provide a fairly prescriptive but practical twelve-step plan, one that embodies some of the best advice we can offer on how to prepare and deliver informative and/or persuasive speeches. Should you wish to review the sequential steps involved and the tasks or considerations important to each, we refer you back to

Table 1 wherein we first presented our plan in its entirety.

Finally, a word or two about applying our plan to your own efforts at speech composition and delivery. Naturally, your first application will seem to go fairly slowly, but as you become increasingly familiar with the tasks and considerations subsumed under each step, you may be amazed at the dispatch and efficiency of your endeavors. And, like any body of prescriptions or guidelines, ours is certainly open to modification as the need arises.

References

Andersen, M.P., Lewis, W., and Murray, J. *The speaker and his audience*. New York: Harper & Row, 1964.

Brooks, W.D. *Speech communication*, 3rd. ed. Dubuque, Iowa: William C. Brown, 1978.

DeVito, J. *The psychology of speech and language*. New York: Random House, 1970.

DiSalvo, V. *Business and professional communication: Basic skills and principles*. Columbus, Ohio: Charles E. Merrill, 1977.

Eastman, M. *Enjoyment of laughter*. New York: Simon and Schuster, 1936.

Mills, G.E. *Putting a message together*, 2nd ed. Indianapolis: Bobbs-Merrill, 1972.

Minnick, W.C. *Public speaking*. Boston: Houghton Mifflin, 1979.

Monroe, A.H. and Ehninger, D. *Principles and types of speech communication*, 7th ed. Glenview, Ill.: Scott, Foresman, 1974.

Oliver, R.T. and Cortright, R.L. *Effective speech*, 4th ed. New York: Holt, Rinehart and Winston, 1961.

Soper, P.L. *Basic public speaking*, 3rd ed. Oxford: Oxford University Press, 1963.

Verderber, R.F. *The challenge of effective speaking*. Belmont, Calif.: Wadsworth, 1976.

Zannes, E. and Goldhaber, G. *Stand up, speak out*. Reading, Mass.: Addison-Wesley, 1978.

Index